In memory of
Pietie,
Unconditional Love)

Leilu Kramer

HEROES ALL - WITHOUT QUESTION

By Louise Olson Krause

Don't grieve for me, I served you well.
I loved you more than you could ever tell.
I am now your guardian angel up above.
I will watch over you, I'll always be around.
I wore my badge with honor every day,
To keep citizens safe and out of harm's way.
So when you see a badge worn with pride,
Remember the canines that have served and died.
Author Unknown

"The one absolutely unselfish friend
That I have found in this selfish world;
The one who has never proven to be
Ungrateful or treacherous, who has
Never deserted me, is my K-9 Partner."

Excerpted from "Ode To A Dog",
Senator George Graham Vest, 1896

Published by:
K-9 Press
926 Honeysuckle Lane, Suite 203
Cape May, NJ 08204-4852
(609) 886-5858
Fax (609) 886-1523
Lulu@dandy.net

In cooperation with:
RJ Communications LLC
51 East 42nd Street, Suite 1202
New York, NY 10017
(800) 621-2556
(212) 867-1331
Fax (212) 681-8002

Layout design:
Budget Book Design
Matt Pramschufer
9 Washington Avenue
Pleasantville, NY 10570
(800) 754-7089

Cover design and layout:
Susan Ferretti Designs
46 Englewood Road, Suite 100
Linden, NJ 07036
(908) 846-7764
Fax (908) 486-7764
sueferretti@comcast.net

Library of Congress Catalog Number: 2003095162
ISBN: 0-9743116-1-8 (paperback)
ISBN: 0-9743116-1-8 (hard cover)
ECPN: 0-9743116-1-8
Printed in the United States of America
This is a Books Just Books book.

First printing: July 2003.

TABLE OF CONTENTS

DEDICATION

October 12, 1985 – July 3, 1997

I want to dedicate this book to all of the working dogs and mounted patrol horses of the past, the present and the future. I realized that these heroes were not getting the credit they deserved. Whenever I would read about a funeral-memorial service, one who has dedicated their life to their partner, I felt the need for more recognition. The aspiration of memorial cards and now this book will rectify that concept. My first memorial cards were for our beloved Greta. That was the beginning, this book is the continuation and may we never forget them in the future. Don't ever under estimate the power of the "paws."

FOREWORD

The partnership between man and K-9 has existed for more than 10,000 years. It is a partnership of love and loyalty which has withstood the sands of time and all the foibles which have been thrust upon it by crime, war, breeding and occasionally human irresponsibility.

This book is offered as a tribute and a remembrance to the love and loyalty of those K-9s that have served with us and partnered us. Their lives are much too short, and are often cut even shorter by some sort of misadventure.

The loss of a partner is devastating to anyone whether you are an Officer of the Law or Military Handler or pet owner. Many people feel completely alone at this time in their life. Some unthinking or uncaring person may make matters worse by saying "Why are you so upset? It was just a dog." No, they weren't "Just a dog." They were our partners.

Our partner was the one who rode with us; protected us, listened to us, comforted us. At the end of our shift, our partner went home and played with our families and loved and guarded them with us.

Our partner may have lived with us "in the field" or gone back to the kennel and waited impatiently for the next time we walked point together; or guarded the airfield or ammunition dump.

For the Military Handlers, from WWII to November of 2000, it was particularly unpleasant. Their partners were considered "equipment" and the handler was not allowed to adopt his or her partner and bring them home. There was no way to explain to their partner why they were left behind to serve and die. This left wounds that would never and have never healed.

In our home, our partners have hunted with and for us. They have guarded us and they have guarded our children. They have provided for us; hearing for those of us who cannot hear, seeing for those of us who cannot see. Rescuing those of us who needed rescue. They were our partners, they loved us unconditionally and we loved them.

This book does not celebrate death. It celebrates life; it celebrates love and loyalty. It celebrates the unconditional, unquestioning love that is given by our partners. Hopefully, it will tell those of you who have lost your partners You Are Not Alone! We do feel and understand your pain and are here for you.

These were our Partners. We remember them and we honor them.

CERTIFIED TRAINING INFORMATION

by: James Cortina, Director of Connecticut Police Work Dog Association, Inc.

The United States Police K-9 Association, P.D.1 trial tests the police K-9 on Obedience, to show the extent of control by the handler and commands at a distance. In the obedience testing the dog will have to do heeling at different paces of normal, slow and fast and also consisting of left, right, and about turns. Verbal and hand signal commands of sit, and down, recall, and drop on a recall at a distance of fifty feet. The obedience exercise is done off leash and the K-9 team must score 70% of the total possible points in the obedience phase in order to continue to the other phases for certification.

Also Agility testing to demonstrate the dog's ability to surmount various obstacles which consists of jumping hurdles, broad jumps, a frame, crawl and catwalk. The hurdles consist of a picket fence, chain link fence, simulated brick wall, window jump, board jump, and shrub jump. Four out of the six hurdles will be used for testing.

The dog will also be tested on search to locate and retrieve articles containing the scent of a stranger and to locate a hidden suspect in a box which is called the box search. The box search consists of 6 boxes with a suspect hidden in one of them and the dog has to indicate which one within four minutes. In the search test the articles selected are usually shot gun shell, (green in color) key on a ring with tab, book of matches, (dark in color) metal gun, credit card, screwdriver, (4-6 inches)or piece of leather.(1/8 to 1/4 inch thick, 3x3 inches, dark in color) The association will choose 2 of the items for testing. Within 3 minutes the K-9 must locate and retrieve 2 items of evidence thrown into a 30 foot square area of grass approximately 12 inches high.

The dog will also be tested on Criminal Apprehension which consists of five parts for certification; recall, false start, apprehension without gunfire, apprehension with gunfire & handler protection. The K-9 is judged on his ability, upon command, to pursue and apprehend a fleeing suspect. The K-9 will also be judged on his ability to release the suspect on command and return to his handlers side. The K-9 will be tested on a recall which is when the K-9 has been commanded to apprehend a fleeing suspect and will be judged on his ability to stop the pursuit on command and return to his handlers side while the suspect continues to run away. A False Start which is when the dog sees someone running away from the handler and is required to stay. attack without gunfire, handler protection and attack with gunfire. These tests show the control of the dog under varied circumstances.

Rotterdam-Rijnmond K-9 Unit

K-9 Disciplines & Certifications in Holland
By: Dick van Leenen
Rotterdame Police Dept. Nederlands
Rotterdam-Rijnmond Police Department
Animal Section - K-9 Unit
Voorwateringweg 99 - Rotterdam - Holland

In Holland, unlike you are familiar in the US, we do not have cross trained dogs or dogs for dual purpose. The patrol dog that also search for narcotics. In Holland we prefer to train each dog for one discipline. Several reasons for that but the main reason is that it can be pretty confusing for the dogs. For instance when I want him to search for a hidden suspect the dog maybe starts a search for narcs. We do not want that to happen and therefore we have only one discipline on one dog.

Because of this system, we also need more good dogs, but that is no big problem when you have so many good K-9's in United States. We have several certifications. All the disciplines have their own strict exam rules and certification. In Holland the rules are so strict that when a combination of handler and dog do not pass their national exam, they do not get the certification and are not allowed to do police work. So no certification means, no work and only training to get the certificate. These are the different certifications:

1. Patrol dog. With this exam the handler and dog prove that they are a good team. They have to show the exam committee obedience, field and building searches and the attack exercises on the decoy.

2. Narcotics (active): These dogs are used to search for narc like heroine, cocaine, marihuana, speed, XTC, etc. All the drugs that are known in the world. Also unlike what they think in the US these dogs can track and find XTC. In the US they think that XTC is not trackable for a dog but in Holland we have learned them to find XTC. The word "active" means that the dog becomes very exciting when he smells the narcs and he will start to bark and try to reach it.

   3. Narcotics (passive) "These dogs are trained on the same drugs as the active dogs but there is one big difference. When a "passive" dog smells a drug he just sits in front of the person that is carrying the drug with him. When this person wants to pass the dog the dog just sits in from of him again and by doing that he just refuses that person to pass him. The word "passive" we use because the dogs do not bark or act like crazy. That's why these dogs are used on airports. sports stadiums and ferry's between Great Britain and Holland, and trains between France and Holland. They do not scare people but do the same work.

4. Tracking dogs: To track persons without biting them when they find somebody. For instance lost kids or runaway inmates.

5. Smell Identification Dogs: These dogs are only used to smell a relation between a suspect and a piece of evidence. I will try to explain this. When a burglar left a screwdriver at the

place of the burglary and he ran away, one of our K-9-offi-
cers come on the scene of the crime and he takes care of the
screwdriver. He puts the screwdriver in a special plastic bag
without anyone touching this screwdriver. In the bag the
smell of the last user of the screwdriver (the burglar) is con-
served. Every people have its own unique smell, just like you
have a unique fingerprint!! We save this screwdriver for
more than three years because the unique smell stays OK for
that long. When detectives arrest a suspect for this burglary
but they do not have real prove they ask the K-9-unit to do
a smell identification test. The suspect has to hold a small
metal pipe. Also 6 other people who has nothing to do with
the burglary has to hold metal pipes. The metal pipes look
all the same but each of them have the unique on them of
the holder. So 6 people who are innocent and 1 suspect. The
7 pipes are put on the ground and the handler and his dog
does not know which pipe is from the suspect. After the 7
pipes are on the ground the handler and his dog comes into
the room. There he gets the screwdriver and he gives the
dog smell of the screwdriver. After the dog got that smell he
walks over all 7 pipes and when he smells the same smell at
one of the pipes he takes that pipe in his mouth and brings
it to his handler. That way the dog proves that there is a relationship between the smell of the screwdriver and one of the
pipes. When this pipe is the pipe that the suspect had in his
hands the detectives can prove that this suspects used that
screwdriver at that burglary. This is fully excepted prove in
court in Holland and its unique in the whole world. Our
country is the only country in the world that uses the dogs
for this kind of police work.

6. Explo-dogs: Search for all kinds of explosives (TNT, Sentex,
   etc.) but also guns and ammunition. Very busy lately
   because of the war against terrorism.

These dogs we have at the Rotterdam-Rijnmond K-9 unit.

TROOPS AND K-9S
ON ANNIVERSARY OF 9/11/01

K-9 handler, T.Sgt. Richard A. Brunet, 380 ESFS is sharing these photos of their ceremony held September 11, 2002.

"Our ceremony had people who worked at Ground Zero. One was a New York Police Officer, another was Chief Retzlaff, an ANG (Air National Guard), who was on his way home. He went to see what happened by hitchhiking to the site and then volunteered his help.

Both told their stories. The Chaplain said prayers and our Wing Commander spoke about the bravery of the people, about the bravery of the families. He also spoke to us about our bravery and how we overcame the hardships and fought for our freedom. They were very touching speeches, everyone was torn up.

They also had a "board" and display of a fire helmet. The board was designed so we could sign and put on display for everyone to see. Sirius' name was mentioned with all the people's names that perished in September 11, 2001. Here are some photos."

/s/ T.Sgt. Richard Brunet, 380ESFS

T.SGT. Rick Brunet (Kennel Master) from Danvers, MA on the left with his dog, Kay (5 yr. old) and S.SGT. Nanes, from San Antonio, TX and his dog, Rico, (2 yr. old). All photos by T.Sgt. Richard Brunet

THANK YOU!

Those two little words can never express the full depth of my gratitude and love for the many people who have helped me to honor the many K-9s and their partners who are presented to you here.

I'm using the word K-9 to cover all the services who have lost a valued partner and wished to memorialize and honor "Those Who Have Gone Before" and now wait for their human partner at The Rainbow Bridge.

I don't want to sound like an Oscar recipient, but in particular, I owe a huge vote of thanks to my husband, Bob, for his never ending support and love; for putting up with me, for taking over some of the household chores, for giving me the time to make daily updates on my web sites: www.k9memorialcards.com and www.petmemorialcards.com . Without Bob's constant and never ending love and support, none of this would have been possible.

I also want to thank all of the local funeral homes, veterinarians, and pet owners who have come to me and ordered cards. They have enabled me to afford the donations of memorial cards to Law Enforcement, Search and Rescue and Military handlers who have lost partners. Thank you to each and every one of you for helping me to help them with their grief for their lost partners. You have helped show that indeed "You Are Not Alone, We do Care."

There are so many people to thank for helping me with this book. Everyone who called or e mailed me about the loss of a K-9 working dog;

Mario Warnaar in Holland, who has been with me from the start, who helped me with my web site. Mario is not only a very valued friend, but also a constant source of wisdom and encouragement.

Tom Johnston, who acted as my proofreader and editor, who worked with me in finding my publisher and constantly kept encouraging me not to give up. He had faith in me when

I had none and thought the book was too big a project. He kept my mind going and helped me organize my thoughts.

Dusty Simon, of Kittering, Ohio. A young man who wants to make Law Enforcement his career. Dusty has constantly searched for and advised me of K-9 losses. Thanks, Dusty, for all you have done, not only to help me, but also the Officers who have lost their partners. Jim Cortina, director of Connecticut Working Dog Association, Inc. who also kept me informed of losses, not only in Connecticut, but around the country. Thank you Jim.

Officer Bruce Bertram in Connecticut, who shared with me his pain in the loss of his partner, K-9 Falk shortly after losing his parents. Bruce gave me an insider's look at "A Day in the Life of A K-9 Handler." The warmth and love he showed for his partner is an inspiration and revelation.

Robert Reiman, my attorney and friend of many years. Without his clear and concise explanations of contracts and legal matters, I would still be swimming in a fog of legalese and doubt.

I am also in debt to the Dandy Company (and particularly to Selena Cunningham and all her technicians), www.dandy.net for their support and donation of the space for my web sites. They have never complained about the time and effort it took to help me retrieve large files of K-9 photos. They have been beside me and supported me all the way. Dandy Company, Thank You! You're the best!

There are many, many others; including K-9 Git Anders' good friend and graphic artist, Sue Ferretti, who lives in Linden, NJ with her husband Jim and their sons. Out of love and in Git Ander's memory, she designed the book's cover. There is also T/St Rick Burnet, who shared his pictures of the 9-11 memorial held in Afghanistan and wrote "Dogs of War" for this book. And also the family of K-9 Git Ander, John & Allison Gillespie and their wonderful children, also a New Jersey resident. We all share their loss.

Each of you know who you are. I wish I could thank each

of you individually. To do so would take a book all by itself.
Please know that you are always in my heart and thoughts.

Again, THANK YOU!

I don't know how to thank Tom Johnston, for sharing his talent and editing this book. Tom, if you weren't there for me...this would have never been possible. I thank you from the bottom of my heart.
Lulu

In Loving Memory of
K-9 SHADOW

February 22, 1968 - June 25, 1985

Handler: Thomas Johnston
Louisville, KY

While I was in Viet Nam, our company received, along with some replacements for some of our casualties, Richard and Shadow.

Richard was a Scout Dog Handler and Shadow (An absolutely beautiful black and silver German Shepherd.) was his K-9 partner. Richard, Shadow and I became almost inseparable. In the spirit of cross training, Richard (and Shadow) taught me how to work with Shadow, what her "alerts" were and how to respond to her.

The day came when my company got caught in an ambush. Shadow and I were wounded, Richard was killed. I was med-evaced, with Shadow, to Da Nang. The doctor there arranged for me to be sent to Okinawa and told me that he had contacted the kennels and they were coming for Shadow to put her down as he thought her injuries were too serious for her to recover.

When the pilot of the med-evac came through, I knew him. We had been friends since 2nd grade. Begging and pleading, I finally convinced him to take Shadow with us. He had two of his crewmen put her between my legs and cover her with a blanket. When we landed in Okinawa, she went to Dr. Mangus' Animal Hospital and I went to Kue Army Hospital.

We both recovered and I sent Shadow home. when I got home 30 days later, Shadow and my Aunt were best of friends.

Shadow lived to be 17 years old, a great family dog, protective and stable. My son learned to walk by grabbing her fur and pulling himself up. All she would do is brace herself, check to make sure he had a good grip, then slowly walk off with Jim toddling at her side.

The day we buried my Aunt, Shadow was with me in the car as we took my Aunt's ashes for their final ride. It was a beautiful spring day, exactly the kind my Aunt had enjoyed the most. We drove all her favorite trails and areas, stopping and picking a small bunch of wild flowers where-ever she used to do so.

Shadow was lying on the front seat with her head on my leg. As I made the turn into the cemetery, I felt her sigh deeply, then her head got very, very heavy. I looked down and realized she wasn't breathing. Shadow had gone to lead my Aunt across the Rainbow Bridge. "Go ahead, Darlin' take her home. I love you."

Remember and cherish those with paws and claws but no voice, which we can understand, to speak or vote for themselves.

A Tribute to Shadow

The one absolutely unselfish friend
That I have found in this selfish world;
The one who has never proven to be
Ungrateful or treacherous, who has
Never deserted me, is Shadow.
Shadow has stood by me in prosperity
As well as poverty.
In health as well as sickness.
She has slept on the cold ground
When the winter winds blew and the
Snow drove fiercely; if only to be
Close by my side.
Shadow has kissed my hand when
I had no food to offer.
She has licked the tears, wounds and sores
That came from our encounters with
The roughness of the world.
She guards my sleep as though
I were a prince.
When all other friends departed,
Shadow remained close to my side.
When my riches took flight and my
Reputation lay in pieces,
Shadow remained as constant in her
Love for me as the sun in its'
Journey through the heavens.

Senator George Graham Vest

May Shadow rest in peace and run in freedom,
Resting in the warmth of the sun
And wanting for naught;
Until I shall cross the river
And we may walk together again;

Forever.
Go, my Darling, go in peace and
In freedom, your tour is done.
I will join you, Shadow;
When my work is done and
My time to rest has come.

Thomas Johnston added

K-9 FALK

Officer Bruce K. Bertram
Danbury Police Department, Connecticut

A DAY IN THE LIFE OF A K-9 HANDLER

By Bruce K. Bertram

As I'm rolling over in my nice warm bed, I peek out from under the covers. I see the rain on the window and hear the pattering on the roof, I don't want to get up. I quietly whisper, "Hey Falk." I notice two sharp, deep brown eyes staring at me from the edge of a plastic portable kennel crate. Within what seemed less than a second, I feel the Yin and Yang. The balance of life, at least for a K-9 handler, of a cold wet nose and a warm wet tongue.

"I'm getting up." I tell him, but his excitement tells me that I'm not fast enough. I talk to him as if he is my best friend. Then I stop and think, not only he is my best friend, he is much more than that. He's my partner, the one who is entrusted with making sure that I'll come home alive and well tonight.

After throwing on a pair of BDU's, a quick name for battle dress uniform, I walk down the stairs; Falk is already at the side door doing circles. I reach to a hook next to the door where a metal chain collar is hanging. On the bottom of the collar, a strip of black leather with a small badge. At the bottom edge of the badge there's an inscription "K-9." "Ok buddy," as I slip the collar onto the now K-9 Falk. We can get some good training in today before our shift starts at four. I wonder to myself, "Why is it Falk always runs to the side door and not the back door where he could lie on the deck and chew a bone or play ball in the grass?" Oh yeah, the police cruiser is parked next to the side door. We set off and drive to a near by field. I call on the radio to a fellow police officer and asked him to meet me at the field.

Within a short time he arrives. He makes his greeting to K-9 Falk and then me, but I'm used to that and to tell the truth, proud of it, a bit like father and son. Then the officer asks "What's up?" "Do you think you could run a track for me?" I ask. With a look like I should be put in an insane asylum, he replies "It's raining."

"Yeah, isn't that great? Dogs love to track in the rain." I'm sure out of respect to K-9 Falk and not me, the officer gets out of his cruiser mumbling something about being nuts and what do you want me to do. After a short explanation, my fellow officer lays a short but nice track. I thank him, say our good byes and begin our tracking training. The morning training went well and K-9 Falk and I return home.

I open the door to my house and K-9 Falk walks into the kitchen where he gives a good shake. As the water, mud and bits of debris hit the ceiling and walls, it crosses my mind that I'd better throw a coat of paint on the kitchen pretty soon. My wife hearing that we had arrived home, walks into the kitchen and upon seeing the muddy foot prints left by our morning trudge through the woods, greets us with "Good morning Falk." Then turns to me and says, "Don't forget to clean up the floor."

It's time for work. Back into the cruiser and to the Police

Department. K-9 Falk and I head for roll call, it's Monday which means inspection day. The sergeant walks into the room and orders all the officers to line up. K-9 Falk and I take our place in the center of the line. The Sergeant walks down the line eyeing us up and down for everything from shiny shoes to a clean weapon. The Sergeant stops in front of me. "Boots look good, service weapon is good, but you have more hair on your pants than your partner does." I just smile and agree.

We get back into the cruiser, and head for the donut shop. Most people think cops like donuts; it's the coffee we like. As I walk into the shop, I'm greeted by the young lady behind the counter. "How's Falk? Do you want the usual?" I reply he's fine and I'm fine too. She hands me a bag with the usual, a small regular coffee and one munchkin. I sit back into my cruiser. K-9 Falk is sitting up with one paw over the front seat. I tell him; "Relax, I got it, I got it. Hold on." Reaching into the bag I pull out the munchkin. "Here you go." Well, he's happy and I see him taking his place in the back seat.

When people ask "What's it like being a policeman?" I tell them "7 hours and 59 minutes of boredom and 1 minute of pure terror." The night is quiet with the light rain still falling. The end of the shift is nearing when a radio dispatch breaks the silence. Two units are dispatched to a burglary in progress. "What do you say Falk? Let's head that way." I'm sure the dispatcher is going to send us also. Before I can shift the cruiser into drive the dispatcher radios me. K-9 Falk immediately rouses to a sitting position. He has learned to recognize my call number. We arrive shortly after the first dispatched units.

As I exit my cruiser one of the officers approaches me and asks if my dog can track in the rain. The officer continues that a suspect had run off into the wooded area and that he didn't know if he was armed. I pop the trunk lid and grab a tracking leash. K-9 Falk upon seeing the leash becomes excited, whining and pacing in the back of the cruiser. As I open the door to the cruiser, everyone steps back. I hear one of the officers say in a quiet voice, "Go get'em Falk."

As I'm hooking on the leash, I ask "Who's my backup officer?" Without hesitation the same officer replies, "Let's go." I bring K-9 Falk to the area where the suspect was last seen. You can tell when the K-9 has found the scent. The ears come up straight and the nose settles in toward the ground. We were off into the wood line. Tracking through the wooded area I noticed that we were headed toward a lighted parking lot.

K-9 Falk slowed his tracking; his head came up as he began to smell the scent in the air in front of us. I was sure the suspect was close as K-9 Falk's tail was whipping back and forth in anticipation of a chance to chase the suspect down. I quietly but strongly command my backup officer to take cover, as the suspect is close. I command K-9 Falk to a laying down position. I yell out: "Police Department with a K-9! Speak to me now or I'll release the K-9!"

All is quiet for a brief moment, and then I hear the breaking of twigs and the crushing of leaves. I see a silhouette of a man running toward the parking lot. Upon seeing him I yell: "Police! Stop or I'll send my dog!" By now the suspect has reached the parking lot. I have a clear view of him and so does K-9 Falk. The suspect is not stopping. All this excitement is just too much for K-9 Falk as he lets out his own commands. I release K-9 Falk.

With the agility of a deer and the power of a tiger, he is through the wood line and onto the parking lot. All I can do now is start heading toward the parking lot and pray the suspect doesn't have a gun. It seems as if every thing has gone into slow motion, as I'm recalling a similar incident where at the end of the track, a gun battle began and K-9 Falk was shot in the neck trying to protect me.

Well, this is the one minute of pure terror. As I reach the edge of the parking lot, I see that the suspect has realized that I really do have a dog and that the dog is out running him. The suspect stops and turns toward my direction, I draw my duty weapon from its holster as I scan the suspect and his movements for any sign of a weapon.

What I see is a teen age boy throwing his hands as high as he can screaming "Don't let the dog bite me!" I call out "Falk, Here!" With only a brief hesitation, K-9 Falk obeys my command to return to me. K-9 Falk had been so close to the suspect that he had to run past the suspect and circle around his back to return to me. As K-9 Falk approaches my side I praise him "At'a good boy." and pat his head as I grab hold of his collar.

My backup officer seeing this "close encounter of a K-9 kind", utters a few words that wouldn't be spoken in polite company and something about the kid having to change his shorts. He then rushes toward the young suspect. The teen is place under arrest and transported to booking. I think to myself if that kid had hesitated for just a few more seconds, we'd be calling an ambulance for him instead. As I walk back to my cruiser, the sergeant approaches me. "Good job, nice police work Falk. Oh, and you too, Bertram." Most people would take offense to being second best to a dog, but to a K-9 handler it just makes us prouder. Kind of like a father when his son hits a home run.

Back at the station as the teen is being booked, the jewelry taken in the burglary is recovered from the teen's pockets. I'm finishing my paper work and K-9 Falk? Well he's under the computer table sound asleep. Done for this shift. "Time to go home Falk."

We walk out the back door of the station and get into the cruiser heading home. I pull into the driveway and open the cruiser door. K-9 Falk jumps out and heads for the bushes, within seconds he's returning, being escorted by his cat. This is an every night ritual. We all enter our house and go into the kitchen where I get the food bowls. "You guys hungry?" The cat is swirling and rubbing around K-9 Falk's face and with one wet lick to the cat's head, he turns her into a resemblance of a punk rocker.

I stare at the two of them "Yeah, big, bad police dog, right?"

Once they are fed, I kick back in my lounge chair. You have to watch your K-9 for a couple of hours after you feed them as they may "bloat." Bloat is when their stomach flips over inside. It can kill your K-9 very quickly. "What do you say Falk, bed time?" Into his kennel cage all curled up. I wonder how he can fall asleep so fast.

I'm startled awake from a dead sleep by something cold and wet. I open my eyes and see two dark brown eyes staring back at me with an expression of anticipation. "Morning already, big guy?" "What do you say? How about some drug training today?"

BIOGRAPHY

Louise (Olson) Krause was born in Michigan. Her family moved to Indiana where she was raised and lived until she met Robert Krause, then an Airman in the United States Air Force. Robert (Bob) and Louise (Lulu) married and moved to Cape May, New Jersey.

Lulu worked as a receptionist for FOMOCO (Ford Motor Co.) while Bob completed his education. They have two children, Eric and Greg. Shortly after Eric was born; Heidi, a Black and Tan German Shepherd joined the family. After their son, Greg, was born; Schatzi, a German Shorthaired Pointer, came to live with them.

As the boys grew up, went to school, then off to college, found jobs and got married, they raised 4 more dogs, 2 at a time. As each of their K-9 companions grew old and then went on to the Rainbow Bridge, they got another. Both for themselves and for the dog who had been left behind grieving. Their sons, in the meantime, succeeded in their endeavors and also presented them with 4 wonderful grandchildren.

They've never suffered from Empty Nest Syndrome as they still have 2 German Shorthaired Pointers in their lives. Chloe, the oldest and Leesy, a young pup just now joining the family (and, incidentally, driving Lulu crazy! She had forgotten just how much of a handful the young of any species can be!).

Bob had planned early on to become a veterinarian, but ended up becoming a Funeral Director. Lulu combined her knowledge of the funeral business and love of K-9s with her compassion for humans who were suffering from the loss of their K-9 companion/partner and "Life went to the dogs."

That's how all this came about. Compassion, caring, respect for public servants and understanding of their grief and need for companionship during their time of grief.

Editor/Proofreader Thomas Johnston, personal remarks:

To the Officers whose Partners are portrayed in this book: I am one of the "civilians" that you folks often don't think care about you and your partners. In this, you are in error. It has cost me tissues and tears beyond count to edit and proofread this book before publication. Although I was never "officially" a handler, my K-9 Partner is here also. Yes, I managed to make some needed corrections, but only after about the 3rd time I reread your story. It was in Shadow's memory and to honor you and your partners that I undertook to proofread and edit this book.

The police are called, with reason, "The Thin Blue Line." Each of you is part of an even thinner blue line.

I hope that you can find it in your heart to accept another K-9 partner and continue to protect and serve. Each K-9 is unique, as are you. You deserve each other and I honor you for your service.

My prayer each night for you and your partner is that your tour be a quiet one and you both go home to your loved ones at the end of your tour safe and sound.

God Bless You and Thank You for all that you do for us.

/S/ Tom Johnston

This book is truly a work of international scope. Some of the entries are from as far away as Australia, Holland and Germany.

For some of the respondents, English is not their primary language. As a result, in every entry, the flavor of the K-9's Partner's phraseology is retained to the maximum extent possible.

The author/publisher lives in New Jersey, as does the graphic artist. The editor/proofreader lives in Kentucky and the printer lives in New York. Therefore, any errors that may be found in this book are probably uniquely mine and I apologize sincerely for them.

As I was preparing this book for publication, I noted that an oft repeated incident in the loss of some of these K-9s was death by misadventure while the K-9 was working "off leash" and away from their handler. There is a new product soon to be marketed in the United States by the Secor Company of Japan.

The product is a GPS signaling device which can be attached to the working K-9's collar. The device will allow the handler to locate the K-9 immediately within 167 feet. I have written to the Secor Company asking if it is possible to develop a hand-held GPS receiver. This new product might well be of interest to some of the police departments and K-9 handlers. The company can be reached by the Internet at: www.secor.jp.com

TJ
Louisville, KY

THE PACT OF THE FIRE

When the world was created, First Man and First Woman struggled to stay alive and warm through the first winter. First Dog struggled also. Deep in the winter, First Dog gave birth to her pups. Each night, she huddled in the brush of the forest, longingly watching the fire which kept First Man and First Woman warm.

First Winter was severe, so cold that First Dog dared not leave her pups to search for food to fill her own belly, fearing that her pups would freeze to death in her absence. She curled around them, but the wind was bitter. Her belly shrank with hunger, and soon she had no milk. The smallest pup perished, and First Dog felt her own life draining away as she struggled to care for the remaining pups. Fearing for the fate of the others, she knew she had no choice but to approach the fire and ask First Woman and First Man to share their food and the fire's warmth.

Slowly, she crept to the fire and spoke to First Woman who was heavy with child. "I am a mother," said First Dog, "and soon you will be a mother too. I want my little ones to survive, just as you will want your little one to survive. So I will ask you to make a pact."

First Woman and First Man listened. "I am about to die.

Take my pups. You will raise them and call them Dog. They will be your guardians. They will alert you to danger, keep you warm, guard your camp, and even lay down their life to protect your life and the lives of your children. They will be companions to you and all your generations, never leaving your side, as long as Mankind shall survive.

In return, you will share your food and the warmth of your fire. You will treat my children with love and kindness, and tend to them if they become ill, just as if they were born from your own belly. And if they are in pain, you will take a sharp knife to their throat and end their misery. In exchange for this, you will have the loyalty of my children and their offspring until the end of time." First Man and First Woman agreed.

First Dog went to her nest in the brush, and with the last of her strength, one by one, she brought her pups to the fire. As she did so, First Woman gave birth to First Child, wrapped her in Rabbit skins, and nestled First Child among the pups by the fireside. First Dog lay down by the fire, licked her pups, then walked away to die under the stars.

Before she disappeared into the darkness, she turned and spoke once more to First Man, "My children will honor the pact for all generations. But if Man breaks this pact, if you or your children's children deny even one Dog food, warmth, a kind word or a merciful end, your generations will be plagued with war, hunger, and disease, and so shall this remain until the pact is honored again by all Mankind."

With this, First Dog entered the night and returned in spirit to the Creator.

Lakota Sioux Legend

2000 AND BEFORE

INDEX 2000 AND BEFORE

In Loving Memory of

K-9 ADAME

October 3, 2000
LODD

A.K.A. "Frenchy"
Caretaker Trooper Richard Crosby
Massachusetts State Police Mounted Unit
a Selle Francais horse - age 27 years,

Frenchy marched in President Clinton's inaugural parade in Washington, D.C., three years ago and most recently helped in the search for missing Warren lifeguard Molly Bish. Adame, a twenty seven year old state police horse, died shortly after he handled crowds outside the presidential debate Tuesday.

The trusted state police worker spent several Fourth of July holidays manning the crowd on Martha's Vineyard. He didn't bat an eye one time at a Lynn rally when a child's balloon bounced off his large head.

After a sixteen year career, the horse named Adame died. October 3, 2000 from a heart attack shortly after controlling the crowds outside the presidential debate at University of Massachusetts at Boston. Sgt. James Condon said it was like losing one of our own. He was one of the bravest horses we had.. Sgt. Condon, is the head of the State Police Mounted Unit headquarters in Acton.

"FRENCHY died in the line of duty." Adame, a Selle Francais (sir name) was one of a dozen state police horses who arrived in Boston Tuesday afternoon to help man the expected crowd of protesters which grew to about 4,000 people. During his shift, state police troopers said Adame showed no signs of discomfort. Caretaker, Trooper Richard Crosby stated that nothing ever rattled him and that he was a solid, solid horse.

Shortly after midnight, Adame and his partner for the night, State Police Trooper Joseph deYoung, headed back with the others to the main staging area, the last stop before the trip home. Adame collapsed at about 12:30 a.m. while walking on an access road behind the JFK Library. His front legs went and then he seemed to sit down. Trooper DeYoung's leg was pinned under the horse for a short time but he was not injured. Emergency medical technicians could not revive the horse at the scene. Adame was buried yesterday at Blue Hills in Canton.

State police troopers who work out of the Mounted Unit headquarters in Acton were visibly upset yesterday at the loss of their loyal member, who they called an A team horse. Adame had worked with the Metropolitan District Commission for eight years before the MDC merged with the state police Mounted Unit in 1992.

Like many of his four legged colleagues, Adame was donated to the state. His caretakers plan to have a headstone made in his honor, which they will set in a nearby field in Acton. Crosby, a state trooper for 19 years, said Adame had a calming effect on the other horses. ``He was like a parent or older brother to them," Crosby said.

Sargent Condon said state troopers in the unit take turns riding the different horses. "Everyone here is devastated," he said. Although Sgt. Condon called Tuesday's crowd nasty, he said neither the conditions nor exhaustion was linked to the horse's death. He said Adame was in good health and was used to that type of work. State police horses patrol state parks and beaches; help in searches for missing people and help control crowds.

In Loving Memory of

K-9 AJAX
Officer Rick Bortnowsky
&

K-9 SZULTAN
Lt. Oscar Lopez
September, 2000

City of Newburgh Police Department
55 Broadway Newburgh,
New York 12550 (845)561 3131
Chief of Police William M Bloom

K-9 cops speak of the bond between officers and their dogs. At a brief memorial service for two City of Newburgh police dogs who died this week, bagpipes skirled in a sunny glade and uniformed police officers fought back tears. Officer Rich Bortnowsky, whose 3 year old German Shepherd, Ajax, was hit by a car Thursday, accepted a plaque from the U.S. Police K-9 Association in memory of the dog. So did Lt. Oscar Lopez, whose 9 year old shepherd, Szultan, was euthanized this week after being diagnosed with cancer.

One officer, who read a poem honoring the deceased police dogs, broke down unabashedly in tears. Lopez, who heads the department's K-9 division, said, "Some people might say, 'All this for a dog?' But it's hard for me to understand that." Unsentimental reasons motivate the police force to have dogs, said Lopez. But you can't stay unsentimental and use a dog effectively.

Lopez said the dogs, which are specially bred German Shepherds imported from Europe, save taxpayers' money in police overtime. "If you hid in the woods, it might take 20 police officers hours to find you. But any one of these dogs could find you in seconds," he said. The dogs can save an officer's life or a suspect's, said Officer Darren Terry, who is in the K-9 division. When a suspect once pulled a gun on him, he would have had to shoot the man if his dog hadn't leaped and knocked the gun from the suspect's hand, Terry recalled. But unlike a machine, the dogs won't work just for fuel. And unlike a human officer, they work neither for money nor for any abstract principle.

"Everything they do for us is out of love," said Terry. "They do it because they're going to get praise from 'Daddy'." "For us to ask what we ask of them, we have to show them we love them," said Officer Rich Carrion. So when an officer joins the K-9 Division, he takes his dog in as a family member. "I don't get my food before he does," said Carrion, speaking of his dog. "If we've been in the car all day, the first thing we do when we get home is to go run and play."

"He was my child," said Bortnowsky, speaking of Ajax. "He was a good dog, a loyal dog," Lopez said of Szultan, who once was pistol whipped in the head by a suspect. Szultan didn't budge and went right on gripping the suspect's leg in his teeth. "I would go through any door or any situation with him (Szultan) without hesitation," Lopez said. Lopez said the department plans to replenish the K-9 force with two more dogs.

In Loving Memory of

K-9 AKAH

October 22, 2000

Partner: Sgt. Dan Johnson
Boone County Sheriff's Dept.
2121 County Drive
Columbia, MO 65202

The Boone County Sheriff's Department said goodbye to one of its most loyal members as well as one of its furriest on Thursday.

Akah, a member of the K-9 patrol who had been with the Boone County Sheriff's Department for five years, died Thursday from cancer.

Born in Germany, this German Shepherd came to Columbia when he was little more than a year old, to live with his owner and handler, Sgt. Dan Johnson. Johnson said Akai was better than any of the dog characters in the movies who portrayed his job, such as in "Turner and Hooch." He didn't make as much money, but he was better. He was very social and loved being around people." Despite his love for affection, Johnson said Akah knew how to get the job done. Nobody wanted to run away from him. Every time I said stop, he would stop. Akah was trained in drug detection, handler protection, apprehension and tracking missing persons. He was definitely a dual purpose dog.

With the loss of Akah, the Boone County Sheriff's Department is down to one K-9 unit, a Belgian Tervuren named Tarko, who was also born in Germany. Both dogs had been very active and instrumental in the success of numerous incidents over the past several years.

Johnson said he will get another dog in January when the training session for police dogs starts again. Akah was cremated and will be buried at Johnson's home. Akah will be missed.

UPDATE:
New partner, Kasper , by Sgt. Dan Johnson

Currently, I am waiting for the next class to open for another K-9 partner. I know there needs to be a cool down time between dogs, but it has been a long winter. My new partner's name is "KASPER." He is waiting at the school, Detector Dogs International in Iowa now. Kasper will be the third dog I have put into service. He should be in service for 10 years, figuring I double the service life each time.

In Loving Memory of

K-9 ANDO

December 26, 2000
LODD

Partner: Officer James Davison
LaGrange Police Department
100 Haralson Street
LaGrange, GA 30240

Statistics / Bio Data
Born: Germany, October 1994.
Age: 6 yrs. old
Physical Standard: German Shepherd
Color: black & tan, 80 lbs.
Beautiful dog!
Employment: LaGrange Police Dept.
Partner: Ofc. Jim Davison, handler for 4 years.
Duties: Multipurpose, patrol/narcotics detection
service dog. Assigned to patrol division.

Ando and his handler Officer Davison are assigned to the patrol division. They assist the Criminal Investigations Division (CID) and the Special Investigations Unit (SIU) serving search warrants and apprehending wanted criminals. They also patrol high crime areas of the city and pro-actively enforce all laws of the state of Georgia.

The team also gives K-9 lectures and demonstrations to the public and assists other law enforcement agencies when requested. Ando was one of four K-9 teams in the LaGrange Police Department and will be greatly missed by all the members of the department.

Ando gave his best whenever called on and loved his job and his handler; he was a great tracker and loved the hunt and catching the bad guys. Some of the highlights of his career included assisting in the apprehension of two murderers, four bank robbers and one of the US Marshal's most wanted fugitives. His loss is a great tragedy to the community and the LaGrange Police K-9 unit.

The K-9 Unit currently consists of three (3) teams. All three teams work in conjunction with the Patrol, Special Investigations Unit (SIU), and the Criminal Investigations Division (CID). The teams assist in the execution of search warrants and felony arrest warrants, vehicle and building searches, tracking of suspects, and the apprehension of fleeing felons.

The teams are high profile and support our Zero Tolerance Program. They concentrate patrol efforts in high crime areas and respond to calls for services. All our LaGrange officers mourn the loss of Ando.

THE INCIDENT:

On December 26th 2000 at about 8:30 P.M. a patrol officer observed a vehicle with no license plate and no seat belts in use riding around in a high drug area of the city. The officer initiated a traffic stop, but the vehicle refused to stop and a pursuit began and lasted for about a mile, ending on a dead end street with both occupants leaving the vehicle and running from the officer into a wooded area.

Officer Davison and Ando responded to assist and began to track the driver. A good perimeter was established but normally our K-9 teams have no cover officer on tracking incidents because of the lack of manpower. To have a good perimeter we have to give up the cover officer, as was the case for this incident.

Ando tracked hard and located a pair of jeans the driver was wearing. As the team continued to track the suspect could be heard moving through the brush about fifty yards ahead of the team. Numerous verbal warnings about the use of the K-9 were given to the suspect with no response. The ground cover got thicker and thicker as the team continued to track the suspect and Officer. Davison decided to go into an area search or directed search off leash.

Officer. Davison gave numerous verbal warnings about the deployment of a K-9 off leash and then began to send Ando out to search a very densely wooded area. Ando went out and recalled twice and was sent out a third time but did not return.

Officer. Davison recalled Ando several times with no response. Nothing could be heard at all. No barking no yelling, nothing. Officer. Davison began to search for his K-9, sensing something was wrong and alerted perimeter officers of the situation.

The other three K-9 teams with the LaGrange Police department were called out and together they began to search the wooded area, continuing to do so for about six hours and concentrating the search on the area within the perimeter. At about five o'clock in the morning Officer. Davison began searching outside the perimeter area and located his K-9 partner Ando in a creek bed, dead from what appeared to be drowning.

Ando was still wearing his collar and black nylon tracking harness with the words POLICE on each side. Further investigation at the crime scene reveled the suspect's footprints, a camo ear warmer, and a black leather jacket that was soaking wet and had creek sand in the pockets. This location was a little over one hundred yards from the area Officer. Davison released Ando last.

LaGrange detectives began an investigation and arrested twenty year old Randal Chambers on December 28th 2000. Chambers had multiple dog bites and scratches on his legs and arms, but refused to talk about the incident. The investigation revealed that Chambers, who has a history of drug arrests, and Obstructing Police, had exchanged crack cocaine for the use of the vehicle. Chambers was charged with numerous traffic charges, obstruction, and killing a police K-9, which is a five year felony and a $10,000.00 fine under Georgia criminal code.

Officer Davison will remain dedicated to the K-9 unit and will be selecting a new K-9 partner in February; he will name him Gator.

In Loving Memory of

K-9 ARCO

September 7, 2000

Partner: Officer Jon Granberry
Grand Prairie Police Department
Texas

Less than a week after their new K-9 arrived in Texas from Holland, the Grand Prairie Police Department lost him to heat stroke. Temperatures in North Texas on Monday were a record setting 111 degrees and officials believe that the dog, Arco, died because of this.

Arco was a three year old Belgian Malinois for whom the department paid $4,750. According to Police Chief Glen Hill, the handler, Officer Jon Granberry, was devastated. "To be in that assignment, you have to have a great love for the animal. Though he only had him for less than 48 hours, there was a bond there," Hill said.

Officer Granberry had kept Arco in a shaded kennel and had wet him down several times in the intense heat. "I believe I did everything I could," he said.

Administrators are talking to the vendor since they feel they were not given adequate instructions regarding the care of Arco. The vendor, Mike Clemenson of Hill Country Dog Center, said, "Anytime a dog comes from a cooler climate like Holland, you have to take that into consideration...I've never had a dog die like this before."

In Loving Memory of

K-9 ARGO

LODD
October 3, 1998

Partner: Officer Brad Thompson
Ft. Worth Police Department
350 W. Belknap St.
Ft. Worth, TX, 76102

Officer Thompson said that Argo was killed during a search for a suspect who the day before had shot a State Trooper during a traffic stop. "K-9 Argo was on point and had lead us into a heavily wooded area and to the suspect's location. Upon contact, the suspect immediately took the team under fire catching Argo in the throat with the first round and dropping him.

Rounds 2 and 3 hit my thigh and chest before I got my first round off at the suspect. Although fatally wounded, Argo then got back up and again charged the suspect."

"I had Argo on long line so I immediately pulled him back to me and placed him in a down position behind me, placing my body between him and the gunman in an attempt to protect him as he had done for me moments earlier." In the ensuing gun battle the suspect was killed.

"We immediately loaded Argo into a patrol unit and took him to the vet where despite our efforts he died the following morning. The only consolation was that Argo died doing what he loved doing and in the arms of the person he loved enough to do it for."

"I have been an officer for 15 years working such assignments as Patrol, Narcotics, Gang Enforcement, Directed Patrol/Tactical, community services and K-9. I am a certified Tactical (SWAT) Officer, Tactical Tracker and Defensive Tactics Instructor. I have had the privilege of training with such units as the German Bundesgrenzschutz GSG9 (Germany's premier counter terrorist unit), the Specialeinsatzkommando (SEK) which is a German State Police Swat Team in Northern Germany as well.

My latest privilege has been the Tactical Tracking course taught by former Rhodesian SAS Officer David Scott Donelan who commanded the Rhodesian Tracking School overseeing all TCU's (Tracker Combat Units). 30 years of fighting terrorists in the bush of SW Africa has made this man a legend and it was my honor to learn from him

In Loving Memory of

K-9 ARON

LODD
May 14, 1998

Partner: Officer Terry Burnett
Metro Nashville Police Department
Nashville, Tennessee

Tuesday, May 19, 1998 at 1315 hours hundreds of Officers from Tennessee and surrounding states assembled at Marshall Donnelly Combs Funeral Home on 25th Ave. As I entered the Funeral Home I observed Officer Burnett standing beside a beautiful casket that held the mortal remains of his fallen partner.

I approached and spoke with Officer Burnett for a moment and then pushed back the tears as I observed Aron lying so peaceful with his training tennis ball at his feet. I some how knew at this moment that I was paying respect to a fallen Officer and not just a K-9 dog.

The funeral procession got started and I estimated that there were approximately 300 to 400 police units, all with lights flashing and many with their K-9 partners running up and down in the back seats as if they knew why they were there.

The procession worked it's way across town with motorists pulling over and many had their hands over their hearts in tribute to Aron. The hardest part of the journey was as the procession passed by the Metro Nashville Criminal Justice Building. The staff of the police department and court house employees lined the street in final tribute to Aron. My tears let go at this point as I knew Aron would have been proud of his fellow workers and the citizens of Nashville.

Once we arrived at the Training Academy, it took several minutes to park all of the police units. It was then that I observed that many citizens were already present waiting for the service. I saw one little girl approx. eight years of age who had flowers in her hand. I learned that she had met Aron some time before and wanted to say farewell to him.

The grave site was covered with flowers from friends of Aron's. They were all so beautiful, truly a sight to behold. The pall bearers took Aron from the hearse and carried him to his final resting place here on earth. Then the Chaplin gave his eulogy, which was beautiful. As Taps started to be played and the 21 gun salute was fired, I realized how lucky we all were that God created these wonderful animals who are able to become true friends and sworn officer's in the fight against crime.

Lined up across the field were officers with their partners seated at their feet, each of whom would lay down their lives at any time to protect both you and me.

Aron, you have meant so much to us all and we thank you for what you gave for us.... your life. You may be gone from this old earth but your spirit will live on and we all will be better for having had you here to protect us.

TRIBUTE TO K-9 ARON

On 05/14/98 at approx. 0900 Hours the Metro Nashville Police Department and all of the Law Enforcement Community lost an outstanding member of our ranks. A lone gunman entered the Regency Bank and robbed it. The quick response of Metro Police Units aborted his escape from the bank and he was forced to run into the woods behind the bank. Officer Terry Burnett and his partner, K-9 Aron, responded to the scene and tracked the suspect into the woods along with fellow officers.

Aron performed his duties with the expertise he was trained with. Aron located the suspect and the suspect opened fire with two semi auto handguns. One round struck Officer Burnett in the foot and Aron positioned himself in between his handler and took gunfire from the suspect that was meant for Officer Burnett. Aron was struck by the gunfire and as officers pulled his handler from the firefight, Aron continued to stand between the suspect and his partner.

Aron forced himself on his back legs only, as his front legs were useless from the wounds he had obtained, from the woods and returned to lay on top of his handler and partner to further protect him.

Officer Burnett had suffered a gun shot to the foot and refused medical treatment until he and other Officers rushed Aron to a local emergency animal clinic where Aron died from his wounds. Aron acted without fear and protected his handler in the most noble fashion. He even returned to his partner with life threatening wounds as he was trained to do. The criminal was killed by the four member S.W.A.T. team, when he attempted to shoot another K-9 and his handler. Aron displayed a courage and devotion to Law Enforcement that many will never understand. The Hendersonville Police Department, it's Officers, and K-9 ''Bo'' salute the valor of Aron and stand beside our fellow Officers of the Metro Nashville Police Department in this tragic and solemn moment.

Officer Aron will be sadly missed by all of us in this community but will never be forgotten. Our prayers to Officer Burnett and his family in his loss, as Aron was not only an officer but a devoted and true friend as he demonstrated today.

In Loving Memory of

K-9 ARPAD

June 29, 1999

Partner: Ad Snoek
Police of Rotterdam
Rijnmond Netherlands

I am a K-9 handler for 18 years and 41 years old. I had a special bond with 3 dogs.. The first was "Waldo"a terrifying dog to look at. When you appeared in front of the kennel he was so angry that it looks like he pulled his lips over his nose. The only thing you saw was teeth. A great dog, he saved my butt at least three times. At that moment, you think that kind of dog only happens once in a life time......wrong!

After that I got another dog, a fine animal, but not that caliber of Waldo, named, "Sandor." When he reached the age of 8, the government changed the rules for the exams for police K-9s. It was too difficult to change Sandor so he could pass the new exams, so he had to leave the force. I got him a fine place to stay, and he died at the age of 14.

Then, I had to get a new dog. It was August 1995. Suddenly

the instructor appeared on the training field with a new dog, his name was "Arpad" He was enormous, 73 centimeters high, had a head like a bull and his weight was over 50 kilograms. I immediately fell in love. I grabbed him from the instructor and said, "he's mine!" So it happened. We became the best of friends. He became a living legend. The power he had in him was unbelievable. No men stood straight when he attacked you. He was my best friend, he was my pal, he was my everything and he was unbeatable.

At least that was what I thought, again wrong. On the 30th of April 1999 (that day our Queen celebrates her birthday) I had to work on the National Festival. I noticed that Arpad was not in his best mood. The whole day it was not Arpad. He was quiet, tired, no power. He was ill! At the vet's, after several check ups, the outcome was terrible. Arpad finally met his awful opponent, CANCER!

Even when I write this letter, the tears are rolling down from my cheeks, Several specialists, medicine and yes, they worked. Arpad became the old one, unfortunately not for long. Within two weeks his weight decreased from 48 to 32 kilograms and he suffered a lots of pain.

Then on the 29th of June 1999, I had to euthanize my everything. He died at 20:03 p.m. that day in my arms, in the company of my wife. That very day, a piece of me died with ARPAD. I never, never, never will forget my friend.

I have a Bronze sculpture of his head in my living room on a very special place. Again I say, thanks to Arpad for being in my life and being my friend. I know I will always be yours. I think there must be a God, even for K-9 handlers, because after Arpad, I was depressed. I thought that I never be so lucky to get a dog like Arpad, or Appie (his nick name) again.

God decided different however. I got myself a new dog named "Ricky." A great dog, very social, also for my family, my wife and five kids, ages 18, 14, 8, 6 and 6 months. ARPAD was not that social, but times they are a changing, even the community, so also the dogs. I am a very lucky guy. I hope that you know what I mean.

In Loving Memory of

K-9 ASKO

May 19, 1981
LODD

Partner: Officer Ken Kramerman
Redding Police Department
1313 California St.
Redding, CA 96001
530-225.4289

Memorial to honor fallen police dogs
Alex Breitler   Record Searchlight

Asko's ears perked and his tail shot up. He'd caught the scent of five escaped inmates on the roof of the old Shasta County Jail. Eager as always to do his job, the German Shepherd police dog followed his nose and leaped over a wall, unaware there was nothing but empty space on the other side. He fell three stories to his death.

Two decades later, Asko, the only Redding police dog killed in the line of duty, will be among 19 dogs honored at a state K-

9 memorial to be unveiled at noon Sunday at the University of California at Davis School of Veterinary Medicine. "He was an exceptional dog," recalled Asko's handler, then officer Ken Kramerman, now a lieutenant in the same department. "It was no different than losing a human partner for me."

The memorial, named "Faithful Partner," includes a star shaped pedestal with plaques listing the names of the dogs, and a statue of a German Shepherd wearing collar and badge. Police dog teams from all over the state are expected to attend the ceremony.

Each of the dogs' stories has a different ending, but all are tragic. One dog was stabbed by a rape suspect during a search. A second was shot while sniffing out a gunman in a park. A third was hit in the head with a pair of pliers by a car theft suspect.

Asko, 3 years old when he died, was imported from Germany and worked the streets with Kramerman for two years before his death. In that time he was credited with 60 arrests and 25 justified bites. He was both a cop dog and a family dog, living at Kramerman's home during the day and working with him at night. Most police dogs get a bit tired on the graveyard shift. Not Asko. He'd stay awake the whole time, his handler said. Even on Kramerman's days off the dog was raring to go. "He'd be at the door looking at me, wagging his tail, saying, 'Come on, let's go,' " Kramerman said.

On May 19, 1981, Kramerman was called at home about 6 AM. He was asked to bring Asko and join in the search for the inmates, who were believed to be armed. The pair went to the roof, which was cluttered with air conditioning units and all sorts of hiding spots. A 3 foot high wall circled the perimeter. Kramerman gave Asko a search command and let him off his leash to follow the scent, figuring the wall would keep him safe. "He wasn't going to walk over and just fall off the edge," Kramerman said. But Asko in his enthusiasm jumped over the wall and fell to the ground. He died a short time later.

Officer Kramerman lost not only his work partner, but his

family dog. "That was part of the job," he said. "It's something you don't think about. You know the risks."

The Department of Justice earlier this year sent letters about the memorial to all law enforcement agencies to collect a list of dogs to be honored. Organizers of the memorial say there are 15,000 police dogs in the United States, including bomb and drug sniffing dogs. "They really enjoy what they do," Kramerman said. "People don't understand how valuable those dogs are. They do the work of basically hundreds of officers."

Kramerman still thinks of Asko occasionally and has pictures of his K-9 friend.

"I lost a partner," he said. "That's what he was."

In Loving Memory of

K-9 ATLAS

July 22, 2000

Partner: Officer Wayne Cooper
City of Miami Police Department
Miami, Florida

On July 22, 2000 at approximately 11:40 p.m., Officer Cooper and K-9 Atlas responded into the area of NW 22nd Ave. & 35th St. in reference to a 'Be On The Look Out' for issued by Officer Jennifer Wing. The BOLO was for a dark skinned Hispanic male that had just committed an armed car jacking of a 1987 Buick Regal, 2 door with tinted windows and gold rims. Office Wing also advised that the vehicle was equipped with an auto kill switch, which would shut the engine off within a couple of minutes.

With this information Officer Cooper began looking for the vehicle within a five block radius. Officer Cooper spotted the vehicle as it turned north onto 19th Ave. The officer turned behind the vehicle just as the security system kicked in and killed the engine. As both vehicles came to a stop, the suspect exited the stolen vehicle. Officer Cooper exited his marked patrol car, and ordered the suspect to stop and place his hands on the car.

The suspect disregarded the orders and ran through an opening in a nearby school fence. As the suspect ran in a south-easterly direction, Officer Cooper gave chase with K-9 Atlas trotting beside him. As officer and K-9 were running behind the suspect, he pulled a blue steel revolver from his waistband firing one round in the officer's direction. Until then K-9 Atlas did not even know why they were running. He was just following his handler's order to "come."

After hearing the shot ring out, K-9 Atlas immediately keyed in on the suspect and gave chase as he had been trained to do as the officer returned fire. As the suspect was about to exit the field, through a gate leading onto 36th St., K-9 Atlas leaped up to apprehend the suspect. The suspect turned and fired another round at K-9 Atlas.

Atlas' momentum forced him and the suspect to fall against the fence. The suspect got up and continued   running. Although wounded, K-9 Atlas regained his composure and continued pursuing the suspect with such tenacity that his handler was unaware of Atlas injuries until he noticed a large pink mass hanging from his side.

Office Cooper recalled K-9 Atlas as he kept an eye on the suspect and directed arriving officers to the suspect's location. Realizing that he had no where to go, the suspect surrendered without further incident. Realizing that K-9 Atlas was seriously wounded and that Officer Cooper's vehicle was some distance away. Officer Wing drove over to the K-9 team, put them in her vehicle and sped them to Knowles Animal Hospital, where Atlas later expired in surgery as doctors tried to repair his ruptured stomach, liver and a collapsed lung.

Although K-9 Atlas lost his life for his actions, it is because of his actions that Officer Cooper still has his life so that he can continue to patrol the streets of Miami and go home at shift's end to his family. Officer Cooper and K-9 Atlas, a 2 year old

Belgian Malinois, were the newest team of the City of Miami's 17 handler/dog team units. On the streets for less than two months, the team was credited with the apprehension of 16 felons before this encounter.

At 54 Lbs., K-9 Atlas was the smallest dog in the unit, but had one big heart. K-9 Atlas was the first K-9 ever killed in the line of duty in the history of the Miami Police Department. K-9 Atlas was awarded the "Medal of Honor" and the "Purple Heart" by the department. Officer Cooper was awarded the Medal of Valor for the actions of K-9 Atlas at the United States Police K-9 Associations National Award Banquet.

During the service for Atlas, Officer Cooper's wife, Brandy, cried in the background as officers bid farewell to the heroic K-9. Seated beside her were the couple's two sons, Daniel, 9, and Jonathan, 7. Just as the ceremony was ending Tony Guzman, owner of Metro Dade K-9 Services, which supplies police dogs to South Florida officers, sprang a surprise.

He marched forward with Tom, a 2½ year old Malinois, Cooper's new partner. ``We've got a new baby,'' cried Brandy. Police dogs live at home with their handlers. Emotional, but holding back the tears, Cooper petted Tom's head as the dog leaned heavily against his new handler's right leg. Tom's tongue was swaying in the heat, and sticking far out of his mouth. ``He looks great,'' Cooper said. ``If he has as much heart as my last dog, we'll get along just great.''

Officer Cooper has expressed his gratitude for the cards and wished that I pass it along. He has a new partner and a foundation has been established by a woman in Ft. Lauderdale to buy vests for our dogs, it's called the Atlas Guardian Foundation.

UPDATE:

June, 2001 A celebration erupted out the Metro Justice Building in Miami. The wife of Miami Officer Wayne Cooper rejoiced after hearing about the guilty verdict against David Soto. Miami Police officers left the court house with smiles on their faces. "I'm very happy," said Officer Wayne Cooper of the verdict.

It was Cooper's K-9 partner, Atlas, who was shot and killed in the line of duty. Now, the suspect, David Soto has been found guilty of four felonies for a car jacking, murder of the K-9 and attempted murder of Officer Cooper.

"He got what he deserved. He got what he deserved. He wrote his own fate and he got it," added Officer Cooper. Jurors said they had to send a message that killing a police dog is similar to killing a police officer. "My dog is part of my family and I treat my dog as a human being," said Juror Sharon Peters. Jurors obviously did not believe that Soto, as his lawyers claim, was just a witness to the shooting. Soto will be sentenced and could face life in prison.

In Loving Memory of

K-9 BAK

February 6, 2000

Handler: Officer Brian Mosley
Defense Protective Service
Pentagon

Years of Service: September 1998 February 2000

Defense Protective Service is sad to announce that Bak died on February 6, 2000. His cause of death is believed to be bloat. Bak and his handler were a team from September 1998 to February 2000.

The Defense Protective Service provides law enforcement and security services for the Pentagon and other Department of Defense facilities throughout the National Capital Region. Defense Protective Service is a civilian police department which formed in 1987.

The K-9 Division formed in 1998. Bak is our first K-9 loss. We currently have seven explosive detector dogs and will be adding more in the future. Our K-9 teams respond to various calls for service, such as, bomb threats, vehicle searches, room and building searches, suspicious packages and K-9 demonstrations.

In Loving Memory of

K-9 BANDIT

1984 - 1988

Partner: Officer Eric Deltgen
New London Police Department
5 Governor Winthrop Blvd.
New London, CT 06320

Bandit was a black and tan, German Shepherd, presumably bred in the U.S. He was a dog obtained from the Connecticut Humane Society, and was to become the first police dog assigned to the New London Police Department.

After many weeks of lost overtime and countless hours in training with Certified Professional Master Trainers, James A. Cortina and Robert Bergeson. As private trainers, as well as some police trainers from agencies that had K-9 units, Bandit was finally admitted into the New London Police Department.

His exact date of birth is not known, other than he was born sometime in 1984. Bandit began his career with the New London Police Department in April of 1986. His handler at the time, Officer Eric Deltgen, had been with the department since 1980. He took it upon himself to learn and train about police dogs, on his own time, with the hopes of getting a K-9 program started with the New London Police Department.

K-9 Bandit was to be the first K-9 to become an active police K-9 in the recent history of the department. A lot of politicking, meetings and pleading went into this accomplishment, and with the help of fellow officer, William Nott, this was accomplished. Nott was training a K-9 named Thunder as well.

The two of us helped each other and continued doing so even after the K-9 unit's inception into the department. We were both K-9 rookies, but we feverishly worked hard at doing it right, asking questions, reading a lot, and going to many schools about the subject.

In time, our dogs, Bandit, Thunder and the dogs to follow would be recognized by many in the field. In time Officer Nott and I would join the USPCA (United States Police K-9 Association), NAPWDA (North American Police Work Dog Association) and eventually have a part in the creation of the CPWDA (Connecticut Police Work Dog Association).

With more hard work and determination we would become certified trainers for the NAPWDA. Sadly though, Bandit's career on the force would be cut short. Barely 4 years old, he contracted cancer and died in 1988. Even with such a short career, Bandit was still able to accumulate some points.

One of his first tracks was in the search of a despondent 12 year old boy who had run away from his home into nearby woods. When the call came, the boy had been missing for several hours, and the temperatures were now in the single digits. It was a late night in February, and if the boy was not found soon, there was a great chance that he would not survive the night.

I still remember the day like as if it were yesterday. We (Myself), Bandit, I can only speculate, and my fellow officers were all nervous.

This was the first big incident involving a New London

Police dog and we wanted everything to end well. The eyes of the boy's family, not to mention the neighbors who had tried in vain to find the boy, were on us.

We began a track from a point the boy had last been seen standing. We had contamination everywhere from the neighbors who had trudged through the area looking for the boy. Even during the track we came upon some persons who had not received word to get out of the area and were still searching. Even with all the distractions, Bandit continued without being phased. I followed Bandit like I had been taught, remembering what had been engraved in my mind. "TRUST YOUR DOG."

The track lasted for about 45 minutes. Can't say how far we traveled, but without warning, Bandit began scratching at what seemed to be a large boulder. At first I didn't know what to make of it, but the when I pulled myself in front of Bandit and peeked on the other side of the boulder, I found that 12 year old boy cuddled in the fetal position. He had somehow found refuge there from the elements, but it wasn't protecting him from the cold. He didn't have any warm clothing and had he been there much longer, hypothermia would have set in.

Long story short, the boy was found, cold, scared and above all safe. He was reunited with his family, and to this day I occasionally get a hardy hello from his family when we cross paths. Bandit got hugs and pets from the family and friends, and he was happy with that. Back home he got a juicy steak. I'm sure he appreciated that more.

Another high point in Bandit's career was when he helped in apprehending a rape suspect. He really didn't do much other than be at the right place at the right time. Fellow officers were chasing a rape suspect on foot, and had lost sight of him in one of our local neighborhoods. Bandit and I were on patrol close by, and decided to assist. We had barely gotten out of our patrol car, when the suspect popped out from one of the backyards. This guy was twice my size, a miniature Hulk, so to speak.

But For Bandit, the bigger they were, the better. Bandit had a neat thing about getting keyed up. You didn't have to say a word, just a light tickle on his collar and he became a fire breathing dragon with a bark that sounded like thunder. In any event, this guy saw us, and when I motioned to him to stand still, he flat out said he wasn't going and that we were going to have to work for it. No need for that.

Bandit got his tickle, and I had all I could do to keep him from dragging me to the suspect. What ever it was, it worked, because without hesitation, the suspect yelled out he was surrendering and to keep the dog away from him.

The suspect was subsequently taken into custody without incident and thankful that he did not have to meet Bandit face to face.

Bandit was a 120 pound German Shepherd, but when he wanted to play hard, he looked like he weighed 190 pounds. I guess that would make one think twice before going on his bad side.

Shortly after that incident Bandit would pass on. I still miss him and wish that he could have had a longer career. I'm sure that if that had been the case, he would have had an impressive career to say the least. Bandit will be sadly missed by all.

In Loving Memory of

K-9 BARO

Born: July 6, 1992
On Duty as K-9: November 2, 1993
End of Watch: June 10, 2000

Partner Sgt. Neal Morgan
Huntington Park Police K-9 Officers Association
P.O. Box 1027
Huntington Park, CA 90255

Baro (born in Hungary) was due to retire July 4, 2000. He became ill and was treated for "Immune Mediated Hemolytic Anemia". The exact cause of this blood disorder was not determined and Baro was treated with medication. Baro recovered from the illness and returned to full duty.

On June 7, 2000, I noticed Baro's abdomen was distended and suspected "bloat," Baro was rushed to the veterinarian's office for treatment. My heart sank as Baro was diagnosed with an aggressive cancer which resulted in an abdominal bleed. His condition was terminal and he never made it. On June 10,

2000, at 1130 hours, Baro was put down. As I held Baro in my arms, he drifted off to sleep and was suddenly gone.

I will never forget the feeling of watching my partner die in my arms. As a handler you learn there is nothing your partner wouldn't do for you. On this day, I realized there was nothing I could do for my partner.

Thank you for responding to my entry on your site. I was having computer problems and did not expect my message had been sent to you. I appreciate your offer for the cards but I don't think it will be necessary. I have been working on making something up on my own with my home computer. I had intended to include Baro's picture on whatever I came up with. It was a project I wanted to take care of personally for Baro. It is also a kind of therapy for me.

It gave me an opportunity to pull out all the photos I could find of Baro. I didn't realize I had as many as I did. The one that I have sent with this e mail, I clipped off our Department's website. I still have a Rottweiler at home who is lonely now and is getting lots of attention. We plan on getting another dog sometime, but we haven't decided when.

There is a big difference between having a pet, and a working dog that is trained to help others. Baro was going to be retired in July.

K-9 "BARO" Information – From Police records:

K-9 "Baro" was born in the country of Hungary on July 6, 1992. He was brought to the United States and selected for duty as a police service dog by the Huntington Park Police Department. He was the loyal partner of his handler, Senior Officer Neal Mongan and a beloved member of his family. K-9 "Baro" passed away on Saturday, June 10, 2000 at 1130 hours after having been diagnosed with terminal cancer. After long years of service, K-9 "Baro" was scheduled to retire from duty in July of 2000.

Senior Officer Neal Mongan and K-9 "Baro" completed their "Police Service Dog I" training on December 31, 1993 certifying them as a Police K-9 Team. They were assigned to patrol duty in Huntington Park to assist the residents and business community in the protection of their families and property. The following is a synopsis of K-9 "Baro's" accomplishments during his time as a police service dog for the Huntington Park Police Department:

Patrol Related Successes:

K-9 "Baro" was involved in the following patrol related arrests: (73) suspect arrests, including four murder suspects and two serial bank robbery suspects. K-9 "Baro" has also assisted with the recovery of handguns and other evidence which have aided in the prosecution of dangerous criminals. K-9 "Baro" conducted perimeter checks of businesses on alarm calls, and assisted patrol officers by guarding 265 subjects during field contacts. This K-9 Team conducted in excess of 333 crime prevention contacts.

In his nearly 6 1/2 years of service to the City of Huntington Park, K-9 "Baro" saved the police department and residents of the community approximately 107,109 "man-hours" during searches for dangerous suspects and clearing buildings. Considering salary and benefit costs of a top step police officer this amounts to a savings of $6,024,881.20.

Police K-9 Patrol Related Competition Successes:

K-9 "Baro" and Senior Officer Neal Mongan represented the City of Huntington Park in local and statewide competitions against police service dog teams from around the country. K-9 "Baro" received the following awards:
* ab3rd Place - Overall in Novice Division / Redondo Beach Police K-9 Trials (1994)
* ab5th Place - Overall in Open Division / Sierra K-9 Trials (1995)
* ab1st Place - Agility Competition / Redondo Beach Police K-9 Trials (1997)

* ab1st Place - Manwork Competition / Redondo Beach Police
K-9 Trials (1998)

UPDATE:

I now have a Belgian Malinois Puppy. He is a little fireball.
Since my partner, Bar, passed away, I have been placed in charge
of our K-9 program. I guess it's the next best thing to having a
leash in your hand and a wagging tail slapping you upside the
head all day. That might not sound like the best job in the
world, BUT IT IS!

In Loving Memory of

K-9 BARON

(K-9 Isko Von Bolser)
January 1991 - July 5, 1997

Partner: Deputy Doug Bolser Jr.
Cliburn County Sheriff's Dept.
914 South 9th St.
Heber Springs, AR 73543

Officer loses partner, friend, when county drug dog dies.

Saturday was a day of mixed emotions for Cliburn County Deputy Doug Bolser. It was the first birthday of his son, Colton, and it was the day he lost his faithful friend and partner of eight years.

Baron, Cleburne County's German Shepherd police dog, died following complications from prostate surgery. He had been ill for several years with a condition similar to muscular dystrophy before the prostate trouble. "The surgery weakened him to a point that he just couldn't recover, I took him in to have him put to sleep because he was in so much pain."

Deputy Bolser talked to Baron on the way to the veterinary clinic and later said that he felt the dog understood what was happening. When they arrived at the clinic, a shot to end his pain wasn't necessary after all. Within one minute, he laid his head over and died. He died on his own terms.

Baron lived at the Bolser's home in Concord with Doug, his wife, Shannon and their two kids, Colton and Shyanne. He went to work with Bolser almost every day for eight years.

"He could read me like a book and I could read him. He had two roles to play. He was a good friend, a part of the family, yet at the same time, he was an officer." He was somewhat of a local celebrity in this area appearing at school programs in Cliburn and surrounding counties. He could be as playful as a pup around school children, yet turn deadly serious if his handler was threatened.

The sheriff's office acquired Baron when he was two years old. These dogs are bred in Germany only for police use and are exported to the United States under very strict conditions. "Isco" was the name given to him by his German trainer and was the name Bolser used when giving him commands. All the commands were also given in German.

He was trained to put his handler's safety above his own and he proved this many times. In one incident, Bolser and another officer answered a domestic dispute call that turned violent. Baron got between the officers and the suspect and wouldn't budge even when the suspect began choking the dog. If we hadn't had the dog, one or both of us would have been hurt. In another incident, a suspect was hidden under bushes. Instead of me going in, the dog went. The man who was wielding a broken beer bottle as a weapon was dragged out of the bushes by Baron. He then stood between the suspect and the officers risking his own life to save the officers.

Special thanks from Officer Bolser and the Cliburn County Sheriff's Department are expressed to Dr. Lee Morris and his staff who worked hard to save Baron's life. Thanks are also given to the two people who made it possible for Baron to come to Cliburn County. The couple, who prefer to remain anonymous, donated approximately $6,000 toward the purchase of the dog. The county has no immediate plans to purchase another dog.

"I cannot even think of replacing him." said Deputy Bosler. The county owns a second police dog, Bandit, who lives with another officer. Baron will be cremated and his ashes will remain with the Bolser family. "He got a lot of drug dealers off the streets and saved myself and other officers from injuries. I just want to say good bye to a faithful friend and partner."

Previous story about Baron April 16, 1994

Drug dog Baron hoarse, but up and running after swallowing ball.

Baron, the Cliburn County drug dog, recuperated this week after getting a training ball caught in his throat Tuesday night. The 4 year old 105 pound German Shepherd was working with his trainer, Deputy Doug Bolser, when the incident occurred about 7:30 p.m. Bolser rewarded Baron after their training session by throwing him a 2 inch ball with a hole through the middle. This ball is called a "Kong."

The ball bounced and entered the dog's mouth, far enough down its throat that he sucked it down. The hole apparently did not provide an air passage. Deputy Bolser had to dig down his throat since the ball was sideways and keep his fist in his mouth to provide an air passageway. Bolser who keeps the dog at his home at Wolf Bayou, 20 miles from Hebert Springs, called the sheriff and headed for a veterinarian's office.

He drove about ten miles with his hand down Baron's throat until he met the sheriff. Then he got in the sheriff's back seat and maneuvered Baron beside him, maintaining the air passage. "It was a very tense situation, it scared me to death." The lawmen took Baron to Dr. Lee Morris, a local veterinarian, who removed the toy in about five minutes.

The sheriff carried the dog into the clinic because Bolser could not risk removing his hand. Bolser said the dog bit him several times during the trip. "He clamped down, he's up and running today, although he is a little hoarse. We are going to get a bigger ball now, the best they make. He's doing ok, but not barking real well yet. He's getting lots of TLC and a few days off."

In Loving Memory of

K-9 BASCO

December 26, 2000

Partner: Officer Mike Meetze
South Carolina Department of Corrections
4444 Broad River Road, P. O. Box 21787
Columbia, South Carolina 29221 1787
803.896.1680 or 803.896.2723 (K-9)

"All Dogs Go To Heaven"

This is my eleven year old Malinois, the first drug detector dog for the South Carolina Department of Corrections. It is with great sadness that I had to say good bye to "BASCO," on December 26, 2000.

As some of you know, he was fighting a medical condition; that he, with all the prayers and medicine could not win. Some of you will remember some of his funny antics and his love for chasing anything that moved, to include a basketball during a real game at a local court. (Boy, that stopped the game!)

But we all loved him and I guess God needed another good dog in heaven. So with much emotion, I bid you good bye, buddy, until I see you again in heaven.

"In God & Dogs, we trust,"

Mike

In Loving Memory of

K-9 BEN

June 6, 2000

Partner: Officer Carlos Vega
Los Angeles Customs Service
Port of Los Angeles   Human Resources Division
425 S. Palos Verdes Street   San Pedro, CA, 90731
Tel: (310)732 3480 Los Angeles, CA

The U.S. Customs Service is mourning the untimely death of one of its most distinguished K-9 officers: A yellow Labrador mix named Ben, who sniffed out more than $1 million dollars of illicit drugs during an exemplary five year career. Ben died in Los Angeles on June 6, 2000 of unknown causes, two days after leading officers to a five pound bag of cocaine in a cruise ship cabin.

He was 7 years old. Ben began his customs career in 1995 at Los Angeles International Airport, and over his five years of service screened nearly a million international passengers arriving in Los Angeles by air and by sea. He also made several appearances on television talk shows and invariably was tapped to represent the Customs Department at demonstrations and media appearances.

One thing about this dog: This dog was very photogenic. "He was our celebrity here," said K-9 Enforcement Officer Rick Spring. "He was just a very pretty dog beautiful color, nice personality. And he was very good. That's what hurt most of all."

He was also selected for a two week course at the custom department's training academy in Front Royal, VA., where 13 of the nation's best drug dogs became the first trained to detect Ecstasy. Results of an autopsy are pending.

Meanwhile, customs officers will present the dog's ashes to his handler, Officer Carlos Vega, in a private ceremony today. Vega also will receive a plaque featuring Ben's picture, with the dog's collar and department badge attached. Vega and the dog had "a super, super bond," Spring said.

UPDATE:

"J'est," a 70 pound Belgian malinois, is a vital element of the Port Police's efforts. Trained to sniff and locate narcotics throughout the 2700 cargo and passenger ships that move through the Port. Certified by the California Narcotics K-9 Association. New to the Port are "Bear" and "Rex". These K-9 officers are specially trained to pick up the scent of explosives and explosive materials.

In Loving Memory of

K-9 BOSS

October 21, 2000
S A R (Search & Rescue)

Handlers: Paul & Karen Hardesty
Parsons, KS

Boss, a Rottweiler, was donated to us in 1992. He was orig-inally rescued by Stan Twodeers. Stan was the original president of Rottweiler Rescue of Tulsa. Stan was killed north of Tulsa on highway 75.

Boss and Bubba were in the van and watched Stan being murdered. For a long time you could not pick up a stick around Boss because Stan was beaten to death. Stan taught all his dogs in Cherokee. I did not speak Cherokee and Boss didn't speak English. I needed to use a choke chain and he learned.

We introduced Boss to SAR soon after we had him. He was approximately seven years old. He was certified in 1994 through Oklahoma K-9 Search and Rescue. We joined Heartland Search and Rescue in 1996. He weighed 100 lbs.

Boss was retired in 1999. He was finally recognized by the Oklahoma Veterinarian Association on January 22, 2000.

Boss worked on the Ossie Decatur case in Tulsa, and numerous missing person cases in Oklahoma.

Boss was put down, (euthanized) October 21, 2000. He had inoperable cancer. He died peacefully in my arms. He hated two things; fighting and guns. He is now resting under his favorite peach tree in our yard, watching the cows that he loved playing.

In Loving Memory of

K-9 BRUTUS

October 29, 2000

Partner : Officer Jim Boie
Palos Hills, IL Police Dept.
8555 W. 103rd St. Palos Hills, IL 60465
708.598.2992

The first police dog for Palos Hills, hit by car, dies.

Palos Hills police K-9 Officer Jim Boie cannot stop agonizing over the death of his longtime friend and former partner, Brutus, the nine year old German Shepherd who was hit by a car while crossing West 87th Street in Hickory Hills.

Brutus, who was the department's first police dog, got out of Boie's fenced in yard in the early evening of Nov. 22. He was struck by a hit and run driver. "It shouldn't have happened, I don't know why he left, and I guess I never will. While he was one heck of a police dog, he was my constant companion for the last seven years." stated handler, Jim Boie. Brutus' career in law enforcement spanned seven years, during which he assisted such agencies as the FBI, Drug Enforcement Administration, U.S. Customs and the Metropolitan Enforcement Group.

Palos Hills Police Chief Paul Madigan said Brutus and Seffe, the department's eight year old female German Shepherd, were instrumental in bringing hundreds of thousands of dollars in drug forfeiture money to Palos Hills' coffers. The Feds used the dogs probably more than the police department did.

Brutus was a good dog; hampered by arthritic hips and failing eyesight, Brutus was retired in May. He had been spending his retirement with Boie and his family, the only family he ever knew. Brutus got out once before and he went over to visit a female German Shepherd, but Jim got him right away. This time he went in the opposite direction. Jim doesn't blame the person who hit Brutus. He said how really dark it is out there, and there is little lighting. They probably didn't see him until it was too late.

Brutus joined the Palos Hills Police Department in 1993, shortly after being certified in patrol work, drug work and tracking by the United States Police K-9 Association. Sgt. Steve Good said Brutus received two awards from the association, one for finding a crime suspect and the other for finding drugs. Brutus always ranked in the top five out of fifty police dogs in the region certified by the association.

Brutus' sniffing abilities helped crack a large money laundering ring that involved more than 100 people, $200 million in drug proceeds and the direct involvement of Mexican banks. Brutus also performed demonstrations at many schools, festivals, block parties and senior citizen functions.

Mayor Gerald Bennett said Brutus "set the standard" for police dogs. Palos Hills was one of the first local police departments to form a K-9 unit and Brutus was their first K-9. He was involved in a number of arrests, and helped his partner disburse large, and sometimes unruly crowds. Brutus set the standard for the rest of our dogs.

The Palos Hills Police Department now has two police dogs

on active duty: Seffe and Boie's new partner, "Rider," a two
year old German Shepherd who had been living with Brutus.
"Rider knows Brutus is gone," Boie said. "I don't think he
knows what happened, but he knows something is wrong. He
won't eat in the same area Brutus used to eat. "We all miss
Brutus.

In Loving Memory of

K-9 BRUTUS

June 16, 2000

Partner: Officer Collin Milligan
Fullerton Police Dept. CA
237 W. Commonwealth,
Fullerton, CA 92832
Phone (714) 738 6800
Police Chief Pat McKinley

Brutus was well known all over Orange County for his K-9 unit work. Officer Collin Milligan could always count on his dog, Brutus. As could police officers across Orange County.

Whether tracking down a gun toting suspect under a porch or sniffing out 15 pounds of meth-amphetamine, Brutus, 7, earned a reputation as one of the premiere K-9 patrol dogs in the county. When the German Shepherd was euthanized this week, three weeks to the day before his retirement from the Fullerton force, he was mourned by more than Officer Milligan, who received more than 30 calls in the last two days from officers in Fullerton, Orange and Anaheim. "It makes me feel good knowing that they care. He was the best partner you could ask for."

Brutus injured his back in March, hindering his ability to run and jump. His retirement was set for July 4. Then, earlier this week, Brutus began gasping for air. He'd developed gastric dilation, a condition that twists the stomach and cuts off oxygen. Brutus was rushed into surgery. But it didn't help, and Officer Milligan decided late Tuesday to put him down.

Brutus was to be honored by the Fullerton City Council next week for a lifetime of service. "If you needed a dog to track a suspect, Brutus would be the dog you'd want by your side," said Mike Scalise, a Garden Grove K-9 officer. "It's hard to describe the attachment you develop. It's truly sad to see him go. Of course, nobody is feeling the loss as much as Collin Milligan, who counted on Brutus 24 hours a day at work and home. "

Officer Milligan, 30, will leave the K-9 unit and return to patrol next month. "I'm not sure I could work well with any other dog," he said.

In Loving Memory of

K-9 CERO

March 25, 2000
LODD

Partner: Deputy William R. Niemi
Ashtabula County Sheriff's Office   Ohio
25 W. Jefferson St. Jefferson, Ohio 44047
Sheriff William R. Johnson
(216) 576 0055

Deputy K-9 Cero

A Tribute
I was your shield, your partner, always a friend.
I took an oath to protect you, right to the end.
I know you're still thinking I should be by your side.
In spirit I am, I'm your courage and your bravery and that
hasn't died.
Life will go on, a new partner a new friend.
A comrade like me on which you can depend.
But hey, got a new job and doing just fine.
God made me an angel so I can watch over my
friends and fellow K-9s

April S. Balint

K-9 Mourners Say Final 'Good Dog' Friday, March 31, 2000

They came from around Ohio, and from Illinois, Kentucky and West Virginia. More than 300 police officers, and 70 dogs. One by one, they walked up to a wooden urn and saluted. Many choked back tears. They came to the small town in Ashtabula County yesterday to pay final respects to "one of our own."

It didn't matter that the fallen officer was a German Shepherd named, Cero, shot to death Saturday while Cero was subduing a man who killed Walter Olson, who was out for his routine dawn walk.

"Cero was as much a police officer as any of us" quoted Deputy Joseph Niemi, brother of Cero's owner, Deputy William Niemi. "Cero sensed the danger, and he died saving my brother's life, and, for that, I thank him. But he also saved other people's lives, because we didn't know who else might have died if not for his sacrifice." The shooter, Levi Ridenour, was killed by Ashtabula County sheriff's deputies in an exchange of gunfire.

Hardened police officers tried hard not to cry during testimonials for Cero at the newly opened Durco Funeral Home in Jefferson as they saluted the urn containing his ashes. Joseph Niemi, the county's K-9 officer, said Cero's attack alerted officers that Ridenour had a handgun hidden under his coat. "After he was shot, Cero crawled back to my brother's side long enough for him to say one final 'Good Dog'," Niemi said.

The moving tribute brought tears to the room crowded with mourners, many with 9mm pistols strapped to their sides. Deputy William Niemi sat with his sobbing wife and children, accepting handshakes and salutes from police and hundreds of local residents. He spoke to the hundreds of people in the funeral home and, through loud speakers, to more than 400 others that filled the parking lot, lawn and sidewalks.

"I'm overwhelmed by the sympathy cards, flowers and letters from everyone," he said. "Cero was a member of my family, and he loved my children and wife, especially my wife. We'll all miss you. Daddy loves you, Cero."

Ashtabula County Sheriff William R. Johnson said the donations that poured in after news of Cero's death would buy vests for his replacement and the county's two other K-9 officers.

After the 90 minute service at the funeral home, a second, longer service was held at the Ashtabula County Fairgrounds.

The funeral procession drove past the scene of the shooting and the county courthouse, where flags flew at half staff. At the fairgrounds, a Cleveland police bagpiper played "Amazing Grace." Two trumpeters played taps, followed by a 21 gun salute that set all 70 dogs in the police cars barking. The dogs then paid their respects, walking to Cero's urn one at a time with their handlers.

In Loving Memory of

K-9 CHARLIE

March 14, 2000
LODD

Partner: Trooper Bobby Brown
Arkansas State Police
Conway, AR

The Arkansas State Police held a service Friday to remember Trooper Charlie and to introduce a new member of the department's K-9 force. About two dozen people, including officers from various agencies, gathered at the Greenbrier Police Department for the service.

Charlie's handler, Trooper Bobby Brown, stood quietly with his new dog, Sartor, sitting at his feet as the service began. "I told Bobby I'd be glad to (do the service), then I had a loss of words," David Dunham, another dog handler with the state police, told the group. Trooper Dunham spoke of the respect all new officers must earn when they start policing a community.

"That respect then turns into trust," he said. That's what

happens with K-9s and their handlers. "These animals, in just a few short weeks, become very tied to you," he said. "Bobby, we are with you, thinking about you." Dunham had a hand in purchasing and training Charlie and called him a "fantastic dog."

Next to the podium where Trooper Dunham was speaking stood a table draped in an Arkansas State Police flag and covered with memorials to the fallen K-9 trooper. Two candles and an ornate wooden box sat in the center. The box held Charlie's cremains (ashes). A stack of sympathy letters written by a local third grade class to Trooper Brown also sat on the table. On the opposite end of the table was a plaque containing an 8x10 photo of Charlie, his K-9 collar, a badge and a purple heart shaped pin with the silhouette of a dog.

As Dunham finished his address, Brown took his place behind the podium. His words were few, mainly saying that he is ready to move on. "Hopefully we'll get this new K-9 (Sartor) on line pretty soon so we can get more criminals off the street." Next came Sgt. Jerry Roberts with the state police. He said mistakes were made by both state and Conway police which resulted in Charlie's death. The mistakes were minor but the consequences major.

"K-9 Charlie went in with the intention that he was going to protect the officers," Robert's said, adding Charlie thought that was what he was supposed to do. Roberts said. Charlie's most recent SWAT training involved him making entry with the first officers. That's what Charlie did on the day he was shot.

Sgt. Roberts said the state police investigation concurred with the Conway Police Department's and it was not the fault of Officer Mike Gibbs, who shot Charlie. There were some Conway officers at the service but Gibbs was not one of them. Robert's said the service was held in Greenbrier not because of any ill feelings between departments, but simply because Greenbrier has a bigger meeting room with more parking available.

Sgt. Roberts then opened the floor to anyone with questions. Greenbrier resident Kitchell Wilson had just one. "I would like to know why it took 20 (officers) to get one person," he said. It was reported that at least that many officers were on the scene of the raid that resulted in the arrest of one person. "We believe in peace in numbers," Roberts explained, adding that officers never know what they'll find when they enter a suspected drug house.

After Charlie's service, the group was given a chance to meet Sartor. The 2½ year old Dutch Shepherd was teamed with his new handler Tuesday and will be leaving him next week to go to school. The dog was donated to the state police by Gerald Goss of LEAD K-9 Training in Lincoln (Washington County) who will be training Sartor.

This period is for the two to get to know each other. Brown has already seen some differences between Sartor and Charlie. Sartor is more dominate with his family's other dog at home, but doesn't chase the cats as much, according to Brown.

Memorials in Charlie's name will help to supply Sartor with a bullet proof vest and other training and safety equipment.

In Loving Memory of

K-9 COPPER
and DEPUTY KENNEY
LODD
November 16, 1999

Partner: Deputy James "Monk" Kenney
Clay County Sheriff's Dept.
Morganville, KS

A sheriff's deputy and his police dog were shot dead as they tried to apprehend an escaped jail inmate, authorities said today.

Clay County Deputy Jim "Monk" Kenney, 62, was killed at about 4:30 p.m. Tuesday when he and his dog, Copper, tried to execute a search warrant at the home of 22 year old Jeffery Hebert, who had escaped from the jail in nearby Cloud County on Monday, officials said.

Kenney and his dog were leading a team of officers into the suspect's home when Hebert allegedly burst out and shot the officer in the head with a shotgun. The six year veteran, who had started the department's K-9 Unit, was pronounced dead at Clay County Medical Center. The dog was also killed instantly. Tiffany Ball, a spokeswoman for the Kansas Attorney General's Office, said authorities do not know what prompted Hebert to open fire. He had been nearing the end of a term for a violation of the probation he received for marijuana possession and DUI charges, officials said.

Hebert had escaped from jail after overpowering two guards. A manhunt ensued that included as many as 40 officers who combed the county. Kenney was leading a small group of officers tasked with searching for the suspect at his Clay County home. Hebert is now being held on $750,000 bail on a charge of first degree murder and misdemeanor killing of a police dog. He could face the death penalty, but Ball said a decision has not been made. The deputy was a retired Wichita Kansas police officer. He trained police K-9s for officers in southeast Kansas. He loved the job so much after retiring he decided to join the small Sheriffs department so he could still work dogs.

In Loving Memory of

K-9 CZAR

September 14, 1999

Partner: Deputy Calvin Purnell
Worcester County Sheriff Office
Maryland
410-632.1111

Deputy Purnell received K-9 Czar in 1998 when he worked with the Ocean City, Maryland Police Department. When he left that department, he was allowed to take K-9 Czar with him. Both Czar and Purnell started working for the Worcester County Sheriff's Office. K-9 Czar died of a brain tumor close to the age of 6.

Purnell now has a new partner and has remained in the K-9 Unit.

In Loving Memory of

K-9 DANN

Born: February 18, 1991
Began watch: October 1992
Retired watch: July 20, 1998
Died: January 20, 2000

Partner: Corporal Ron M. Renken
Grant County Sheriff's Department
P.O. Box 37
Ephrata WA 98823
(509) 754 2011 ext.468

Dann was a pure bred German Shepherd import. He was born February 18, 1990 in Czechoslovakia. He was able to escape the country into eastern Germany to a kennel that specialized in Schutzhund sport dogs. Schutzhund is a sport that is real big in Germany, there dogs are taught various skills such as Man Tracking, Handler Protection, Obstacle Courses and many other skills.

During the Schutzhund Tournaments the dogs are graded

on their ability to perform the given task. Sort of like people at a Martial Arts event. As the dog progresses through the given task, they are given a title. Dann was given the title of Schutzhund 1. I met Dann for the first time on October 22nd, 1992 when I traveled to Bakersfield CA. He had been purchased from the Tony Bairos Kennels by my department.

By now Dann had learned another skill. That was the ability to find Illegal Narcotics. I was receiving 2 dogs in one. The next 3 weeks were spent training. For me it seemed like Dann had a good idea of what he was to do. The training was actually for me and believe me, it wouldn't have hurt us to stay another 3 weeks. The training was vigorous with not enough time in a day to cover all of the things that needed to be covered. I was totally awed by the amount of work a K-9 officer must put in to keep himself and his partner in line.

Tony would always tell us, "remember that these guys are dogs, their brains are this big" holding up a golf ball for comparison. I felt like my brain must not have been much bigger.

When we returned home he went to work with me as a Patrol Deputy assigned to the Ephrata patrol district for the Grant County Sheriff's Department. He immediately became part of the family and moved into my home with my wife and 4 children. Never did I have to worry about him around the kids and my wife has enjoyed the fact that as we slept, Dann was guarding us.

Dann has been a lot of help for me in my duties. I honestly feel that I have received the most benefit from having Dann as my partner though I know that he has also contributed to everyone in my Department and the citizens of Grant County in Washington State. If anything, his company during a long graveyard shift in the middle of January has been a treat. I always had a friend that I could count on as a listener. When the times got tough he was there. His presence defused many a bad situation and he helped me find people that had gotten away from the other deputies. Dann has never let me down.

During my 14 years as a law enforcement officer I have had

the opportunity to work with many shift partners. Some of them I would regard as the best in the trade, however none of them have or will ever be a partner like Dann. He was with me when I was happy and when I was sad. He has never left my side. The sadness I feel from having to retire him after 6 years of work can only be felt by another K-9 officer that has had to do the same. Any type of bond known by man can not match the special bond that develops between an officer and his K-9 partner.

Even though I am more than happy with our career together, I feel that we didn't get a chance to achieve the goals we had set. But that is the life of a K-9 team and it is part of the program. Dann has taught me a lot in life and I will continue to use these lessons as I continue with my career in law enforcement in addition to walking through my steps of life.

Because Dann was 8 years old and his time to be with me on patrol was at best maybe 4 more years, my Department chose to retire him due to a condition called Intervertebral Disk Disease. It is possible that a new dog will be purchased. I have put in my request to receive hm. I know that a new dog will not be like Dann, as dogs like him are very unique and difficult to find.

UPDATE:

Dann died on January 20th, 2000. I have yet to be assigned a new dog to work with me however I have Dann's wife (Wasichu) and his daughter (Cinnomen) at home. Cinnomen has many of the same traits as Dann and she reminds me so much of him but she just isn't him. For the longest time I kept his cremains (ashes) in my patrol car while on patrol, but have since moved him into my home.

So often I feel like he is still sitting in his seat behind me when I work. I can even hear his howl at times when I run with my lights and siren. I still believe that someday I will see my friend again. Life at work and home has been so much different since the day Dann moved on.

In Loving Memory of

K-9 DARBY

March 21, 2000

Partner: Sgt. Frank Moore
Caseyville Police Department
10 West Morris
Caseyville, IL 62232
618-344.2151

Darby, 6½ year old K-9 officer for Caseyville died of melanoma cancer. He was diagnosed in February 2000. Darby had 21 catches, found over 350 lb. of marijuana and an immeasurable amount of cocaine.

He was loved by his partner and the entire city of Caseyville. He will be sadly missed by all.

In Loving Memory of

K-9 DENY

March 12, 2000

Partner Deputy Mark Loveland
Onondaga County Sheriff's Dept.
407 S. State St .
Syracuse, New York 13202
315. 435 3044

Deny, the bomb sniffing K-9, was killed by a car on the Thruway Sunday.

Deny, the four year old bomb detection dog with the Onondaga County Sheriff's Department, was struck and killed by a car on the Thruway Sunday night, about two hours after breaking free during an exercise session. "We're all reeling from this," said Sgt. Bernie Podsiedlik, administrative Sargent for the road patrols.

A Thruway maintenance worker who read Tuesday that the dog was missing told authorities he had removed a dead animal matching Deny's description Sunday night from the westbound lane of the Thruway, about a half mile from Exit 34A. Deputies had spent most of Monday combing the area around Hancock Field searching for the dog, whose 60 foot lead unlatched about 7 p.m. Sunday while handler Mark Loveland was letting him exercise. The department used a helicopter and infrared scopes Sunday and Monday, trying to catch a glimpse of the dog, one of eight in the unit.

The 85 pound dog was hit about two miles from Hancock. Although the accident report wasn't available Tuesday afternoon. The car that hit Deny had to be towed. Deny was wearing a large chain link collar but didn't have any identification linking it to the sheriff's department. Tags are not kept on the dogs. If they're working, a suspect could grab it or it could get caught on a fence while the dog is jumping over and it could hang itself. The department is now trying to come up with a way where they can weld something onto the collars so it doesn't dangle down.

The SPCA shelter in Mattydale arranged Tuesday to inject microchips for free into the K-9 unit's seven remaining dogs this month so that the dogs will be quickly identified if they become lost and are turned in to the shelter. Although the sheriff's department notified the SPCA, dog wardens and the Air National Guard Monday, the state police on the Thruway use a different radio system, so they just wouldn't have heard the transmission. Otherwise, they might have known about this sooner.

Deny was one of four bomb sniffing dogs and had worked extensively in schools throughout the county, checking for bombs during a spate of threats last year. Deny was buried Tuesday afternoon near the aviation unit on Cessna Drive, where other police dogs are buried.

Donations are arriving to get another K-9 for Deputy Loveland.

In Loving Memory of

K-9 DERREK

August 8, 1998

Partner: Sgt. Dave Molinet
Evansville Indiana Police Dept.
Special Operations Platoon K-9 Unit
15 New MLK Jr. Blvd. Evansville IN 47708

My K-9 partner Derrek was shot and killed by an armed subject wanted for Carjacking, Kidnaping, and Armed Robbery on
August 8, 1998. K-9 Derrek tracked the subject for several
blocks before locating him as he was hiding in an old work van.

The suspect also shot at me during this confrontation and
was convicted of Attempted Murder as well as the charges I
have already listed. K-9 Derrek received numerous awards for
this apprehension including the USPCA's 1998 National
"Catch of the Year".

The City of Evansville filed a lawsuit (which it won at trial)
against the suspect for the cost of Derrek. The suspect was
ordered to reimburse the city $100,000 for the loss of K-9

Derrek.

The Incident:

On August 8th at approximately 2:30 AM, officers Brent Melton and Gerald Carter were attempting to stop a vehicle that they believed might contain a subject wanted on a drug dealing warrant. After a short pursuit the vehicle finally stopped and both passengers, a black male and female, fled on foot. The female was caught by the officers, but the male got away. Upon returning to the suspect vehicle with the female suspect, the officers heard voices and banging coming from the trunk.

When the officers opened the truck, officers found two hysterical, nude, females. The officers quickly learned that the B/M suspect had carjacked this vehicle from the victims at gunpoint and had fired a shot through the side of the car window during the carjacking. The female suspect had driven the vehicle behind a feed store where the male suspect ordered the victims to hand him their money and jewelry and take their clothes off. The suspect then locked the nude females in the trunk.

Just minutes after these officers had stopped the car. Sgt. Molinet arrived and initiated a track with K-9 Derrek for the B/M suspect with other officers setting up a perimeter. K-9 Derrek picked up the track southbound, between some houses, in the south alley, between some more houses, before turning eastbound on the south side of Adams Street. K-9 Derrek continued tracking eastbound for about a block, crossing Garvin Street, and was turning back southbound between some houses when perimeter officers spotted the suspect running south across Monroe about three or four blocks further southeast of K-9 Derrek's location.

A perimeter car transported Sgt. Molinet and K-9 Derrek to the spot where the suspect was last seen. The perimeter officer did not know exactly where the suspect had crossed the street, but K-9 Derrek quickly picked up the track in the front yard of 631 Monroe.

Officer Jeff Kingery followed the K-9 team from this point on. K-9 Derrek tracked south through the backyard of this house, crossed the alley, went on for a short distance before shooting into the backyard of 632 Jackson. Officer Sawn Smith was standing in the middle of the backyard (about 10 ft. behind a large work van). K-9 Derrek ignored Officer Smith and pulled right past him and jumped in the back door of the work van. K-9 Derrek quickly worked his way to the front of the work van and lunged to his right.

At that instant, Sgt. Molinet heard four or five gunshots and saw the muzzle flash from the suspect's gun; the last shot had been fired at him. After the second shot, Sgt. Molinet heard K-9 Derrek yelp one time.

The work van had walls separating the front (passenger) compartment from the back compartment. The back compartment had large wooden shelves, from the top to the bottom, on either side. This left just a narrow isle leading to the passenger compartment of the van and it was full of trash and junk. All Sgt. Molinet could see of the passenger compartment was the middle console. With all of the clutter in the back of the van, Sgt. Molinet could not see K-9 Derrek or the suspect, who was hidden in the front passenger side.

Sgt. Molinet immediately shouted for the suspect to come out and show his hands. The suspect did not comply so Sgt. Molinet began shouting for K-9 Derrek to return to him. Perimeter officers arrived and surrounded the van shouting orders to the suspect. Sgt. Molinet continued shouting for K-9 Derrek to return to him. After a few minutes, perimeter officers were able to remove the suspect from the van. Sgt. Molinet immediately ran into the van and observed K-9 Derrek lying motionless on the floor of the van between the two seats.

K-9 Derrek was rushed to a nearby 24 hour vet clinic where he was pronounced dead a few minutes later. K-9 Derrek had been shot one time with a .38 cal. handgun. The bullet had shattered the right shoulder, ricocheted between two ribs, punctured a lung, entered the heart near the top and exited the heart near the bottom. The vet stated that K-9 Derrek had died in a matter of seconds.

Officer Smith stated that he had been sitting on the perimeter when he heard the dogs next door start barking. He knew the suspect was running in his direction and figured that the dogs might have been barking at the suspect. He had gone to the backyard and had heard a noise in or near the van. He was about to climb up into the van to investigate when K-9 Derrek arrived and jumped in the van. Officer Smith stated that K-9 Derrek probably saved his life that night.

The suspect was transported to Welborn Hospital where he was treated for various injuries, among them a dog bite to his left shin. He was transported to headquarters where he was booked for Attempted Murder (class A), two counts of Kidnaping (class A), two counts of Armed Robbery (class B), Carjacking (class B), Criminal Mischief (class D), and Battery of a Police K-9.

On Tuesday, August 11, K-9 Derrek was given a funeral, with full honors, at the Evansville K-9 Unit training grounds. Several hundred people attended including a large number of out of town K-9 units.

Cpl. Tim Nussmeier and Lt. John Haller delivered the eulogy praising K-9 Derrek as a hero. Derrek was laid to rest in the Evansville K-9 Cemetery directly behind Sgt. Molinet's first K-9 partner (K-9 Pit). He will be sorely missed.

ADDITIONAL INFORMATION

K-9 Derrek was a six year old German Shepherd that had been working with Sgt. Molinet for just over four years. He was cross trained for explosive detection in addition to patrol work. He was a large, mostly black dog, weighing about 80 pounds. K-9 Derrek was a very social dog and especially loved kids. He often played with Sgt. Molinet's daughter, Laura, age 5 and other neighborhood children in the backyard.

Just three weeks prior to his death, K-9 Derrek had finished first place overall at the United States Police K-9 Association Region 5 Field Trials; competing against approximately 50 K-9 teams from Indiana, Kentucky, Ohio, Michigan and Illinois. K-

9 Derrek's ability to successfully track and find suspects has led the Vanderburgh County Prosecutors Office to appeal an antiquated (1927) Indiana Law that does not allow a police K-9's track to a suspect to be admissible in court.

A track K-9 Derrek ran on an armed robbery suspect in March of 1998 led the Prosecutor's Office and the Attorney General's Office to appeal this law based on the number of successful tracks K-9 Derrek had run. This was undertaken before K-9 Derrek's untimely death.

A change in Indiana State Law (brought about by his abilities as a police K-9) would benefit all Law Enforcement Officers in the state of Indiana and be Derrek's biggest legacy.

K-9 Derrek was given the "Monza" award by the United States Police K-9 Association at their 1998 awards banquet. The "Monza" award is given annually to a police K-9 that exhibits bravery and heroism in the act of fulfilling it's duties as a police K-9. Additionally, the Indiana Association of Veterinarians awarded K-9 Derrek its first ever "Hero Dog" for the year of 1998.

Also K-9 Derrek was posthumously awarded the "Gold Metal Award" for his actions in this incident at the February meeting of the Evansville Police Merit commission. He was the first K-9 from Evansville to receive this award. In addition K-9 Derrek's apprehension was deemed the August "Catch of the Month" for Region 5 of the United States Police K-9 Association (This encompasses the states of Indiana, Ohio, & Kentucky). This catch was also deemed the "Catch of the Quarter" for the third quarter of 1998 by USPCA Region 5.

The USPCA further decided that this was the top catch by a K-9 team in the United States in 1999 and awarded their highest honor, the National "Catch of the Year" for 1998. The Evansville Police Department also awarded K-9 Derrek it's "Catch of the Year" for 1998.

Derrek was a member of the Evansville Police Dept. K-9 Team that finished second at the USPCA National Dog Trials in 1994, 1995, 1996, & 1997. In 1995, K-9 Derrek placed

11th overall at the National Dog Trials.

The citizens of Evansville contributed over $13,000 towards the purchase of a replacement for K-9 Derrek. The City of Evansville filed a lawsuit against the suspect for the loss of K-9 Derrek. After a jury trial, the suspect was ordered to pay $50,000 compensatory and an additional $50,000 punitive damages to the City of Evansville. This makes K-9 Derrek the first $100,000 K-9 in the history of the Evansville Police Department.

K-9 BEN

My new partner Ben teamed with three other K-9's from our department and won the 2002 United States Police K-9 Association's National Department Championship. It is the first time we have won the championship since K-9 Derrek was killed.

We now have 5 K-9 patrol teams on our department. All of these dogs are German Shepherds. A typical tour of duty for the K-9 units on our department is third shift. The officers call in service and try to stay available for K-9 runs. They will back up officers on runs but they are seldom dispatched as the primary car to a run.

We do not get stuck taking a lot of reports, doing accidents, or handling a lot of B.S. runs because we have to be available if a K-9 run comes out. A lot of smaller departments do not have this luxury and their K-9 handlers have to act as regular motor patrol officers and cover a beat or district in addition to handling their K-9 related duties.

On a slow night our officers will do some form of training such as running a practice track or making a narcotics hide. There is seldom a night that our K-9 officers are not called for some type of K-9 related search.

Most of our searches come in the form of tracking a felony suspect or a building search for a felony suspect. All of our dogs are also dual purpose (patrol as well as narcotics work). Each of our 5 teams does about 50 narcotics searches a year.

We also have two K-9 teams that are strictly narcotic detectors. One is a German Shepherd and the other is a yellow lab. They do not do patrol work. They do about 150 searches in a year. Most of the time one of them works day shift and the other works second shift. The officers are assigned to our drug interdiction unit and work the highways and high crime areas doing traffic stops. They have an additional human partner assigned to them to assist on the traffic stops.

We are just now training an explosive detection dog. He is a black lab. He will work day shift and be available whenever our bomb technicians are called to a run.

All of our units are required to be tested and certified annually by the United States Police K-9 Association (USPCA). However there are a lot of other K-9 organizations that do certification tests also. I may be prejudiced but I believe that the USPCA is the best organization.

/s/ Dave MOLINET

In Loving Memory of

K-9s DUNNE
1994 - 2000

K-9 SPOOKY
1992 - 1998

K-9 DUNNE
Partner: Officer Superintendent Edward Flaherty
Waterbury Connecticut Police Department
236 Grand Street
Waterbury, CT 06708

K-9 Dunne was a yellow lab male, Narcotics Detector. He had a long career with many assists in drug arrests in Waterbury, CT. Dunne also served New York City Police Department from 1989 until 1994 when he was given to the Waterbury Police Department.

K-9 Spooky was a shepherd/Sheltie mix female, and a great Explosives Detector. Officer Flaherty also had K-9 Lenny from 1989 - 1994, he was a black lab male and was the original K-9 started for the program. He had many notable seizures in his career.

In Loving Memory of

K-9 ERNY

October 12, 2000
LODD

Partner: Deputy Mike Mayne
Escambia County Sheriff's Department
Pensacola, FL

A sheriff's deputy was wounded and his K-9 partner of 16 months killed in an early morning shoot out with a suspect who was killed after pulling out a handgun and firing as deputies tried to arrest him, police said. The incident began at approximately 2:40 AM Thursday when deputies received a report of a suspicious, armed man in the 600 block of Palm Court. After a K-9 team was sent to the area, the suspect, Gregory Allen Kidd, 32, was cornered. As deputies attempted to place him under arrest Kidd pulled out a handgun and began firing, police said. The identity of the deputy who shot Kidd has not been released. Deputy 1st Class Mike Mayne, who did not fire his weapon, received a gunshot wound to the leg and remains in Baptist

Hospital. Mayne's dog, Erny, a three year old German Shepherd was shot and later died in an emergency veterinary clinic. Autopsies on the suspect and the police dog are being conducted today. As is standard in shooting incidents, the Florida Department of Law Enforcement is investigating.

THE INCIDENT:

On October 12, 2000 at approximately 0238 hours, deputies responded to the area of Massachusetts Avenue and Kelly Avenue in reference to an armed suspicious person call. Deputies made contact with a Yellow Cab driver who advised that he had picked up a white male subject at the Conoco station at N. "W" Street and Beverly Parkway. The male pulled a handgun on the cab driver and made statements he was on a rampage then fled North into a residential area, Court.

Deputy Mike Mayne responded with K-9 Erny. Deputy Mayne began tracking the subject, with Deputy Kevin Coxwell providing backup during the track at 0338 hours, Deputy Mayne continued the track and located the individual lying in tall grass in a fenced lot behind 622 Palm. Deputy Mayne and Coxwell ordered the subject to surrender and show his hands.

When the subject failed to do so, K-9 Erny was deployed followed closely by the officers who attempted to take the subject into custody. The subject pulled a handgun and fired on the officers. One round struck Deputy Mayne in the right lower leg. A second round struck K-9 Erny killing him. Deputy Coxwell returned fire at the subject with his service Sig Sauer .40 caliber pistol. The suspect was hit and pronounced dead at the scene. Deputy Mayne was transported by EMS to Baptist Hospital for treatment of his gunshot wound. he is in good condition.

An autopsy has been conducted and the identity of the suspect has been made using fingerprints. He is identified as Gregory Allen Kidd of Pensacola. Kidd was currently wanted by the Escambia County Sheriff's Office for Robbery with a weapon and Possession of a weapon by a convicted felon. He was further suspected of having committed other area robberies in recent weeks. Kidd had an extensive history of violent crime and had been incarcerated in the state prison on several occasions.

Deputy Mike Mayne has been employed by the Escambia County Sheriff's Office for eleven years. He is currently assigned to the Patrol division working out of the Warrington precinct on midnight shift. K-9 Erny was three years old and had been partnered with Deputy Mayne since May 1999. Deputy Kevin Coxwell has been employed by the Escambia County Sheriff's Office for two years. He is currently assigned to the Patrol division working out of the Warrington precinct on midnight shift. Deputy Coxwell has been placed on paid administrative leave which is standard sheriff's office policy. The Florida Department of Law Enforcement is the lead investigative agency. The sheriff's office will be conducting a separate but parallel investigation of the shooting.

K-9 Erny is the second patrol K-9 to be shot and killed in the line of duty. In March 1998, K-9 Wolf was shot and killed as he apprehended a car thief who had fled into a wooded area. The suspect in that case was arrested as he exited the wooded lot when pursued by the Sheriff's Office SWAT Team.

In Loving Memory of

K-9 FALCO

February 18, 2000
LODD

Partner: Deputy John Schoen
Hoyt Sheriff's Department
Hoyt, KS

K-9 Falco, a Belgium Malinois was shot and killed in the line of duty. The shooter killed his parents, shot the deputy and the K-9, set his house on fire and died in the blaze.

The bark of police dogs echoed through Holton Cemetery as law enforcement officers from across the state paid their last respect to Falco, a K-9 officer killed during a standoff last week. K-9 units, which are law enforcement teams composed of an officer and a dog, traveled to Holton High School from as far away as Garden City and Nebraska for a service in memory of Falco.

Officers dabbed their eyes as taps played during a flag folding ceremony and the official retirement of a fallen K-9 Officer's service number. After the service, a procession of more than 30 squad cars and police vehicles with lights flashing wound through the streets on their way to bury Falco, 2½ years old in Holton's pet cemetery. "It's like losing a real officer," said Rob Dunham, a deputy who works with K-9 officers for the Atchison Sheriff's Dept. "I've been to other funerals for officers, and this was just as big as any of those."

I have a new partner. His name is 'NEKO.' He is a male Belgium, 2 years old. We have just started his training. He will be a duel purpose dog, narcotics and apprehension.

In Loving Memory of

K-9 FRED

Born: March 18, 1990
Died: May 27, 2000
LODD

Partner Sgt. Rusty Sullivan
Aurora Police Dept.
350 No. River St.
Aurora, IL 60506-4154
630/859.100

In the early 1990s, a 33 year old burglar was facing armed police officers after breaking into an Aurora building. Apparently not intimidated, he refused to surrender. But when Sgt. Rusty Sullivan, then a patrol officer, let loose his partner, a 110 pound German Shepherd named Fred, the crook immediately gave up. "He was crying like a baby, because he didn't want to mess with Fred, red," Sullivan said.

Sullivan on Tuesday reminisced about Fred, one of the Aurora Police Department's first two police dogs. Fred was put down Saturday, days after his quality of life dramatically diminished because of an unusual skin cancer he was diagnosed with nearly five years ago. Fred was born March 18, 1990, in Czechoslovakia. He and Ajax, a retired police dog who lives with Sgt. William Lomax, joined the Aurora force in March 1992. Both dogs and their human partners graduated from the Illinois State Police Academy K-9 division in June 1992.

Fred was 5 years old when he retired in September 1995, at the time Sullivan was promoted. He continued to live with Sullivan, his wife, Mary, and their 10 year old son, Matthew. Because Matthew was just 6 months older than Fred, the two "grew up together," and thus Fred displayed what Sullivan called a "Dr. Jekyll and Mr. Hyde" personality. Kind and gentle with children, he was fierce when commanded into action on the job. "When I needed him, he knew it was time to get down to business," Sullivan said.

There was the time Sullivan and Fred were the first to arrive at a shooting scene and entered a basement occupied by a throng of people in a known gang house. "He and I were able to control 20 plus people until we were able to get some assistance," Sullivan recalled. "He saved my butt. There was no question about that."

During his 3 years on the force, Fred made his share of successful drug searches, helped on drug raids and even participated in homicide investigations. He demonstrated his skills at local schools. And Fred achieved some measure of immortality when he was featured on a trading card. "He wasn't just a family pet, he was a partner," Sullivan said. "He put his time in, like the rest of us, and he did it well."

In Loving Memory of

K-9 GATOR

1978 - 1992

Partner: Deputy Michael Fox
Montgomery County Sheriff Dept.
330 W. Second St.
Dayton, Ohio 45422
937 225.4357

K-9 Gator joined the Montgomery County Sheriff's Department in 1980. He became Mike's partner after Mike lost K-9 Brutus. Gator retired in 1984. Mike left the K-9 Unit and presently is a Lieutenant in the department.

Gator was placed on active duty March 2, 1980. During his first three months of duty he made five apprehensions. He was an excellent patrol dog and proved himself numerous times during the course of his service.

The trophies were awarded for criminal apprehension work during the United States Police K-9 Association Region 6 Field Trials (USPCA) in June of 1982. He won top dog honors in the protection/apprehension work.

In Loving Memory of

K-9 GREIF

March 28, 2000

Partner: Cpl. Jerry Wright
Berkely County Sheriff Office
Moncks Corner, South Carolina
(formerly of Bonneau Police Dept., SC
Now Chief Jerry Wright)

The Berkeley County Sheriff's Office in Moncks Corner, South Carolina, mourn's the death of its first and oldest K-9. Greif, who died of cancer on March 28, 2000.

Everyone, along with Greif's handler and best friend, Cpl. Jerry Wright will miss Greif and are thankful for the years of continuous service, loyalty and love Grief gave us.

Greif was a fellow officer and a member of the Thin Blue Line. Originally, Greif came from Europe and was imported from Europe through Advanced K-9 in Bowling Green Kentucky.

He was the Berkeley County Sheriff's Office first dual purpose K-9. During his service, Greif had more than 2 million dollars worth of narcotics and narcotics related seizures. He also had numerous tracks where he found wanted felons, missing children and Alzheimer patients.

Greif was as comfortable 'out' with the family as he was at work. Col Wright was fond of saying "I would have been out of a job if Greif had thumbs. He would have been able to drive himself around and wouldn't need me as his driver to get to the action."

He is and will always be missed.

In Loving Memory of

K-9 GRINGO

Gringo von Wernbert Koblitz Sch I
Born in Germany   August 1, 1988.
Arrived   Cheektowaga July 1991
End of watch: October 24, 2000

Partners: Officer Daniel Smith & Officer Kevin Retzer
Cheektowaga Police Dept. NY

The Cheektowaga Police Department regrets to announce the passing of retired K-9 dog, Gringo on October 24, 2000. He was 12 years old.

Gringo served more than six years with the department. He was noted for his apprehension of criminals involved in drug activity in our town as well as his assistance to other agencies in Western New York. Gringo von Wernbert Koblitz Schutlz Hund I (Gringo for short) started his career in law enforcement in June of 1991. He was a pure bred German Shepherd, raised and trained in Germany before he was imported to America. He received further training in drug detection at the Amsel Kennels owned by Owen Tober.

Gringo earned the distinction of an internationally certified narcotics' specialist, a ranking that is recognized anywhere in the United States as well as 40 countries around the world. He was the only police dog in New York State to pass the qualification test in 1992.

Officer Daniel Smith and Gringo performed numerous K-9 demonstrations for community groups showcasing Gringo's skills at drug detection. They also participated in the advanced K-9 Patrol and Narcotics Dog Handler Seminar as guest instructors for drug dogs nationwide.

Throughout his career, Gringo assisted in numerous arrests and recovered more than five million dollars of narcotics. He will be greatly missed by his handler, Officer Daniel Smith as well as the officers of the Cheektowaga Police Department. Breton, the department's current dog, is carrying on the high standards set by his predecessor, Gringo.

Gringo died of old age, October 24, 2000. It took us some time to get a stone and plaque made for him. He was cremated by our dog warden and one of our retired lieutenants, who is a wood worker, made a casket for him. Gringo's handler was Police Officer Daniel Smith. Gringo was special because not only was he a great drug dog, also apprehended a number of fleeing felons, and he also was great with people and kids. Kids could climb all over him.

Memorial services for Gringo will be held on Friday, January 26, 2001, at 9:00 A.M., in the front of our police station. He will be buried near our police memorial in front of the station. We have a volunteer to play taps from a VFW post. The Chief and the Town Supervisor will say a few words. Neighboring K-9s and officers will be present and file by the casket. The prayer and poem, "The Time Has Come" will conclude the service.

The donated memorial cards from the F.A.S.T. Co. have Gringo's picture and Guardians of The Night poem on the back.

Officer Daniel Smith has welcomed a new partner, "Breston" since Gringo retired. Gringo was lucky to have two families. After retirement Gringo joined "Chew Toy," a.k.a.; Kevin Retzer, and his family, and their two pets. He is missed by many. Gringo is also dearly missed by Kevin Retzer and his family who were there to care for him at the end of his life.

Gringo is the father of K-9 Rose, who is Kevin's K-9 Partner. Kevin wrote: "I put Gringo down. Gringo died in my arms after I realized he was living for me. He had multiple health problems. One of the meds he was taking for Arthritis became toxic in his system and shut his Liver down. He was in extreme pain. I made the decision I knew he wanted me to make. It was very hard to do, but it was the right thing to do. I was blessed in that I was able to say good bye before hand. I also let a lot of other people who loved him have the opportunity to say good bye. By the way he has a resting spot in front of the station."

"He was the best partner that I ever had." Quoted Daniel Smith, K-9 Officer, Cheektowaga Police Department

In Loving Memory of

K-9 HANNA

July 7, 2000

Sheriff Officer Brian Howarth
Union County Sheriff's Office
10 Elizabethtown Plaza
Elizabeth, NJ 07207
908.273.6064

My K-9 partner, Hanna, passed away in 2000. She was my
first partner. We were teamed up in early January of 2000 and
went off to our 16 week training. While we were in training, my
wife and I had our first child, Timmy, in February of that year.
Hannah was right there to welcome her new 'brother' home.
We continued our training during the day, and while it was
exhausting for both of us, Hannah still came home at night to
lay by Timmy's crib and watch over him. Hanna and I graduated from Patrol Training on June 16, 2000 and took to the
streets immediately that night chasing two suspects within hours
after graduation.

She was a great partner, friend and family member, always ready to work at a moment's notice. Two weeks after graduation, Hanna's attitude changed. She was always tired, didn't want to eat, but she still wanted to work. She was diagnosed with stomach intestinal cancer only 2 weeks after graduation. She passed away on July 7, 2000. Now she is keeping watch on Timmy from above. She is still greatly missed by us.

I did get a new K-9 partner 2 weeks after her death. Udo and I have been inseparable since that day. Hanna now sits on a shelf on the same wall that she always liked to lay by in our living room. Her pictures hangs above the urn with her bright new shiny badge.

In Loving Memory of

K-9 HOND

October 10, 1999

Partner: Deputy Marc Newsom
Polk County Sheriff's Office
455 N. Broadway Ave.
Bartow, FL 33830
863-534.0980

Hond, an 8 year old, retired Polk County Sheriff's Office K-9, died Thursday morning at a Bartow veterinarian's office, where he was being treated for a systemic infection.

Sgt. Steve Pry, who's in charge of the PCSO K-9 unit, said Hond had been taken to the animal hospital Tuesday night from his home in Fort Meade when his handler, retired Deputy Marc Newsom, "noticed he wasn't feeling well."

Sgt. Pry said Hond suffered from "some kind of an infection that spread to other organs and they couldn't control it. I hated to see it happen. He was a good dog. It's like losing one of the family."

Hond, a five year veteran with the sheriff's office, began his career in November 1994, with K-9 Deputy Howard Martin. He was a Belgian Malinois. Sgt. Pry described him as having an average weight of 55 to 60 pounds, or somewhat lighter than a German Shepherd, weighing in the 75 to 80 pound range.

Belgian Malinois dogs are short haired and usually have a tan or light brown coloring. "They come out of the Dane breed," Pry added. "They are a herding dog and are very intense and a very high drive breed." In 1996, Newsom became Hond's handler until they both retired in October of 1999. By department policy, when a deputy retires, the dog also retires, if the dog is up in years, or if it isn't feasible to assign the dog to a new handler.

Hond was credited with 105 arrests during his career. He was the first sheriff's office K-9 purchased by the Lakeland Association of Realtors association's fund raiser for local K-9 units. A spokeswoman for the association said the group has bought several dogs for the sheriff's office and the Lakeland Police Department.

"He was a very sociable animal," Pry said of Hond. "We would send him to schools to do demonstrations. He lived with his handler as all of our dogs do."

The sheriff's office currently has 19 K-9 teams. Hond was purchased from The Netherlands, where he was KNPV titled. During his career with the PCSO he became nationally certified and was cross trained both in narcotics and patrol.

Sgt. Pry said most K-9 deaths come after they retire with their handlers. "All of the K-9 officers understand what it is like to lose one," he added.

In Loving Memory of

K-9 ISMAR

LODD
January 30, 2000

Partner: Officer James Swanson
Leesville Police Dept. LA

Several people gathered to mourn the death of the Leesville Police Department K-9, Ismar, Wednesday at a memorial service. Chief of police Bobby Hickman delivered the story of the K-9.

K-9 units from all over the state of Louisiana, including Alexandria, New Llano, Rapides, Savine, LaSalle and Vernon Parish Sheriff's Departments, Ft. Polk Military Police and officers from Rosepine, Anacoco and other departments joined the lineup at the burial site. During the services, officers placed a small white rose on the casket of their fallen comrade.

K-9 Ismar was killed in the line of duty during a standoff. He was shot and killed on an operation to arrest a man whom police said held his daughter and mother captive with a handgun.

Leeville police said they responded to an emergency call in this small western Louisiana town and found 56 year old Douglas Mayo holding his 26 year old daughter and his 73 year old wife at gunpoint in a house. Police said they persuaded Mayo to release his captives about a 45 minute standoff, but authorities still could not convince him to surrender.

When five officers and their K-9, 2 year old Ismar, a male Belgian Malinois, stormed into the house, Mayo allegedly shot Ismar in the face, killing the police K-9 before officers could arrest him. The women were not hurt.

Ismar was an important part of the department and will be greatly missed by the chief, Officer Swanson and the 30 officer police force.

The memorial service was held at the Municipal Golf Course followed by a burial ceremony.

K-9 Ismar cost the department approximately $10,000 and worked for approximately four months. He was trained to detect drugs, search building and catch suspects.

Mayo is being held on $34,500 bond and charged with aggravated assault, aggravated kidnaping, injuring and killing a police animal, weapons possession and aggravated assault on a police officer.

In Loving Memory of

K-9 JEEP

WW II

Partner: Howard Killen
668 Lingerlost Road
Killen, Alabama 35645

(Photo, Jeep with correspondent, Ernie Pyle)

Memories of his wartime dog put man on the move.

At the edge of a winding two lane road, a small grave lies under trees providing shade against rising summer heat. Howard Killen thought it was a fitting place for his old war comrade. "Old Jeep was a good dog," Killen said. "Probably saved my life a time or two," Killen was in the U.S. Marines 3rd Division during World War II and served as a scout dog handler in the Infantry. "Since I was a country boy and grew up with dogs, I had a good chance to be accepted," he said.

Before going to the Pacific, Killen served as a dog trainer at

Camp Lejeune, N.C., where the dogs underwent extensive training to transform household pets into animals able to survive combat. As a Private First Class, Jeep outranked his handler who was a buck Private.

When the war ended, Killen got permission to bring the Doberman home to Florence after the dog was decommissioned and retrained to be a pet. Killen later moved to Tennessee and left his dog with a relative in Florence.

Jeep died on Memorial Day 1954 and was buried in his owner's back yard on Royal Avenue, Killen returned in 1972. It's been 48 years since his death, but he has never forgotten about Jeep.

In recent weeks, those memories have intensified and created a desire to reconnect to the past. It started after a friend showed him old pictures during his time in the Pacific. They showed the famous war correspondent Ernie Pyle with Jeep and Killen. Only Killen's fingers are shown in the blurry picture, but he remembered the moment. "It just brought back memories to me," Killen said. "I guess I go tenderhearted about it."

Last week, Killen's nostalgia reached a peak. The new residents at the old Royal Avenue house were surprised with a visit from the veteran. Killen wanted to dig up the old dog and bury it near his home. He showed them the 1954 Florence Times newspaper article telling Jeep's story as proof. They agreed. "I came back the next day with my pick and shovel and dug him up," Killen said.

After five decades, everyone except Killen had forgotten about the unmarked backyard grave. He remembered the exact spot between the house and a tree. Now, Jeep has a new burial place. This time with a marker and in a nice cool shady spot that is just right for Jeep's final resting place.

Dogs have been used in the American military and in combat since the First World War. They are credited with saving thousands of human lives. The dogs were used as messengers, mine detectors, scouts and guard dogs. At night, they stood guard against surprise attacks. In the daytime, it was the dogs that often first sensed the enemy's presence. "You could tell by his reactions that someone was there," Killen said.

There are several memorials honoring the soldiers and their K-9 helpers including the Doberman War Dog Memorial in Guam, where the dogs were used extensively. "We put the dogs out in front of the troops," said Dr. William Putney, DVM, a retired Marine Corps Captain and author of "Always Faithful," a book chronicling the use of War Dogs in the Marines. "Having the dogs increased the distance between the troops and the people in the jungle."

Dr. Putney is a veterinarian who was assigned to the Marine Corps' War Dog Training School in 1943, after his graduation from Auburn University. He was the commanding officer of the 3rd War Dog Platoon, in the Marine's 3rd division in the Pacific. "The dogs caught them before they could get to us," said Putney, who is retired and living California. "The dog would alert us to the ambushes."

In 1994, Putney established the War Dog Cemetery on the U.S. Navel Base on Guam. Killen's earlier dog is buried there. A sniper got him just a foot or two from his owner's head.

After the war, Jeep made a good transition to peacetime and made a gentle pet for Killen's family. The three foot Doberman has remained in the back of Killen's mind for years since the war's end. Killen just completed the second volume of his book, "Possum Creek Tales." In it, he documents life in Possum Creek, a community between Killen and Lexington, where the biggest industry was a molasses mill and its biggest employee was the horse that turned the grinder.

In the latest book "The Possum Creek Flash," the author describes life away from Possum Creek after joining the Marines and being sent to fight for survival in the jungles of the Pacific. There's a picture of Jeep in the book.

Jeep's memory will be passed on to all who read the story of Killen's life. After facing the horrors of war and returning home for a normal life together, Jeep's story and Killen's life are insep-arable.

In Loving Memory of

K-9 KAI

LODD
March 5, 1994

Partner: Deputy Andy Thomas
(Now, Det. Thomas)
Bannock County Sheriff Department
5800 Fifth Street
Pocatello, ID 83204-7128
Seen on "America's Most Wanted " June 22, 2002

Notation by Andy Thomas

Although this incident took place over four years ago, it is still in my mind as if it happened last night. There is no way that I could ever try to explain, nor would I even attempt to explain, the feelings that take place between a K-9 handler and his partner. The kind of bond that I shared with Kai is a bond that I will never share with any kind of animal again as long as I live.

The thing that I found surprising while going through this incident was not only the bond that I shared with Kai, but also the bond that K-9 officers share with one another.

During this difficult time in my life, I was contacted by K-9 officers all over the United States. Officers who had never met me nor had they ever heard of Andy Thomas or Kai before, took the time to call me and wish me good luck in the future and to tell me how sorry they were about the past. Although these incidences are many, I remember every conversation as if it were yesterday and those are the conversations and the people which helped me get through what I would say has been the hardest time of my life.

At this point in my career I am no longer a K-9 officer, but that doesn't mean that I don't respect and have the utmost admiration for each and every K-9 team that is out there today. Since Kai's death, there has been a law in the State of Idaho passed which makes it illegal to harm, harass, or tease any police K-9 or horse in the State of Idaho. Idaho has also passed a law making it a felony to try to kill or severely wound any K-9 in the State of Idaho.

THE INCIDENT:

On March 5th, 1994, K-9 Officer Andy Thomas was called out of his residence at approximately 3:04 in the morning. Dispatch advised Officer Thomas that other officers, along with Idaho State Police, were out with an individual who was armed with a firearm, walking up and down a U.S. highway. Dispatch explained that the sergeants on the scene were asking for a K-9 unit to respond and asked Officer Thomas and his partner, Kai, to assist them.

Shortly after being notified, Officer Thomas and Kai responded to a location which was approximately 40 miles from his residence in rural Bannock County, Idaho. Officer Thomas explained that during the several minutes that it took him to respond to the call, he listened to the radio traffic of the incident from the officers who were already on the scene.

Officer Thomas noticed that some of the radio traffic between the sergeants and the patrolmen at the scene gave him the sense that the situation was very much escalated from the normal, everyday call. Several minutes had passed before Officer Thomas arrived on the scene and he happened to arrive at the same time that the Patrol Commander, Tom Canfield, arrived.

At this time, Officer Thomas, Patrol Capt. Tom Canfield, and Patrol Sgt. Kevin Fonnesbeck gathered behind a patrol car, at which time Sgt. Fonnesbeck briefed Capt. Canfield and Officer Thomas on the situation. He explained to Officer Thomas that their patrol officers had dealt with the suspect in question, a Gerald Cox, earlier in the evening, at which time Mr. Cox was displaying a firearm that was taken away from him by patrol officers.

At the time of the first contact, officers did not have enough to take Mr. Cox into protective custody nor had Mr. Cox violated any laws. However, the officers were able to take the firearm into custody until Mr. Cox could, at a later date, come down to the station to pick up the firearm. After officers left, several hours had passed when a Bannock County Deputy Sheriff received a call of a man walking down a highway in front of a home with a firearm. The officer responding to the scene, Officer Michael Dahlquist, had not put the two scenarios together until he arrived at the scene and found Mr. Cox standing on the side of the highway with something behind his back.

As Officer Dahlquist started closing in with his vehicle toward Mr. Cox, he raised a very old long barreled firearm. It was undetermined what kind of firearm Mr. Cox had in his possession, but there was no mistaking that it was a firearm. At this time, Officer Dahlquist backed out of the area and started communicating with Mr. Cox via the public address system while at the same time, Officer Dahlquist was asking for backup.

After Officer Dahlquist requested backup, Officer Bob Laumann from the Idaho State Police, along with patrol sergeants from the Bannock County Sheriff's Office were dispatched to assist Officer Dahlquist. Officers started to arrive at the scene shortly after the first call for backup, at which time Officer Dahlquist started asking Mr. Cox to place the firearm on the ground.

Mr. Cox appeared to be intoxicated or, possibly was high on methamphetamine because of his abnormal state of paranoia.

Officers at the scene had negotiated with Mr. Cox for approximately three hours by the time K-9 Officer Andy Thomas arrived. It was apparent that Mr. Cox was not going to put down the firearm nor did he have any intentions of giving up. At this time, Patrol Capt. Tom Canfield and Officer Andy Thomas talked about the different scenarios that they could use to disarm the subject by using non-lethal force. It was determined that the only type of non-lethal force that could be used to try to get Mr. Cox to surrender would be the use of Officer Thomas' patrol K-9, Kai.

At this time, a plan was discussed to have the officers on the far right of Mr. Cox distract him by talking to him and ordering him to put down the firearm, while Officer Thomas and Capt.Tom Canfield would be at the far left of Mr. Cox, at which time K-9 Officer Kai would attempt an apprehension on Mr. Cox from behind.

Officer Thomas noted that Mr. Cox had placed the gun in his weak hand, which appeared to have been his left. Mr. Cox was screaming at the officers to the left of his location and pointing at them with his right hand. He did several gestures with his right hand while holding the gun with his left hand with the barrel facing down toward the ground in a backwards motion.

At this time, Officer Thomas felt that this would be a prime opportunity to send in Deputy Kai because Mr. Cox was completely unprepared for this type of scenario. Officer Thomas then made sure that Kai had target acquisition; and after noticing the dog was locked onto the target, Officer Thomas whispered into Kai's ear, giving him the command to apprehend.

K-9 Kai left from Officer Thomas' side with his tail up high, his hackles up, running full speed at his target, Mr. Cox. It is still unknown by Officer Thomas what alerted Mr. Cox to the presence of Kai, but Mr. Cox turned, noticed the police dog coming in, and switched hands with the firearm, shooting once at Deputy Kai.

K-9 Kai let out a loud scream, going up into the air on his back haunches, while at the same time, Mr. Cox took the firearm and struck the top of Kai's head with the barrel, causing Kai to go to the ground. Kai then regained his composure and started to come back up for a second time, at which time Mr. Cox was pointing the firearm now toward the group of officers, then in the direction from which the dog was sent.

At this time, five of the officers returned fire, shooting a total of 11 rounds toward Mr. Cox, one of which happened to hit Kai in the side of the mouth, taking off the lower side of the jaw. Simultaneously, as K-9 Officer Kai was shot, the suspect, Gerald Cox was also shot. He received three gunshot wounds, two to one elbow and one to the other elbow. The left side elbow was hit once with a 9 millimeter round and then a second time with a 12 gauge slug round. The other elbow was hit with a 9 millimeter round.

The suspect immediately went to the ground, at which time he was handcuffed and placed into custody. The Life Flight helicopter was called, along with a local ambulance service. Minutes later an ambulance arrived and administered first aid to Mr. Cox.

At the same time, Officer Thomas was administering first aid to his partner, Kai. As Officer Thomas arrived at Kai's side shortly after the shooting, he noticed that Kai's eyes were extremely dilated and glossy looking. Officer Thomas sat and talked to Kai for several minutes and other officers at the scene noticed that Kai's eyes were starting to constrict and go back to normal size.

At this time, it appeared that Kai had come out of shock and was starting to be more aware of his surroundings and his handler, Andy Thomas. Officer Thomas noted that the day prior to the shooting, all the K-9 officers in his department had gone through a course of advanced first aid dealing with gunshot wounds to their dogs. Officer Thomas was able to keep an airway established on Kai while, at the same time, taping his lower jaw back up to his mouth, preparing him for the 30 minute Life Flight ride that they both would take.

Approximately 25 minutes after the shooting, Life Flight landed and transported both Kai and Officer Thomas to Bannock Regional Medical Center in Pocatello, Idaho. Waiting at the medical center was another Bannock County K-9 Officer, Tom Foltz, who transported Kai, Dr. Gerstner, and Officer Thomas to Hawthorne Animal Hospital. During the ride to the hospital, Kai quit breathing and had to be given CPR by Officer Thomas and Dr. Gerstner until they arrived at the veterinarian center.

At the Hawthorne Animal Hospital, Kai was taken into an operating room and examined; at which point it was determined that the trauma to his throat and lower jaw was too massive and could not be repaired. At this time, Officer Thomas quit doing CPR on his partner and Kai was pronounced dead.

Shortly after the shooting on May 5, 1994, all the officers were involved were cleared and given Letters of Recommendation for their bravery during this incident. Officer Thomas and Officer Kai were given Medals of Valor, along with distinguished Medals of Honor through the Bannock County Sheriff's Office.

Later on that week, Kai was cremated, and a large ceremony was held for him in the county seat of Bannock County, Pocatello. Close to 100 K-9 officers drove to Pocatello and gave their respects to not only Bannock County and Andy Thomas but to the fallen hero, Kai.

Shortly after Kai's funeral, Bannock County celebrated the opening of a brand new Sheriff's Office and jail facility. In front of the facility is a large monument with a picture of Kai the poem, A Call to Give Your All engraved on the back.

During the first month after Kai was killed, Officer Thomas received hundreds, if not thousands, of letters from not only local citizens but people throughout the United States who had heard about this horrific incident and took the time to write to give their condolences. At the same time, an elderly female in the community donated the money for another dog to replace Kai.

A short time later, Kai was replaced by another German Shepherd male by the name of Zaire, who remained the partner of Deputy Andy Thomas for approximately one year, until the time he was promoted into the Detective Division.

In Loving Memory of

K-9 KASTOR

November 4, 2000

Partner: Cpl. Dan Redd
Republic Police Department MO
221 North Main,
Republic, MO 65738
417. 732 2642

The Republic Police K-9 Unit consisted of handler Dan Redd and Kastor. Officer Redd and Kastor started working together as a team November 1996 after completing an extensive training course.

The K-9 Unit is trained to sniff out illegal drugs as well as locating and apprehending suspects. The K-9 Program is active in assisting and working with the local schools in drug awareness.

Since the beginning of the K-9 Program the team has been a highly visible presence on the streets of Republic. As well as regular calls for service and duty shifts, the team is on call 24 hours a day to assist patrol officers of the Republic Police Department as well as other agencies.

It is hard for me to believe that this November 4th, Kastor will be gone for a year. I remember this time last year and the hard times he was having. He was a trooper till the end.

I remember him fighting so hard to keep going even though I knew in my heart he was hurting. He had cancer and the day we (my wife and I) decided he need not suffer any more was the worst day of my life. I was at his side when he left this earth.

Even now as I write this I have a hard time keeping the tears back. You would think that after a year one could handle the situation better; Kastor, to me, was more that a partner, he was part of my family. In fact I think I spent more time with him than I did with my human family.

I believe you asked in your letter a little about him, He was 90 Lb. and 7½ years old at the time of his passing. He is buried at a Service Dog cemetery in a place of honor for service dogs at the Rivermont Memorial Gardens, Springfield, MO. I stop by his grave as much as I can.

Where he is buried is a new site just started for Service Dogs in July of 2000, Kastor was the second K-9 buried there. Rivermont provided his final resting place along with his service free for Service Dogs and as far as I know this is the only such location in Southwest Missouri.

At this point there are no plans to obtain another K-9 for the department, no funds for such. Also shortly before Kastor passed away I was promoted to Cpl. and now that Kastor is gone I have been told that since I am now a supervisor that someone else would be the handler if another dog was obtained. My answer to that was I would take a demotion if that is what it would take to again work with a police K-9.

In 26 years of Law Enforcement, the 5 years I spent with Kastor has been the best and most rewarding part of my career. I still have children coming up to me while on duty asking about Kastor, they remember him at the schools. Most were not aware he was gone. Kastor's body is gone from this earth however his spirit lives on as far as I am concerned.

/s/Dan Redd
Republic Police Dept.

In Loving Memory of

K-9 KEESHA

Sept. 16, 1992 Oct. 20, 1999

Partner, Deputy Doug Rollison
Leavenworth Sheriff's Dept.
Leavenworth, Kansas

Training That We Received
March 15, 1996 Drug Detection and Tracking
Detector Dogs International Omaha, NE
May 16, 1997 Drug Detection and Tracking
Detector Dogs International Omaha, NE
June 15, 1999 - Drug Detection Team
North American Police Work Dog Association Raytown Mo. Nationals

A Tribute To Keesha
Life began on September 16, 1992
"She started as a 'dog' but ended as a 'True Deputy'
that we all loved."
Keesha started her Law Enforcement career at the Atchison

County Sheriff's Department in 1996. This was her second car that she patrolled. She worked for Atchison approximately 3½ years. We worked together for the Leavenworth County Sheriff's Dept. in 1998. That is where Keesha was working when she died.

Keesha was eulogized with "Guardians Of The Night. Just to remind you of the events that led to her death, we were at our south station getting gas and I always let her out to take care of business and we would go play in a nearby field. This time she took off after something and was killed on the highway. The driver left the scene and called it in anonymously. It really helped in our time of sorrow to know that someone was thinking about our loss on the other side of the nation.

I now have Kai and have had him since December 1999. He is a little over four years old. He came from Czechoslovakia and has all his commands in Czech. He is certified in narcotics, tracking, and article search. He is doing really well at aggression work; we just haven't been to a seminar to get him certified. We still miss Keesha very much. We have a memorial set up for her in our living room.

Personal note: If it weren't for Doug's phone call, thanking me for cards, I would have never continued this passion. Thank you Doug, get home safely from Qatar.

In Loving Memory of

K-9 KILO

January 10, 2000

Partner: Deputy Brad Metz
Shawnee County Sheriff's Dept.
Shawnee County, KS

K-9 hepatitis is similar to the disease that affects humans, but in dogs the cause isn't known. No cure exists for K-9 hepatitis.

Kilo was placed on a daily regimen of drugs designed to slow the disease's progress. He continued in recent months to ride on routine patrol and serve as a bomb sniffer. But Sheriff's Sgt. Scott Baker said the department found it necessary to retire Kilo on Jan. 10.

Sgt. Baker said he and Metz decided to euthanize Kilo on Thursday morning, when the dog didn't want to eat and wouldn't get out of his doghouse.

Sgt. Baker said deputies first noticed Kilo was sick in mid October after he lost about 17 pounds in a month. Veterinarians at Kansas State University diagnosed him as suffering from K-9 hepatitis, an inflammation of the liver.

In Loving Memory of

K-9 KODA

August 13, 1986 - April 30, 1997

Partner: Officer Rick Osborn
Sacramento Police Department
900 - 8th Street
Sacramento, CA 95814

Koda was an asset to Sacramento Police Department. He won numerous awards and loved to compete in local K-9 trials. He apprehended many felons. He also backed up fellow K-9's, for example when he helped his friend & fellow K-9 officer K-9 Sammie. The first K-9 team on scene was Officer Dave Kidd and K-9 Sammie. As Sammie was getting ready to go in to apprehend the suspect the suspect kicked Sammie in the ribs breaking two of his ribs .

Rick and Koda then showed up on scene. Koda was sent into the room and the subject closed the door unaware that K-9 Koda was in the room too. The room was pitch black & all that could be heard was someone being slammed up against a door repeatedly. Rick attempted to get into the room, fearing for his partner. When Rick was finally able to get into the room Koda had the suspect apprehended.

The continuous slamming against the door was Koda slamming the suspect against the door. Koda caught a bad guy and backed up a fellow K-9. Sammie did recover from his injuries & penal code 600 PC came into effect thanks to Officer Dave Kidd of the Sacramento Police Department. This penal code makes it a felony to cause any type of injury (such as K-9 Sammie received) to a horse or dog being used by a police officer.

Good work Sammie and Koda.

There was another time when a vehicle stop had been made because the car that was stopped had been a suspect vehicle for having drugs. When Rick and Koda arrived on scene, Rick gave Koda the command to start searching. While searching the inside of the van, Koda decided to do what seemed to be jumping jacks. The Detectives on scene knew that there were drugs in the vehicle. Well, Koda's Jumping Jack routine ended up to be Koda "alerting" to the 100 Kilo's of cocaine hidden in the head liner of the van.

When Koda wasn't busy being a protection dog or a narcotics dog he enjoyed showing his respect to upper management with a salute. On his off time he enjoyed going to Island Lakes for a swim and a good hike.

He loved his family and playing ball. But most of all he enjoyed the quiet hikes with Rick and going and hanging out with the cows at "Auntie Stacy's."

Unfortunately age caught up with Koda and after a short lived retirement, he was put to sleep due to the pain he was in from arthritis and other medical problems. To this day we have a portrait of Koda hanging over our fireplace so that he can help his successor "Devo" watch over our family.

THE SPIRIT OF A GERMAN SHEPHERD

I was standing on a hillside, in a field of blowing wheat
And the spirit of a German Shepherd Dog was lying at my feet
He looked at me with kind dark eyes, ancient wisdom shining through.
And in the essence of his being his love shone clear and true.
His mind did lock upon my heart as I stood there on that day.
And he told me of this story about a place so far away.
His tale did put my heart at ease, my fears did fade away.
About what lay ahead of me on another distant day.
"I live among God's creatures now in the heavens of your mind.
So do not grieve for me, my friend for I am with my kind.
My collar is a rainbow's hue, my leash a shooting star.
My boundaries are the Milky Way where I sparkle from afar.
There are no pens or kennels here, and I am not confined.
But free to roam God's heavens among my shepherd kind.
I nap the day on a snowy cloud, gentle breezes rocking me.
And dream the dreams of Earthlings and how it used to be.
The trees are full of liver treats and tennis balls abound.
And Milk bones line the walkways just waiting to be found.
There even is a ring set up, the grass all lush and green.
And everyone who gaits around becomes the Best of Breed.
For we're all winners in this place, we have no faults, you see.
And God passes out those ribbons to each one, even me.
I drink from waters laced with gold my world a beauty to behold.
And wise old dogs do form my pride to amble at my very side.
At night I sleep in an angel's arms, her wings protecting me.
And moonbeams dance about us as stardust falls on thee.
So when your life on earth is spent, and you stand at Heaven's gate,
have no fear of loneliness for here, you know I wait."
~author unknown

In Loving Memory of

K-9 KODI

March 4, 2000
LODD

Partner: Officer Craig Pesko
Pontiac Police K-9 Unit Michigan
110 E. Pike St.
Pontiac MI 48342
810.857-7870

Kodi's Statistics
Pontiac Police K-9 Unit
Registered Name:
Warrick vom Frolich Haus
Handler: Craig Pesko
Breed: German Shepherd
Weight: 90 lb.
Sex: Male
D.O.B. August 24, 1997
K-9 Certified: Sept. 6, 1998

"I will protect you with my last breath ..."

Standing before a small white casket, Steve Kulakowsky pushed the words past the knot in his throat. "There is no greater love than this, that I would lay down my life for you." His voice breaking, the Flat Rock police officer rushed to finish his eulogy for Kodi, the Pontiac police dog who died in the line of duty.

Officers from dozens of metro Detroit police departments stood rigidly at attention at a Taylor Pet Cemetery Tuesday during a military funeral for Kodi. At the sides of many, K-9 officers whined and fidgeted against taut leashes as Kulakowsky read from "Guardians of the Night," a tribute to fallen police dogs by an unknown author.

"Together we will experience a bond only others like us will understand." Kodi's owner and handler, Pontiac Police Officer Craig Pesko, wept behind dark sunglasses as taps sounded a farewell. Later, Pesko quietly declined comment.

Other K-9 handlers said it's difficult to understand the bond between police officers and their K-9 partners. "Craig has no kids," Kulakowsky said. "The dog was what he had. I can't imagine what it's going to be like for him to get back in the cruiser and not hear Kodi barking." Kodi, 2½, died Friday during surgery to repair spinal damage caused by a two story fall the dog took during the search of a building in Pontiac Thursday night. He had been on the force for about 18 months and assisted in tracking, drug detection and searches. His work was steady, always top notch. The dog had apprehended car thieves during manhunts, and uncovered drugs on several occasions.

More than 130 police officers, police dogs and others attended the funeral, where Kodi joined more than 20,000 animals buried at AAA Pet Services cemetery in Taylor. The officers wore black bands around their badges, identical to the badges and bands fastened to each police dog's collar.

"When our time is done, you move on in the world. If we

should meet again on another street, I will gladly take up your fight."

Kodi will always be missed. He was a full blooded German Shepherd and his commands are given in German. Kodi was a Full Service Police Dog and was trained by his partner, Officer Pesko, with the assistance of other officers. Kodi was trained in Drug Detection and Evidence Detection. Kodi especially loved showing off his skills at K-9 demos.

Kodi's success has been possible due to the outstanding teamwork shared by his fellow officers.

In Loving Memory of

K-9 LASER

November 16, 1991 - December 1996

Partner: Officer Andy Niederdorfer
West Hartford Police Department
103 Raymond Rd.
West Hartford, CT 06110
860.523-5203

K-9 Laser was born on November 16, 1991. He was West Hartford's first K-9 starting service in 1992.

Lazer was imported from Czechoslovakia and was trained with Officer Andy Niederdorfer as his handler at the Suffolk County Police Department in New York. Laser went on to receive cross training in Narcotic Detection with a trainer from the New London Police Department and was certified through the Connecticut Police Work Dog Association and NAPWDA.

During his three year career he performed over 100 tracks, 82 building searches, 25 evidence searches and made approximately 30 criminal apprehensions. He was narcotics certified for one year and performed 59 searches in that time with 37 finds.

Being West Hartford's first K-9, a strong effort was made to introduce him to the community. Laser visited numerous schools, civic and youth groups totaling some 180 public demo's in that three year span. The department had 10,000 baseball cards made (10 different cards each with Laser on them). All 10,000 were handed out within one year at demos and by officers from the police department while working the streets.

He was also featured two years in a row in the Town's community calendar. During his three years on the force he had received over 275 letters of appreciation and commendation from other Police agencies, civic groups and citizens. One year on his birthday the department received 10 birthday cards in the mail for him.

He won Awards for Criminal Apprehension and Narcotics Detection for actual cases worked from the New Haven German Shepherd Club and was a runner up for the Daniel Wasson Memorial K-9 Award in 1994.

Laser was forced to retire early due to health problems but served the West Hartford Police Department for three years. In that time he made numerous criminal apprehensions and narcotic finds for the West Hartford Police Department as well as several neighboring Towns and Cities.

Upon his retirement local businessmen and the local newspaper combined to throw a retirement party for Laser where all school children and residents could come out and wish him well. K-9 teams from around the state came out for the retirement to give a demo to the crowd and film was donated so the children could have photos taken with Laser.

Laser went into retirement on December 31, 1995 and had to be put down a year after retirement in December of 1996. He has been and always will be missed.

In Loving Memory of

K-9 LAZER

September 15, 2000

Partner: Officer Kari Bauer
North Huntingdon Police Department
11279 Center Highway
North Huntingdon, PA 15642
724.863-3806

A Tribute To Lazer:
(Andy Starnes, Post Gazette)

"He was my best friend, my son, my world," said Bauer, 34, who had been Lazer's partner and handler since he started in 1993. Looking stricken, she sat stoically at the service at Oak Hollow Park, then tearfully accepted condolences from fellow officers and friends."He went on vacation with me. He was home with me. He was with me all the time," said Bauer, who hid her tears behind a pair of sunglasses. The service had all the trappings of the typical funeral. It brought together folks who hadn't seen each other for some time. Some of the officers took group photographs, but some of their police dogs behaved like skittish relatives who hadn't seen each other since the last funeral. They barked fiercely at each other as they waited for the parade to begin. "It is important to be here," said Homestead Patrolman David Smoley. "Lazer was a fellow police officer." Some officers came on their own time, before starting or after finishing their shifts, while others were being paid. Nearly all were driving municipal vehicles. Homestead K-9 officer Jeffrey DeSimone said his department had four officers, two dogs and three cars at the memorial service. He said three of the four officers were there on their own time. The fourth officer got permission to leave his daylight shift early so he could attend the service. At about 12:45 p.m., three police motorcycles led a cavalcade of about 40 vehicles, mostly patrol cars with their lights flashing, slowly out of the North Huntingdon police station. The procession traveled through the community of Irwin to a picnic grove in Oak Hollow Park, a township park, about 10 minutes away. There, on a little table, was a photograph of Lazer flanked on each side by vases of fresh roses, carnations and irises. His dog collar and police badge hung off the frame. His leash lay on the table, alongside some photographs, a framed poem and a little box containing the remains of Lazer, who had been cremated. As guests settled into folding chairs, the voice of Elvis singing "You'll Never Walk Alone" blared from a set of speakers. Police handed out memorial brochures that contained poems for fallen K-9 dogs. A lone bagpiper, Charles Gledich, played "Amazing Grace" as he marched through a column flanked by about 30 K-9 officers with their dogs. Several poems were read. Two Norwin Senior High School band members played taps. Most of the dogs were well behaved until a triple volley was fired from the opposite hillside. Gunfire made them jittery, sending them into a chorus of barking. Admittedly uncertain about what his role should be, Fischer called the chaplain of the Pittsburgh police to get some ideas for his eulogy to the crowd of more than 125 people, mostly police officers. He ended up talking about the difficulties of being a police officer, manpower shortages and burnout, departmental and office politics, and concerns that hang over most departments about who gets promoted and who doesn't. "Lazer's only concern when that collar and badge went around his neck was to 'protect and serve.' It never occurred to him that he didn't get promoted or demoted. Budgets, shortages, politics never entered his mind. Whether people understood him or not was not a concern," Fischer said. "He was a living example of single minded devotion." Sombo seemed ready to deflect any criticism about the event. He defended the department's decision to hold such an elaborate memorial service, saying that K-9 Lazer was well known and much loved in the community. Some merchants' signs along Route 30 seemed to support that. On several placards in North Huntingdon was posted:"K-9 Lazer. Gone but not forgotten."

In Loving Memory of

K-9 LORD

February 27, 2000

Partner: Cpl. Ken Weed
Daphne Police Dept.
1502 U.S. Highway 98
Daphne, AL 36526
251.621 3095

The tragic death was caused by a ruthless driver, seen by a witness, who swerved from one lane to another to hit him and leave the scene. What kind of person would be so cruel as to deliberately hit such a beautiful creature and drive away? The loss of a family member is always painful when it is as unexpected and horrific such as this event. It is done.

Now is the time to think of all the sunshine and smiles that Lord spread to all with whom he had come into contact. He was one big dog with a broad smile and lapping tongue that would light up children's and adult's hearts where ever he was located. His stately appearance, his strong gait, his sauntering style made for appealing sights of his presence. He had charisma!

Memories:

Long lasting memories of a friend will never die until the last thought of him has perished with the last brain wave.

With us forever!

Your friends of the Daphne Police Department, the Baldwin County Sheriff's Office, the Alabama State Police, the Drug Enforcement Administration and other surrounding law enforcement entities will miss you Lord. The loss of K-9 Lord is a heavy and dark cloud surrounding those who knew him.

It is with sympathy that we grieve with Corporal Ken Weed and his family for the loss of their family friend. It is with deep satisfaction that we will remember Lord and his partner, Ken.

From: The team.

In Loving Memory of

K-9 MAC

LODD
October 14, 1982 - Memorial Ceremony 2000

Partner: Patrolman Robert Parrish
Trenton Police Department
225 N. Clinton Avenue
Trenton, NJ 08609

There was a ceremony in this year of 2000, to bring closure for Officer Bob Parrish.

On October 14, 1982, Patrolman Bob Parrish and his K-9 partner, Mac, responded to a burglary in progress at a tavern. On their arrival, the officers at the scene reported seeing the silhouette of a person on the premises.

Patrolman Parrish and Mac entered the building and conducted a search as they were trained. It was in the basement that a suspect armed with a knife lunged from a utility closet. As he was trained, Mac pounced on the suspect and during the ensuing struggle, Mac was stabbed in the chest and mortally wounded.

Patrolman Parrish rushed his partner to the veterinary hospital, where Mac died from his wound shortly after arriving. Mac will always be remembered by the Trenton Police Department for his service and the extreme sacrifice he made in the performance of his duties. Mac's presence on the scene likely saved an officer from serious injury from the armed suspect who was predisposed to attack with his knife.

As the result of Mac's death, New Jersey passed legislation making it a crime to assault a Police Animal.

In Loving Memory of

K-9 MAJOR

Oct. 1981   Sept. 1991

Partner: Sgt. George T. Cayer
Rumford Police Department
Rumford, ME

A Tribute To Major

I was and still am very proud of him for all that he did for my agency and me. As always he was there when I needed him, ready to put his life down for mine if needed. He was a machine when it came to obedience, trained in all aspects of police K-9 work. At home he was a house pet, watching over my wife and at the time one daughter.

He is sadly missed and could never be replaced. Some day in the future I will have another K-9 to work and spend long hours with.

Thank you for giving these fallen heroes a place where they can be remembered in everyone's lives. Major was almost ten years old when he passed on (October 1981 to September

1991). He was endorsed by the Rumford, Maine Police and the Maine State Warden Service for Search and Rescue operations. During my time with Major, I was Deputy Game Warden and spent many of days and nights in the field.

Sincerely grateful,

/s/ Sergeant George T. Cayer

In Loving Memory of

K-9 MARCO

January 18, 2000

Partner: Officer Cory Smith
American Fork Police Dept.
98 North Central St.
American Fork, UT

With community donations, many coming from children, the American Fork Police Department has received more than $10,000 in donations to purchase a new police service dog to replace Marco, a 4 year old Belgium Malinois, who died January 18 during a routine procedure to repair an abscessed tooth.

Officer Smith lost his partner, Marco after the operation on his tooth, he died from complications from undigested food. Officer Smith has a new partner, Nik. Marco cannot be replaced, but working with Nik helps.

In Loving Memory of

K-9 MAVERICK

Date Certified: March 26, 1997
Date End of Watch: February 12, 2000
LODD

Partner: Deputy Theodore "TJ" VanBebber
Sonoma Sheriff Department
Santa Rose, CA

RESOLUTION NO. 24426
RESOLUTION OF THE COUNCIL OF THE CITY OF
SANTA ROSA NAMING THE DOG PARK IN DE TURK
ROUND BARN PARK IN HONOR OF MAVERICK.

WHEREAS, the city of Santa Rosa has constructed a park at
8th & Donahue Sts. Which includes a dog park area; and
WHEREAS, Maverick was a valuable member of the K-9
Corps of the Sonoma County Sheriff's Department and fre-
quently worked with the Santa Rosa Police Department; and
WHEREAS, Maverick was killed in the line of duty in the

City of Santa Rosa; and

WHEREAS, the Board of Community Services has recommended that the dog park in DeTurk Round Barn Park be named in honor of Maverick.

NOW, THEREFORE, BE IT RESOLVED that the dog park located in DeTurk Round Barn Park be named in honor of Maverick

IN COUNCIL DULY PASSED this 30th day of May, 2000

The Sonoma County Sheriff's Department is sad to report that they have lost a K-9 in the line of duty. The department's K-9, Maverick was struck by a motor vehicle and killed while pursuing two armed suspects that were in possession of a half pound of amphetamine and a loaded handgun.

Maverick, a male German Shepherd was donated to the Sheriff Department on March 26, 1997.

K-9 Maverick was one and a half years old and assigned to Deputy T. J. VanBebber as his partner. They went through an extensive training program which included Field Searching, Suspect Apprehension, Handler Protection and Obedience Training. Maverick was a fast learner and was certified to start working patrol within six weeks. Outside of his field work, Maverick represented the department in several K-9 demonstrations. Because of his friendly demeanor, he was repeatedly asked to perform in demonstrations in local schools.

During his short, but productive career, Maverick was responsible for apprehending several felony suspects. He was best known for apprehending three suspects following a vehicle pursuit from a Shots Fired call. After the vehicle stopped, three suspects fled on foot. Maverick pursued the suspects with Deputy VanBebber. Maverick tackled two of the suspects, knocking them to the ground. He then pursued the third suspect, catching him by the leg and holding him until Deputy VanBebber arrived.

On Maverick's last night on patrol, Deputy VanBebber and Maverick were patrolling the area of west Santa Rosa, which is classified as a high crime area. Maverick was well known in this area by the criminal types.

Another deputy had made a traffic stop on a vehicle suspected of being involved in criminal activity and that deputy requested a back up. Deputy VanBebber and Maverick responded. As they arrived on the scene, the two suspects who were being detained could hear Maverick barking from the patrol vehicle, which was a trademark of his.

The suspects, with the arrival of the K-9, started to become uncooperative with the deputies. The suspects then fled on foot with Maverick in hot pursuit. During the foot pursuit, the suspect dropped a large quantity of drugs and a loaded hand gun.

While crossing a busy street a vehicle swerved to miss one of the eluding suspects and struck Maverick who had almost caught up to that suspect. Maverick was immediately rushed to a nearby veterinarian clinic where he was pronounced dead a short time later. Maverick died on Feb. 12, 2000. Although his career was cut short, he was killed in the line of duty, doing what he loved best, "Chasing Bad Guys."

"I lost my partner, He was one tough cop. The kind of guy who got hit by a car. He nearly caught a fleeing drug suspect from behind."

Update:
TJ trained another German Shepherd, "Colt." They are back on the streets together, making them safer for all.

In Loving Memory of

K-9 MAX

January 24, 1991   December 29, 2000

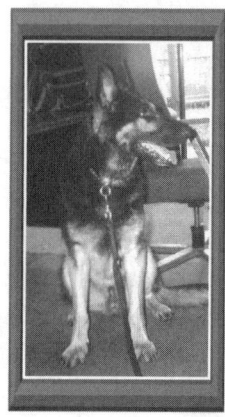

Partner: Officer Terrence O'Connor
New Castle Police Department
New Castle Headquarters Bldg.
3601 North Dupont Hwy.
New Castle, DE 19720

Max was born in Kiev, Russia , 60 miles from the Chernobyl Nuclear Plant, in what is now the Ukraine. He was imported to the United States and worked as a Police Service Dog for 5½ years. Max made numerous apprehensions and drug finds. Max was known for his "very independent" personality. He was nicknamed "butt head."

Max retired three years ago due to stress related problems. He was very sociable with children and a cherished member of our family!

Max was well loved by members of the police department and by citizens we contacted as part of our daily routine. He was born January 24, 1991 and died of pneumonia related to pancreatic cancer on December 29, 2000. He was my first police service dog.

I would like to thank Amy Kevis and Chip Shepherd for being with us when I had to put Max down. His final moments were peaceful.

Max we miss you!

God Bless You........Max!

In Loving Memory of

K-9 NERO

September 19, 2000

Partner: Officer Phillip Aufiero
New Castle County Police Dept.
Delaware

Nero, a veteran New Castle County police dog praised for his many acts of valor, died Tuesday night after a brief illness. "I am profoundly saddened by the loss of Nero. He was much more than just a police K-9. He was a loyal friend and employee." stated Col. Jack Cunningham.

The end came peacefully for Nero at 6:30 p.m. " I let him out, he came back in and laid down. I laid down next to him and he put his head on my lap and just closed his eyes. He is irreplaceable," said his partner, Officer Phillip Aufiero.

In August 1992, Nero saved his life when a robbery suspect pulled out a pistol and tried to shoot Officer Aufiero. Nero hit him and knocked the gun out of his hand. They had a ten year career together.

Nero was responsible for seizing more than $1 million in drugs, cash and property. As a result he was the recipient of countless commendations for merit and valor.

He was born in Budapest, was picked up in Raleigh, NC when he was only 18 months old. He only understood Hungarian. His handler had to learn to speak the commands in Hungarian.

In addition to catching criminals, Nero was credited with finding several lost children and missing Alzheimer patients.

Nero was always a big hit at community functions and with the school children we visited in Middletown during the past five years. He was an old guy, but loved to work. When Officer Aufiero would go out, he would always want to go.

The K-9 veteran was forced to retire from the force late last month after undergoing emergency surgery. After the operation, the dog's health declined. About the only thing he didn't like was the vet. He was happy with Aufiero and he was happy with him. Officer Aufiero only wanted him to come home.

In Loving Memory of

K-9 PAX
Pax Von Langemark

August 23, 1977 - September 15, 1989

Partner: Officer Ken Kramerman
Redding Police Department
1313 California St.
Redding, CA 96001
530.225-4289

Pax was 3½ years old when he began his career with the Redding Police Department. He was a Sch III imported from Germany. He took the place of Asko who was killed in the line of duty. Pax worked the street as a patrol dog for 8 years until I was transferred to detectives. He was credited with numerous misdemeanor and felony arrests. He performed many K-9 demonstrations and was always a hit while visiting schools. He was an excellent patrol and family dog. Pax was laid to rest in 1989 after suffering from a degenerative spine disease.

Pax came after Asko and was the last working K-9 Ken had at the Police Department, he is now LT. K. Kramerman.

In Loving Memory of

K-9 QUANTO

LODD
November 16, 1999

Partner: Officer J. J. Thurne
Jacksonville Sheriff's Department
Jacksonville, FL

The shooting plays continuously in Jacksonville police Officer J.J. Thurne's mind: Releasing his K-9 partner Quanto to chase after an armed robbery suspect. Quanto tiring as the suspect beat him with his hands and legs. The numbness in his hand, not realizing part of his trigger finger had been torn away after a shot was fired. Quanto lying on his side and not moving after a nudge. The 21 year Jacksonville Sheriff's Office veteran remembers it vividly each time he tells the story since he was shot last week by a robbery suspect who had escaped from jail.

It's a story he's told many officers who have stopped him in the hallway at the Police Memorial Building, where he returned to work part time yesterday. "You look back and wonder what you could have done to prevent this or make it come out in a different light," he said. "If I could trade a finger for the dog, there wouldn't be a question. The dog is the hardest thing to deal with."

After a week of grieving, planning a memorial service for his partner of two years and meeting with doctors, Thurne, 41, is learning to be a "lefty" and looking forward to meeting his new partner. But Thurne knows the new dog won't be able to replace the one he lost in the shooting. Gary Lee Neil, 22, who is accused of shooting Thurne and killing Quanto, is being held at the Duval County jail. He is charged with attempted murder of a law enforcement officer, killing a police dog and escape.

Police are still searching for the driver of the dark blue Chevrolet that Neil jumped from that night. Thurne said an officer never knows whom he will encounter on the street. That night, he didn't know it was the same man he and Quanto helped arrest in January after a shooting at a Burger King restaurant on San Pablo Road and chase by police. He remembers struggling with him then. It wasn't any different last week, Thurne said.

The man continued to fight even after Quanto bit him on the leg for the third time. Thurne grabbed the man and started applying pressure around his neck when the suspect reached back to grab his gun. It was then they struggled for the weapon and the gun fired. Thurne felt his hand go numb, but he didn't realize he or Quanto had been shot.

The bullet plunged through the middle knuckle of his right index finger and came out above the top knuckle. The struggle continued as Thurne tried to get control of the gun. Before they went to the ground, the man tried pointing the gun toward his chest. "I knew I was in trouble," he said. Though Thurne was tiring, he kept fighting, "'Cause I know I was going to die if I didn't," he said. Thurne tried to fire as the suspect dashed into nearby woods until he noticed his finger was nearly torn away. By the time he switched hands, the man was gone. Other officers found him hiding in a garage a few blocks away.

Thurne, a father of three children ages 12, 10 and 6, didn't tell his youngest what happened for days. The others took the news hard. "He [Quanto] was big and mean, but you knew when his feelings were hurt," Thurne said. "He's just like a child. With the exception of the dog, I feel I came out smelling like roses considering the alternatives." Thurne's been shot at before, he said. But he now thinks there may be other alternatives to handling dangerous situations and isn't sure how he'll react the next time he's faced with sending his dog after a suspect.

For now, he is working administrative duties until he recovers and has another surgery to replace the bone in his right index finger. He hopes to regain the use of his finger.

Quanto, 4, will remain at the city morgue until his burial, which could be in a few months. Thurne said they are waiting for the new police academy to open to bury him on site. "He was a pretty amazing dog," he said, proudly. "Quanto was doing his job. He was getting tired. He ultimately saved my life."

In Loving Memory of

K-9 SAM

December 2000

Handler: Sgt. Ian Carnegie
Royal Army Veterinary Corps Dog Unit
British Army in Bosnia-Herzegovina

The RAVC is a technical support Corps, small but competent. Deeply involved in all aspects of military animal activity and related matters but with little opportunity for high profile publicity.

Few watching the ceremonial duties of the Household Cavalry or The King's Troop RHA are aware of the RAVC's involvement in the procurement and veterinary management of their much admired horses. The discovery of terrorist arms and explosives caches are attributed to the security force and not the dogs, procured, trained and serviced by the Corps.

RAVC personnel enjoy a challenging and varied employment role involved in all aspects of the use of animals for military purposes, from their procurement, through their initial assessment and training, the maintenance of their health and fitness throughout their service life, to their retirement from the service. The RAVC provides the service lead in the development of good husbandry and training practice, preventative medicine and care in the maintenance of service animals. Corps personnel advise commanders on the best utilization of Service animal resources and the development of good practice to ensure that they are used to their fullest potential.

Army dog Sam wins a posthumous 'VC'
By Graham Tibbetts - Daily Telegraph UK

An Alsatian (German Shepherd) that disarmed a gunman and held rioters at bay in separate incidents while serving with the British Army in Bosnia Herzegovina is to be posthumously awarded the animal equivalent of the Victoria Cross. The courage of Sam will be recognized when his handler, Sgt. Ian Carnegie, is presented with the Dickin Medal on his behalf at a ceremony next month.

Sam, who died of natural causes, aged 10, two years ago, helped Sgt. Carnegie to defuse two flash points in 1998 while serving with the Royal Army Veterinary Corps Dog Unit. In the first, a volley of shots rang out as the 1st Battalion The Royal Canadian Regiment patrolled Drvar. Troops saw a gunman run into a bar. In the medal citation, Sgt. Carnegie said, "After a chase, Sam brought down the suspect and I disarmed him, retrieving a loaded pistol."

Six days later, again in Drvar, a mob was besieging a compound where Serbs were taking refuge. Sgt. Carnegie said, "By threatening the mob with our pistols and dogs, we forced our way into the compound. We kept the rioters at bay until reinforcements arrived."

In Loving Memory of

K-9 RECON

LODD
March 17, 1998

Partner: Deputy Jim Gibson
Snohomish County Sheriff's Office
Washington

Moments after capturing an alleged drug dealer who tried to flee authorities Tuesday night, a Snohomish County sheriff's K-9 dog wandered into freeway traffic and was struck and killed. Now deputies are trying to determine if the suspect they arrested hurt the 3 year old German Shepherd named Recon, causing the dog to become confused.

The incident happened between 6:30 and 7:30 p.m. on I 5 near 44th Street in Lynnwood. Recon and his handler, sheriff's deputy, Jim Gibson, were assisting the Snohomish Regional Narcotics Task Force in a drug bust at a nearby Park and Ride lot when the suspect broke loose.

The suspect, an Alaska man, ran off, climbed a seven foot

fence and crossed six lanes of freeway traffic, before the dog was able to catch and stop him. Gibson, arrived a short time later and called the 3 year old dog away from the man.

"Recon, just looked like he was dazed like I've never seen him before," Gibson said, adding he thinks his partner may have been choked before roaming into traffic. "It's like losing a son," Gibson said of the dog, who had lived with his family for more than a year. It's also like losing a deputy, Sheriff Rick Bart said. "In every way I considered Recon one of my deputies. I will aggressively look for a charge against this man, if he assaulted my deputy."

It is a felony to assault a law enforcement officer that includes a police dog. The woman driver who struck Recon is very upset too, Bart said. She was driving at normal freeway speeds, but there was nothing she could have done to avoid the accident, he said, adding he's glad she wasn't injured.

The suspect was treated at Stevens Hospital in Edmonds for minor dog bite wounds and booked into the Snohomish County Jail for investigation of delivery of a controlled substance and several outstanding warrants, said sheriff's Lt. Dan Howard. Authorities confiscated approximately 1 kilo of cocaine.

The suspect allegedly flew in from Alaska to make the delivery at the Parkand Ride lot, where he was met by authorities, Howard said.

In Loving Memory of

K-9 REX

January 28, 2000

Partner: Cpl. Bob Negri
Mid West City Police Dept.
100 N. Midwest Blvd.
Oklahoma City, OK 73110-4310
405.739 1300

"I've traveled the pathways beside you,
I've made you the lord of my day,
But now that I've gone on before you,
It's only to show you the way."

Rex, the second drug dog trained for the Midwest City Police Department, died at the age of 7, during surgery for cancer. Corporal Negri knew if Rex had to retire due for medical reasons, and would not be able to work, he would be very unhappy. He lived to work. Rex did not suffer.

His training started in 1992. Career began in the streets in

1993. They conducted 1,588 searches, made 901 arrests, resulted in 1,848 criminal charges filed. They seized $257,688 in street valued narcotics and $1,061,331 in cash property and vehicles.

Losing Rex was like a family member died. He was wonderful with his family, especially the children. He was not just a pet, but a partner that spent ten hours a day working together. He is sadly missed.

I now have a new dog, a German Shepard, "Billy" 2½ years old. My son helped me pick him out, its almost like Rex has been reincarnated into Billy, same attitude and good nose.

In Loving Memory of

K-9 RINGO

April 17, 2000

Partner: Officer William Lowe
Norwalk Department of Police Service
297 West Avenue
Norwalk, CT   06850
203.854 3000   Chief Harry Rilling

At a time when the Police Department is evaluating the future of its K-9 unit, it is mourning the loss of one of its few "officers." Ringo, a 7 year old German Shepherd, had to be put down Monday because he had an inoperable tumor in his chest, according to Sgt. Andre Velez. Ringo was partnered with Officer William Lowe.

Flags flew at half staff at the West Avenue station this week in tribute to Ringo. "We feel we've lost a valiant servant to the city and feel badly for Officer Lowe," said Deputy Chief Mark Palmer. "I know he developed a close bond and relationship with Ringo. I know it's very hard for Officer Lowe and his family. Lowe could not be reached for comment Friday.

Ringo's death leaves the department with two K-9s, Nik, a Belgin Malinois, & Max, a German Shepherd. Both have patrol and narcotics training. Officer Ashley Gonzalez, who handles Max, also handles K-9 Zasko, who is set for retirement and only works when Max does not, Palmer said.

Chief Rilling had Palmer evaluate the K-9 unit last month after Finance Director Jack Miller reported that it cost the city $22,000 annually for each dog. Rilling says it cost much less than that, but could not give a specific figure.

Deputy Chief Palmer said the department has no immediate plans to replace Ringo and will make do with the two K-9s. "I think at this point with two active police dogs, we don't see a deficiency in the services we can provide," Palmer said. Rilling said he is still awaiting a final report of the evaluation before he makes a decision on whether to expand, reduce or leave the K-9 unit as is. Many K-9s are used in dangerous situations where officers cannot be used, including building searches in hostage situations or finding suspects hiding in crawl spaces or basements, Palmer said. And the dogs can sniff out drugs in a car or house, he said.

Ringo, who came from Belgium, joined the department in 1995 after K-9 Aron retired in 1996, Sgt. Velez said in a press release. Ringo participated in more than 300 searches, including sniffing out a pound of hidden cocaine last June. He was the first K-9 in the city to be nationally certified for narcotics detection and minimum force apprehension.

In Loving Memory of

K-9 ROADIE

May 2000

Partner: Sgt. Tim Fell
Miami Dade Police Department
9105 Northwest 25th Street
Miami, FL 33172 1500
Telephone: 305.471 3165

I had to retire Roadie after nine years of working the streets. He was just old and he was living in pain. I came home one day from work and he couldn't get up. After several days at the vet, it was decided to put him to sleep so I had no choice. Still miss him.

In Loving Memory of

K-9 ROBBIE

October 15, 1992 - January 12, 2000

Partner: Dick van Leenen

Rotterdam Police Dept. Nederlands
Rotterdam-Rijnmond Police Dept.
Animal Section - K-9 Unit
Voorwateringweg 99 Rottterdam, Holland

Het gebed van de hond
Ho mijn meester,
Kies mij als vriend,
en ik zal van al je vrienden de trouwste zijn.
Geef mij een thuis,
en ik zal de beste bewaker zijn.
Geef mij een naam,
en ik wil nooit nog een andere.
Geef mij een bevel,
en ik zal je gehoorzamen.
Geef mij voedsel,

en je zult nooit ontgoocheld zijn.
Geef mij een liefkozing,
en ik zal gelukkig zijn.
Geef mij uw affectie,
en ik zal je mijn leven geven

The station is both Mounted Police and the K-9 Unit. We share the same building and we have the same staff. Robbie was born on October 15th 1992 and I was his only handler. Robbie was not an easy dog and was not very social. I used to say that he hated everything that walked on two legs excepts my wife and I. For us he was fabulous!! Always friendly and protective, always ready for training and hard work and the best "partner" any cop could have. He was my partner, my buddy, my guardian angel!

In the years we worked together he did more than twenty "K-9 arrests" and protected me against attacks from criminals. He also searched and found several criminals after crimes. December 1999 Robbie got heavily injured when he lost his balance on an obstacle course on K-9 unit training field. The injury was so bad that we had to euthanize Robbie on January 12th 2000.

That day we lost more than our dog. That day we lost family! Every day we look at Robbie. My wife bought me a beautiful oil painting of him which hangs in the living room. Every day we look at him and he looks at us, and we know he is there!

I'm working with my second dog, Rex. Keep on the good work! I would be very honored if there is a place in your memorial webpage for "my Robbie." Thank you very much. I think he deserves it!

First of all I can tell you something about myself. I'm a K-9 officer with the K-9 unit from the Rotterdam Rijnmond PD in The Netherlands. So that answers your question about my nationality. I'm Dutch. Although me and my wife are Dutch we speak a lot English because of our great friendship with K-9 officer Greg Thomas and his wife.

Greg is on the K-9 unit of Gilbert, AZ. We met each other on the internet and became friends forever. Our love for the dogs and the police work with dogs brought us together and now we visit each other regularly. Last August they were with us in Holland and last April we were in AZ.

In 2003, Greg will visit us again with some other K-9 officers from Maricopa County and our K-9 unit. This will make a great exchange program for them. After that, in November 2003, we will visit Arizona again for lots of K-9 training. So you see, Dutch and U.S. K-9 officers are great friends!

K-9 team in front of a chopper is from ASU who are used to transport us when neccesary. Our K-9 unit of the Rotterdam Police Department has six K-9 teams. Every K-9 team has 5 dog handlers, Next to that we have about 8 handler trainers with special dogs, like narcotics, explosives, tracking, etc.

Dick received the memorial card of "Cosmo," the former partner, my good friend, officer Greg Thomas of the Gilbert Police Department. We, in Holland, know very well how important those "partners" are in fighting crimes. My first K-9 Robbie, died on January 12, 2000. During his life he had many good arrests for the Rotterdam Police Department. And of course Robbie was my first big love!

It's a coincidence that all my dogs names begin with an R. because police department buys them when they are about 3 years old and half way there for police exams, the first owner give them a name and that name they already have when they arrive at K-9 unit. So it is just a coincidence that all the name had an R. But it's very common in Holland to give a police dog a very short name, like Nero, Robbie, Rex, Rambo, Rico, Rudy, Max, etc.

Rambo is my current and fully operational patrol dog. With him I passed on Dec. 4th the National Dutch K-9 exam and with him I'm going on patrol now. But he is only three years old and he has very, very much to learn still so during the patrol he and I are busy in making him "street wise" as I like it to call it.

Rex is also my current patrol dog but he is not operational

because he injured his right knee in training, about seven months ago. During his long attack on the decoy (100 meters) he suddenly got crippled and the orthopaedic vet found that one of his knee bands were ruptured. Now he is still recovering and I hope he will be back in full service the next month. If the vet reports that he definitive is not good enough for active duty, he will get his retirement and we will keep him as a house-dog. I will keep in touch with our lives here in Holland.

In Loving Memory of

K-9 ROCKY

LODD
January 18, 2000

Partner: Officer Steven Schaumleffel
Quitman Sheriff's Department
Quitman, AR
501.362-8143

Found shot and left at the side of the road. $1000 REWARD offered to apprehend killer. Anyone with information call: 501 589.3512 or 24 hour Heber Springs dispatcher 501.362.8291

Rocky was trained by Greg Durham, Durham Haus Working Dogs of Arkansas. His other name was Sam. Rocky was stolen from a locked kennel at the police station. To date, the killer has never been caught.

From late 1999 to present, there have been other K-9 deaths, including the Mountain Home K-9. No more information on this sad case.

In Loving Memory of

K-9 ROCKY

1986 - 1996

Partner: Officer Eric Deltgen
New London Police Department
5 Governor Winthrop Blvd.
New London, CT 06320

Rocky, a black and tan German Shepherd was waiting for me. Officer Nott and I were training him, he was donated to the department. Rocky was not as formidable as Bandit, and was much smaller. He was the type of dog that would have made a great house pet, not really suited for police work, But we were short of dogs, we didn't know any better at the time and we worked him.

We learned a lot with Rocky, but above all we made him into one hell of a police dog. His specialty was article recovery. For fun, I would use pennies or any small item for him to find. Whether it be in a back yard, parking lot or even in the water, he would find it. I lost track at the number of keys he found for people who lost them, even in the snow. Officer Nott and I would joke about Rocky saying that he was really a retriever in disguise as a German Shepherd.

Amongst his finds, Rocky was responsible for finding a rotisserie fork that had been thrown high in a tree. The fork had been used in a serious stabbing and when the suspect fled, it was thrown in a tree. After being released in the general area, Rocky located it. That fork would later become instrumental in obtaining a conviction. I used to practice article recovery exercises by planting a knife in a tree and have Rocky locate. I guess all that hard work paid off.

In another incident Rocky located a loaded .380 Cal. weapon that had been used in a drug transaction gone bad. The suspect had fled from police and had been able to discard the weapon. The suspect was eventually apprehended, but without the weapon, officers searched the path, taken by the suspect during his attempt to flee. They could not find it. Rocky was called to the scene and in less than two minutes, found the weapon that had been buried near an abandoned building. The weapon was loaded and ready to fire. That too was instrumental in obtaining a conviction.

Rocky used to like to chase bad guys too. In one instance he chased down a car thief that just couldn't be caught. This guy ran like a gazelle and always managed to slip away. This time, however, Rocky and I happened to be in the vicinity where he had been spotted. He was seen driving a stolen car, and we headed to intercept. This guy just happened to cross our path. He tried to flee with the car, but lost control, crashed into a fence.

Before you could blink, this guy was out and running. Of course cops being what they are, we all started to run after him. We forgot that we had a police dog at our disposal. Suddenly realizing that we were being out run, and there was a K-9 , I called Rocky from about 50 yards out. He jumped out of the cruiser where he had patiently been waiting. I commanded him to pursue the suspect. In a flash, he passed by us and continued another 70 to 80 yards beyond and apprehended the suspect in full stride.

All of the cops that were there were mesmerized. So much in fact, we almost forgot why we had been running.

Another time, we were doing what we called sneak attacks in the projects. This consisted of several officers approached one of the high rise buildings from one side, while the other officer approached from the back. Usually what happened, as the officers approached from the front, the bad guys who shouldn't be there, would run out the back into the arms of the waiting officers.

This time Rocky and I were the ones in the back with open arms. As it turns out, two subjects did exactly as expected and ran into us as we were entering the back hall of the building. At first they were cooperative especially seeing that Rocky had a watchful gaze on them. I was able to pat down the first guy without incident, but when I went to pat the second, he suddenly turned and sucker punched me, made a run through the courtyard towards another building. Rocky immediately responded and gave chase through the court yard, through a crowd of about 40 people that had gathered and continued on after the suspect that had struck me. The suspect used a steel door to strike Rocky and tried to close it on him in an attempt to keep him away. That only made Rocky more angry. The suspect then tried to flee through the halls of the adjoining building, but before the operation began I had locked all the access doors. Thereby, locking the suspect inside the hallways of that building.

I still clearly remember the loud roar coming from Rocky just as he entered the hallway of that building after having been stuck by the door. I also remember the suspect continuing to fight with the dog and once I got there, fight we did. Seemed to last forever. But all that said and done, I also remember the suspect losing the fight and crying like a baby in its aftermath.

When this all began, the suspect had been fully clothed. When it ended, the only thing left unscathed were his underpants. The greatest part of all was hearing the residents of the projects cheering the dog as we were battling it out. Rocky earned his respect that day and many who lived in the project knew his name.

As to the suspect, he ended up with better than 40 puncture wounds, did three years in jail and was never returned to the projects. Rocky stayed on patrol with me for about five years. During his career, he was either directly responsible or assisted in over 100 felony arrests. Some being narcotic arrests, even though he was not trained for narcotics. That's where a lot of the article search came into play.

Finally, he located hundreds of dollars in stolen merchandise and or other crime related items.

Rocky was also the recipient of several USPCA citation awards, also certifying with the NAPWDA several times, excelling in Tracking Article Recovery and Area Searches and Passive Gun Fire. He saw many street battles and as a result eventually had to be retired due to what we believe was post traumatic syndrome stress.

Here is a dog that would love to do school demos, be petted by children of all ages, but now had become unsteady. The liability became too great. So Rocky retired, became a couch potato and eventually ended up with a couple who cared for him like he was their child.

Rocky eventually died in 1996 from complications of Lymes disease he had contracted when he was working the streets.

In Loving Memory of

K-9 RUDO

October 6, 2000

Partner: Officer Jay Turner
Muncie Police Department
300 N. High St.
Muncie, IN 47305

On a cold, windy evening, Jay Turner and the Muncie Police Department lost a hard worker, a partner and a friend. Rudo, a 1½ year old German Shepherd who was Turner's K-9 dog for the past 6 weeks, died during a K-9 unit demonstration at Heekin Park about 8 p.m. Friday night. Captain Tony Mench said an autopsy revealed the dog died from a tumor on the aorta, something that is very difficult to detect. The tumor continued growing until it burst Friday night, causing Rudo to bleed to death. Nobody knew what happened until after the autopsy. We have never had this happen before, so we're at a loss.

A memorial service was held Sunday afternoon at the

Fraternal Order of Police Lodge on Butterfield Road. Mench said K-9 officers from the Muncie, Delaware County, Anderson and Randolph County police departments attended.

The bond that is formed between a K-9 officer and his dog is unique. They spend every day together and get emotionally attached. To an officer, their dog is not just a partner, but a best friend.

A prominent community benefactor who recently died donated the money to buy Rudo. The benefactor wished for his donation to be anonymous. Maybe Rudo will be a pet for him in heaven. The captain said he was going to throw Turner "right back into the saddle" by getting him a new dog and having him finish the K-9 training classes. But for now, everyone hopes a much loved member of the department's K-9 unit will not soon be forgotten. Donations for a headstone or memorial marker for Rudo are being accepted.

In Loving Memory of

K-9 RUDY

May 21, 1990

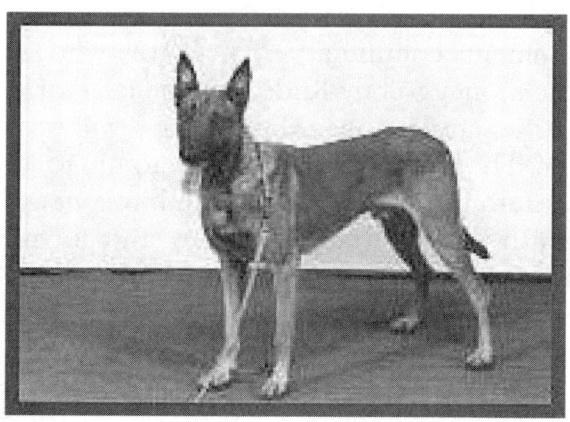

Handler: Mario Warnaar
Soesterberg A.F.B. 298 Squadron
334 Squadron of the Royal Netherlands Air Force
(RNLAF) 32 TFS "Wolfhounds"
of the United States Air Force (USAF)

Rudy, a Belgian Malinois, was my second buddy we worked together for the rest of my air force career. We worked together from May 1982 to August 1989. We have obtained several air force and police certificates and diplomas. Rudy was one of the best dogs the Soesterberg AFB kennel had and so became that in 1985 we took part of the preliminary rounds of the Air Force K-9 dog championship, but weren't lucky/good enough for the final contest.

One of my Soesterberg colleagues became that year champion; it was the fourth time of his career. At this moment the Air Force K-9 championship is held every year at Soesterberg AFB.

Every year the SP organized near the baseball field the "Police Day", at this day the security police and several Dutch law enforcement agencies, like the Customs, local Police and the Royal Netherlands Marechaussee, gave demonstrations. We as K-9 section were also given demonstrations, and after the official day we all had a big barbecue.

In times of war, as part of the Ground Operating Squadron, the dog handlers operate as explosive specialists advisers, in concerted action with NBC (Nuclear, Biologic and Chemical) specialists.

A special thank you to Mario who helped me with my website that became a book.

In Loving Memory of

K-9 RUGER

1992   Oct. 6, 2000

Partner: MIKE ANDREL
Darby Twp. Police Department
Sharon Hills, PA

Ruger died of Cancer. We had no warning at all that week he was just great tracking a burglary suspect to a house and found drugs the next night and was just unbelievable. I found him that Friday morning at the bottom of my basement steps. His buddies, Toby my oldest who is 12 and still kicking and Jaeger his son. It was like he wanted to be with them before he left. It is still a very hard thing to deal with but I know he is in a better place watching over us .... Mike

FROM A PUPPY, TO A PARTNER, TO A MEMORY

Although October 6th was one of the worst days of my life, our friends and partners do not live forever. On that day, I lost my friend, buddy, family member and police K-9 Partner Ruger. As both a K-9 Officer and trainer both for sport and police, we must all prepare for this day. I know this is something that is not talked about, but this was important to me and anyone else that can share with this loss.

It all goes back to a day in April 1992. This little fur ball came in from Germany on the Lufthansa flight. His name was Ruger (vom haus Dexel). The challenge was on! He was a puppy with attitude, part John Belushi. His accomplishments were multi times Sch H 3 and he was DPO II and WPO 4 times; he was also a Drug Dog. Ruger was following in the footsteps of Toby (alex vom haus dexel), my first Schutzhund dog raised from a puppy to Sch H3 FH V rated, and also a retired police dog, who is still kicking at 12 years old. There are not enough pages in the magazine to explain this relationship.

Ruger was more than just a police dog. No, he didn't make any major bust or catch a fleeing robber that shot at him, but there were two incidents that come to mind that I will always remember. The first involved a car stolen from a neighboring town. The pursuit started, and into Philadelphia they went. After going down a dead end street, the two suspects fled; fortunately, one tripped and was taken into custody ten feet from the car. But the driver got away. So the call went out for a dog (K-9) but none were working the street this night at 2:07 AM. So, the Sharon Hill Police asked their dispatch to contact Darby Township's K-9 team, which was Officer Mike Andrel and K-9 Ruger, who at this time were home and asleep.

After receiving the call, we responded to the scene and started the track from the car. After tracking down the street, into the woods, and over two hills into a small group of trees, Ruger came upon a large pile of leaves; he was coming to a stop and downing on what turned out to be the subjects chest. The only words we heard were, "Please get the dog." At this time Ruger was just crawling, but after given the command to Platz, he remained still. The subject was taken into custody. While going back to the car, Ruger was jumping and barking, for he knew he had done a good job.

The second incident was on a Sunday night. While on routine patrol of one of our parks, we came upon a suspicious van that stopped and started to back up the street. After turning around, the car headed to one of the main roads in our township. After turning on the main road (Hook Road), I activated my lights and hit my siren a few times, but the van continued on and then turned onto a side street. With the vehicle still not responding to my lights or siren, I called to radio that I was attempting to stop a vehicle and, providing the registration, I requested other cars.

On Sundays we usually have three cars working, but this night there were only two, and our other car was on the other side of town. Answering the radio that the other car was en route, the minivan now turned down another side street toward a local bar known for drug dealings, where numerous shootings have occurred. The van stopped right behind the bar and the driver jumped out. I immediately jumped out and ordered the driver to get back in the car. He started toward the bar and had both hands in his pockets.

For a police officer, this makes your hair go up on the back of your neck. He would not take his hands our of his pockets, so I immediately pulled my weapon and again ordered the driver to show me his hands. He continued to walk toward the bar. Having my patrol car door open and my cage open, without any commands Ruger jumped out of the car and went around to the other side, and started to come to the front of my patrol car. Seeing the dog, the driver stopped immediately. Again, not knowing that Ruger was out of the car, I glanced over and saw it was Ruger, my patrol dog. The driver then immediately took his hands out of this pockets, raised his hands and said, "Get that dog."

Ruger started to go toward him, and given the command to Platz, he followed. In the distance I could hear sirens from incoming police vehicles. I had contacted the dispatcher that my K-9 was out of the car (which is our department's policy).

Still, with my weapon on the driver, I order him to the ground and then handcuffed him. Ruger crawled up beside the driver, growling the whole time. The driver just kept saying, "Please hold the dog."

The driver was searched and drugs were found. This was part of a domestic in which the wife was looking for the van. The driver was taken to headquarters and processed. Everything happened so fast; if it weren't for Ruger, things might have turned out differently. Later that night, I looked in the rearview mirror and saw Ruger's familiar head, his one ear up and the other off to the side. I thank God for having a partner like him.

These are just two incidents that will always stand out in Ruger's career, and in my life. But there were all the schools we visited over his six years. It was the kids that loved Ruger or Ruper or Ruger or all the other names they had for him. To see the kids at all the demonstrations he did, and to see the parents that is what makes a K-9 special (yes, you could pet Ruger and he was fine with groups and crowds). But the thanks go back to so many people, all the old members of the Greater Philadelphia Schutzhund Club, Jim Hill, Rich Rosen, Bill & Mary Beth Talley, Frank Fisher, Patsy, Ed, Debbie and many more.

They all helped form Ruger's foundation and personality. He was not the best sport dog, but on the street Ruger was very serious and very special. More thanks go to all the members of Delaware Valley Police and Schutzhund Club, especially Brian & Michele Jones. I must thank DPO Judge Mike West for giving Ruger the opportunity to be my first DPO dog and qualifying for the World K-9 Police Dog Team. Thanks to Wendell Nope for giving Ruger the opportunity to be part of one of the most prestigious teams in the world, the United States Police K-9 team not once, but twice, Ruger receiving a qualifying score in both events, and for being a part of the 100 year anniversary of the German Shepherd in Germany; this will live on forever.

In Loving Memory of

K-9 SHAKA

May 1989 - 1996

Partner: Officer Eric Deltgen
New London Police Department
5 Governor Winthrop Blvd.
New London, CT 06320

This was Officer Deltgen's third K-9, previous was K-9
Bandit and K-9 Rocky. Shaka was a full black German Shepherd.
He had been imported as a pup, from England, from the same
kennels that supply the British police with their dogs. Shaka was
born in May of 1989 just outside of London, England.

Having been bred specifically for police work, Shaka showed
all the good qualities of a police dog as a young pup. He loved
to hunt, search for the man, and especially loved hide and seek
games. This would become instrumental later when doing
building searches. During a building search, Shaka would
become so entangled with the search, that once he had found
the man hiding, be it a closet or room, he would literally suck

the oxygen out of that room.

Shaka weighed about 115 lb., and had the pull of a bulldozer. Once during a training exercise, he pulled a 250 lb man out of the bathtub he had been hiding in. No matter how hard this man tried to stand up, or keep tugging back, Shaka would always bring him down.

Shaka had a shiney black coat, and bright white teeth. On patrol that would work to his advantage especially at night. The bad guys wouldn't see him until it was too late or until they were up close. It was amazing the reactions I got to observe.

Shaka also certified with the NAPWDA, excelling in Building Searches, Area Searches, Criminal apprehensions, and Passive Gunfire.

Shaka came on patrol in 1991 while Rocky was still patrolling. I was lucky for a while because I was able to patrol with two dogs. Rocky was still the main or primary dog, and Shaka was the trainee. It was amazing on how many things Shaka picked up from Rocky during the course of a shift.

Shaka was well liked by the community as he had a great deal of exposure to the public. At the time there was a great emphasis on neighborhood policing, especially in the downtown sections of the city. It was not uncommon to see Shaka and I walking a beat visiting all the retailers that were on our beats. It got so that certain merchants would have treats for Shaka, and every time we walked by one of them, Shaka would literally haul me into their establishment. After a while it got to that I began wondering who was walking who.

After Rocky retired, Shaka became the main and last partner I would have. We were also responsible for over 100 assists and arrest. Shaka had several apprehensions, but many of his catches, or arrests, as I like to call them were mainly due to his impressive stature. When he looked at you, you knew he meant business. That in itself deterred many would be fighter.

Unfortunately before we knew it, because of political reasons, the K-9 unit would be disbanded. It would be another five years before we would see it re emerge again, but by that time,

I would be promoted and therefore not eligible to have another K-9 partner. Shaka was retired and came home to stay with me.

He did not take lightly to retirement, often showing me his displeasure by leaving me welcome home gifts after a day's work. He absolutely hated to see me go off to work and leave him behind. I guess in the long run it was to do him in, as about a year and a half into retirement, he developed stomach cancer and died about 7 months later. He fought until the very end. At one point we thought he might have beat it, but it wasn't meant to be.

Shaka was great with children. He loved going to schools and doing little demos, and even playing tag. Today still I get asked about Shaka. Sometimes by the same ones (now grown up) that used to play with him at these school functions.

Shaka left part of himself behind in people's memories, not to mention mine. He is missed by all.

In Loving Memory of

K-9 SHIERKHAN

September 1, 2000
LODD

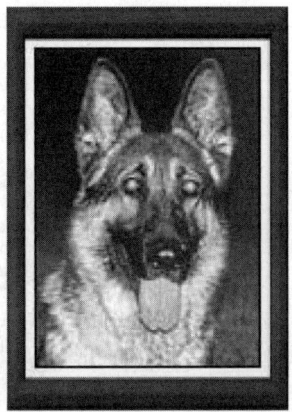

Partner: Officer Mike Lewis
Seattle Police Dept K-9 Unit
WA

A Seattle police dog that befriended countless elementary school children and caught eighty-three bad guys was killed on the job last week.

More than 250 police and K-9 officers from many other states and Canada, as well as civilians and others turned out at the auditorium of the former Sand Point naval base to honor the four year old German Shepherd, Shierkhan and to pay tribute to the Police Department's close knit K-9 unit, including Shierkhan's handler and partner, Officer Mike Lewis.

Some K-9 officers came from police agencies as far away as British Columbia. The forty five minute service included songs, prayers, a video presentation, an appearance by the department's honor guard and remarks from Seattle's police chief, Gil Kerlikowske. Officer Bruce Wind, a former K-9 officer addressed the guests. "To some of you, it may seem a bit strange: a memorial for a dog, but why are we really here? We are here to show support for Officer Mike Lewis. We are here because cops stick together. We are family, and one of our own is having a tough time right now."

Yesterday's service also was an opportunity to reflect on what many outside the department don't realize; how crucial police dogs are to officers what a vital role they play in police work. The ability of a police dog to track something that the rest of us can't even see is amazing.

We're all going to miss Shierkhan, but the citizens of Seattle are going to miss him the most. There will be a lot of bad guys who are going to get away because Shierkhan is no longer here." Sgt. Carol Minakami, who heads the department's fourteen member K-9 unit, said that Shierkhan possessed the self confidence and balance that good police dogs must have. The animals must be gentle and relaxed enough to give demonstrations to schoolchildren but aggressive, sharp and fast enough to catch criminals.

You can look at one hundred dogs and only get one good police dog. Shierkhan, who had served with the department since January 1998, died last Friday night after he was hit by a car on Interstate 5 while tracking a suspect in a robbery and car jacking. The dog's death was only the second dog fatality in the roughly thirty year history of the department's K-9 unit.

Shierkhan's death has deeply affected Lewis and every other K-9 officer. That is the one thing all handlers dread.. We're closer to our dogs than we are to most people. You end up sharing dangers together. You're working even more closely as a team than with a human police partner. The dog leads you. He's an extension of your senses. You're using those things so both of you can go home at the end of the night.

Like the department's other police dogs, Shierkhan lived with his handler, Lewis, who is married and has three young sons. Yesterday, Lewis told the audience how grateful he was to have worked with "the best partner   the best friend that anyone could ever have. "I miss you," Lewis said. "I'll see you in heaven, someday."

In Loving Memory of

K-9 SOLO

LODD
June 5, 1998

Partner: Deputy Robin Eckel
Monmouth County Sheriff's Office
50 E. Main Street
Freehold, NJ 07728
732.431-7138

Emi Marmorstein has lived in a sprawling colonial style house in this summer resort town for forty-eight years. In that time, nothing that has happened on the quiet side street a few blocks from the Atlantic Ocean rivaled the drama that played out Thursday and Friday.

Marmorstein and many other residents were ordered to lock their doors and stay inside as police squared off with an armed robbery suspect. One suspected of having ties to fugitive cop killer Joanne Chesimard and the Black Liberation Army, who barricaded himself in a Newark Avenue apartment.

After police bombarded him with a water cannon, stun grenades, and tear gas, and after he reportedly gunned down a police dog, Donald Bunting, 48, finally surrendered Friday.

"I found out it was over because they let me out of my home," Marmorstein said. "What an ordeal!" By 2 p.m. Friday, Marmorstein had joined throngs of people from his neighborhood to swap stories about the chilling 22 hour standoff. It was scary," said Donna Malone, who lives next door to the squat, red brick apartment building where Bunting took cover. "This was quite an experience."

A state police spokesman said Bunting has ties to the Black Liberation Army and has "maintained periodic contact" with Chesimard. in 1977, Chesimard, who uses the name Assata Shakur, was convicted of killing Trooper Werner Foerster and injuring another trooper who stopped her and two friends on the New Jersey Turnpike in 1973. Chesimard escaped from a state prison in 1979 and has been living in exile in Cuba.

Bunting himself had been a fugitive since Monday, when he and LeRoy Adams, 53, allegedly attempted to rob the occupants of an Asbury Park home and then exchanged gunfire with police, officials said. Jones was caught, but Bunting escaped.

On Thursday, police received word that Bunting was hiding out in the apartment at 319 Newark Ave., where he has been a "periodic resident," police said. Thursday afternoon, a Monmouth County emergency response team cordoned off a block of Newark Avenue and ordered some nearby residents to stay inside. A few were evacuated, and others who weren't home when authorities set up their barricades were barred from returning.

Malone and her parents stayed with neighbors after being evacuated Thursday night. Emergency response workers had to sneak back into the Malone residence during the night to retrieve her father's heart medication. Later Thursday, state police arrived. By nightfall, officials realized the building's phone lines had been snipped from inside. Through Thursday night and Friday morning, police   and later, Bunting's cousin used a bullhorn to unsuccessfully try to talk him out.

"This morning, at 6:30 a.m., we heard a big boom," Malone said. State police later explained that the noise was a tear gas bomb going off. Police said Bunting endured an estimated 50 barrages of tear gas, as well as the deafening noise and blinding light of stun grenades. "He had barricaded the furniture and he withstood the tear gas" using a makeshift gas mask of wet towels and a carpenter's mask, said Alton Kenney, first assistant Monmouth County prosecutor. "It was a siege . . . and we were prepared to wait as long as it took to get him out."

At about 8:30 Friday morning, officials sent Solo, a German Shepherd from the Monmouth County Sheriff's Department, into the building. Two shots were fired and the dog was killed, Hagerty said. Authorities also used water from nearby Fletcher Lake to try to flush out the suspect. Officials sprayed high powered hoses through the front door and second floor windows early Friday afternoon. "These hoses apparently led Mr. Bunting to consider surrendering," said state police spokesman John Hagerty.

The final surrender came after officers drove an armored personnel carrier up to the apartment building and used explosives to blow open the downstairs door. Inside the doorway, they placed a robot with a video camera. The robot also had a microphone that police used to communicate with Bunting. At 1:50 p.m., he surrendered peacefully.

Throughout the standoff, "he acted in a paramilitary fashion. He never exposed himself to open fire; he remained calm throughout," Kenney said.

Bunting was transported to the Monmouth County Jail in Freehold, where he was being held without bail. Police say he had been convicted in 1989 of drug charges and was in a state prison from 1989 to 1994.

As police and emergency personnel dismantled the barricades around Newark Avenue, a cluster of neighbors gathered on a nearby street corner. Among them was a woman pushing a baby carriage. "It was a long night," said the woman, who had to sleep at a neighbor's house Thursday night. If there was a silver lining, she said, it's that the standoff and evacuation drew the neighborhood closer. "We all stayed together," she said.

Service was held on June 10, 1998 in Freehold, NJ

In Loving Memory of

K-9 ROSE & K-9 DANNY

January 2000 - March 1998

Partners: Officer John Zimmers and Officer Bruce Stewart
Texas City Police Department
Texas City, TX

In the summer of 1991 the Texas City Police Department enacted the county's first K-9 Division. There were three handlers originally. They were Officer John Zimmers, Officer Bruce Stewart, and Officer Donald Halstead. Officer Zimmers' partner was a narcotic dog named Rose, Officer Stewart's partner was a patrol dog named Danny, Officer Halstead's partner was a patrol dog named Hondo.

Officer Halstead resigned from the police department and his partner also left with him.

In 1995 K-9 Rose retired from active duty with the K-9 Division. In 1996 Officer Cyr was assigned to the K-9 division. Officer Cyr's first partner was a patrol dog named Claus. A few years later, in 1997, K-9 Danny retired from active duty with the K-9 Division.

In March of 1998, K-9 Danny had passed away due to complications of his health. In February of 1999, K-9 Claus was retired due to an injury received due to years of service. In January of 2000, K-9 Rose passed away due to health complications.

In Loving Memory of

K-9 TAZZ

October, 1999

Partner: Sgt. Scott Kirkpatrick
Ocean City Police Department
Ocean City, MD
410.723-6640 Ext. 8181

He may have been named after the Tasmanian devil, but the Ocean City K-9 officer could be as sweet and gentle as a puppy. The department will bid farewell to Tazz tonight in a memorial service following the death of the K-9, a result of cancer.

The illness and loss of the dog has hit the police community hard, especially PFC. Scott Kirkpatrick, the owner and handler of Tazz. "The cancer hit him so hard and so fast," he said. "It was probably the toughest decision I have ever had to make in my life." Kirkpatrick added of the decision to put Tazz to down last week.

Though the dog showed no signs of pain, the disease was not curable, forcing the department to make the choice. "I didn't want him to be in pain."

Tazz and two other K-9 dogs were brought to Ocean City in 1993, courtesy of the Ocean Grand Ball Association. Knowing his commands only in the German language, both Tazz and Kirkpatrick had their work cut out for them. Both attended a 10 week training session comprising more than 400 hours of instruction. "Basically, he knew how to do everything, and I didn't." Following the training, Tazz was bilingual and Kirkpatrick had a new friend. "He's been here so long, he's always with me."

Last year, Kirkpatrick noted, the K-9 gave his best performance, leading the department to 15 arrests, including several large drug busts. In 1998, Tazz led officers to a quarter pound and a half pound of marijuana in separate incidents. His career total exceeds 50 apprehensions.

Tazz was a remarkable tracker. He was the best one in Ocean City. The German Shepherd was always anxious to work, even on the day Kirkpatrick paid that visit to the veterinarian, only to learn that Tazz had contracted lung cancer.

Doctors told Kirkpatrick the disease came as a result of environment exposure. While aggressive on the job, the dog could join children and the community with no worries to officers. In the many cases Tazz handled , he bit only one suspect and only because the suspect refused to surrender to officers. Kirkpatrick compared the K-9's aggressive temperament to a light switch,; it could be turned on and off at his command.

The death has left the department saddened over the loss. Many looked at Tazz as another officer. The dog will also be missed by the community as many throughout Ocean City knew his presence and abilities. He's just like another officer, actually Tazz is more well known through the community than I am. They just know I am the guy at the end of the leash." Tazz died at the age of 9. The memorial service is to be held at 5 PM at St. Luke's Roman Catholic Church, 100 Coastal Hwy.

In Loving Memory of

K-9 TEKA

LODD
April 7, 2000

Partner: Gary Trumbly
Niceville Police Department FL
212 N. Partin Dr.
Niceville, FL 32578
850 729 4030

Niceville Police Department lost their K-9 Teka on April 7, 2000. K-9 Teka had just located a small amount of marijuana in a vehicle on a traffic stop along SR20 in Niceville. After finding the marijuana, she was struck by a passing van. The female driver slowed down, but never stopped.

Gary and another officer rushed Teka to the Emergency Vet Clinic. Another officer tried to get the van to stop. Teka was dead before she got there. She had a hell of a nose and was our partner. We will not forget her.

UPDATE:

We had Teka cremated so we could keep her with us. When I went to pick up her ashes, the proprietor said, "I have someone for you to meet." There stood this huge chocolate lab who weighs 105 lb. My first reaction was " Does he come with a saddle?"

This beautiful dog was going to be put down that day because he bit the finger of a woman who was shaking her finger at him!" What a waste that would have been. Pat, my wife went to see "Buddy" (we kept his name)...and she fell in love with him. Buddy is doing K-9 work and averages 2 apprehensions a night.

We are also adding to our family, a black and tan German Shepherd puppy which I also will train. We are getting pick of the litter, so now Buddy will have a "buddy" to play and work with.

In Loving Memory of

K-9 TY

May 23, 1997

Partner: Warren Neff
Ft. Riley, KS

My name is Warren Neff and I am an officer with the Overland Park Police Dept. in Kansas. I was directed to your site by Officer Robbie Fischer who is a handler with our department. I am a former Military Police Dog Handler and I really appreciated your article on "Robby." The Malinois that sparked the bill to save these K-9 soldiers.

I wish that I knew where I put my picture of my Partner Ty so I could send it to you. I'll keep looking. I just wanted to let you know what happened to him. After 8 years of serving his country and 3 years protecting me, Ty died on the 23 of May, 1997. We were stationed at Ft. Riley Kansas which is next door the Kansas State University.

Once Ty passed on he was sent to the K State Campus for up and coming veterinarians to "experiment" on. My K-9 supervisor, Sgt. Charles A. Mailloux, as well as the rest of us, were very upset with this choice. Sgt. Mailloux took this upon himself and took issue through the chain of command. He was able to have Ty returned to his post and he received a semi proper burial with a nice looking headstone in the Pet Cemetery on Ft. Riley. He was not buried with the rest of the fallen soldiers in the cemetery, but at least he was not used for training at that school.

During his burial ceremony, a fellow soldier, SPC Eric Von Yahn, composed the following and I wanted to share it with you. It's not a whole lot but, it meant a lot to me, Ty's last handler.

"I first met "Ty" in October of 1996, he was a very happy dog with a personality all his own. "Ty" had two missions to fulfill in his life. His first was to aid in the apprehension of people who broke the law and his second mission was to provide an undying loyalty and sense of protection to his handler. Ty was a truly usable and essential member of the law enforcement activity on Ft. Riley." I stand before you today, to say that Ft. Riley has lost a committed, energetic, and professional soldier through the death of "Ty". A soldier who dedicated his life to law enforcement and country above all else.

You may see our K-9 vehicles on Patrol late at night or in the early morning hours. If you look close and the light is just right, you can see a wagging tail or the face of our partners. It is often said K-9 handlers and their partners "OWN THE NIGHT." I think it's safe to say that as the sun goes down, that this evening "Ty" has earned the right to own the night eternally.

In Loving Memory of

K-9 URIAH

1990 - May, 1998

Partner: Trooper Lynch
Connecticut State Police
1995

K-9 Uriah won the highest honor given to a Connecticut K-9 team, the Daniel Wasson Memorial K-9 Award. This award was established by the   Connecticut Police Work Dog Association. Uriah won the award for sustaining multiple stab wounds during the tracking and apprehension of an armed felony suspect. Uriah recovered from his injuries and returned to duty.

Uriah retired in September of 1997. He died of liver failure May 5th 1998.

In Loving Memory of

K-9 VALCO

July 17, 2000
Dutch Shepherd
LODD

Partner: Officer James Thomas
Indianapolis Police Dept. K-9 Unit
50 North Alabama Ave.
Indianapolis IN 46204

Police are mourning the death of a K-9 gunned down by a confused officer in a raid on the home of a suspected 85 year old drug dealer. Police said. Rookie police dog, Valco, a Dutch Shepherd, became the first police dog killed in action in the city's history during a raid on the home of Charles Howard on Monday night. Valco got away from his handler, and one of officers thought it was a strange dog coming at him.

This is not the first time another officer has shot a strange animal, but it is the first time since the K-9 unit was established in 1961 that a police dog has died in the line of duty.

It happened at about 9 p.m. as plain clothes officers were preparing to serve Howard, a senior citizen with a history of drug arrests dating back more than a decade with a warrant charging him with marijuana possession and possession of drug paraphernalia.

Police had decided to bring Valco along for an extra measure of security as police dogs are often used in drug arrests. The dogs are used for both for their commanding presence and if a suspect runs, a dog can chase him better than officers can.

Dogs can break free , but Valco, who joined the department's K-9 unit less than a year ago, broke free of his handler at precisely the same moment officers were preparing to rush Howard's door. One of the officers saw the dog running toward him, wrongly believed that it was an attack dog sent by the suspect, and shot and killed him.

It was not immediately clear what, if anything, the department planned to do to honor the slain K-9. The department feels that something should be done. Regardless of the circumstances, Valco did die in the line of the duty.

In Loving Memory of

K-9 VELLO

April 3, 2000
LODD

Partner: Officer Mike Hovda
Olympia Police Dept.
900 Plum St.
Olympia , WA 98501
360.753-8300

"Vello and Hovda had been nominated for the Red Cross award and were considered by several sources to be the top contenders for the prize this year. The team had received a missing person's report last year and was able to track down an Alzheimer's patient who had wandered away.

One blast from a shotgun. Authorities said Amos drove his white four by four pickup truck around the locked gate that stood at the entrance to the 2 mile long driveway of the woman's home. Leaving his girlfriend in the truck, Amos allegedly approached the dog and shot it once with a shotgun.

He then dumped the dog into the bed of the pickup, drove off with him and tried to hide his body miles away in a wooded area, authorities said. Brown said that Amos knew he was killing a police dog. In fact, he had allegedly met the dog and made threats toward Vello during past encounters with Hovda and his estranged wife, authorities said.

In addition, Vello had become a well regarded member of the force after undergoing three surgeries on his spine, said Sue Larson of the American Red Cross. "As a team, the dog and Officer Hovda had come through a lot of adversity," she said. "The dog has been very successful in his career," added Machan. "He is missed not only by our agency but by some others around that we do work for." Amos is now charged with killing a police dog, a class C felony, which could mean up to five years in prison and first degree theft, which is punishable by up to 10 years in prison. He also is charged with various domestic violence offenses that could put him behind bars for life, Brown said.

A strange twist at court. After Hovda, who had been the dog's handler for about three years, discovered the dog missing and reported it, Lewis County authorities went to the home where Amos lived with his girl friend, 42 year old Mary Chichester. Brown said the sheriff's department found blood and fur on the pickup. That was enough to get a search warrant for Chichester's home, where the sheriff's department allegedly found more evidence, officials said.

The case got stranger at Amos' first court hearing Wednesday when police found Chichester sitting in the audience and arrested her because the search of her home turned up illegal weapons. Chichester has past convictions for domestic violence and is not permitted to keep guns, Brown said. After being arrested at court, Chichester allegedly told police about witnessing the dog shooting. This new information prompted Amos to later get up in court and admit to shooting the dog, Brown said. Amos also later led police to the K-9's body, which probably would never have been found.

Police grieve. Meanwhile, the death has filled many people at the Olympia Police Department with grief. Spokesman Dick Machan said that Hovda is on leave and too saddened to talk. "Obviously, in any of these kinds of things, the dogs are kind of like family so it's a big loss," he said. "And it's affected people very hard, the same way it would with anybody that you have around a lot. "Chichester, meanwhile, faces weapons charges. Vello joined the department in 1995 after K-9 Aron retired in 1996, Velez said in a press release.

The person who shot K-9 Vello was prosecuted and sentenced to serve time and pay restitution. Vello was a great loss to department and especially Officer Hovda. Many cards and well wishes were sent in honor of Vello.

GOOD NEWS: K-9 Conan just finished training school and received exemplary scores. He has been on the job with successful tracks and apprehensions.

10/15/02 UPDATE: I am working patrol now. Have been since. Enjoying every day, thanks to Vello. He is still with me. He school me in the art of finding people and I think he still guides me at times. I still train with our new K-9, Conan. He is a great police dog and has a lot of the same personalities as Vello. I also train with Lacey's K-9 Kuda.

The handler is Bob Lions and when I was in K-9, Bob had Baron. Baron has since passed away and now he has Kuda. So I am still involved a little but it certainly is not like having a partner, 24 hours a day.

Nov. 2002: I have been thinking about all the things Vello did for me. I just thought I would share one or two. Vello was injured about the second year of his career. He had two discs go out in his back. He barely could walk. I had to make a decision to try and fix it or put him down.

Knowing Vello and his strength and the love he had for his job, I decided to let the doctor try and fix his back. After three surgeries on his back, carrying him around for months while he recovered, he came back to the road and never lost that desire to work. In fact, he earned the Red Cross Life saving award before his death.

He found a patient that walked away from a hospital and lost his way in the woods. When Vello found him in the middle of the night, The elderly gentleman was near death. If it had not been for Vello and the speed he found him, he would not have made it and we would have never found him. I received the award for Vello after he was killed.

Vello's last track for a suspect was for an auto thief. He ran over fences, through yards, across streets and into his own house. Vello couldn't jump anymore because of his surgeries, but it didn't stop him. I would lift him over things to help him and he would track like nobody's business to help me. Vello found the house and in fact went right to the door. The suspect was taken into custody. This was his last track. Like every handler, there are just some things you won't forget. I just thought I would share it with you, it might give people a better insight of how powerful the bond is between the two partners. Vello will jump right out and talk my ear off, like he always did when we were on tracks. I'm finding out he still does. Baron and Vello worked together and trained togther all the time. They were backing us up or we were backing them up. They did a lot of Tag team tracks together.

In Loving Memory of

K-9 WAYLON

January 10, 2000

Partner: Officer Steve Purney
Topeka Police Department
Topeka, KS

Waylon, a male Belgian Malinois, had been a K-9 cop with the Topeka department since 1995. Waylon made numerous felony apprehensions during his career as a patrol utility dog, said LT. Jerry Young. Young said Purney released Waylon to give him a break Monday while they were on the former Topeka State Hospital grounds at S.W. 2nd and MacVicar.

Waylon chased a rabbit onto S.W. MacVicar and was struck by a pickup truck, whose driver stopped at the scene, Young said. Waylon was taken to Animal Emergency Medical Services and later to Western Hills Veterinary Service before police concluded his injuries were too serious to overcome. Waylon was euthanized at about 11:15 a.m. Thursday, Young said. He said a funeral service for the dog would be scheduled for a later date.

Two veteran police dogs, one suffering from hepatitis and the other from injuries received in an accident, were put to sleep separately Thursday morning. Authorities reported the deaths of Topeka police K-9 officer Waylon, the partner of Officer Steve Purney, and Shawnee County Sheriff's K-9 Officer Kilo, the partner of Deputy Brad Metz. Kilo, a 7 year old Belgian Malinois, had a drug related name but was the sheriff's department's primary deputy dog used to sniff out explosives. He had joined the department in 1994 as one of the first explosives detection dogs used in Kansas.

In Loving Memory of

K-9 XANTHOS

November 3, 1998   October 28, 2000

Partner: Wim Verbeek
Politie Diest
BELGIUM Police Dept.

Xanthos was born on November 3, 1998. He died on October 28, 2000. He had an obstruction in his stomach. Xanthos was in education of drugs. He did very well. It's a great loss for our family because Xanthos was our family dog. Max, our other dog, misses his friend too. In Belgium we speak Dutch, French and German. In this part of the country we speak Dutch.

UPDATE:

Today we bought a new German Shepard.. His name is Falco and he is 6 months old. We will certainly not forget about Xanthos, because no dog can replace him. Tomorrow I'm going with the dogs on a training camp for four days. My function is police officer in the police department of Diest Belgium, mostly I go on patrol with Max.

In Loving Memory of

K-9 YOGI

SAR
1989 1998

Partner: Jerry Nichols
Law Enforcement Bloodhound Association
LEBA
P.O. Box 471267
Aurora, Colorado 80047 1267

Yogi was born on September 18, 1989, and named "Fosgate's Fozzie Bear." When soon to be partner for life, Officer Jerry Nichols went to pick him out of the litter, he had every intention of naming him "Fred." That was soon thrown out by his son, Eric, who liked the name "Yogi" much better, sure fit him!

Yogi was placed in the K-9 Unit in 1990 after being placed on a trial basis by one of the department chiefs. Yogi and Jerry worked very hard, and Yogi became not only a good trailing dog, but he also excelled at Decomp work. Jerry and Yogi attended many training seminars learning something new at each one. Yogi even learned what rattlesnakes smelled like and that they are bad and should be avoided! He never forgot this lesson. De-snaking is a great tool and it can save a dog's life. No dogs are bitten and no snakes are hurt in the process.

Yogi made many appearances and he loved to be around children. As with most bloodhounds he had the gentlest of temperaments. Yogi survived 'Bloat' and worked with severely dysplastia hips. He logged many miles in the work he did, yet never slowed down.

As a team, Jerry and Yogi worked 476 cases for over 70 Federal, State & Local Agencies in 8 states. Due to their work, they have been instrumental in Appellate Court decisions in Colorado, regarding bloodhound evidence. The picture is from Yogi's last active manhunt. One Denver Officer was killed and another ambushed.

Yogi passed over the "Rainbow Bridge" in June of 1998 as a result of cancer. Only one week before that, he worked a homicide case, and he was happy to be working.

2001

INDEX 2001

In Loving Memory of

K-9 AJAX Badge # 905

October 31, 1995 - September 9, 2001

Partner: Officer Phillip L. Howell
Put-in-Bay Police Department
P.O. Box 268 Catawba Ave.
Put-In-Bay, Ohio 43456-0401
419.285-4121

A trumpeter's "Taps." Blasts from the American Legion's 18 gun salute. A bagpiper's "Amazing Grace", all aimlessly drifting into the wind. It is a scene that, in light of national activities, will be replayed thousands of times over the next few weeks. But for the close knit Put in Bay island community, Thursday morning's memorial service was a time to remember one of their own, Officer 905, "A very special dog who thought he was king."

Ajax, a 5 year old German Shepherd, was Put in Bay's first K-9 cop. "This is a tribute toward Ajax and all of the lost K-9s and officers throughout the U.S. and especially the tragedy we had in New York City Tuesday. It is a sad day for us." said Put in Bay Police Chief Jim Lang. "Today, the village has lost a valuable asset to law enforcement and a loyal friend," said Father Jeff Nordhaus, from Mother of Sorrows Catholic Church.

Ajax died Sunday. "The tragedies of this week are unbelievable," said Put in Bay Mayor John Blatt. Few, if any, of the 150 or more police officers, emergency medical personnel, island residents and passers by in attendance had dry eyes. Six police dogs, heeled at their handlers' sides, barked with the saluting guns. When Ajax's memorial was planned Monday, more than 300 officers were expected. Many canceled as their services were needed for security at airports, power plants, and elsewhere across Northwest Ohio.

"A lot of the island children thought of Ajax as their friend. But the saddest part is that Ajax would have been able to serve four to five more years on the islands as an active narcotics certified police dog," said Maj. Robert McDowell Jr. from the Huron County Sheriff's Department. McDowell, owner of M&M K-9 Boarding Kennel, helps officers from across the country train police K-9s. McDowell helped Howell get Ajax, "a narcotics tracking machine." "Phil worked his heart out training with Ajax all last winter getting prepared for what he would face on Put in Bay this summer," McDowelll said.

Ajax served from Memorial Day weekend through evening duties Sept. 7, 2001, tallying more than 65 narcotic arrests during that time, Howell said. Those arrests included drugs ranging from LSD and cocaine to marijuana, ecstasy and oxycontin. Ajax also helped the Ohio Department of Water craft seize a boat with drugs and check incoming ferries and planes from Canada's Pelee Island, Howell said.

Island officials said they are looking to find another K-9 narcotics dog to help patrol the island. McDowell said if Howell can obtain a dog within the next few months, the dog can easily be ready for patrol at the beginning of Put in Bay's 2002 summer season. Ajax will be laid to rest near Oak Harbor, Howell said.

Special thanks to: Brenda Cullen reporter and Tim Fleck, photographer, and their paper, Sandusky Register for contributing to this memorial.

UPDATE:

Alex takes over the Put in Bay beat of Ajax who died Sept. 9, 2001.

For about an hour, three year old Alex sat quietly on the floor, legs crossed with gentlemanly poise. But when it was time to play, the pure bred German Shepherd bared his sizable teeth and attacked his "hidden ball box" like a whirlwind, ultimately shattering the Plexiglas window to get to the ball, something most dogs never do. "He's got good ball drive. He's obsessed with the ball," said Huron County Sheriff's Office investigator Robert W. McDowell Jr. "If a dog has good ball drive, they will make good drug dogs."

Training centers around Alex's enthusiasm at playing ball, McDowell said. When Put in Bay Police Officer Philip Howell plays ball with Alex, the dog learns the ball is his toy. Later in the training, the ball will be put away while Alex watches. Alex learns that by pawing, digging, scratching and barking at the barrier separating him from his toy, Howell will reward Alex by getting the ball and playing with the dog. Alex is a quick learner, Howell said. After this is mastered the ball is hidden with marijuana and the dog learns to associate the drug's scent with his toy.

"We start with marijuana because it is the drug with the strongest odor," McDowell said. McDowell, owner of M&M K-9 Boarding Kennel, trains dogs in narcotics detection and tracking. He is helping Howell train Alex to be South Bass Island's next K-9 officer. "He's like a vacuum cleaner with his nose down on the ground tracking a scent," Howell said.

Alex replaces Officer 905 Ajax, who died Sept. 9 after becoming ill during a drug bust Labor Day weekend. Ajax was so well liked by island businesses and residents for his drug busting and safety services they donated around $5,000 for Howell to purchase and transport Alex from his home in the former Czechoslovakia, Howell said. He arrived in the United States Oct. 19, 2000.

Island residents expect Alex to take up where Ajax left off, especially during tourist season. "Ajax made a serious impact on the drug habits of summer visitors (with more than 63 arrests in four months) and I anticipate that by next summer, Alex will be fully trained and ready to go," said Mayor John Blatt.

Alex's training began in his native country, and he brought to the U.S. a working knowledge of suspect apprehension, tracking and off leash obedience, McDowell said. This means it will only take about one month for Alex to train with Howell, and for Howell to acclimate himself to giving commands in Czech for Alex to become a certified police dog in Ohio. Howell and McDowell said it will take 60 days of intense training for Alex to become state certified in narcotics detection.

Police dogs in Ohio have to be certified every two years but the dogs must practice their skills on almost a daily basis to perform best. Alex's temperament also fits the people friendly attitude that is a must on the island. "It is a must that a dog on Put in Bay is non aggressive around people because thousands of people are walking around the island everyday who may walk up to Alex and pet him," McDowell said. "But if Phil gives Alex the right command, he will light up like a firecracker."

In Loving Memory of

K-9 ARGO

October 5, 1991 - May 6, 2001

Partner Sgt. Paul Shaughnessy
C.M.H.A. Police Dept
Cuyahoga Metropolitan Housing Authority P.D.
5715 Woodland Ave.
Cleveland, OH 44104
216.739 7837

It had all the trappings of a police funeral; the procession of cruisers with flashing red and blue lights, the honor guard, the final volley of gunshots. The only difference was that when the kilt clad policeman played "Amazing Grace," the air was filled by the sounds of bagpipes and barking dogs. Man and beast alike paid final homage to a fallen comrade yesterday as Argo the police dog was buried at an animal cemetery in Richfield.

We look at this as seriously as if one of our human officers would have died. Argo is going to be missed by our department. After nearly a decade of tangling with violent criminals, Argo died from a chest infection early Sunday afternoon.

The robust German Shepherd had served the CMHA police, assisted numerous other departments and saved his handler, CMHA Sgt. Paul Shaughnessy, from death or serious injury at least a half dozen times. Last weekend, Shaughnessy tried to save Argo, rushing him to a veterinary clinic because he was not eating.

Shaughnessy spent Saturday night at his partner's side, went home the next day and expected to return that day to bring Argo home with him. Instead, he had to plan a funeral. More than sixty people attended yesterday's memorial, including about forty police officers from departments throughout Northeast Ohio, as well as two dozen police dogs and their handlers.

When a police dog goes down, police come from all over. Police are a close knit group, and the K-9 units are even closer.

When Argo wasn't patrolling with Shaughnessy, Argo was a fixture at the Justice Center because his partner had to testify frequently. They had thousands of arrests. That's why you saw him in court every day. Nobody gets away.

Last November, Argo tracked down a juvenile who was a suspect in a homicide and car jacking. The youth had eluded sixty Cleveland police officers during a chase and subsequent search. Shaughnessy said he was nearly beaten to death last year by a man who already had been imprisoned twice for assaulting police officers. But Argo leapt from the patrol car and brought the attack to an end. "I have no doubt that guy would have killed me."

In Loving Memory of

K-9 ARKON

August 25, 2001

Partner: Officer Steve Endrie
Fond du Lac Police Department
180 S. Macy St.
Fond du Lac, WI 54935

Approximately 200 people attended a memorial service for a police dog that died from cardiac arrest. They included about 60 law enforcement officers, representing jurisdictions such as Winnebago County, Fond du Lac County, Oshkosh, Manitowoc, Manitowoc County, Ripon, Wisconsin Dells and Racine. Twenty to thirty police dogs from other K-9 units came with their handlers, most of whom know Arkon's handler, Officer Steve Endries, from training workshops. Arkon, one of five dogs serving with the Fond du Lac Police Department, died Saturday.

Endries said during the ceremony Wednesday at Rienzi Cemetery's pet burial grounds that Arkon had been "a loyal partner and best friend" to him for nearly six years. Mount Horeb Police Officer Blaine Hall said that part of the loss that is hard to deal with is the bond of trust built up between a police dog and officer. "You learn to trust the dog with your life," Hall said, adding that more than once on duty, his own police dog, Sierra, "made people change their minds" about getting violent with him.

Winnebago County Sheriff's Department Officer Greg Weitz said many people don't appreciate police dogs as much as they should. "The dogs are a lot more valuable to a police department than people realize, and it's nice to see people give them some recognition," he said.

In May of 1996 K-9 Arkon along with handler Officer Steve Endries joined the unit. Then in November of 1997 the City Council continued to show their support of the K-9 program by funding two additional dogs bringing the unit's current level to four dogs. Yalco and his partner Tina Braun joined the unit in May of 1998. K-9 Manto and handler Officer Bill Ledger completed the four team unit in September of 1998. All four K-9s are dual purpose patrol & narcotics detection dogs. The K-9s are also trained and certified as reasonable force (find & bark) dogs.

Officer Steve Endries and K-9 Arkon have been partners on the Fond du Lac Police Department since May of 1996. Arkon was a dual purpose five year old male German Shepherd imported from Germany. This K-9 team works along with the officers on patrol and on emergency on call type basis.

Arkon was trained to protect his handler and other officers who are nearby when needed. Arkon was extremely useful when searching buildings, fields, parks, etc., for fleeing or hiding suspects who may be armed. Arkon could be used to track the direction of travel of a fleeing suspect through terrains where Arkon could use his nose to locate the suspect. Upon finding the suspect, Arkon would bark to advise officers of the find.

AWARDS:

DPO 1 Title   September 1998

Arkon successfully completed passing scores in tracking, obedience and officer protection phases. Arkon and Officer Endries were nominated for the Outstanding Apprehension Award by the Wisconsin Law Enforcement K-9 Association in October of 1998.

In Loving Memory of

K-9 ARNO

August 16, 2001

Partner: Cpl. Joseph Welda
Walker Police Department
P.O. Box 988
Walker, LA 70785
225.664-3125

Arno, the police dog, died Thursday of an unknown ailment after three years of active duty with the Walker Police Department.

The department is totally devastated, Arno did it all; the tracking, officer protection, drug searches, crowd control. Arno, a 5 year old Belgian Malinois, lived with the family of his police handler, Cpl. Joseph Welda. The Belgian Malinois is a breed related to the Belgian sheepdog that is well suited for police work.

Welda called Burns Wednesday night to report that Arno was ill. Welda took Arno to a veterinarian Thursday morning and then brought him home to recuperate. When Welda's wife, Beverly, returned home at 3:30 p.m., she discovered Arno's lifeless body.

Although the dog was taken to the LSU School of Veterinary Medicine for an autopsy, officials do not suspect poisoning. Burns said the Welda family members were very attached to Arno. Their 15 month old daughter, was crying "dog, dog, dog" on Friday.

Arno was one of two police dogs with the 10 member Police Department. Hondo, also a Belgian Malinois, was a gift from the Livingston Parish Sheriff's Office. They are members of the force.

The city purchased Arno from a Kaplan trainer through a federal grant, Burns said. The police chief said he has already contacted town officials about buying another police dog, which may cost about $5,000. That doesn't include the cost of training with the assigned police trainer.

In Loving Memory of

K-9 AXEL

April 21, 2001

Partner: Officer Stephen Shepard
Tacoma, WA Police Dept.
Tacoma Police Union 901 S. I St., Suite 201
Tacoma, WA 98405

Tacoma police lost a trusted friend over the weekend. Axel, the recently retired police dog, died Saturday after his vital organs began failing, a police spokeswoman said Sunday. Veterinarians decided to put the German Shepherd down when it became clear he wasn't making the recovery from prostate surgery they had hoped for. Earlier this month, the Tacoma police union asked the public to help pay for mounting medical bills.

Axel started acting sluggish a couple of months ago and his condition began to worsen, police said. Veterinarians found a tumor in his prostate, which was later found to be benign. With his death, police intend to use any remaining funds to help pay for future retired police dog medical bills. Officers were unable

Sunday to say how much money had been collected.

Axel was set to retire in a couple of months but was forced into early retirement because of the illness. In his 4½ years with Tacoma police, Axel racked up 220 arrests, police said. Officers plan a memorial service for this week, though they didn't have a firm date Sunday. Donations for the retired police dog fund are still being accepted at any Key Bank branch.

TRACKING BAD GUYS IN HEAVEN

Police dog, Axel, passed away April 21, after a tiring struggle to recover from surgery. Axel provided courageous and loyal service to his fellow officers and citizens of Tacoma. In addition to apprehending 220 felons, he protected and saved countless lives. We are blessed for having Axel with us for over four years.

Officer Stephen Shepard and his family grieve his loss, as well as all those whose lives he had touched. The K-9 Unit wishes to thank the men and women of the Tacoma Police Department, who provided financial and emotional support. The Tacoma Police Union, Phoenix Central Labs, Arc Northwest, and the businesses and citizens who donated so generously for Axle's medical care.

We will be forever grateful to the doctors and staff of the 56th South Durango Animal Emergency Hospital for their constant loving care, compassion, and expert medical treatment for our beloved Axel.

A memorial is planned for May 10th for Axel. We will use your cards, which will provide a keepsake reminder for all who attend. Officer Shepard is doing well...he has good and bad days, as might be expected. We have found a new dog for him, with whom he has begun training. The new dog is providing a much needed respite from his grief. Steve has named him "Elvis." He is an excellent tracking dog. They look forward to many years of partnership.

Thank you again for your thoughtful donation during our difficult time.

/s/Sgt. Karen Kelly

Tacoma WA. Police Department, K-9 Unit

In Loving Memory of

K-9 BART

December 13, 2001

Partner: Peter Bryce
K-9 Specialist Protection
3 Oak Training Kennels
Botley Rd., Bishops Waltham
Southampton, England S032 1DR UK

My boy's name was Bart, a long coat German Shepherd Dog. He died on the 13/12/01 at 10:40 hours. He had a ruptured spleen. also a tumor from his kidneys to his liver. The vet let him go while under the anesthetic. He was with me for ten years, good and bad times.

I lost a friend yesterday. A friend I had loved for ten years. His passing has left a void which will never be filled again. He was part of me, my companion and protector, my ears and my eyes. We did not need words. We anticipated each other. We were one, beside each other every day throughout the years. His only purpose in life was to please me. We worked and relaxed together. For those short years, we were inseparable.

The end was quick with no warning. We had no time to prepare. For my friend this was a blessing as the pain was short, but my pain will last much longer because I had no time for good byes.

My handsome, majestic friend has gone ahead of me...........Wait for me, Bart, as you have done before. I will walk through that door one day and you will be by my side once again.

In Loving Memory of

K-9 BLITZ

Born in Canada   October 11, 1987
March 26, 2001

Partner: Detective Bob Valencia
Overland Park Police Dept. KS
12400 Foster St.
Overland Park, KS 66213

A member of the Overland Park Police Department in Overland Park, Kansas and currently a member of the K-9 section, trainer, Bob Valencia recently had to put to down his police K-9 BLITZ who was 14 years old. Blitz was the first dog on the department and Bob's trusted friend for many years.

The lieutenant of the Corps read Blitz's eulogy and the fact that Blitz had a love for fast food. Another lieutenant read, "The Rainbow Bridge." The fast food story was also told.

Bob spent his last five dollars on Arby's roast beef, and when Bob was out of the car, Blitz decided to help himself. Just one of the many memories of Blitz. The chief presented a plaque to

Bob. It hurt him deeply when he made the trip to the vet that one last time and held Blitz in his arms. As he watched his eyes close I'm sure he felt as if his heart was breaking.

Our police department buried Blitz in front of the station. We have been assured, that when our dog's time comes to pass on, the department will honor them properly.

In Loving Memory of

K-9 BLONDIE

December 31, 2001

Partner: Officer Sean Mulligan
Seattle-Tacoma International Airport WA
U.S. Customs Service
1000 2nd Ave. Suite 2100
Seattle, WA 98104

What government worker helps keep us safe and expects nothing more than a rolled up towel in return? The answer is found at Sea Tac Airport. They're man's best friend, but not if you're a drug smuggler.

Last year alone, U.S. Customs Service K-9 teams detected hundreds of tons of illegal narcotics, worth several billion dollars on the street. Since 1970, customs has been using specially trained dogs, usually rescued from animal shelters, to detect illegal narcotics in packages or luggage entering our country. The K-9s can inspect several hundred packages or bags an hour. "If we had to hand pick through all the bags, if we had to stop each individual and speak to them, we would be here all day just to do one flight," said Sean Mulligan.

Officer Mulligan and Blondie, a golden retriever rescued from an animal shelter, went through four months of training together. If she smells drugs in someone's luggage, she'll simply sit down. As a reward, she gets to play with a rolled up towel. The officers don't mind letting their partners enjoy their reward. After all, these K-9 cops work hard, and never complain. The dogs' skills are well known among smugglers.

In fact, customs officers watch for nervous reactions when the dogs come in to the baggage area. "As soon as the dogs come out here looking for narcotics, we're also looking at the passengers as well. If you start seeing passengers moving away from the dog, that kind of gives you a clue," said Luis Sanchez. The dogs have to have at least a 95% success rate at finding drugs to stay on the job.

A sad update to that story.

K-9 enforcement officer Sean Mulligan lost his partner, Blondie, to cancer on New Year's Eve. Blondie was a customs dog for 5 years. In that time, Blondie was responsible for several busts, including discovering 57 pounds of marijuana on a Canadian fishing boat in 2000. Officer Mulligan says Blonde's greatest accomplishment though, was visiting thousands of school kids at countless schools in the area and educating them about the dangers of drugs. Sean says the kids don't always remember him, but they always remember Blondie.

On New Year's Eve, I lost my loyal partner, "Blondie." She was diagnosed with cancer on December 13th. My wife and I were able to spend Christmas with Blondie. Blondie was a 7 year old Golden Retriever. We started working together in 1997. At the time I was assigned to work for U.S. Customs in Calgary, Canada. Blondie was discovered at a animal shelter in California.

Blondie got sick on Nov. 27th, 2001. On Dec 6th, she had surgery to remove a tumor from the right side of her heart. The results came back, the tumor was malignant. Exactly one year to the day, Dec. 13th, I lost my dad to cancer.

Blondie was released from the vet hospital on Dec. 14th. She came home with me to recover. She "officially" retired on Dec. 23rd. The best Christmas present was just that Blondie got to spend Christmas with me and my wife.

Blondie's health and attitude was great. We spoiled her with gifts and her own turkey dinner. It didn't take her long to learn how to enjoy the "retired" life, going for rides, going on walks and even watching football games on the couch.

TO HONOR BLONDIE:
Irish Blessing
May the roads rise to meet you,
May the winds be always at
your back,
May the sun shine upon your face,
The rains fall softly upon the fields,
And until we meet again,
May God hold you in the
hollow of His hand.

In Loving Memory of

K-9 BLUR

LODD
July 27, 2001

Partner: Officer John Allovio
Waco Police Department
721 North 4th Street
Waco, TX 76701

A Waco police officer shot and killed a police dog Friday during a search for a robbery suspect. Officers attempted to pull over a car about 3:15 a.m. at the intersection of West Avenue and North Ninth Street. The car was reported stolen in Dallas. The car's driver, Bradford Carr, 23, of Waco fled from police. Officers followed until Carr stopped the vehicle and fled on foot in the 800 block of Harlem Avenue, spokesman, Anderson said.

Officers surrounded the area, and with the assistance of a police dog, they began a yard to yard search, he said. As the K-9 and its handler approached the fence of one yard, Carr stood up and surrendered, Anderson said. An officer, hearing the commotion, approached the scene from behind the K-9. The dog, sensing a threat to its handler, bit and held onto the approaching officer's left arm. The dog released the officer upon his handler's command.

Another officer, with his gun drawn, approached from the same direction, and the dog again bit and held onto his left arm. Before the handler could order the dog to stop, the officer shot the K-9 in the side. K-9 Blur died at the scene. He shot on an impulse. It was a very quick reaction to the seriousness of the situation. He fired one shot, and that killed the dog.

Police would not release the names of the officers involved. Both bitten officers were taken to Hillcrest Baptist Medical Center, where they were treated and released. Anderson said one officer's wounds required stitches. The dog, a 3 year old Dutch Shepherd named Blur, was purchased by the department in May.

The dog was trained to use its mouth to restrain anyone it perceived as a threat to its handler. You can train and train and train, but then you get out into a high stress situation where everybody is tense and the suspect is believed to have a gun, and the unexpected can happen.

We will have to work this into our training in the future. The dog's body was sent to a veterinarian to check for rabies. Waco's police dogs are used mainly to sniff out narcotics, but they are also used to locate weapons and track people. The dog's death has been difficult for the department. Sure it was only a dog, but it is still one of the officers.

For the K-9 officer, this was his partner. Officer Allovio lived with him as part of his family. He's taking it very hard.. It is also hard for the officer who fired the shot. It is a bad situation all the way around. Anderson said it was too early to determine whether a memorial service will be held for Blur.

Both injured officers were on medical leave Friday. Waco police Sgt. Dennis Kidwell said there will be an investigation into the shooting, but said that is routine in such cases. Carr remained in the McLennan County Jail late Friday on charges of evading arrest and aggravated robbery, a jail spokeswoman said. Bond was set at $11,500.

"Blur was not just a dog, he was an officer, he was one of us, one of the family."

In Loving Memory of

K–9 BRIX

November 18, 2001

Partner: Correctional Officer First Class Sam Stottlemyer
Frederick County Sheriff Department
7309 Grove Rd.
Frederick, MD 21704
301.694-1532

Corrections Officer First Class Sam Stottlemyer and Brix begin a search at the rear of the Frederick County Court House during a bomb scare in May 1998. Brix, a dog the Frederick County Sheriff's Office used to detect explosives, died Sunday of complications from cancer that had gone undetected.

"We're all kind of stunned because there were no signs that anything was wrong." Brix and his partner, Correctional Officer First Class Sam Stottlemyer, had finished working about 2 p.m. when the dog collapsed and was rushed to Glade Valley Animal Hospital, where he "died in Sam's arms," Sgt. Robeson said.

Although a necropsy will be conducted to confirm the cause

of death, Sgt. Robeson said initial indications are that the dog had cancer of the heart and spleen, which caused the heart to rupture Sunday.

Plans are being made to hold a memorial service for Brix, a 6½ year old, all black German Shepherd who was in great demand for his explosives work throughout the Western Region of Maryland as well as in Pennsylvania, Sgt. Robeson said. Sheriff Jim Hagy said this is the first time since he's been in office that a K-9 has died while still an active working patrol dog. "He's been a valuable member of our agency and an ambassador for the Frederick County Sheriff's Office," Sheriff Hagy said.

Rep. Roscoe Bartlett, (R 6th), donated the money for the K-9 to the sheriff's office in October 1996 after a pipe bomb was found at the Frederick County Detention Center. Contacted Monday morning, Dr. Bartlett said, "It's always sad to lose a dog we love."

Sgt. Robeson said Brix was particularly busy after the disaster at Columbine High School. In the days following the school massacre, Brix was called out to conduct 28 explosives scans throughout the area.

Brix also came to Officer Stottlemyer's aid during a fight at the jail when an inmate swung at him. "Brix was a good dog. He'll be missed," Sgt. Robeson said.

Sykesville Police Chief John Williams, formerly head of Frederick County's K-9 unit, trained Brix and Officer Stottlemyer as partners in explosives and patrol work. "This certainly is a traumatic time in Officer Stottlemyer's life. These officers spend as much time with their police dogs as they do with their families. And these dogs actually do become a part of the family."

In Loving Memory of

K-9 BRUNO

August 20, 2001

Partner: Officer William Proulx
East Hartford Police Department
497 Tolland St.
East Hartford, CT 06108
860.528.4401

The town's most celebrated police dog, Bruno, afflicted with crippling spinal arthritis, had been ailing for some time. On Monday morning Officer Bill Proulx drove to a veterinary hospital in town where arrangements had been made for Bruno to be put to sleep.

But before stopping at the vet's Officer Proulx, accompanied by his children Ryan, 10, and Nicole, 7, took his retired K-9 partner around East Hartford in his police cruiser for one last patrol. In the past two weeks his condition had deteriorated to where he could not stand without assistance and Proulx, after much soul searching, decided it was time to end his partner's suffering. The dog was 9½ years old.

You reach a point when you realize they are staying alive because of you and that's when you have to do the right thing, not for you, but for them.

In the world of K-9's there are the good and the very good. Bruno was incredibly very, very, very good! A 4 time, First Place winner in the CT. K-9 Olympics, he has had two books written about him: Dogs With Jobs and Everyday Heroes and was recently featured in the June 2000 issue of Readers Digest. In January on CPTV, he starred in the television series, Dogs With Jobs, which has been seen by audiences around the world.

On the job his record of service was equally impressive. Despite being shot at, battered, punched and injured in the 6 years he was on the force, Bruno, at the time of his retirement, had been credited with 1100 arrests, half of which were felonies, the recovery of 9 lost children and 3 Alzheimer's patients and numerous demonstrations.

With his aggressive bark and sharp bite that targeted legs and buttocks, he was a criminal's worst nightmare. In fact, many in that particular line of work felt you were no one unless you'd been bitten at least once by Bruno.

In 1995, the only year he placed 2nd in the K-9 Olympics he was the only police dog selected by a panel of judges from the Connecticut Chief of Police Association to receive the Daniel Wasson award for disarming a gunman at a local motel and saving Proulx's life.

A member of the 56th K-9 Training Troop, he graduated first in his class from the Connecticut State Police Academy in May, 1994. Friendly and spirited off the job, he possessed a dignity and presence that seemed to embody all that was best in his kind. He enjoyed his work, put his whole being into it, and in the process brought recognition and fame not only to the EHPD and Proulx, but to our community.

Because he was one of the few K-9's whose career was regularly documented by The East Hartford Gazette, residents especially children and seniors, were treated to a personal, inside look at what life on the streets is like for policemen and their K-9 partners. And they responded accordingly with adoration, lots of affectionate pets and friendly greetings and, at holidays, gifts of homemade cookies.

Bruno won the hearts and earned respect of many in and outside of East Hartford, not because of headlines but because he definitely was that rare and genuine bright and shining star. He will be missed by many.

(photo taken by James A. Cortina)

1996 Connecticut K-9 Olympics

AWARDS:

1994 Officer William Proulx & K-9 Bruno won Daniel Wasson Memorial K-9 Award Outstanding Achievements K-9 Policing
1995 Officer William Proulx & K-9 Bruno won 2nd place award
1996 Officer William Proulx & K-9 Bruno won 1st place award
1997 Officer William Proulx & K-9 Bruno won 1st place award
1999 Officer William Proulx & K-9 Bruno won 1st place award

In Loving Memory of

K-9 BRUNO

May 23, 2001

Partner: LT. Ethan A. Hazard
The Pine Knoll Shores Police Department
100 Municipal Circle
Pine Knoll Shores, NC 28512
252. 247 4353

So many people fail to understand that the death of this "dog" was actually the loss of a partner and police officer. I have now lost 2 officers that were mine as a chief; one was a "human" police officer killed in the line of duty, I feel the loss no less with Bruno.

We have a saddened police department. LT. Hazard has a 10 year old boy that is also devastated. Bruno was the complete K-9; talented, loyal, fearless and a loving family pet. Bruno earned countless awards for successful drug raids, finding lost children and the elderly, locating escaped prisoners and valor. Bruno proved himself repeatedly.

He always served his partner and community with pride and professionalism. Intelligence, loyalty and fearlessness were his police traits. Loving, face licking "good boy" was his soul. He will be a partner for life. His death is still under investigation.

Bruno was found hanging outside his kennel at his handler's home on the morning of May 23, 2001. We may never know exactly what took place or how Bruno was lost to all of us. The difficult thing is that he is gone and we must pull it together and go on.

Bruno would have it no other way.

/s/ Mary M. Muhlig, Chief of Police

The following is included to show how tenuous life can be and just how "hardened and callused" our police officers actually are. These are Chief Mary's own words. (ed.)

The Highway Patrolman and local police at the scene of the accident thought the driver of my vehicle was dead (Yup, I was the driver). I was traveling north on a two lane highway, speed limit 55 MPH. Someone going south decided to cut across the median and try to drive through my vehicle to get to a side road, it did not work! I saw the car coming and that was it. I couldn't go anywhere, just wait for that dreaded sound of impact.

The impact (it boned me in the driver's side door) spun my car around and threw it into another vehicle stopped at the side of the road, that person was also transported to the hospital but thankfully was ok, if my vehicle had not hit that car I would have probably flipped and gone down the embankment.

I can remember coming to and trying to figure out where I was, it turned out that the impact broke my seat and shoved my seat half way into the passenger side. I was literally looking up at the roof of my car. My legs came up under the dash and shattered the dash and were up under what was left of the dashboard and side of the car (the metal from the outside of the driver's door was partially inside and up against the left side of my body).

My right side (kidney area) slammed into the center console and smashed it and somehow I was partially on top of the passenger's seat. The steering wheel was broken in half and the rear of the car was pushed up almost to the back of the front seats.

Anyway, I had a major concussion, torn muscles in my thoracic spine, left shoulder, deltoid area, and others. Lovely bruises on my face and legs (but no broken bones-amazing).

The worst thing was my beloved Gabby was in the car too and in all the mayhem of trying to get me out of the car some very nice people who had stopped were trying to get Gabby out and she got away from them. She ran across four lanes of traffic into the woods.

I would not let them keep me in the hospital and went searching for my "child".

The local police were WONDERFUL – they formed search parties and in freezing temps we looked and looked   through the woods, through the water and mud FOR 3 DAYS! The local newspaper ran an ad for me with Gabby's picture and I had flyers printed up and posted in every mailbox with, of course, a reward offered. People would see her and she would run away. It was awful because I was always just 5 minutes late getting to her.

Finally, friends were due in to get me and take me home and to a hospital when the Chief of the Shallotte Police Department called and said "I see her and she's about 1 block from you right now". She had gotten herself inside a huge fenced in area and the entire police department drove through front yards and backyards and surrounded Gabby. I, at long last, got my hands on her!!!

Everyone was crying out in the middle of this field! I know the neighbors probably thought we were after some big time criminal after we tore through everyone's yard!

Gabby had some cuts on her paws and had lost 2 pounds.. but she was fine! I just could not thank that police department enough, they were a very small department with old, old, old equipment.

I went and got them a new scanner and printer and Gabby and I delivered it on the way out of town (police departments cannot accept gifts so I told the Chief to consider it "found property").

I don't know how Gabby made it, but finding her sure helped me to make it! Anyway, staying out of the hospital did not really help my condition but Gabby was more important than my problems at that time. After months and months of procedures and 20 plus injections in my back and shoulder it was determined that nothing could be done for my shoulder and upper back.

I went through withdrawal to get off all the narcotics (that was pure hell and some other time I'll tell you about oxycotin hell). I went through rehab in Charlotte for a month and I am as good as I can be right now. I have some permanent disability but not enough to keep me from work!

It has been a long haul and friends and loved ones like you guys helped me make it. Well, I guess I need to get to work but I did want to fill you in a little.

Update:

The accident is a mystery for me and the investigating trooper, the other driver simply said she wanted to turn down that side street and just did not see me! No drugs, alcohol or functioning brain cells I guess (smile). It could have been worse so I just continue on and try to remember how much stronger I am for it (that which does not kill us makes us stronger).

Well, I am heading out to check my town and patrol. Gabby is a 7 year old mixed breed schnauzer / lab "wanna be police dog".

In Loving Memory of

K-9 BUCK

July 9, 2001

Partner: Sgt. Mark Day
Renton Police Department
1055 Grady Wy.
Renton, WA 98055
253.852-121

Buck was born in Frankfurt, Germany on April 30, 1990. He was the son of a Frankfurt Police K-9 nicknamed the " Red Baron." His dad was a highly decorated officer (so they tell me.) He was brought to the United States via West Virginia by Jack McDonald (a legend in Police K-9 training in Washington.) We tested about 40 dogs including Buck.

I knew he was the one the first time I laid eyes on him. We loaded him on a plane and brought him to Renton to start his career. Jack McDonald trained Buck and I and together we became the last team trained by the legend himself (Jack retired after we graduated).

Buck was commissioned on January 28, 1992. His first night on patrol he tracked a burglary suspect from Hazen High School and located him in a chicken coop; his career was well on its way!

His career consisted of arrests for rape, arson, kidnaping, burglary, and even two homicide suspects. He had over 200 arrests during his career. My recollection tells of even a time he tracked a burglary suspect who had left the scene in the back of a pickup truck.

Can you imagine the surprise when we showed up on her doorstep after she had gone to bed and arrested her for the crime? He found a kidnapper in Auburn who had taken a 4 year old child in a car jacking attempt. Christmas morning 1996, he tracked a stolen vehicle suspect in Tukwila near the Duwamish River. He found the suspect who jumped into the water with Buck attached to him. After a lengthy rescue attempt, I am sorry to say the suspect would not allow himself to be rescued.

There was the time during a violent struggle with a felony assault suspect that Commander McClincy was introduced to Buck when he nibbled on her back side when she got between him and the suspect. (I don't think she ever forgave me or Buck for that!)

He captured two homicide suspects, one for Tukwila and the other for Seattle PD. The capture for Seattle was his last before retiring in March 1997. Buck was a favorite at K-9 demonstrations and Citizen's Academies. During a demonstration for children at the library he somehow got some chewing gum stuck in his fur. The senior librarian covered him in peanut butter saying it would get the gum out. Have you ever seen a German Shepherd with peanut butter and chewing gum all over him? It was very funny!

Buck sired 37 puppies. Many are currently working law enforcement dogs today. His son Rico took his place on the force at the Renton Police Department.

Some of the pups became partners for individuals who are sight impaired and others are just family members. When I see the offspring, I see so much of him in their mannerisms and actions. I guess what I really cherish the most is when I was struggling to fight the cancer that had me on the ropes. He was always there. Buck helped me tremendously to face each day of therapy with determination and hope. He, or so I would like to believe, he understood what a battle I was in for.

Just like at work, Buck never left my side or let me give up. On July 9, 2001, the partner that shared so much of my life lost his own battle to cancer. He left suddenly and in my arms.

I miss him so. I did not believe I could hurt so much as when it happened. I can never put into words what my time with him meant.

In Loving Memory of

K-9 BUDDY

July 30, 2001
LODD

Partner: Officer Mike Davis
Bremerton Police Department
239 Fourth St.
Bremerton, WA 98337
360.478-5220

On 7/30/01 at 0145 hours, officers responded to a City of Bremerton park to investigate a report of someone shooting a gun. One officer spotted the suspects who started running through the park toward where Officer Mike Davis and K-9 Buddy where waiting. K-9 Buddy engaged the suspect, who then shot Buddy. The suspect then shot at Officer Davis.

Officer Davis returned fire, hitting the suspect. K-9 Buddy was rushed to Central Kitsap Animal Hospital where he was pronounced dead.

The suspect is in critical condition. The suspect's gun was

stolen last year in a burglary.

Officer Davis and K-9 Buddy were a new team, having replaced K-9 Zaro. K-9 Buddy was turning out to be an excellent dog, well ahead of where he should have been on the learning curve. In his two months of service, he had over 10 captures.

The arrests included the drivers of several eluding vehicles, an escapee from Mission Creek Youth Camp, several DV assault suspects and a suspect in a drive by shooting who fled after a pursuit. He will be sorely missed.

Memorial service was held on August 8, 2001 at 2:30 PM at the Bremerton High School

Follow up:

Trial begins for suspect in Buddy shooting. Aaron Williams, also accused of trying to kill a Bremerton police officer, didn't fire any shots stated his lawyer.

More than a year after a nighttime shooting at Lions Field that took the life of Bremerton police dog Buddy, the trial of 22 year old suspect, Aaron Williams of Bremerton got under way in Kitsap County Superior Court. Williams' defense against charges he tried to kill a Bremerton police officer after killing his K-9 partner may hinge on the darkness of Lions Field the night of the shooting and whether there were dog bite marks on Williams' arm.

Those were the two main themes that emerged Monday as Williams' lawyer cross examined the first prosecution witnesses in the trial arising from a July 30, 2001, shootout in the East Bremerton park. In the lawyer's opening statement, "It was not Mr. Williams who fired any of the rounds alleged to have been fired."

Police dog Buddy died of a bullet wound early that morning. His handler, Officer Mike Davis, testified that two shots also were fired at him. And Williams was hit in the side as Davis shot back.

Kitsap County Prosecutor Russ Hauge set forth the evidence against Williams for Superior Court Judge Anna Laurie.

She is hearing the case without a jury, at Williams' request. Hauge said police were sent to the park after Williams or his companion, Maurice Jackson, fired off a full clip of 9 mm ammunition in a residential street near the park. They were celebrating Williams' 21st birthday, he said.

The celebration turned deadly after the two ran to the park. Officer Davis confronted a person there. He ordered the person to stop. Buddy was at Davis' side. He was looking at me, waiting for a command. When the person ran, Davis gave the command, "pauken ù" German for "get 'em." Buddy ran around a fence and "contacted" the person.

One or two shots rang out and the dog was mortally wounded. Davis testified he saw it happen in the dim illumination from a street light and a light on a nearby house. He said he chased the suspect into a darker part of the park, clicking his flashlight on and off as he went. He saw the person had stopped with his arm extended toward him. He heard two shots and saw one muzzle flash. Davis then emptied his own gun at the moving suspect, 10 shots. Within one to three seconds of his last shot, he saw Williams lying on the ground, flailing around, wounded.

Officer Clay Schultz, backing up Davis, testified as to what happened next. "Where's the gun?" Williams said, "I threw it," Schultz saw a gun on the ground, jammed and inoperable.

Williams' lawyer questioned Davis at length about what and how he could see as he fired at the figure in the flickering flashlight beam. He asked where the officer and the suspect were standing during the gunfire. He asked if it's possible Williams was shot while already on the ground. Davis said he doubted it. Muenster also asked Schultz if he saw any bite marks on Williams' arm, and was told no. He asked Davis about where Buddy was trained to bite a suspect and was told the first point of contact, unless it's the head or neck. Davis testified he saw Buddy going for or grabbing the suspect's arm.

Hauge asked Davis about whether the dog might have struck Williams with an open mouth bite then relaxed and held him by the arm of his shirt. Davis said that's possible. There was no medical evidence presented in the first day's testimony as to whether Williams did or didn't have any bite marks.

In Loving Memory of

K-9 CAESAR

May 10, 1994 - May 16, 2001

Partner: Patrolman Tommy Royal
Springfield Police Department
321 E. Chestnut Expressway
Springfield, MO 65802-3899

Caesar retired early because of physical reasons. He continued to live with Officer Thomas Royal to the end of his life. Officer Royal is no longer in the K-9 Unit, but continues his career in the department, keeping us safe in this country of terrorists.. Sherry, wife of Officer Royal, also works at the Springfield Police Department. Losing Caesar was like losing a member of our family and we appreciate having his memory shared by others.

In Loving Memory of

K-9 CAO

January 11, 2001

Partner: Officer Keith Stevens
Crown Point Police Department
Crown Point, IN

Cao never got the attention of her more famous counter-part, Udo, but the 4 year old German Shepherd didn't lack for heart and courage, her police department co workers said. The three year department veteran died early Thursday after suffering a seizure.

The dog had been on the job with Officer Keith Stevens Wednesday night and seemed normal just before she died. Stevens said that she was just laying where she normally lays. She got up and collapsed and she was gone. An autopsy performed Thursday at the Purdue University Animal Hospital could help determine whether the dog ingested poison. With it being a police dog, we have to make sure it's not somebody throwing something over the fence.

Cao, an American bred shepherd, was trained to sniff out drugs and track missing people. She'd spent her whole career with the Crown Point department and during that time helped take a total of 140 pounds of marijuana off the street and locate suspects in several burglaries and a battery case. On occasion, she'd been loaned to federal, state and county law enforcement agencies to help solve crimes. Cao did a lot of good work for a lot of people.

Like the rest of the department, Cao had been awarded a police badge. They are members of the department just like everybody else. Cao's death leaves the department with two police dogs, Udo, owned and handled by Officer Charles Sprague, and Enzo Stevens' newest dog.

Udo and Sprague got nationwide attention last year when the pair were nearly separated after Sprague left his former department to work in Crown Point. An outpouring of sympathy for the close bond between police dogs and their handlers resulted in Crown Point city officials agreeing to buy the dog from its former owners and grant ownership to Sprague for life.

Stevens said Thursday that he understands that bond only too well after losing a dog he described as attentive, loving and playful. That's why she was so good at narcotics detection. Cao's reward afterward was to get to play.

Officer Stevens never realized how much he loved Cao because she was always there. When something like this happens you're just floored, especially the way it happened. A four year old healthy dog. It's just unbelievable she's gone. Results of the autopsy are not expected for several days.

Memorial Service Jan. 26, 2001.

Crown Point, IN is Lake County seat in northern Indiana. No results from autopsy.

Update:

To all the people at the F.A.S.T. Company, Thank you so very much for the memorial cards that you sent. It was amazing to see that kind gesture coming from people I have never met before. It has touched us all deeply. The cards did arrive in time for the memorial as we wanted to wait for her remains to return.

The memorial will be held on Jan. 26, 2001 at our police station. Unfortunately the cause of Cao's death has not been explained as of yet. We have to send away samples of tissue to a lab in Oklahoma for further testing. If we get an explanation we make sure to let you know. Thank you for everything, your thoughtfulness will never be forgotten.

Thank you

/s/Keith

In Loving Memory of

K-9 CARO

September 30, 1992 - December 28, 2001

OFFICER KEVIN MELCHIOR
AND POLICE K-9 CARO

Partner: Patrol Officer Kevin Melchior
St. Louis Metropolitan Police Dept.
St. Louis, MO
314 .444-5524

TRIBUTE TO CARO

On December 28, 2001, retired St. Louis Metropolitan Police K-9 "Caro" was put to sleep. Caro was taken to the vet because he had not eaten for two days but everything else seemed normal. During the examination the Vet felt a mass in Caro stomach area. It was decided to do exploratory surgery.

During the surgery both of Caro's kidneys were tumors the size of cantaloupes. Because nothing could be done to keep Caro in the quality of life that he was used to, he was put to sleep.

Caro was a Police K-9 until September of 2000, when his handler P.O. Kevin Melchior was transferred from the K-9 section. P.O. Kevin Melchior handled Caro from September 1993 until September 2000. When Caro was retired, Kevin and Linda Melchior purchased him so he could become their pet. But he wasn't a pet, Officer Melchior could not let Caro see him in his uniform because Caro would get extremely excited and try and find his police car, to go to work.

K-9 Caro was one of the most decorated Police Dogs that the St. Louis Metropolitan Police Department has ever had. He received numerous awards from the United States Police K-9 Association, The German Shepherd Dog Club, and The Human Society for both his work on the street and during dog trials. Caro was the only 3 time Champion of the USPCA Region 16, Field Trials. Throughout his career Caro conducted numerous K-9 demonstrations to thousands of people. He truly loved doing these and then letting the people pet him afterwards. Caro could not resist giving the kids a kiss as they left.

Caro you were one of the best, you did almost everything that I ever wanted you to do, and did it with style and personality. You will be missed; not only because you were my best partner, or that you were a great Police Dog, but also because you were my best friend.

POLICE K-9 CARD
Breed: German Shepherd
Color: Dark Sable   Weight: 82 lb.
DOB: Sept. 30, 1992 Birth Place: Hungary
Graduate K-9 School December 16, 1994
Dual Trained   Patrol/Narcotics
U.S.P.C.A. Region 16
"CHAMPION"
1996, 1997, 1998
USPCA Certified PD1   1995, 1996, 1997, 1998
USPCA Nationally Certified PD1, 1995, 1996, 1998
USPCA Nationally Certified Narcotics Detector   1998
USPCA   Regional 16's Narcotics
Find of the Year 1995 1996

Handler, Officer Kevin Melchior
Police Officer   February 25, 1980
K-9 Handler   April 27, 1987
Police Dog Trainer   June 28, 1991
Member of
USPCA NAPWDA DAD/DAC MPCA

In Loving Memory of

K-9 CHASE

December 31, 2001

Partner: Patrol Officer Robert Gooding
City of Beacon Police Department
1 Municipal Center
Beacon, NY 12508
845.838-5000

Beacon is a small river city along the Hudson River, about half way between New York City and Albany. Beacon is five square miles with a population of approx. 15,000. Our department has 38 officers, and currently there are four K-9 teams working. They are trained in routine patrol methods, suspect tracking, and narcotic identification.

Chase was with the department from 1989 to 1996. I was not his original handler in the department. I worked Chase from 1993 to his retirement in 1996. He was retired when I was out on a job related injury. He will always be remembered.

In Loving Memory of

K-9 CHIEF

October 8, 2001

Partner: Sgt. Julie Hoffman
Topeka Police Department
320 South Kansas St.
Topeka, KS 66603
785.368-9551

This morning at 1:30 A.M. my partner since 1994, Chief, died in my arms after a long battle with cancer. I never knew being a K-9 handler could be so painful, but losing a partner and best friend is beyond words. God, I know there are no criminals in Heaven, but please make sure Chief has a place to play.

God speed Chief.

My partner, my love, and my heart have gone to the angels.

Sgt. Julie Hoffman and Angel K-9 Chief

Officer Hoffman has been on the department since 1983. Chief has been in the department since 1994. Chief was one of the oldest working police dogs. Julie is formerly from Elizabeth, NJ.

In Loving Memory of

K-9 CIRO

AKA; CIRO DE-LUXE
Born: May 15, 1995
Died: December 16, 2001

Partner: Officer Howard Knauf
Melbourne Police Dept.
650 N Apollo Blvd.
Melbourne, Florida 32935
321.259-1211

Proud servant of the Melbourne Police Department in Melbourne, Florida from February 1997 to June 2001. A patrol dog crossed trained for drug detection. He lived to work for his partner, Officer Howard Knauf. Ciro was retired in June of 2001 when he suffered a broken leg during training. The bone never healed strong enough so that he could continue his service without physical impairment or risk of further serious injury. Ciro was the ball craziest dog I have ever seen. This is what made him a fantastic drug dog but unfortunately played a major role in his death. He would destroy the average toy within half an hour and was only allowed to have a solid 3 inch rubber ball for a toy. He would literally spend an entire 10 hour shift chewing this ball nonstop. Any waking moment he could be found gnawing at this thing and he was never without it. One day Ciro got hold of a kong which was left unattended by my new partner and he chewed the top off of it and swallowed it. When the toy became lodged in his intestine he became ill and numerous trips to the vet didn't reveal the problem until his intestine ruptured. Ciro died on the operating table. Ciro's life as a working police K-9 was as colorful as they come.

In over 4 years of police service he was called to duty on 522 separate occasions. 53 of those resulted in apprehensions. Although our city is not considered a Mecca of drug smuggling, his two largest drug finds were 2 kilo's of cocaine and almost 50 pounds of marijuana. Ciro was to be considered all business at all times, even at home, but this did not preclude him from being a loving member of the family by my wife and children. When Ciro was forced to retire I felt that my family was in great hands and I never worried about their safety as long as he was home with them. Ciro only weighed 74 pounds but he had a huge heart and was fearless. He proved this to me as my partner when he took down a 300 pound bad guy on one occasion and later, when he was beaten by another criminal during a physical apprehension, never letting go, before I could come to his aid. When a K-9 handler tells you that he puts his life in the hands of his partner, this is what he is talking about. A courageous, fearless and fierce partner that puts his life on the line for his owner/handler. Ciro's pet peeves were handcuffs, velcro and anyone trying to take his picture. His personality was that if he wanted to play, you WILL play. He is sorely missed by myself, my family and all that knew him. My friends and fellow dog handlers keep his memory alive by reliving his antics and speaking of him often.

To let you know how good Ciro was with drug detection....every one of our narcotics detectives would request

Ciro before any other K-9. If Ciro said there was dope, then there was dope. He had a great reputation within the whole county. God Bless You CIRO. I am honored that you would put my Ciro in your book.

UPDATE:

I am still a dog handler with Melbourne Police Department and will continue to do so until I retire in 13 more years. It is the best job in the whole dang place..I love it! My current partner is named ROSCOE.

In Loving Memory of

K-9 CIROS

October 15, 2001

Partner: Trooper Mike Fiore
Massachusetts State Police
Special Operations K-9
MSP Stoneham Barracks, 166 Pont St.
Stoneham, MA 02180
781.279-1283

From Sgt. Robert McCarthy, Eastern MA Supervisor of MA State Police Special Operations K-9 Unit: I have some sad news concerning Ciros. Last week, Mike and Ciros were involved in a pursuit of bad guys that ended in New Hampshire. The chase ended in a car accident involving Mike and Ciros.

Ciros sustained back injuries that were deemed inoperable, leaving Mike with the heartbreaking decision of having to put his partner to sleep. Mike put Ciros down on Monday. He is now searching for a replacement, but no dog will ever fill Ciros' collar.

An example of K-9 Ciros' work

Trooper Mike Fiore and K-9 Ciros did a bang up job on a day shift recently in Malden. A robbery suspect was doing a fine job of eluding the police in the area of Rt. 99. The suspect would be seen running and then seek cover, until flushed, and the process would start all over. When Ciros got involved in this ordeal, the suspect decided he would be safer hiding in a house. The police surrounded the house and Ciros was put on a building search. After a few minutes, the suspect was located hiding in a corner, with a Rottweiler on his chest. One in custody for Malden Police Department for a host of charges.

Trooper Fiore and Ciros were then summonsed back to the scene by the Malden detectives. Ever the good cop, Trooper Fiore knew he had to connect several pieces of this puzzle. The detectives had a victim, and a suspect, but they still needed assistance looking for the implements of the crime.

Mike and Ciros backtracked their route during the earlier pursuit. A knife, duct tape, hat, mask and gloves were all located and submitted as evidence.

K-9 Ciros will be fondly remembered as a loving 'leaner' when you patted him, he leaned his whole being onto you what an affectionate being!

Note from Officer Fiore:

I want to thank you so much for the Memorial Cards for Ciros. The Guardians of the Night Poem says it all. Many of us have lost pets that are very dear to us and hold fond memories of them.

The loss of a K-9 partner hits you two fold. During the off hours spent at home with family and friends they are pets, social butterflies seeking attention and love of family. During the work hours they are the point man using their hunting skills to locate and apprehend criminal suspects that are dangerous threats to searching officers.

Ciros has been my Hero many times searching woodlands and vacant buildings for those that have committed criminal acts against others. He truly was a champion in his K-9 work and his ability to socialize with everyone. He will be sorely missed and I will hold onto the great memories of him as a partner, a friend and great listener.

Many folks have seen the memorial cards and thought they were a nice tribute to him. Everyone that has read the poem has shed a tear or two. I have also viewed the website and you are doing an awesome job of letting others know the true heroes our four legged partners are. I have posted your web address at work for others to view. Keep up the great work and thank you very for giving Ciros a space on your site.

 Thanks Much,
 /s/ Mike Fiore
 Mass. State Police K-9 Section

In Loving Memory of

K-9 CYR

February 19, 1996 - May 20, 2001

Partner: Constable Steve Kaye
Saskatoon Police Service
P.O. Box 1728
Saskatoon Sk S7K 3R6 Canada

Police Service Dog CYR was born on February 19, 1996. His partner and friend was Constable Steve Kaye. Kaye and Cyr had worked together protecting the citizens of Saskatoon since April 1998.

On May 21, 2001, members of the Saskatoon Police Service were attempting to effect an arrest on firearms related matters when the suspect fled the area in a truck. A chase ensued which ended on Highway 41. The male suspect exited his vehicle discharging shots into the air and was commanded by police several times to drop his weapon. In an attempt to disarm and subdue the subject Police Service Dog CYR was commanded to attack.

Cyr took on the challenge of subduing the subject without hesitation as he had done a million times before. He did it because he was asked to. He did it to protect his partner and the community. There was no fear...only determination...to do what was right.

The subject discharged his weapon killing Police Service Dog CYR. Cyr died instantly, and at that moment we lost a colleague, a partner, a friend and a police officer. Cyr, for your courage and strength we remember you. You have paid the ultimate price to protect us. We will never forget you.

A memorial service for Saskatoon Police Service Dog "Cyr" will be held Thursday, May 31, 7:00 p.m. at the Francis Morrison Library Auditorium. This is a private memorial for Police Members and family. Media representatives will not be allowed access to the auditorium.

UPDATES:

May 29, 2001 Police Acquire Grandson of Slain Dog.

In Sherwood Park, Alberta at 11:00 a.m., May 30, 2001, Constable Steve Kaye of the Saskatoon Police Service will receive a young dog named "Blue" for training as a police dog. Blue is the grandson of Cyr, Constable Kaye's slain K-9 partner.

Kaye describes Blue as a clone of Cyr and added that the young dog has tremendous potential to succeed as a police dog. Blue has been living with a foster family, the Robinsons at 8 Gilmore Avenue in Sherwood Park. Paul's son Garret Robinson has been Blue's caregiver. Garret will present Blue to Constable Kaye.

Blue was owned by Heartridge Training Academy in Sherwood Park, Alberta. Peg O'Neill of Heart ridge knows how difficult it is for a child to relinquish foster-ship of a dog, her daughter had been prime care giver to Cyr before he became a member of the Saskatoon Police K-9 Unit. Heart ridge will be supplying Garret with a new K-9 companion.

Nov. 2002

I have a new partner, but not without a bunch of more heart aches. I originally had a long haired male named ROCKY who was a wonderful powder keg of excitement and enthusiasm. He was coming to terms with being the number two creature on the planet. After five days of training, he keeled over from a heart attack.

Not good for my little guys to see Dad doing CPR on another dog, only weeks after Cyr passed away. Despite everyone's best efforts, Rocky passed away also.

That was the day I damn near said, "Enough of this, my kids don't need this roller coaster ride anymore than I do."

After much thought I agreed to look at another guy, JAGO. I have been together with JAGO ever since. He is a big male who loves his dad and a few others. He is an amazing tracking dog with a huge heart that he pours into everything we tackle.

"Forever Watchful"
In Memoriam Police Service Dog Cyr

My eyes are your eyes,
To watch and protect you and yours.
My ears are your ears,
To hear and detect evil minds in the dark.
My nose is your nose,
To scent the invader of your domain.
And so you may live,
My life is also yours.

In Loving Memory of

K-9 CYRO

1993 - May 27, 2001

Partner: Chief Deputy Vernon Brown
Wayne County Sheriff Department
Iowa
641.872-1566

Cyro was born in Holland, in 1993 and came to America in 1995. He began as a corrections officer from June to Dec. 1996. Mark Beauregard became his handler. In 1997 Jim Olson became his handler for the Marion County Sheriff's Department.

In 1999 Cyro began to work for Wayne County with Deputy Vernon Brown and stayed until his death. He was a talented dog and a dedicated police officer.

He loved to work and live with Vernon, a match made in heaven. He wanted to be with Vernon, no matter what he was doing. He wasn't happy staying home from work with the house dog, Missy, a German Shorthaired Pointer.

He loved to ride in the patrol car and bark which intimidated many people. Inside he was a puppy who loved his toys and chew rawhides. He had a great nose for drugs. His talent will be missed, but the love he gave everyone will be missed most of all.

We love and miss him very much.

He had an official funeral service, with speakers, music and honor guards and was laid to rest in a ceremony that included soft music, a few poems and kind words from a Methodist minister.

Several people, including officers from other counties who brought their own police dogs, gathered in the yard behind the sheriff's office in Corydon for a memorial service to the 8 year old German Shepherd that died of cancer. "Cyro was faithful and true to the last beat of his heart."

He helped deputies sniff out drug dealers and drug stashes and chase criminals. On occasion, he worked on interstate highways helping officers and state troopers go through vehicles suspected of carrying drugs. "He could find even the smallest amounts," said Vernon Brown, his handler and chief Wayne County deputy. But, it was Cyro's friendliness with children, his unwavering will to work, his gentle personality that made him popular, according to Brown. "He was special," said Brown. The dog was buried in the yard, Brown said there will be a marker placed at the site.

UPDATE:

Deputy Brown is looking for another K-9 not replace Cyro, but to love and work with. Received a wonderful email from Lori Brown, sister to Vernon to say that the cards were received and appreciated.

Vernon is using a K-9 that used to be a prison dog trained in everything. We have a friend who retired from Oakdale prison system in Oakdale, Iowa. She has moved to Wayne County and we are using her dog, Araas, and we love him. Although we continue to miss Cyro, like mad!

In Loving Memory of

K-9 DEKE

February 21, 2001

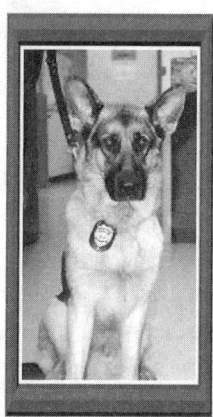

Partner: Office Russell Douglass
Laurel Police Department
Laurel, MS 39367

The accident occurred on February 21, 2001. I was in route home at 05:30 AM. The fog was very dense. A log truck "with no logs" had pulled onto the road and had no trailer lights working. I did not see the truck until seconds before the impact. The pole of the truck came though the front window of my personal car and though the plastic kennel that Deke was in and though the back glass then lodging in the trunk.

When I came to, the log truck had moved and continued leaving the scene of the accident. I immediately began looking for my partner. The rear passenger door of my car was open and the kennel was shredded. My partner was gone. I called out, but it was no use. He would not respond. I attempted to get out of the car, but I was trapped in the front seat.

Two young men on their way to work stopped to help and stayed with me until the fire rescue arrived. The guys from my shift began to arrive and started a search for Deke. Later at the hospital in the ER, I was informed by another K-9 handler that Deke was found across the road at the nearest house to the accident scene. I was then told that Deke was dead. I was crushed. I was saved and my partner had been killed.

I believe that Deke was trying to get help for me because, he seemed to be heading to a house close to the accident. It is hard and thank you for sympathy. I returned to light duty a month later as I had only minor injuries. I have a new partner Rex. Thank you again.

In Loving Memory of

K-9 DOC

November 7, 2001

Partner: Detective Ed Roman
Cuyahoga County Sheriff's Department
Narcotic Unit
1215 W. Third St.
Cleveland, Ohio 44113
216.443-6000

Doc was a really good dog, he made me look good. Doc and his good buddy, Marlie, a black lab who is trained for narcotics only were friends.. Marlie's handler, Dave and I are partners in the Narcotic unit.

A little about Doc:

He was in service for our department from June 15, 1995 until a sudden illness of kidney failure. He passed away on Wednesday, November 7, 2001. He was both patrol and narcotics certified through NAPWDA and the State of Ohio. He would have been eight years old on January 1, 2002.

We have two GSD females right now, just pets, but I will get another K-9 like Doc, after this giant hole in my heart is healed.

UPDATE: K-9 Sabre is helping fill that empty hole in Ed's heart. He is a Belgian Malinois.

In Loving Memory of

K-9 DRAKE

LODD
July 16, 2001

Partner: Deputy John Palermo
Harris County Sheriff's Department
1301 Franklin St.
Houston, TX 77002
713.450-1623

The Harris County Sheriff's Department has changed its K-9 units policy after the death last month of a drug sniffing dog left in an air conditioned vehicle. LT. Ricky Williams of the Harris County Organized Crime and Narcotics Task Force said Monday that dogs can no longer be left alone in a vehicle for more than 10 minutes.

The policy change comes after a black Labrador retriever named Drake died last month while his handler was attending a mandatory training session. At the time of Drake's death, department policy allowed deputies to keep their dogs in air conditioned vehicles while they attended court, training sessions and other functions where the dog was not needed. Until we figure out what happened to Drake, we have changed the policy.

On July 16, Drake's handler, Deputy John Palermo, attended a required street survival training session at a church near Katy, Williams said. The day was hot and humid, and Palermo did not want to leave Drake in a kennel all day at his home. Instead, he brought the dog, which the county paid $5,000 for, to the session and left him in an air conditioned Chevrolet Tahoe. He checked on the dog at every break At 11 a.m., the dog was fine. At noon, he was dead.

Palermo was devastated. An autopsy report on the cause of Drake's death is not complete. At first it was thought the dog died from poisoning, but that has since been ruled out. Drake, who was almost 2 years old, had been with the department for about 5 months.

In Loving Memory of

K-9 DUTCH

LODD
September 13, 2001

Partner: Officer David Sawlaw
Rantoul Police Department
109 E. Grove Ave.
Rantoul, IL 61866
217.892-2103

On September 13, 2001 at approximately 2200 hours Dutch, a Dutch Malinois, died in the line of duty working as a K-9 for the Rantoul, Illinois Police Department. Dutch had 6 years of service and over 1000 drug seizures for the Village of Rantoul. While searching a three story building for a burglary suspect, Dutch fell off the roof. According to officers present, Dutch and his handler K-9 Officer Dave Sawlaw were clearing the building.

Apparently Dutch heard a noise on the roof and ran out a door leading to the roof. As his handler gave the command for him to stop Dutch had already leaped 15 feet away from the building and off the roof, falling three floors. A nearby ambulance crew responded and transported Dutch to Heritage Animal Hospital, Champagne, IL, where he was pronounced dead.

Memorial service was held Thursday, September 20, 2001.

Black ribbons draped the walls of the Rantoul Police Department on Monday to honor Dutch, a dog that assisted with 957 drug arrests, tracked down 27 suspects, and helped with the seizure of more than $150,000 in cash and 23 vehicles over the last six years, according to police records. Dutch died late Thursday when Rantoul police responded to a burglary in progress at White Hall, 801 Commerce Drive. White Hall had been the largest building owned by the military until the construction of the Pentagon. According to a police report, officers from Rantoul, Ludlow, Thomasboro, Fisher and Gifford helped to secure the 500,000 square foot building while a K-9 team searched for the intruders.

During a search of the three story building, Dutch gave chase to apparent intruders on the roof before he fell into an open courtyard inside the building. Police Chief Paul Dollins has said that he will ask the village board to spend up to $6,000 to buy a new police dog. Mayor Neal Williams said he wholeheartedly supports Dollins' request and would put it on the agenda for the Oct. 2 village board meeting.

Chief Dollins has said he would give Officer David Sawlaw, who was Dutch's handler, full discretion in choosing a new police dog. "He's going to have to live with the dog and work with the dog, so he should have the most expertise as to the kind of dog that would be best,"

Rantoul has a second police dog named Rocket that works with Officer Jim Sullivan.

UPDATE:

We made a trip to Texas on Friday and Saturday to look for Dave a new dog. We found one in Springfield, Illinois. So Dave has a new partner to train. I think it is helping him get through this.

Thanks again.

/s/ Officer Jim Sullivan

In Loving Memory of

K-9 ELLIOTT

December 21, 2001

Partner: Officer Stephen Piersa
City of Hartford Police Department
50 Jennings Rd.
Hartford, CT 06120
860.527-6300

This is Elliott. I was his partner for almost six years. I deeply regret to inform all that Elliott was put to rest today, the 21st of December 2001, after a brief illness.

He was a gentle giant to all, except for those who turned up their noses to the law and sought to commit crimes against society. Elliott especially loved children, visiting schools, public events of all kinds and social visits to a children's hospital to make the sick smile, even if just for awhile.

I was and still am very proud to have served alongside my trusted and faithful partner, Elliott, who not only protected me, but every single citizen, with every breath he gave. He will truly be missed by me and my loving family.

Elliott's many memories will never fade from my heart. He will never be replaced. For thousands of years, we have bestowed titles, laurels and praise upon the "warriors" that have protected our homelands. From ancient Rome; where the conquering General was proceeded into the Senate by flower girls covering his path with rose petals, to our Generals of today, that are given ticker tape parades as they return victorious from battle or conflict. As a nation, we tend to place the symbols of peace upon the head of the warrior, as we blindly turn our heads from the true peace makers of the world that walk among us every day. We look but never see those that protect and serve unless we become the victim. They ask for little, but give so much. It is said that a man has no greater love, than to give his life for another. This is so true for the police K-9.

So here today, I attempt to honor and pay tribute to my hero, who has given us his service and his love, through injuries and pain without complaint. Elliott was a true champion! I will always love you Elliott!

In Loving Memory of

K-9 ENZO

March 2001

Partner: Officer James Harlow, Ret.
Christian County Police Dept.
501 S. Main St.
Hopkinsville, KY 42240 2319
502 887 4135

Enzo, the city's first police dog, has died of complications of age and years of hard work. Many who knew this strong and intelligent animal will not forget him; most of all, the man who was his handler and who loved him until the day he died has the most memories, and it's those memories which are now helping him handle the death of his dog at age 12, old for a dog and especially for a working dog.

Enzo came from Germany to Hopkinsville, and city police officer Jim Harlow became his handler when the dog was about 3 years old. Both Harlow and Enzo retired in 1996, and the dog has made his home with Harlow since that time. He built him about an acre chain link pen with an air-conditioned dog-house. But Enzo spent most of his time in the house with Jim.

For about a year Enzo was having trouble getting up and down. He was in pain and was receiving pain killers and corti-sone shots, but it got so bad he couldn't get up at all. His heart was almost gone, so he had to be put down.

Harlow and another retired policeman buried Enzo in his yard on a hill under a tree, and had a little ceremony. Now only Meeka remains to fill the empty place at the Harlow home. Meeka is Enzo's daughter. Jim Harlow is really worried about her. She's always been with Enzo and doesn't understand where he is. She keeps looking for him, and she is grieving. Jim is spending a lot of time with her, and bought her about $20 worth of new toys, but still she grieves. If she doesn't do better, he plans to go out to the pound and get another dog for her to play with.

Among the many who have good memories of Enzo are some of the people at the New Era. Harlow used to occasional-ly bring the dog in to visit at the paper, and he would go around visiting with different ones. He especially liked the women and would lay his head in their LAP to be petted, with some he'd crawl in their lap to be loved and to love back.

When the visits were over, Harlow would open the front door, and the dog would almost fly through it and into the back seat of the police cruiser. He was instantly on duty again and ready to work. It was at that point that the loving nature switched instantly to police dog, and some of the people who had just petted him would touch the window of the car and be greeted with snarls and growls.

He was such a good dog, he never really hurt anyone, but he did such a good job. Just his presence made such a differ-ence. He took good care of Harlow and he tried to take good care of Enzo.

Many people still remember him, and I have been constant-ly asked about how he is doing. It is so hard to tell people he's gone. Explaining that he had hundreds of letters from school children, Harlow said many still remember him from when he would take the animal to the schools for law enforcement demonstrations.

Enzo touched a lot of people, he had an excellent record, he was a good dog, a great tracker, he found lost children, and he was my protector. He had a good life, and now we must celebrate that life and live with those good memories.

In Loving Memory of

K-9 Exe von Baphomet

November 18, 2001

Partner: Hartmut Hauser
Trainer
Bavarian village near Munich Germany

A long worse time has passed since we have heard from each other. There was the most horrific day of September 11, 2001. There was nothing in me which I could say or write because I don't find words for this evil day.

Yesterday another beloved K-9 entered the Rainbow Bridge to wait for me on this very special day. Pia & Exe, the little black one from Gaby were fighting. Pia destroyed the arteria right at the right side at Exe's' throat. There was nothing I could do .

We tried to reanimate her with heart pressure and breathing her in the nose, but after all, it was useless. She bled to death within a few minutes. Gaby was with me when I put her to the last rest in my Garden. I honored her with that very special trumpet solo that they play when heroes are buried. I do not know the name, but maybe you know what I mean and will tell me the title.

Well, should close, cause tears are running over my face again.

/s/Hartmut

Previously

I live in a small upper Bavarian village near Munich. Finding your link, "Feelings" and reading them was one thing. Congratulations.

There is no better way to tell about the loss of a beloved partner. I know this very well because I lost 4 beloved friends during the last twenty five years. All of them have been GSD (German Shepherd Dogs). The last one was "Rex" and it was also the most worst loss. He died with his head on my chest while I was sleeping after night shift.

Pia is the Mother of both Aicka and Bax. Aicka is the half sister of Bax. They are out of the Kennel of Gaby Ramoser.

In Loving Memory of

K-9 FALK Von BATU

June 11, 2001

Partner: Officer Bruce Bertram
Danbury Police Department
120 Main St.
Danbury, CT 06816
203.797-4611

K-9 Falk was imported from German as an untrained dog in 1989, and joined the Danbury K-9 Unit on January, 1990. K-9 Falk was trained by his handler, Officer Bruce Bertram. K-9 Falk was the first recipient of the prestigious Daniel Wasson Memorial K-9 Award. He was also awarded Danbury Police Department's highest award, The Medal Of Valor, among many other medals and awards.

K-9 Falk, after being trained as a dual purpose K-9, was credited with making many hundreds of arrests, both in general patrol work and in narcotics and also the recovery of thousands of dollars in stolen property. In 1992 while searching for a shooting suspect, K-9 Falk was shot through the neck by the suspect at the start of a gun battle between Officer Bertram and the suspect. Despite the severe wound K-9 Falk continued to function as an outstanding police dog and was credited with saving the lives of five officers including his handler. K-9 Falk returned to active duty seven months later and continued to served Danbury's K-9 Unit until he was retired in 1996.

On K-9 Falk's last day of work before retirement, he responded to a call for assistance from Ridgefield Police Department to search a large building for a burglar hiding inside. K-9 Falk located the suspect and physically apprehended him. The Ridgefield Officers stated that they were proud to be able to give K-9 Falk a retirement dinner. After getting used to civilian life K-9 Falk enjoyed retired life in the home of his handler.

K-9 Falk passed away at home in June of 2001 after suffering a stroke. Plans are being made for a police memorial service for K-9 Falk at the Danbury Police Department where his ashes will be buried. The expected date will be Police Memorial Day in May of 2002.

AWARDS
Medal of Valor Award
Daniel Wasson Memorial Award, plus others

In Loving Memory of

K-9 FERRO

vom Sickenger Moorwerk
LODD
December 14, 2001

Partners: Deputy Greg Premo
Deputy John Reding

Pierce County Sheriff's Dept.
930 Tacoma Ave. South
Tacoma, WA
98402
Pierce County Sheriff's Dept.
K-9 East Precinct
271 John Banaola Way East
Puyullup, WA 98373

As Pierce County sheriff's deputy, John Reding toiled with paperwork late Wednesday, he listened on the scanner as his former partner chased after a suspect. He could tell Ferro was excited by the yip in the 5 year old German Shepherd's bark. "He gets so jacked up in the cars," said Reding, who was Ferro's handler until three weeks ago when he transferred out of the department's K-9 unit. "I got to know his yip after almost five years."

Suddenly, a voice screamed over the radio. Another deputy's patrol car had accidentally hit Ferro in Parkland while he chased a fleeing man across Pacific Avenue South near 112th Street East. Reding dropped what he was doing and rushed to be with his friend. Two hours later, Ferro died in Reding's arms, but not before Reding stroked him and whispered into his ear.

"It made me feel like something happened to one of my children," a sorrowful Reding, the married father of three girls, said Friday. "You go through so much with that darn dog that the bond is unbelievable." Reding has been a dog handler for four years.

Ferro, a purebred from eastern Germany, was one of five Pierce County sheriff's dogs. He was the county's most famous crime fighter, man, woman or dog, having been featured several times on the TV show "COPS." He'd also recently survived a week lost in the Mount Baker Snoqualmie National Forest near Greenwater.

Ferro helped capture hundreds of criminals, including suspects in killings, kidnaping, rapes, burglaries and armed robberies. "That dog was amazing," Reding said. "He was a tough dog with a lot of heart, a lot of personality." Ferro lived for riding in the patrol car, but he also enjoyed hauling around large objects, playing tug of war and racing to fetch. And like most dogs, he loved to be petted. "He'd go to sleep in your arms just like he did the other night," Reding said. "He died at work and that's the way, if he had any human thoughts, I think he would have been happy doing, dying at work."

The department plans a public remembrance for Ferro on Thursday. He will be cremated and his ashes given to Reding, who is more saddened than upset at Ferro's death. When Reding transferred out of the K-9 unit he had wanted Ferro to step down as well, but another deputy needed the German Shepherd's help. "I wanted Ferro to retire also, that way he'd have a good, long life," Reding said. "But it was nice for the guys in patrol because they all loved Ferro."

Memorial Service

Once inside Covenant Celebration Church, several hundred people sat in attendance many of them police officers and K-9 handlers from around the Northwest. The Tacoma Scots Band played in Ferro's honor. Other K-9 dogs in attendance bore the pipes stoically, although none appeared terribly happy. "Ferro died doing what he did best, chasing bad guys," Maj. Tom Miner of the Pierce County Sheriff's Department told the audience. The dog boasted 152 misdemeanor and felony arrests, and successful tracks that led to the apprehension of dozens of other criminals. He and his handlers searched countless darkened buildings, fields and forests where other deputies could not safely go. Ferro captured a national audience after five appearances on the television show "Cops." Last summer, on camera, he managed to capture one bad guy who fired at deputies during a pursuit. He even endured his own trial in the wilderness in May, when he disappeared while chasing a suspected car thief in the rugged woods near Mount Rainier. During the chase, he became separated from his handler, John Reding. Despite a search by dozens of search and rescue workers and other tracking dogs, Ferro was missing for seven days. He was found in the same spot where he vanished, more than 20 pounds lighter. In a month, however, he was back on the job. "I kept him safe; he kept me safe," Reding said yesterday. "He had a lot of heart."

Ferro and Reding began their service together Jan. 1, 1998. During his off hours, Ferro lived with Reding, his wife, their three young daughters and a leggy blonde named Heide, another German Shepherd the family laughingly called Ferro's girlfriend.

But on Dec. 13, shortly after midnight, Ferro's luck ran out.

His new partner, Deputy Greg Premo, had stopped a man for speeding in a car with bad license plates. The man jumped out of the car and ran into a gas station. Ferro quickly sniffed him out and chased him across the street. That's when Ferro was struck by another patrol car coming to help. Deputies rushed him to an emergency veterinarian, who worked for two hours to try to save his life. Numerous deputies crowded into the animal hospital, first to hold a prayerful vigil for his recovery, then to mourn his passing.

Reding completed his tour of duty in the K-9 unit last fall, and Ferro was assigned to Premo. The two had only been together a few weeks at the time of Ferro's death. The two had already developed a strong bond, and Reding said Premo has profoundly apologized to him for Ferro's death. "I told him, 'Don't worry about it,'" Reding said. "It was something that just happened." Reding's three girls, ages 12, 10 and 8, are still grieving the loss of the dog they called their "baby boy."

Sympathy cards have flooded in from all over, even from police in New York, where officers surely have a more profound grief with which to deal. Yesterday's ceremony likely would have been unbearably solemn for a mischievous dog such as Ferro, who was 5 when he died. Around station houses, he delighted in shredding any stuffed animals he could find. He was especially merciless when it came to his nemesis, a stuffed monkey that hung from the ceiling in one precinct. For that creature, Ferro would uncoil an awesome vertical leap of almost 8 feet to bring the monkey down to earth.

"The dog just didn't want to quit," Sgt. Paul Schneider told those at the service. Mainstream religious wisdom has long debated whether animals have souls; many authoritative sources say they do not. But yesterday, from the grief written on the faces of those in attendance, to the tender way they stroked their own dogs, it was clear Ferro had gone to heaven. He is survived by his handlers and their families; his girlfriend, Heidi, and at least two litter-mates, Frankie and Felicia.

In Loving Memory of

K-9 FURLOW

July 3, 2001

Partner: Officer John Green
Montgomery County Police Headquarters
2350 Research Blvd.
Rockville, MD 20850
240-773.5000

This K-9 unit was established in 1961, it is made up of 13 officers and 17 dogs. Since 1961, 91 dogs have served in this unit. The county uses a variety of breeds, including German Shepherds, Labrador retrievers, Malinois and Bloodhounds.

The dogs get yearly physicals with a contracted veterinarian. They are fed high protein diets supplied by the country. They live with their handlers and are a part of the handler's family. Once the dogs are retired, they stay on as pets with their handler and family.

In Loving Memory of

K-9 GIT ANDER

LODD
September 26, 2001

Partner: Sgt. John Gillespie
Union County Sheriff
10 Elizabethtown Plaza
Elizabeth, NJ 07207
908.273-6064

In German, Git Ander means Get Under
(K-9-GIT in on cover of this book)

A police dog that searched for survivors in the rubble of the World Trade Center was shot to death by two Plainfield officers who mistook it for a vicious stray attacking a young suspect. Git Ander, a 7 year old German Shepherd that served with the Union County Sheriff's Office, was killed Wednesday by officers Ronald Fusco and Craig Montgomery.

The incident began around 7 p.m., when Git Ander's handler, Sgt. John Gillespie, and several other area officers were pursuing a car that had been reported stolen. When Gillespie saw some suspects bolt from the car, he chased after the driver while Git Ander, who had a sheriff's badge on his collar, went after and subdued a 12 year old girl, who ran in the opposite direction. When they arrived a short time later, Fusco and Montgomery thought the dog was a stray and tried to pry it off the girl's leg.

When the dog bit Fusco, the officers shot it 11 times. Gillespie, who had apprehended the driver, arrived on the scene as his dog was dying. Union County Sheriff Ralph Froehlich said the dog performed as it had been trained when it subdued the suspect. Froehlich said Git Ander turned on Fusco because he tried to separate the animal from the girl, a command that can be given only by the handler.

No charges have been filed in the shooting, but it is under investigation by Union County Prosecutor Thomas V. Manahan because it involved police use of deadly force.

Neither the girl nor the officers were seriously injured. The driver of the car, Brian Tinsley, 18, was charged with possession of a stolen car and eluding police. The girl and another passenger, a 17 year old male, were also arrested.

The Union County Sheriff's Department K-9 Unit, commanded by Sergeant John Gillespie and Sergeant Ronald Malcolm, is a special branch of the Search and Rescue Unit of Union County. Since its inception in 1983, the K-9 unit has been commended for its expertise in searching for missing persons or fleeing felons, evidentiary searches of burglarized buildings and arson scenes, narcotics detection, bomb and weapons searches and crowd control. The unit is also involved in community relations work and gives demonstrations to schools.

Git Ander, World Trade Center Hero - Killed In the line of duty.

After searching for survivors in the rubble of the World Trade Center, Git Ander, a seven year old German Shepherd returned to duty as a police K-9 in Plainfield, New Jersey. Git

Ander was a member of the Union County Sheriff's Department K-9 Unit.

According to an Associated Press report, on the night of September 26, 2001, Git Ander and his handler, Sergeant John Gillespie, arrived at the scene of a reported stolen car. The suspects fled on foot. Sergeant Gillespie pursued the eighteen year old driver while Git Ander was ordered to chase after and apprehend the other passenger who was a twelve year old girl. Git Ander apprehended the passenger. As he was trained to do, Git Ander held onto the suspect by holding onto her leg. The dog had been trained not to release his hold on the suspect until his handler arrived on the scene and commanded him to do so.

Minutes before his handler showed up, two other police officers arrived on the scene. Despite the fact that Git Ander wore a police badge on his collar, Officers Ronald Fusco and Craig Montgomery fatally shot the dog eleven times. Sgt. Gillespie arrived just as his dog was dying. Officers Ronald Fusco and Craig Montgomery later alleged that they thought the dog was a stray.

Sheriff Froehlich of the Union County Sheriff's Department explained that the dog had been trained not to separate from the suspect until a command from his handler was given. Even in the face of repeated gunfire, the dog faithfully followed his handler's commands. "Unfortunately, Git gave his life doing what he was supposed to," said Sheriff Froehlich. He added that, "He was our most popular dog because he was so easy to deal with. "The kids loved him because he was this big hairy thing they could throw their arms around and hug." The well known Union County Sheriff's Department K-9 Unit has been highly commended and is well recognized. Git Ander and other K-9s from the unit arrived at the World Trade Center two hours after the attack on September 11, 2001.

The heroism of Git Ander has gone unrecognized. Officers Ronald Fusco and Craig Montgomery looked at him as a stray and shot him to death while the dog was conducting official police duty.

Git Ander, a heroic K-9 police officer was gunned down for following orders. He deserved respect from his fellow officers. Eleven shots within minutes is an uncalled for act of excessive, deadly force, even if the victim hadn't been a hero and was just a stray. The unharmed twelve year old suspect was later arrested.

No charges had been filed against the two officers who shot Git Ander to death.

UPDATE:

Despite clear and convincing evidence, Union County prosecutor, Thomas V. Manahan did not file any charges whatsoever against Plainfield Officers Montgomery & Fusco who recklessly and needlessly shot to death K-9 Git Ander.

Despite the attempts of the police and prosecutor's office to withhold from the public a police videotape which showed the incident, NJ News 12 obtained a copy of it and extensively analyzed it. What was revealed on the videotape was even more shocking than previous reports of the shooting. News 12 reported that Officers Montgomery and Fusco fired a total of 18 shots at Git Ander at point blank range. The 18 consecutive shots can be clearly heard on the videotape.

In addition to Git Ander wearing his police badge, the Union County K-9 Police Van which was clearly marked and visible was parked less than 10 ft. away from the spot where the officers gunned down Git Ander.

Within seconds of the shooting, Sgt. John Gillespie arrived on the scene and attempted to talk to Officer Montgomery when he saw Git Ander on the ground dying. The videotape clearly showed Officer Montgomery lashing out and forcibly and physically knocking Sgt. John Gillespie down to the ground.

Even before the investigation had been concluded, prosecutor Manahan publicly defended these officers. Union county prosecutor Manahan closed the case and stated that the Plainfield police officers were justified in shooting Git Ander and he blamed Sgt. Gillespie for losing sight of his dog.

Plainfield Public Safety Director, Michael Lattimore, told News 12 NJ that he was pleased that his officers had been exonerated and the Plainfield police chief, Edward Santiago, supported his officers' shooting of Git Ander.

It is an outrage that the Union county prosecutor did not file charges against these officers. It is equally appalling that Plainfield police chief, Edward Santiago and Public Safety Director Michael Lattimore condoned their officers' conduct.

In Loving Memory of

K-9 HOOVER

April 25, 2001

Partner: Dan Davis
Salt Lake County SAR Official Search & Rescue Team
1632 Roosevelt Ave.
Salt Lake City, UT

On April 22, 2001, a very special dog named "Hoover" went to sleep for the last time. Over sixteen years old, Hoover had an extraordinary life and a very special human partner that made sure his last days were comfortable and full of love.

Hoover was adopted as a young pup at the Humane Society of Utah by Dan Davis. He was very quick to learn and Dan knew he had chosen a very special dog. They began training for search and rescue and soon Dan and Hoover were certified as a team by Salt Lake County Search and Rescue. The team also worked for Dear Valley Resort as Avalanche Rescue support.

Hoover's keen sense of smell and his intense love of humans led him to find eleven lost people. As if saving human lives wasn't enough, Hoover's gentle nature, rugged good looks, and intense desire to please made him a natural for the film 'Waste Utah" campaign in the early 90's and for his starring role as "Fuzz" in the movie "Little Heroes". Hoover has appeared in many other films and has made special appearances with two of Utah's Governors, several famous actors, and has even co hosted a KJZZ Movie Festival.

Hoover will be missed by many and remembered by anyone that was fortunate enough to meet him and see his big brown eyes and constantly wagging tail. Dan Davis asks that donations to the Humane Society of Utah be sent in memory of Hoover.

In Loving Memory of

K-9 IRON

April 30, 1997
Medal of Valor Awarded May 13, 2001
LODD

Partner: K-9 Officer James Losee
Norfolk Police Dept. VA
Police Administration Building
100 Brooke Ave. Norfolk, VA 23510

K-9 Officers Ron Godwin and James Losee were checking equipment and gathering keys one night last spring when they struck up a conversation, which turned to the subject of awards. Godwin was about to receive a commendation and wanted to see Losee's medal for a shootout in 1997. Losee had shot and killed a suspect who fired at him and his six year old Belgian malinois, Iron. The dog was gunned down.

After that night, the story mostly was recounted for investigators and the attention was all on Iron. That was fine with Losee, because Iron probably saved his life. The dog was buried with full police honors. His funeral drew widespread attention and was attended by K-9 officers from across the state and as far away as North Carolina.

His death inspired cards, letters and awards from across the country. His name was placed on a wall at the American Police Hall of Fame in Miami. But Iron and Losee were never officially recognized by the Norfolk Police Department. Losee didn't have a medal.

That's not right, Godwin thought. Something should be done. He would nominate Losee and Iron to the department's awards committee. But first, he wanted to hear the details. It would be four years before most of Losee's colleagues would hear the details of the running gun battle.

It took four days and several drafts before Godwin's nomination letter was perfect. A month later, he heard that the awards committee had voted unanimously on a medal of valor. Losee, who now patrols with a German Shepherd named ZAK, accepted his medal at a ceremony earlier this year. He also received a white and gold police cross for Iron, who is buried in Garden of the Pines Pet Cemetery on Salem Road in Virginia Beach. Lobo, a Norfolk police dog hit by a car in 1983, rests beside him.

Losee still insists that Iron was the hero that night. Godwin thinks Losee was, too.``It takes a lot of guts to stand there and fire back,'' Godwin said. ``I thought it was an extremely brave thing to do.''

UPDATE:

Note from Officer Losee.

Just a short note to let you know that K-9 Zak is now retired. His last evening on the street was Saturday. He served me for 4 great years and we made many arrests. He will now retire and is our home security K-9. I have a new dog named Jaymo. He is from the Netherlands. I think we will have a great career together also.

In Loving Memory of

K-9 IVAN

January 17, 1997
End Of Watch: March 1, 2001

Partner: Officer Hanspeter Merten
Sacramento Police Dept. K-9 Division
900   8th St.
Sacramento, CA 95814

The Sacramento police dog, K-9 Ivan, was injured Tuesday
when he fell from a second story building. He later died from
the injuries. The decorated dog was a two year police veteran.
K-9 Ivan was a four year old German Shepherd who had been
with the Department's K-9 unit for two years. He and his partner, Officer Hanspeter Merten, were credited with the arrest of
over 50 dangerous felons.

One of the more notable apprehensions was of three wanted felons at one location. The three felons were located hiding
at different locations, attic and bedrooms, and were wanted for
charges that included homicide, kidnaping, and parole viola-

tion. K-9 Ivan earned several awards at K-9 trial competitions during his two years with the department.

K-9 Ivan was an asset to the community he served and will be sorely missed by the Sacramento Police Department.

Memorial service was held March 7, 2001.

Ivan was bought by the Sacramento Police Department in November of 1998. He was born on January 17, 1997 in Czechoslovakia and brought to North Carolina in November of 1998. From the day Ivan got off the plane at the Sacramento airport he was an instant hit around the police department.

Ivan would let anyone play with him at work or at home. He loved it when people would throw his "Kong" toy for him to chase. Ivan quickly caught on to police work. He became fully certified in just under 8 weeks.

During his two years on the department he is credited with over 50 felony arrests and who knows how many people he stopped from running from the police or those who decided to surrender instead of meeting Ivan up close. Ivan was known throughout the city for his wolf like face and loud bark from the patrol vehicle. He always knew when he was at work and when it was time for play at home. It was like he had an on/off switch. Ivan became an important part of our family.

He went to the snow and came camping with my family. One day, Ivan and I decided that we were going to climb 10,000 ft. Mt. Tallac in the Lake Tahoe Basin. Ivan and I made it in just under 4 hours and we had a great view of the Sierra Nevada's from on top of the mountain. Ivan would go for daily walks or jogging down by the American River in Sacramento. He loved being outdoors and exploring new things.

Ivan was loved by everyone at the police department, in the community and especially his family, and he will be truly missed. I know Ivan will be waiting for me at the gates above us with a "Kong" in his mouth, waiting for me to throw it one more time. Once again thank you for all that you have done for my family. It is people like you who make this world a much better place.

In Loving Memory of

K-9 IZZY

1990   April 11, 2001

Partner: Det. Ed Stewart
Stowe Police Detective
Lamoille County Sheriff's Department
Hyde Park, VT

The identification card was signed with a tiny paw print because the card holder couldn't write. Izzy the police dog, who passed away last week after 11 years with Stowe Police Detective Ed Stewart, could do almost anything else. "If Izzy could drive, she wouldn't need me at all, I don't think we even scratched the surface of her capabilities."

Izzy was with Stewart from the time she was eight weeks old and had reached the equivalent of a doctorate in saving lives, finding people, sniffing out drugs and tracking criminals. Last week Izzy passed away after a short bout with a cancer. She was, perhaps, the best friend Ed Stewart has ever had, and a great friend to the community.

"Our last trip together was to New Hampshire to have her cremated," Stewart said. "And even then, she was there for a rescue. We drove by an accident and stopped, and were the first EMT on the scene. I had to reach over Izzy to get my rescue kit. It was like she was there even after she was gone."

Izzy came into Stewart's life after he, through the Stowe Hazardous Terrain team, had come into contact with the New England K-9 rescue group on some search and rescue operations. "I was so impressed with what they did, and their dogs did, that I wanted to join," he said. "Of course, first you have to have a dog."

Ben was Stewart's first dog, and partially trained when the Fidelco Guide Dog School called to offer him Izzy. "We went down to look at him, knowing I think that if we looked, he would be coming home," he said. What Ed and wife Judy found was a slightly undersized, but frenetic black German Shepherd named Izzy.

A year later Ben was given to a game warden, and Izzy, already certified to search by air scent, was well on her way to a career that would take her and Stewart all over the country, including a trip to the 1996 Olympic Games in Atlanta. "She's taken me a lot of places," Stewart said. "A lot of people who knew Izzy have no idea who I am. We were in an airport in Nashville and Dolly Parton came over and signed her rescue vest, she probably wouldn't have done that to me."

Since Izzy passed away Stewart has received dozens and dozens of e mails. "If they had heard that something had happened to Ed Stewart," he said, waiving a thick sheaf of copies of the e mails, "they probably wouldn't have known who I was, but Izzy..."

A few years ago Stewart started grooming a smallish black lab named Cinder as Izzy's replacement. "Izzy started training her about a year ago," Stewart says of the active black lab from Covered Bridge Kennels in Stowe. "When you are looking for a working dog you have to try to pick out the one that is the biggest pain in the neck, the most active, the most curious. The one that always has to be doing something."

Izzy eventually was certified for air search, tracking, drug detection, searching for bodies, searching for living persons under rubble and in disaster situations, and she pursued those activities all over the country. Stewart and Izzy found numerous lost people, saved a number of lives and found an incalculable amount of drugs. The team, highlighted by Izzy's calm presence, visited a number of schools and helped bridge the sometimes broad gap between the police and the community.

With dogs trained to operate in dangerous situations there is always the specter of a sudden and violent death, but Izzy survived all those situations. "The last few weeks she had lost a little bit of her spark," Stewart said. "We had taken her to the vet several times, but they couldn't find anything. Wednesday we were home with her and she passed away. With a dog like this you are always sending her into dangerous situations, so you're always a little prepared."

After 11 years of being together almost constantly, Izzy's absence is not easily replaced by Cinder's exuberance. "We are a team, and it's like any loss," Stewart said. "We flew maybe 70 or 80 thousand commercial miles together and many more in armed forces aircraft. We did 20 to 25 searches a year. But it was different because we were together almost 24 hours a day, there are few relationships like that."

In Loving Memory of

K-9 JACK

August 5, 2001

Partner: Charles Barnett
Unit 18 Midwest Search & Rescue
Moore, Oklahoma

HOW I BECAME INVOLVED WITH SEARCH & RESCUE

When I was a boy, I wanted to be a police officer. In 1984 I went to work for an investigation firm in Oklahoma City. I had a K-9 partner, "Shep" that I trained for the company. That same year, I was "let go" because of new state laws. In 1988, I went to college and received a degree in paralegal in 1990. While I was attending school, I met my wife, Krissie. We were married in December of 1990. I had to give up my partner, Shep who was donated to the Luther Sheriff's deputy. My wife felt sad for me and bought me a black lab, Samantha.

Over the next few years, we had a daughter. Krissie received her degree in nursing. I worked at night and was at home during the day. Sam would often go into the baby's room and look in the crib. As Molly, our daughter became older, Sam became very protective of her and would keep her out of mischief. Sam also was a very loving dog who liked everyone. In 1994 Sam became epileptic. We tried everything and spared no expense. I had her put down. I stayed there with her and made a promise that she would never be forgotten.

In 1994 I joined a group, Amateur Radio Emergency Services. On April 19, 1995, the Federal Building was blown up in Oklahoma city. Krissie and I were both called out to the scene. I could not believe what I was seeing. In 1998 I joined the Heartland Search and Rescue. A black lab puppy, Jack was donated to me by a family from Moore, OK. Over the next year or so, I trained him. On May 3, 1999 I was called out to help find victims in Moore. I had Jack with me. I don't know how many people we found. It seemed like it was one right after the other.

Jack was inducted into the "Oklahoma Veterinary Medical Association Pet Hall of Fame on January 22, 2000 for his work during the tornados. Soon after we joined MidWest SAR. In May Jack helped find a drowning victim. Molly, who is now 8 years old, helped in training Jack by hiding for me and others. That is where we came up with the support slogan for search and rescue, "Get Lost." I never became a police officer, but I have one heck of a partner. His big sister, "Sam" would be proud of him. Well, that is how I became involved with SAR. My parents live near us in Oklahoma City.

I never really went into the paralegal work, as I still work with my hands. I do commercial construction and maintenance. If I get called out for a search, I am one of the lucky ones who still gets paid for the day. All of my equipment is bought and paid for by me out of my own pocket. We have a 1978 GMC Jimmy that we use as a field car. It is equipped with 5 gallons of water, dog food, first aid kit, bed-roll, tent, fire extinguisher, food, television and all kinds of radio equipment, pick, shovel, rope for repelling and swift water rescue equipment. The truck is in the process of being repaired because I was a little too close to the tornado last year. That tornado had winds up to 318 MPH, killed 40 people and left thousands homeless.

I have other ideas that I am going to try. I am going to start talking at a few schools and let them know what search teams do and who they really are. I have even put our logo and name on the side of my truck windows. We are planning to fix the truck up for car shows. It will include a modified motor and lift kit as well as oversized tires. We feel this will also help letting people know who we are. Our team members are limited, Jeff with K-9 Frog, Darcie with K-9 Toad and of course, K-9 Jack and I . Our newest team member is K-9 George, a Chow-Golden mix that was rescued from a puppy mill by my wife.

` Charles Barnett, Unit 18, MidWest Search & Rescue, Moore, OK

Support SAR - "GET LOST!"

UPDATE:

Since Charlie wrote the above, you can see, he lost K-9 Jack, and has a new partner, Buddy.

In Loving Memory of

K-9 JAKE

August 3, 2001

Partner: Officer Jim Gilchrist
Geauga County Sheriff's Department
13281 Ravenna Rd. — P.O. Box 22
Chardon, OH 440.286.4031

Jake, age 2 years, German Shepherd , killed by auto.

I lost my BEST friend last August in a Horrific car/dog accident that I will never forget. Within days, you sent me completed cards to pass out to friends and family. I don't know you, and had not heard or your service. The following week, my mother was diagnosed with terminal cancer. I was physically and emotionally depleted upon her death on November 26 2001.

During this time we all suffered from the murder and destruction now referred to as "9/11." Words have no meaning here. Just too much loss. I've lost so much,... but yet, I have so much... a strange but comforting thought.

I've been back to work since January 2002. I have a new

partner, "Kety," a wonderful Holland Shepherd, I love her so. The Sheriffs Office has been very good to me on my K-9 issue as well as my personal front. "The government can be good when managed by good people"

I cannot tell you how many times I have looked at your card and cried, missing him. I will always miss him. He deserved so much more. What you did for me and my three boys cannot be described in mere e-mails. We passed out those cards so proudly to everyone that knew "Jake." You provided us a gift during a most sad and lonely time, you were one of the miracles my family received during those difficult times.

In Loving Memory of

K-9 KAHLUA

March 9, 2001

Partner: Officer David Rey
Glassboro Police Dept. NJ
1 S. Main St.
Glassboro, NJ 08028

Kahlua, my partner, protector and friend passed away on Friday March 9, 2001 at 5:15 PM. The staff at the University Of Pennsylvania attempted to save Kahlua's life after a blood clot was found in his lung. He fought valiantly to the end, but was unable to overcome this obstacle. I was with Kahlua until the end. I am thankful that I could hold him in my arms as he passed. He was truly a K-9 with 9 lives.

It was the community who reached out to help Kahlua in his time of need. Those individuals gave us two years of extended service. I don't know if these individuals will ever know how much their love and support meant to me. I will never forget. I can only hope to give back to the community what they gave to me.

I would especially like to thank the members of The Glassboro K-9 Unit and my loving wife for all of their support and strength.

Eternally grateful, Ptl. David Rey K-934

Kahlua, who had diabetes and inflammatory bowel disease, gained fame when a TV news program reported that an 11 year old Mantua, New Jersey, girl, Erica Collins, heard about Kahlua's case and raised money at her school to help pay for his medical costs. A grateful Rey had only words of praise for the Pennsylvania team. It was such a great experience.

Through a call over the police scanner Saturday to all Gloucester County police, it was announced that Kahlua, the famous K-9 Rottweiler from the Glassboro Police Department had died in the University of Pennsylvania Animal Hospital. It was still unclear Saturday night what caused Kahlua's passing, but the K-9 was diagnosed with diabetes last year, which required twice daily insulin injections, five days a week. Kahlua may also have been suffering from inflammatory bowel disease. He was operated on March 24, 2000, where doctors removed a foreign body from his stomach and intestines that was said to have equaled the size of a basketball.

Kahlua's handler, partner and friend, Ptl. Dave Rey was unavailable for comment. Their friendship and partnership began in 1993, when the two began working together and together they have apprehended over 49 suspects and have answered well over 200 police calls.

In 1996, the two were called in to assist the state police which ended up successfully tracking and apprehending two suspects. One of the suspects was later charged with vehicular homicide.

In Loving Memory of

K-9 KANTO

December 13, 2001

Partner: Deputy Robert Andrews
Plymouth County Sheriff Department
K-9 Unit
Obery St.
Plymouth, MA
508.530-6328

Kanto was a world traveler and a dedicated worker for the Plymouth County Sheriff's Depart. The 75 pound German Shepherd was also Deputy Sheriff Robert Andrews' best friend and constant companion.

On Wednesday night, Kanto was struck by a hit & run driver and killed. The driver of the car never slowed down, Andrews said. Even though Kanto had been off his leash, Andrews said the driver should have at least stopped. "If you hit something, you should stop." a heart broken Andrews said Thursday.

Duxbury police are investigating. It is illegal to hit a dog without reporting it to police. It is also illegal to have a dog outside without a leash, and Andrews may be liable for damages, Duxbury police Lt. Roger Banfill said. "If the dog is loose and he gets hit, it is the fault of the dog, & Andrews is responsible for damages to that vehicle," Banfill said.

Kanto came to the United States from the Czech Republic 3 years ago after going through two years of police training. Andrews paid $3,500 for the dog. The sheriff's office paid for Kanto's upkeep, including food & veterinary bills. Each dog used by the sheriff's department is owned by the officer. Andrews learned 30 Czech command phrases to communicate with his new comrade.

Kanto was soon an integral part of both the Plymouth County Sheriff's K-9 unit and Andrews' life. Kanto's specialty was finding lost people & recovering evidence. We found several little kids. We found bad guys, good guys, elderly people, stuff like that. "He loved my son and I very much. He was just a good dog. He was unique, and he was very good at what he did," he said.

On Wednesday night, Andrews had taken Kanto outside to let him run in his kennel in the back yard. Once his run was finished, Kanto usually kept close to Andrews and would follow him around the house to the front door and then back inside. But Kanto either heard a noise or smelled a squirrel and bolted from his owner's side toward Franklin St. where he was struck. "I tried to talk to him and he didn't respond and I knew right at that point he was all done," Andrews said.

Kanto will be cremated. His ashes will be kept in an urn at Andrews home, until Andrews himself dies. "In my will I'll put that he's buried with me," Andrews said.

In Loving Memory of

K-9 KOPPER

Niko's Koppertone of Rib Mountain
October 8, 1996 - July 27, 2001

Partners: Officer Jerry Nichols
and Milica K. Wilson
LEBA
Law Enforcement Bloodhound Association
P.O. Box 471267, Aurora, CO 80047-1267
303.369-6784

It is with deepest sadness that I inform you of our partner's crossing the "Rainbow Bridge." Niko's Koppertone of Rib Mountain, Kopper, lost his battle with cancer. It came on literally over night and it hit hard and fast. While he put up a good fight, unfortunately the cancer won out. I apologize for taking over a week to announce this, but Jerry and I have been trying to deal with his loss.

It is especially hard since Kopper had not yet reached his 5th birthday. For those of you who knew, our heartfelt thanks for your prayers and good wishes. As you all know, it is most difficult to lose a partner, and they truly are family members.

Kopper died in my arms which was comforting, it is the letting go that made it unbearable. He was my dog and then I shared him with Jerry, who saw his potential.

Milica

In Loving Memory of

K-9 LUCKY

End Of Watch June 25, 2001

Partner: LT. Ron Taylor
The Blaine County Sheriff's Office
210 First Avenue South
Hailey, Idaho 83333

On March 14, 1990, Lucky became a most valuable member of the Blaine County Sheriff's Office. Lucky, a twelve year old Golden Retriever, was a mellow and good natured dog; good around children from pre school up. He loved his public relations work with the Sheriff's office.

On June 25, 2001, Lucky passed away as a result of a tumor in his pancreas. During the eleven years he was with the Sheriff's office he became a big part of the community and the activities the community had for drug prevention. As a result of his participation and interaction with adults and children he made a positive contribution to the entire population of Blaine County.

In October 1992 Lucky was presented a plaque by Governor Cecil Andrus, for the Red Ribbon K-9 of the year, in recognition of commitment to drug prevention efforts in his community.

In March 1994 with Lucky's' efforts he helped with a bill in the legislature that became a law. To protect Police Dogs, making killing and otherwise mistreating police dogs a felony.

In October 2000 Lucky was presented an award from K-9 Companions for Independence, in recognition of years of dedicated service in keeping his community safe.

During Lucky's' career his sniffing work helped to get 29 search warrants where drugs were located. He did 783 sniff searches in Blaine County and out of the county. Those sniff searches were school lockers, vehicles, airplanes, postal mail, luggage, businesses, apartments, residences, storage sheds, and the outdoors. He gave a lot of demonstrations in the county, at other counties and out of the State of Idaho. He was called on by many agencies for assistance.

During his lifetime he had 7,086 training sessions. With his strong commitment to help keep his community safe, he got two million dollars of drugs off the streets of his community and helped seize eleven million dollars in property. His first search was June 8, 1990 and his last search was on June 19, 2001.

In Loving Memory of

K-9 LYDA

July 4, 2001

Partner: Officer Mike Liechti
Savannah, Police Department
Savannah, GA

Lyda served Savannah well, but briefly. The K-9 sniffed out about a dozen drug offenders since joining the police force in May. She accidentally hanged herself by her leash on the Fourth of July. Police Chief Derald Lammers accepts part of the blame. " Never dreamed anything like this would happen, but it's still hard not to beat myself up about it," he said. After Lyda created a hole and escaped her kennel, Chief Lammers got the call, caught her and tied a leash to the opposite side of the cage where he secured Lyda with a choke collar.

Minutes later, Officer Mike Liechti, the trained handler responsible for the dog, returned home and found her struggling, but still alive. He performed a form of CPR, but it was too late. "It just crushed me and the kids," Officer Liechti said.

"They're still asking where Lyda is."

It wasn't the first time Lyda had found her way out. Her escapes had become routine. The 2 year old Malinois dog, similar to a German Shepherd, would tear up her cage and officers would patch it with steel wire panels the best they could. "We did everything we could without spending money, but she was smart and determined Chief Lammers said. "Hindsight is 20/20, but there was still nothing in the budget. The money should have been made available to get a kennel built."

Officer Liechti assumed fireworks frightened the dog last week, because thunder had set her off before. To calm her during storms, he took her into his home. "I took this very seriously" Officer Liechti told city council members. "I knew it was a big responsibility and I put 110 percent into it. I did everything I possibly could."

Councilwoman Friday Ramsey said the city shouldn't rush into purchasing a replacement K-9 for the force. The price tag for Lyda's transportation from Holland, training for her and Mr. Liechti and equipment was nearly $15,000. "Maybe we jumped too quick the first time," Ms. Ramsey said. "I'm not doubting anyone's ability; I just want to get all our ducks in a row. "It was a very expensive accident. And accidents do happen, but we need to learn from this incident. We spent a lot of money and I'm just saying we should take our time and really look at this."

Councilman Bob Wilson argued that the majority of Lyda's expenses were covered by donations. "A lot of the money came from the community," he said. "They supported this. And we owe it to them to take the steps to get a new dog and do it right this time."

Officer Liechti found a dog for $5,000 with the same certification for drug detection and search and seizure missions Lyda had. The owner agreed to turn over the dog to him in August with the promise of full payment in October when Savannah's new budget year begins. The city council voted unanimously to allow the money to come out of the already tight police budget then.

"It's a significant amount of money, but a really good deal," Chief Lammers said. "We'll have to cut buying and updating other equipment, but it's a worthwhile program. Since the community supported it from the beginning, it's our top priority." Chief Lammers gave $1,000 from a department fund raiser as the down payment and the school district will donate another $1,000 from its anti drug education grant.

Like it's predecessor, the new dog will serve area law enforcement programs, such as the Missouri State Highway Patrol, the Northwest Missouri Narcotics Enforcement Team and the Andrew County Sheriff's Department. "If we're going to do the program, we need to do it right," Officer Liechti said. "We need a top of the line kennel and equipment. You simply can't pinch pennies on a program like this."

Mike Ramsel, L&M Auto Center owner, solicited funds for the first dog and said he would raise the money needed and build an appropriate kennel for the next K-9. "I loved the dog almost as much as Mike (Liechti) did," Mr. Ramsel said. "And I've seen her work and it's impressive. We need this here."

In Loving Memory of

K-9 MAKO

May 5, 2001
LODD

Partner: Deputy Dennis R. Cunningham
Manatee County Sheriff's Dept.
515   11th Street West
Bradenton, FL 34205 7722
941.747 3011

Everything happened so quickly...reactions were to save the officer. A real tragedy! A Manatee County deputy shot and killed a K-9 Corps dog early Saturday after the K-9 attacked him. Mako and Deputy Jeff Dunn wrestled after the dog mistook him for a car jacking suspect. The dog bit the deputy in the arm and hand and would not let go, even after being ordered by his K-9 handler.

Dunn shot Mako, who may not have heard the commands or was confused in all of the commotion, sheriff's spokesman Dave Bristow said. "There were lots of lights and sirens going off," Bristow said. "Nobody feels as bad about this as Dunn. He's a K-9 handler himself." Dunn was taken to Manatee Memorial Hospital, where he received 14 stitches.

This is the first time in decades that a deputy has had to shoot a police dog, Bristow said. Any time a deputy is involved in a shooting, the department usually conducts an internal investigation. The shooting occurred shortly after 12 a.m. near Ninth Street East and 35th Avenue in Bradenton. Deputies were searching for a car jacking suspect, who forced a man out of his truck and drove off in it. The deputies spotted the vehicle in the same area, after the owner called 911. Deputies chased the suspect, later identified as Kenneth Whitfield, for 10 minutes. He ran from the car, and K-9 units were called in to look for him.

Whitfield was captured and charged with car jacking, fleeing to elude and having no valid driver's license. This was not the first violent incident for Mako and his handler, Deputy Dennis Cunningham. Outside of the Outer Limits nightclub last October, Cunningham and Mako were attempting to clear the parking lot. After Cunningham signaled for club patron Craig Holloman to leave, Halloman ran over the five year veteran and Mako with his car, reports said. Cunningham could see his attacker smiling while running him over, he said in his report. Cunningham got up, drew his weapon and ordered Holloman out of the car, but the deputy was hit with the car again. Holloman, who had gotten out of his vehicle, did not have the car in park.

A correction to the story as follows:

Deputy Cunningham released K-9 Mako on the suspects of the truck as they ran from it. K-9 Mako followed the passenger and Cunningham followed Mako. The driver turned and got back into the truck. Deputy Cunningham grabbed the driver to keep him from running the truck into a deputy or starting the chase again. No one realized another deputy was on the other side of the suspect's vehicle. Mako came around the truck and grabbed the deputy by the hand. Deputy Cunningham got in a brief struggle with the other potentially armed suspect.

When he got a back up unit to grab the suspect. Cunningham went for Mako, but it was too late. Deputy Dunn had to do what he did not want to. Deputy Dunn and Cunningham are very good friends and continue today. K-9 Mako did what he was trained to do. The suspects created the confusion ultimately leading to Mako's untimely death.

Mako spent three years certified on the road with 75 apprehensions and numerous narcotic alerts. He recently spent 4 hours tracking a burglary suspect through a residential neighborhood, catching him in a house. This ended a crime spree of that area.

The arrest totals are amazing considering that Deputy Dunn and K-9 Bronco accumulated 80 plus apprehensions during the same period. The two K-9 teams worked the same times together and frequently helped each other on tracks. The arrest totals are only the arrests the K-9 found during his service. "THEY WORKED HARD FOR THEIR COMMUNITY TO MAKE IT SAFER. "

In Loving Memory of

K-9 NERO

April 1998 - September 14, 2001

Partner: Officer Todd Haller
Terre Haute Police Department
17 Harding Avenue
Terra Haute, IN 47807

K-9 Nero died at the age of 3, due to medical reasons. He will be missed by everyone in the department.

As a recording of "Taps" played overhead Tuesday in Terre Haute City Court, a police honor guard saluted during a memorial service for one of their own. Soon, one by one, fellow members of the city police department offered their condolences to a teary eyed Officer Todd Haller, whose partner of two years died Friday after emergency surgery.

Nero, a 3 year old police dog, was more than just a K-9 drug sniffer. He served as Haller's companion and friend, long after their work day concluded. "Some may look at our partners as just dogs that are highly trained," but they are much, much more, said Officer Dan Parker, who oversees the department's K-9 unit.

"Nero definitely loved only one person and that was Todd," Parker said, fighting back tears as he eulogized the dog. They "were not only partners, but inseparable," he said. Nero was euthanized Friday following emergency surgery for gastric bloat, said Dr. Floyd Lee, a veterinarian at the Cross Clinic in Terre Haute.

For unknown reasons, a dog's stomach can fill with air and easily rotate itself, cutting off circulation to the organ, said Lee, who was among about 50 people attending Nero's memorial service. The affliction is more common among large dogs than small. Even with surgery, the condition can be life threatening, and in Nero's case the stomach tissue had deteriorated beyond repair, Lee said.

Nero's death was the first for the Police Department's K-9 unit, which was established about four years ago, Parker said. Nero, one of four dogs assigned to the department, was born in April 1998 and acquired about a year later when Parker traveled to Europe to transport 12 police dogs back to the United States for an Indiana kennel.

He came with one talent, to bite, Parker recalled. "He's the reason I carry a suture kit, by the way," Parker said, bringing a laugh from the audience during the otherwise somber ceremony.

Nero's difficult personality proved a challenge for his new handler. Haller, at first nervous about his new role, said it took a few months for the 100 pound K-9 to warm to him, but before long it was the "beginning of a true friendship."

At home, Nero had his own log retreat, a large insulated dog house made with cedar logs and finished off with carpet inside, Haller said. During the workday, the two often reported to schools, businesses and even state agencies, where Nero would perform his public service, looking for drugs. With a fixed stare, the dog would alert his handler to hidden narcotics, and wouldn't move until told.

Nero and his handler were part of an estimated 1,000 plus searches during the dog's lifetime, including one Haller remembers fondly. As Nero sniffed for narcotics in a car, the dog found more than he bargained for while his handler briefly looked away. When Haller turned around, his dog's mouth was filled with a Big Mac sandwich, a treat he'd found in a fast food bag inside the car. Haller ordered his K-9 companion to return the burger to the bag, and the dog immediately complied. But his antics didn't end there. At times, the four legged officer seemed fascinated with machine guns, once knocking down a SWAT team member by his gun during a raid on a Terre Haute home, Haller said. And he was always reliable at slobbering on a clean uniform.

However, when it came down to serious business, Nero was one of the best in the state, Parker said, explaining that Nero and his handler had recently placed third in a K-9 Olympics competition in Muncie. Hours after the dog was honored Friday in Terre Haute for the accomplishment, something was noticeably wrong. Haller's four legged partner became sick, bloating in the mid-section. Even emergency surgery wasn't enough to save the dog.

"It was like losing a child," said Kris Wagner, Haller's fiancee. And for the department, it was like losing one of their own. A member of the honor guard stood stoically next to a photograph of a wide-eyed, perky eared Nero during Tuesday's 40 minute memorial service. The eulogies, including a brief one from Haller himself, brought tears to some officers' eyes. Many wore black bands across their badges.

For now, Haller's squad car will have a noticeably empty back seat. But hopefully not for long. Even as early as today, Haller and Parker planned to make the trip to a Peru kennel to look for a new police dog. And Haller, an eight year member of the force who never intended to be a dog handler, is eager to do it all over. Even if that means the back seat of his squad car will become a chew toy once again.

In Loving Memory of

K-9 SUNDANCE OBY

October 10, 2001

Missed by Mary Anderson & Senior Police Officer Richard
DeJoode
Narcotics Unit, Des Moines Police Department
25 E. First St.
Des Moines, IA 50309
515.283-4824

Oby, the Des Moines Police Department's drug sniffing
golden retriever who retired in 1996 after six years on the force,
died Wednesday. A favorite with schoolchildren who traded his
"Cop Collectible" card, Oby was instrumental in the seizure of
more than 128 pounds of illegal narcotics with a value of more
than $860,000. He also was given credit for the seizure of near-
ly $725,000 from traffickers.

Officers draped medals of appreciation over his shoulders
when he retired at the age of 8. Cake was served at his retirement party. Oby's tenure at the department occurred during

the height of the city's gang problems and gang generated drug trade. Oby had his own photograph identification card that he sometimes wore on a chain around his neck. Using a golden retriever whose most notable characteristic was his wagging tail represented a shift for Des Moines police when Oby joined the department in 1990.

The department had used larger dogs capable of defending their handlers. After one of those dogs attacked a police officer, who was hospitalized with serious injuries, the department looked for a more gentle breed. Oby got the nod.

Since his retirement, Oby had been staying at the home of Mary Anderson, a civilian who works in the Police Department records section. Anderson said Oby couldn't get to his feet Tuesday. "He was put to sleep this morning," Anderson said Wednesday.

Born 10, June 1988 in Elkhart, IN, Oby became a certified police K-9 in July 1990. He was affectionate, loving and gentle. He loved attention and truly enjoyed his work as a drug sniffing K-9. Oby was responsible for putting several criminals in jail and also for keeping millions of dollars of illegal narcotics from our streets.

Oby was the center of attention with school children and assisted in educating them about drug awareness. He retired from the Des Moines Police Department in September 1996. He enjoyed his retirement with Mary Anderson, Police Records Clerk and his playmate Maggie. His playmate Maggie passed away December 4, 1999 and Oby joined her on October 10, 2001.

Both Oby and Maggie are buried in Warren County, Iowa at a beautiful pet cemetery. They are buried along the cemetery's "Wall of Honor" for service dogs. A monument was erected at the site in honor of both Maggie and Oby.

In Loving Memory of

K-9 OTTO

May 3, 2001

Hillsboro Police Dept.
102 South Main St. P.O. Box " N"
Hillsboro, KS 67063
620.947-3440

"A piece of me died." quoted by Jessey

K-9 Otto died Thursday at home. After initial suspicion of foul play, a K State autopsy confirms that Otto died of natural causes at his home. It is not only a loss to the department but to the community as well.

Otto, a German Shepherd dog, joined the Hillsboro police department in October 1997. He immediately began obedience and drug recognition training in Wichita with trainer Brad Agnew. He graduated from training school April 1998. Law enforcement officers Otto and Jessey Hiebert also underwent training together so Hiebert could learn how to properly groom and handle the dog. All of Otto's commands were given in German.

According to Chief Kinning, after Otto was found dead, the event was reported to the Marion County Sheriff's Department and investigated for possible foul play. There are Kansas statutes relating to Otto. The dog's death was investigated as if it were the death of an officer. The dog was taken to Kansas State University for testing, and results came back, stating that the dog died of gastric torsion, commonly known as a "twisted gut."

He was our most popular officer. He visited every school in the county. He will be missed. Otto not only worked in drug detection, but he also was an invaluable public relations tool. A memorial service for the police dog will be held Friday, May 11, at Hillsboro Memorial Park, with pastor John Ryding speaking at the service.

Chief Kinning said he had been contacted by the Wichita Police Department regarding the service. The WPD had wanted to bring the bagpipes to Hillsboro, but they had a prior obligation. Chief Kinning said he was later contacted by the Kansas City Police Department. If possible, the department will bring bagpipes to the service Friday.

Marion County Sheriff Lee Becker also expressed his regrets at the loss of the drug dog. The K-9 drug work, however, will not end with Otto's death. Chief Kinning said a fund has already been started for the purchase of a new dog as a memorial to Otto. Sheriff Becker said the Sheriff's Department would donate $500 from the drug dog fund toward the purchase of a new drug dog. Anyone wanting to make a donation to Otto's Memorial Fund may do so at the Emprise State Bank in Hillsboro.

The service:

Area law enforcement respond to the loss of a K-9 comrade. Arriving in a procession of almost 20 vehicles, about two dozen law enforcement personnel and 35 civilians bid farewell Friday to Otto, the Hillsboro Police Department's K-9 drug dog that died of natural causes May 3. Law enforcement officers from at least seven communities and McConnell Air Force Base including five of the K-9 variety gathered on the east side of the Scout House in Memorial Park at 11 a.m. for a solemn tribute to the popular K-9.

Hillsboro Police Chief Dan Kinning said he wasn't surprised by the strong turnout. In fact, it could easily have been much larger. We received many condolences. A lot of departments sent us teletypes saying they wanted to be there, but it was May Day and All School's Day in McPherson. It was also the kick off for the River Festival in Wichita, so the highway patrol and a lot of departments were tied up.

The service included brief comments from Officer Jessey Hiebert, Otto's handler, plus written messages of condolences from Attorney General Carla Stovall and U.S. Rep. Jerry Moran, and a brief meditation from John Ryding, HPD chaplain and pastor of the Zion Lutheran Church in Hillsboro.

Chaplin Ryding noted the unusual nature of the gathering a first for him in 24 years of ministry. He said Otto was "faithful and dependable, and will be missed by all." Two memorial plaques were presented to the department, one from Kansas Specialized Dogs, the organization that trained Otto for duty, and one from the Peace Officers Association.

The service ended with a "final call" for Otto radioed via the PA system in HPD's K-9 unit vehicle. It noted the dog's three years of service and called for Otto to "rest in peace." Chaplin Ryding followed the final call with "Taps."

As they dispersed, more than a few of the law enforcement officers wiped tears from their eyes. Several comrades and guests shared words of condolence to Officer Hiebert afterward, some with a handshake, others with an embrace.

Chief Kinning said his department had originally planned on marking Otto's passing with "a little prayer" and by presenting a memorial plaque to Officer Hiebert. "It kind of took on a life of its own," he said.

The event received media attention far beyond Hillsboro.

KAKE TV 10 was on hand to cover the memorial program. Earlier in the week, the Wichita Eagle had carried an article about the emotion surrounding Otto's death. Chief Kinning said he also had been interviewed by a reporter from the Kansas City Star. Reportedly, the story had gone out over national news. "I wasn't expecting that much media attention," he said. "I know the Eagle had been looking for a small town story and this sort of fit the bill for them."

Chief Kinning is aware that not everyone in the community understood or appreciated the groundswell of attention Otto's death generated. He was more than just a dog, he was a police officer, by law. Also, he was a member of the community. Everybody knew the dog, especially the children. I think if school hadn't been in session, we probably would have had a good turnout of children." He said the gathering was never intended to be a "funeral." "It was a memorial for the officers and whoever in the community wanted to say good bye.

A fund has been established at Emprise Bank in Hillsboro to receive contributions for acquiring a new K-9 officer for the department. Chief Kinning said Otto's trainer has already offered to donate a replacement dog. Such dogs normally cost between $5,000 and $10,000. If this particular dog is selected, Kinning said about $3,500 still will be needed to train it for duty. About $1,400 had been donated by Monday afternoon. If the money can be raised, Chief Kinning thinks the local K-9 unit could be back in service in as little as three months. Otto's remains were cremated and the ashes likely will be placed in Hiebert's custody.

UPDATE:

Jesse is looking for another partner, not to take Otto's place, but to protect us all.

In Loving Memory of

K-9 PAL

July 2, 2001

Partner: P.O. Michael O'Brien
Yonkers Police Department
730 E. Grassy Sprain Rd.
Yonkers, NY 10710

On July 2, 2001, K-9 Pal came to an accidental death. K-9 Pal and his partner, Patrol Officer Michael O'Brien were very busy as a K-9 team. They were responsible for numerous felony arrests. K-9 Pal and Mike also put on several K-9 demonstrations to school children throughout the city. Pal's bravery and dedication were outstanding. This K-9 team will be missed by the department.

In Loving Memory of

K-9 PUFF

November 15, 2001

Fire Stations "The House Of Dragons"
133 North 10th Street - Philadelphia, PA 19107

Fireman's Prayer
When I am called to duty, God
Wherever flames may rage
Give me strength to save a life
Whatever be its age.
Let me embrace a little child
Before it is too late
Or save an older person from
The horror of that fate.
Enable me to be alert
And hear the weakest shout,
and quickly and efficiently
To put the fire out.
I want to fill my calling

To give the best in me,
To guard my friend and neighbor
And protect their property.
And, if, according to your will,
I have to lose my life,
Please bless, with your protecting hand,
My family and my wife.

Puff is missed by everyone who ever met him. 'Puff' was a fixture in Chinatown for 16 years. Puff, "the dragon fire dog," who for sixteen years, brought love, smiles and extraordinary companionship to his Chinatown firehouse and neighborhood, was to be put to sleep today. He was 16 years old and the fire dog of "The House of Dragons," the fire station of Engine 20, Ladder 23 and Medic 1. Puff became a part of the Chinatown family for sixteen years.

During a major winter storm, Firefighter Vern Yeager went with him even though he was so big. Puff's declining health broke the heart of everyone. Puff could barely walk, he couldn't even jump out of the bed the last time I went to the station. Usually when he saw me he would just jump out of bed and get all excited. From the look in his eyes , I knew he was suffering. We are going to miss him a lot.

We have a lot of wonderful memories of Puff, a dog who was obedient and very easy to train. When the fire bells went off, he would bark and get excited as he watched us run around like crazy. He always waited patiently for our return. When we'd come back he'd always be wagging his tail. We'd block the traffic to come back in the station and he would block the traffic with us."

Slightly overweight," Puff was a big eater who especially loved Chinese food. The neighbors would come and bring him Chinese food all the time. He loved it. He was chubby because he was constantly being fed.

After the firefighters get Puff's cremated remains from the veterinarian, they will set up a special place for them in the firehouse and build a memorial to the dog. He was worth his weight in gold.

Our fire house, nicknamed the "House of Dragons", due to our location in the Chinatown section of Philly, is designated as Engine 20, Ladder 23, Medic 1 by the Fire Department. Puff's had many "Partners." Firemen come and go in station houses, and quite a few have passed through our doors during Puff's tenure. Some took more of an interest in Puff's needs than did others, but each cared for and loved him in their own way. He is sorely missed by all!

In Loving Memory of

K-9 QUENT

November 23, 2001

Partner: Officer Gary Gear
Porter County Sheriff's Department
157 S. Franklin St.
Valporaiso, IN 46383

The Porter County Sheriff's Department suffered a great loss when K-9 Quent was struck and killed by a car in front of his handler's residence. All who knew Quent are greatly saddened.

None, however were as grief stricken as Officer Gary Gear and his fellow K-9 handlers who have worked closely together as a team. Officer Gear and Quent had worked together as partners for over two years, and had been involved in a number of drug arrests. Our thoughts and prayers go out to Officer Gear. In Memory Of Quent

Don't grieve for me I served you well.

I loved you more than you could ever tell.

I am now your guardian angel up above.
I will watch over you, I'll always be around.
 I wore my badge with honor every day,
 to keep citizens safe and out of harm's way.
So when you see a badge worn with pride,
 Remember the K-9s that have served and died.
unknown author

Update:

Officer Gear is no longer in the K-9 program. He decided to devote more time to training new officers.

In Loving Memory of

K-9 RANGER

1992 - October 30, 2001

Partner: Officer Lynn Morrow
Eden Prairie Police Department
Eden Prairie Public Safety Services
Eden Prairie, MN 553444
952.937-2700

For five years, kids in Eden Prairie Schools would get excited when Eden Prairie Police K-9 Ranger would come. Oh, yeah, Ranger didn't come by himself. Officer Lynn Garry, now Morrow, came along with the deal, too. "Kids who saw me without him would recognize me and say, 'I know you. You came with Ranger,'" she said Monday.

Ranger hasn't been in local schools since 1998, when he retired from the police force. Officer Morrow moved on to other duties. Today, she is an investigator and liaison officer at Eden Prairie High School. Last week, one of her duties was to say goodbye to Ranger before he died of cardiac arrest. Ranger was nine years old. Ranger had a malignant tumor a month ago, explained Morrow. It was removed in surgery, but the aggressive form of cancer still spread. Although he was sick, Ranger's death wasn't expected when it came on Oct. 30.

Despite the events of that hard day, Investigator Morrow said, "I'm glad I didn't have to make the decision about whether or not to put him down. "He would have given his life for me," she added. "I didn't want to make the decision of taking his life."

On the force, Morrow and Ranger started out together in 1994. From the start, Ranger was a standout, graduating as top dog in his St. Paul Police training class. Ranger lived with Morrow, just as other Eden Prairie K-9 partners do with their officers.

Ranger originally came from Holland, not even one year old when he first started the training process. "He was a little bit younger than other K-9s," Morrow said. "He had a lot of puppy energy."

Three months of intense training at the St. Paul Police Department K-9 facility, though, turned Ranger into a great partner for Morrow. "It's a lot of work," she admitted, "but it's really rewarding. It's amazing how well trained and knowledgeable those dogs can get." By the end of training, the two were true partners. "If I was crabby, he knew it," Morrow explained. "If I was scared, he knew it."

When Ranger and Morrow would take off for an Eden Prairie school to do a demonstration, she explained they would show the kids his obedience training as well as an example of how he could track down narcotics. Back at the station, Morrow said Ranger would often hang out while she would fill out reports. Usually, someone at the police department could be persuaded to play tug of war or catch with Ranger. He was so at home at EPPD that "he would sit in on roll call with me," Morrow said.

Described as a "super social" dog, Ranger would quickly become a hard worker when it was crunch time. "There were cases I was on where I know if he was not barking, I would have had a problem," Morrow said. Besides performing well on the job, Ranger did well at regional and national competitions.

In 1995, Ranger placed third in obedience in his region and 15th overall at nationals. The next year, Morrow's K-9 partner placed third in article search in the region. In 1997, he was fourth overall in the region and 24th at nationals. Perhaps even more impressive is the fact that Ranger placed in the top five in narcotics each year of certification. Morrow explained that K-9s have to be certified every year, both to preserve public safety and ensure continued agility, obedience, and tracking ability.

Throughout the entire time with Ranger, she talked about how amazing it is to see what dogs can do out in the field. "K-9s are great tools for the department," Morrow said.

For a little while longer, the Morrow household still has a police K-9 in the family. Husband Jim handles Jet for the EPPD. Jet is set to retire sometime next year. "I think Jet really misses him," Morrow said.

In Loving Memory of

K-9 RENO

March 2001

Handler: "AJ" Albert J. Haines III
Air Force USA

I handled Reno from 1994 to 1997. He was whelped November of 1988, and his brand number was 163P. Reno expired in March of this year. He had an irregular heartbeat and expired while under anesthesia.

I first met Reno in early 1994 when I was stationed at Tinker AFB, in Oklahoma City, Oklahoma. My first impression was he looked so intimidating because he was so large, being 105 lbs. I quickly learned that despite his training as an explosive detector dog, he was just a big, happy puppy at heart. We learned each other's personalities in short order, and formed a bond that will never be broken.

Our first real away mission from the base was to Dallas, Texas, for the World Cup Soccer Games of 1994. For 45 days we provided explosives detection support to the Dallas PD.

Daily we searched the Cotton Bowl Stadium and it's surrounding buildings, with several other K-9 teams, to make them safe for the games. Texas being Texas, it was hot, real hot.

To get around the large complex, we used golf carts. Reno especially liked riding around on the passenger seat of the carts because he got to feel the wind in his face as we sped about the grounds. One day, during one of our searches, Reno discovered the set of elaborate fountains just outside the stadium, and dove in. It was just deep enough for him to sit in and still have his head above water.

This became a daily ritual, and I could see the look of anticipation on his face every time we approached that fountain! He was in heaven! Once back in Oklahoma, we fell back into our daily duties of policing the base. Reno would sit in the back of the patrol car and keep watch as we went around the installation. We would walk through the many large buildings on base, and Reno became a welcome sight. He was very friendly with people, and all who met him enjoyed his visits, so much so people would forget my name, I was just called, "Reno's handler".

Reno and I shared all of our time together at work, and on my days off I would come in and take him out just to play. We even jogged together, he could easily do 2 miles, which couldn't always be said for his handler. We also trained with the Oklahoma County Sheriff's Bomb Squad and they quickly learned how talented Reno was. Captain Heady of the bomb squad began to ask for Reno by name when they needed help off base with bomb threats. We were on 24 hour recall, and during my time at Tinker, Reno and I searched countless businesses, schools, and public buildings.

Later, during the Oklahoma City Bombing, Reno and I were called into action, arriving downtown at 0930 hrs, and Captain Heady put us to work clearing buildings and cars for additional explosives. The glass on the ground had become so thick in some places it looked like snow. Reno had no problem with me throwing him around my shoulders and carrying him from spot to spot. After April 19, we were assigned to the U.S.

Marshals for 30 days to provide further explosive support for the ongoing rescue, and the recovery missions.

Following the bombing Reno and I were sent on many Presidential searches in such places as Arkansas, Iowa, Illinois, Texas, and Oklahoma itself. These were the "cush" missions, as the Secret Service kept both Reno and I in nice hotels during our stay. Reno loved having his own bed, and he would always choose his bed first, I got the one he didn't want. We got to go to many of the sites the President was going to be at and clear them of explosives, it was always a good time for the both of us.

I guess to offset the luxury of the Presidential missions, it was inevitable that a real world military mission would come up. In 1996 we were sent to Saudi Arabia in the wake of the Kobar Barracks bombing, which killed several of our fellow airman. We were re-deployed to the country of Qatar, just west of Saudi, where we worked round the clock searching everything coming onto the base.

After 2 months of 120 degree heat and living in a tent, Reno and I were re-deployed back to Saudi, to the dubious luxury of a newer, larger tent in 110 degree heat, where we spent an addition 2 months searching for explosives. As homesick as I was, it was comforting to know Reno was there by my side, oblivious to the political climate we were in and just happy to be with me.

He was such a great conversation partner, he would listen intently to my daily woes, never interrupting, and always went along with my suggestions. I don't care what other people say, in their own ways dogs do understand what we say to them. Living, sleeping, and eating with Reno 24 hours a day, 7 days a week made me a believer.

Life settled down upon our return to Oklahoma, and we went back to our now mundane daily duties. Unfortunately only a month after being back, Reno suffered a gastric torsion, in which a dog's stomach flips over inside, and is fatal if not corrected immediately.

Our military vet was away, so I rushed Reno, lights and sirens, off base to a waiting animal hospital. After a tense few minutes, the vet was able to stabilize him, but not before damage was caused to his spleen, which had to removed. For two weeks, I visited him everyday in the hospital, and nothing beat the feeling of seeing his joy when I came. As sedated as he was he would still try to get up to greet me, then just lay there and wag his stub tail as I talked to him. He quickly recovered, and we went back to work again. But time had caught up with us, and as much as I loved him, I knew that I wanted to pursue a career outside the military, back in my home state of New Jersey.

As our time together grew short, I heard about the new bill that was being considered in Congress which would allow handlers to adopt their dogs. I took up the matter within the military, but found that the military really wasn't interested in the bill, and was actually somewhat hostile to the whole idea. I was told conflicting statements by different people, and outright lied to by others. I decided to look outside the military for help.

I heard about the Volunteers for Animal Welfare group in Oklahoma City and attended one of their meetings, where I met a very special lady, Cynthia Armstong. After telling her about my plight, and how the military never retired their dogs, just put them to sleep, she set out to do everything she could to help us. Letters of support came in from senators, representatives, and the Governor of Oklahoma himself, Frank Keating, pledging their support.

Sadly the military continued their resistance, again stalling people, making up absurd stories of ex military dogs going insane and killing people, and just plain lying. They claimed Reno was no more than a piece of equipment, and had about as much feeling as an F 16 fighter plane, and that just like when the plane was no longer needed, Reno too would be destroyed.

As a final gesture, I asked to be notified when Reno passed away, so I could at least provide a small memorial to him at the local pet cemetery in Spencer, Oklahoma, where other workings dogs had been buried. The effort to save my partner continued long after Reno and I parted, Mrs. Armstrong never giving up.

I moved back to New Jersey and bought a house, and became a police officer.

In July of 2001, Mrs. Armstrong called me with the excited news that the military many be close to letting me adopt Reno. But only 2 days later she found out the sad truth, that Reno had passed away in March while undergoing surgery in Texas. He was twelve years old.

It was like losing a family member, and I had really envisioned him lying in the shade under one of the large shade trees on my lawn. I know Reno, he'll find shade where ever he is, even in heaven. If anything good can come out of the whole affair, it is that the laws are slowing changing, and the military will have to be held responsible for their mistreatment of their dogs.

The more the public learns about the military's K-9 program, the more they will demand it be changed. Hopefully they will also change the status of these four footed soldiers back to living, breathing creatures, and not just equipment. They deserve it.

In Loving Memory of

K-9 REX

May 1993 - August 7, 2001

Partner: Officer Bo Curry
Montgomery County Police Headquarters
2350 Research Blvd.
Rockville, MD 20850
240.773-5000

Rex was born in May, 1993 and started police work in 1994. He was an outstanding tracker and was Bo's Pride & Joy. He had numerous street apprehensions to his credit, including a couple of burglars who were wanted in high-profile cases. This case was known as "The British Bandits." They used a British accent and would break into expensive homes while people were sleeping and steal cash and jewelry.

Rex could track anything. I knew when he could not keep up with the tracking, something was wrong. He developed some neurological problems and had to undergo surgery to his spine. He died as a result.

UPDATE:

Officer Curry returned to patrol in January with new partner, Greger.

In Loving Memory of

K-9 Robbie

July 23, 2001

Partner: Chief John Garner
Lewisport Police Department
P.O. Box 22
Lewisport, KY 42351-0022
270.295-3345

The first police K-9 in Hancock County history, Robbie, died Monday due to kidney failure and possibly cancer. Robbie was an 8 year old Belgian Malinois.

He was responsible for many drug related arrests and seizures. Even in his last month, when he was feeling bad, he was ready to go. He had the heart of a champion.

Seven years ago, the Lewisport mayor suggested a K-9 unit would benefit the community and Garner received Robbie from the TASK K-9 Academy in Texas. Garner took him in as his own and on the second day of duty, Robbie managed to help retrieve $16,000 worth of stolen church equipment. He came in and proved to be an asset from the start. He would find whatever you needed him to find no matter what.

Robbie became involved in the community by helping out the school's DARE program. He loved to go to the schools and let the kids pet and play with him. Chief Garner believes having the dog helped spread the anti drug message to the kids. Robbie lived at home with Garner and his wife and children. He liked to play ball with the family and would often just sit with them. He was a member of the family. The Garner children grew up with him.

Getting a K-9 in Hancock County was a big deal seven years ago because the Lewisport Police Department was a one man agency. Many regional law enforcement agencies got dogs after hearing of Robbie. The Hancock County Sheriff's department got Ulan, a K-9 that worked with Robbie, two years ago. This showed what kind of positive impact Robbie had in the community. K-9 Ulan's owner, Deputy Sheriff Chuck Jones, said Robbie was one of the best dogs he knew.

"A K-9 is worth its weight in gold. They give it their all and all they ask in return is a little affection. The impact of losing a dog an officer worked with on the job is significant. Having a dog that will take a bullet for you is something completely different. If I were to lose Ulan, it would be like losing a kid."

Robbie was put to sleep Monday at Town Square Animal Hospital and then buried at Garner's house. There are no immediate plans to replace Robbie, though Garner doesn't rule out the possibility of getting another K-9. "You've got to get over the loss." Garner said tearfully, "You can't replace him." Garner plans to collect all the photos and articles about Robbie so he can show people about his special dog. "You don't realize how he helped until he's gone. He did a lot for the department."

A memorial service for Robbie will be held at 1:30 p.m. Monday at the Lewisport Fire Department.

In Loving Memory of

K-9 Robbie

LODD
January 1999 - October 15, 2001

Partner: Sgt. Jeff White
B.I.A. Law Enforcement Services
New Town, ND 58763-0309
701. 627-3314

"He was my partner, my best friend." Robbie the Fort Berthold Drug Dog to be honored by New Town, Local law enforcement and Bureau of Indian Affairs.

Police dog handlers from other reservations will gather in New Town today to pay tribute to Robbie, A Fort Berthold Drug & patrol dog who died earlier this week. The funeral service for the fallen K-9 officer Robbie, will begin at 10 AM in the New Town Civic Center.

Elbo Wood Works of New Town is making a casket for Robbie. Robbie died in a fire at his handler Jeff White's home near Parshall Tuesday. The incident is under investigation.

Jeff White is an officer for the Fort Berthold Bureau of Indian Affairs Law Enforcement Department and has been Robbie's handler since the Fort Berhold agency added a K-9 unit about a year and a half ago. Robbie, 3 yr. old Belgium Malinois was a multi purpose dog, but mainly worked drugs and patrol. He lived and worked with White.

Officer White and Robbie worked locally, but also went on a number of special assignments for the BIA. Throughout his career, Robbie was responsible for numerous drug arrests from Indiana to Wyoming. He was also used in 3 Special Response Team Deployments, one in Nevada and 2 in Wyoming. White and Robbie were also sent to a search and rescue operation in South Dakota.

Robbie was a very friendly dog and was in demand by several law enforcement agencies in his home area. His services were also requested by all the local schools where he performed locker and area searches.

The Fort Berthold BIA Law Enforcement established the K-9 unit because people in the local communities had concerns about drug problems, former BIA Police Chief Elmer Four Dance said in an interview last October. "Robbie was the main reason we made a lot of drug arrests. He found a lot of drugs we would not have found."

Robbie who was born in the Netherlands, followed commands in Dutch. White learned the commands at a 5 week training school for dogs and handlers in Indiana. Robbie was the only police service dog on the Fort Berthold Reservation. He was buried today at the Gerald White's residence near White Shield.

In Loving Memory of

K-9 ROBBY

1993-2001

Partner/Handler: LCPL Shawnn Manthey
Headquarters, Marine Corps Base
Quantico, VA

Robby was born in central Europe. He had his basic training at Lackland A.F.B. for two years, then worked with U.S.
Marines at Quantico, VA. He saw partners come and go, but is
last partner was LCPl. Shawn Mathey. He trained at least two
hours a day. (Photo by Sgt. Mikay Niman)

In the invasion of Guam in 1944, Marine Capt. William W.
Putney led a patrol to root out some entrenched Japanese. "I
took a squad of men and two BARs [Browning Automatic
Rifles] and a flamethrower and three dogs," the retiree recalls
by phone from California. "We got to the area, and I gave the
signal to be extremely careful. A shot rang out from the distance, and the dog right in front of me name of Cappy, a
Doberman I saw him fly into the air. I could see the hole in his
chest, he was dead. "If it hadn't been for Cappy right in front

of me, I would have been the target."

The dog's handler, a Marine named Terrell, "picked the body up and held it in his arms with blood all over his face he was crying, just rocking back and forth. He'd lost his buddy." Today, Cappy is buried on Guam with 28 other dogs who gave their lives for the liberation of the island and who were credited with saving hundreds of American soldiers. A life size bronze sculpture of a Doberman, provided by veterans, guards the cemetery. In a sense, it's a far reaching symbol. From the sands of Iwo Jima to the frozen wastes of Korea, from the steaming jungles of Vietnam's Annamite Cordillera to the deserts of the Persian Gulf, thousands of valiant American dogs of war have covered themselves with glory.

After the war, Putney became chief veterinarian of the Marine Corps and successfully "detrained" 550 war dogs, returning them to civilian homes to live out their days.

Then, in 1949, he watched in dismay as military dogs were reclassified as "equipment." No longer could they be adopted; instead, at the end of their usefulness to their country, they would be euthanized. This was U.S. policy for 50 years. Putney was outraged. "Thousands of these dogs have needlessly been destroyed," he says. "To employ an animal for our own use and then, when they can no longer serve us . . . cast them on a garbage heap is the worst kind of animal abuse."

Earlier this month, however, Putney and other dog lovers applauded as President Clinton signed a bill allowing military dogs to be adopted at the end of their "useful working" lives by former handlers and others qualified to care for them safely and humanely. "A victory for common sense," declared Rep. Roscoe G. Bartlett (R Md.), who ramrodded the dog bill through a unanimous Congress. "These military dogs deserve a dignified retirement in loving homes in return for their unique and irreplaceable service to our country."

A farmer and dog owner, the conservative congressman had learned about the Defense Department's policy in a Stars and Stripes Digital article in September. The article mentioned a

U.S. Marine Corps dog named Robby, sick and nearing the end of a distinguished career. Robby, Bartlett feared, was facing euthanasia.

The Few, the Proud . . .   "Get him! "On command, Tanja leaps forward, a tan and black blur of pure canine muscle and fang streaking toward the suspect. The "suspect" in this demonstration at the Quantico Marine Corps Base - where Robby lived until recently - is running like crazy. Suddenly Tanja is on him, teeth clamped onto his right arm, wrestling him to submission. "Out!" commands Marine Sgt. Terrell Lambert. The dog retreats instantly to his handler's side.

"Sir, at this time I am going to move forward and search you," the handler shouts at the suspect. "Do not move or my dog will bite you again!" The suspect freezes, hands up. Lambert moves forward and carefully begins searching him. The dog, a German Shepherd, watches intently from a distance. Suddenly, the suspect makes a move on Lambert. Tanja, without any verbal signal, charges on her own accord and again subdues the suspect in a maelstrom of snarling and biting.

A few moments later, the demo over, Lambert and Tanja are happily petting and nuzzling. Like any carefree lad with his pup. The kennels at Quantico, home to half a dozen award winning teams of dogs and handlers, are where Bartlett, early one autumn morning, came to visit ....Robby and his handler, 26 year old Lance Cpl. Shawnn Manthey.

It was upsetting for everyone. Robby, an 8 year old Belgian Malinois, tried to go through his paces but failed. Beset by bad hips, arthritis in his front elbows and a painful growth on his spine, he couldn't catch the suspect when his handler ordered him to attack. When he finally did get in a bite, his gums bled. Finally, the dog was in so much pain the demonstration had to be halted. The congressman, full of admiration for both dog and handler, returned to Capitol Hill with fresh ammunition for his effort to rescind the 1949 law. Manthey, he knew, wanted to adopt the dog but could not do so unless Bartlett succeeded with the new legislation.

The key was for the military to be able to transfer liability to new owners when it adopted dogs out - and Bartlett wrote this into the law. "The fear that these dogs might pose a danger or a legal liability after adoption is understandable, but unwarranted," he said. Putney's 550 post WWII dogs had been returned to civilian life with "not a single instance of those adopted dogs biting anyone," he noted, and police dogs routinely live at home with their handlers and families.

While Bartlett lobbied for the new law, a "Help Save Robby Campaign" appeared on the Web, complete with a picture of the dog and handler Manthey and a poem,

"For Robby"
Where once a life was his to save
It is now our turn to try
To give him back some happiness
But you will not let us - Why?

By the time the legislation passed and the president signed it into law on Nov. 6, however, Manthey's wife was pregnant and the young handler realized he couldn't afford the high dollar medication the dog needed. "Me and Robby were partners so long," he says, "I don't want him getting jealous of the baby or my other dogs." In late October, Robby was shipped back to Lackland Air Force Base in Texas, where the nation's military dogs are trained at the 341st Training Squadron and where, when their lives in the field are over, they return to help train new handlers. And to die.

Lassie in Combat.

American war dogs like Robby and Tanja, called military working dogs, or MWDs, in peacetime are the stuff of legend. The 10,425 canines who served in WWII saved countless GIs. They included heroes like Chips, who stood guard at the Roosevelt Churchill conference at Casablanca and later, in combat in Sicily, broke away from his handler to attack a pillbox and capture an enemy machine gun crew.

In 1990 Disney produced a TV movie called "Chips the War Dog." In 1999, the Discovery Channel's "War Dogs: America's Forgotten Heroes" documented the exploits of the 4,000 dogs who served in Vietnam, leading jungle patrols, spotting ambushes, pulling their handlers to safety. The documentary lamented the fate of hundreds of dogs left behind at the end of the war. "Without Toro," says Vietnam dog handler Carl Dobbins in the documentary, "there's no way I'd have made it back to the United States. I wouldn't have made it probably three months without Toro."

Today, America's roughly 1,800 military dogs and their handlers are engaged mostly in military police work apprehending suspects, searching buildings, securing perimeters. The Quantico dogs and their handlers are also loaned out to the Secret Service, State Department and other federal agencies for bomb and narcotics detection work. When President Clinton visited India last spring, Lambert and Tanja went along, searching vehicles and rooms the president would use to make sure they were bomb free. The dog stayed in the hotel room with me," the handler recalls. "We were on call. We'd play around, throw the ball around. When I'd go for a jog, she'd accompany me. She was my partner. It's a very close bond, like having a very, very close friend you know you can count on."

Dogs are currently deployed with U.S. peacekeeping forces in Kosovo, the closest thing we have to a war zone right now, where they work in security, VIP protection, crowd control and bomb detection. Should America go to war, Lambert and other handlers say, their dogs can be quickly trained to lead patrols, spot tripwires, sniff out the enemy at distances of up to 1,000 yards, serve as couriers and perform other assignments under combat conditions.

At long last, such steadfast and often heroic service is being recognized, as memorials to America's war dogs spring up across the country. Streamwood, Ill., decided to add one to the town's War Memorial after citizen Jennifer Pfannkuche got the idea from reading a children's book on war dogs. "Dogs have been serving our country in combat for 200 years since the American Revolution, and they've never been acknowledged," said another citizen, Carolyn Pentecost, who mailed 1,000 letters seeking financial support for the Streamwood memorial. At a dedication of another memorial, at March Air Force Base in Riverside, Calif., earlier this year, Putney watched "200 dog handlers from Vietnam, and you could see the tears on their faces some didn't even get a chance to tell their dog goodbye."

Next spring, Simon & Schuster is planning to publish Putney's book, "Always Faithful: A Memoir of the Marine Dogs of World War II." During that war, dogs were recruited just like soldiers. They came from among people's house pets, according to the Quartermaster Foundation's Web site, www.qmfound.com. The American Kennel Association and a group called Dogs for Defense mobilized dog owners to donate quality animals to the armed services. Thus, when it was time for the dogs to demobilize, most had homes to go to.

This is not true of today's military dogs, who are kept in kennels from puppyhood and work with several handlers over their careers. Today, it's not that simple.

Troubling Transitions.

In the wake of the new law, calls are coming in to Lackland, from military dog handlers and others, wanting to adopt dogs. Spokesman Gary Emery says the 341st Training Squadron is studying how to implement the law "so that we're doing the right thing for the animals and the people that will adopt them." Despite assurances from Bartlett and Putney, the military, including the very handlers who love the dogs, remains concerned about safety. "I don't think you can really deprogram these dogs," says Lambert. "The training might get toned down, but she'll always have it in the back of her mind." "These dogs have a rough transition to their older years," says Sgt. Brice Cavanaugh, Quantico handler of an award winning Belgian Malinois named Irac. "I'd rather see a dog put down than have the handler take him home and have him bite a small child out of fear and pain."

It's not yet clear how many dogs will be available for adoption. The squadron needs to keep about 150 on hand for training purposes. During the past three years, about 200 dogs a year have been euthanized. "Our policy is that the only time we euthanize military working dogs is to ease the pain and suffering of an animal with a terminal disease that's untreatable," Emery says. Army Col. Larry Carpenter, 48, the squadron's chief veterinarian who grew up on a farm in South Dakota, admits to loving animals and has two dogs and three cats at home. He says he has never euthanized a military dog "where the dog was not ready to die. They usually have serious medical problems. "We try to make a decision on the quality of life of a dog, and his ability to work. We have 12 and 13 year old dogs that still have the drive, the heart to work; and work is what they love." In the end, Carpenter says, the death decisions are made the same way they are in a private veterinary practice. "You come to a decision where the dog doesn't have a quality of life that can sustain it, so you end up putting the dog to sleep as an act of kindness."

Each corpse is autopsied, for medical research, and then cremated. There's no graveyard at the squadron.

Dogs that can be adopted under the new law will be those not needed for training work and still healthy enough to enjoy life. These dogs Carpenter will evaluate and then match with qualified applicants. It will be, he's sure, tricky. "If I look at a dog from a medical standpoint," he says, "I can say that he's likely to bite, but I can't say that a dog won't bite.

Some dogs are very aggressive and may not be adoptable just because that's their personality." This is worrisome, he says. In a civilian adoptive setting, "there is a significant danger that the dog could do what it's been trained to do, which is protect and attack. Given a situation where breeds are being banned for aggressive behavior, this is one of the main problems in adopting out these dogs. They don't have to be ordered to attack; they do it without command. Put yourself in the position of having children and living next door to a dog like that."

Rep. Bartlett isn't worried, however. "These dogs are not a hazard," he says. Under his law, the military must provide a report on each euthanized dog. "We can have hearings," he says, "and they'll have to get up there and explain why they killed that dog."

As for Robby, he is now in a "nice kennel" at Lackland, Emery says, adding he is receiving top quality medical care and is being evaluated for use as a training dog.

Semper Fi

In another war dog book that came out last year, "K-9 Soldiers: Vietnam and After" (Hellgate Press, $13.95), author and Vietnam veteran Paul B. Morgan described the courageous exploits of his German shepherd, Suzie. They walked point together through the jungle, made parachute jumps, saved downed chopper crews. Morgan had acquired Suzie not from the Army but from a priest, Father Tu, in exchange for a pistol and silver rosary beads. "God protects dogs from the knowledge of death," Father Tu had observed, "so they will be brave and serve their fellow man. "Because of the unconditional love, devotion, humility and honesty, all dogs are rewarded in the afterlife with the equivalent of Heaven.

Poems by Janis Dibert

FOR ROBBY
You say he is just another dog
Who served his master well
And on his fate of euthanasia
We really should not dwell
Where once a life was his to save
It is now our turn to try
To give him back some happiness
But you will not let us - Why?
You say he is U. S. property

And when his job is through
He must die, he cannot go home
There is nothing you can do.
Dog is God spelled backward
And just like his son
He must now forgive you
For you know not what you have done.

SECOND POEM

DOCTOR JOHNSON'S ORCHARD
Today I'm coming home at last
To rest my weary head.
To lie among the apple trees
In Doctor Johnson's bed.
I'd hope to have some green grass
There's plenty there it's said
And during life I only heard
Of Doctor Johnson's bed.
It seems that many years ago
Doc Johnson felt it wise
And gave a final resting place
To friends in doggie Guise.
Some of us were family pets
And some worked for mankind
But each of us was special
And hard to leave behind.
I will not be alone at all
And truly I'm not dead
I'm merely napping waiting for you
In Doctor Johnson's bed.

ROBBY HAS GONE HOME

FRIDAY, JANUARY 19, 2001—

As fireworks flew in our nation's capitol; eleven-year-old

Robby, known to the Dept. of Defense as "military working dog number W005," the Military Working Dog whose illness and dedication to his handler incited a firestorm leading to the passage of the first war dog retirement bill (HR 5314/Public Law 106-446), was being euthanized at Lackland Air Force Base in San Antonio, Texas, where he had been "under evaluation" since October.

The decision by the Air Force was not totally unexpected. Still, it was a very unpleasant surprise, both to Congressman Bartlett's office and to members of the "Save Robby Campaign". Bartlett contacted the Secretary of the Air Force, asking for a "stay of execution" until there was conclusive evidence that Robby's medical condition was indeed beyond hope.

Meanwhile, Ms. Nicole Miller of the Congressman's staff contacted Save Robby founding member, Dr. Bill Putney, DVM and sent him Robby's medical records. Ms. Miller also contacted Tom Johnston, Chairman of the "Save Robby Campaign" to see if there was any possibility of finding a home for Robby should he be released from the military.

Johnston contacted Beverly Gainer and Mary Thurston of Austin, Texas and a home was found for Robby, conditional on Dr. Putney's decision after having reviewed Robby's medical records and consulted with Colonel L.G. Carpenter, the veterinarian at Lackland Air Force Base.

After reviewing the records and speaking with Colonel Carpenter, Dr. Putney said that Robby's arthritic lesions on his spine had worsened to the point where he was in constant pain, and the medications were no longer helping. The only way to keep Robby from being in pain was to drug him to a comatose state. Considering this, we sadly agreed that it would be best to let Robby go home.

The Save Robby Campaign had been in the middle of trying to get an update on Robby's condition when it received news of the Air Force's plans for euthanization. Initial requests from Congressman Bartlett's office for an update on Robby's physical condition after the holidays were rejected on the grounds of national security. Then, late Thursday afternoon, the Air Force made a sudden turnabout and agreed to fax Robby's latest health report to the Congressman - at the same time mentioning that he would be killed the next morning.

Robby served his country well, above and beyond the call of duty. Because of him, thousands of compassionate citizens were moved to speak out on behalf of all the war dogs. Because of Robby, we now have the first retirement law for war dogs on the federal books.

But there remains much to be done. HR 5314 (Public Law 106-446) merely gives the military the option of retirement, and judging by how they handled Robby's situation, it seems they will resist implementing the law as long as they can think they can get away with it.

For years the Air Force knew Robby had a progressive, deteriorating arthritic condition, and, with the signing of the law in November, they could have released the dog to his handler to live out his final months in a normal home. Instead they choose to keep him at Lackland Air Force Base "for evaluation."

We bid farewell to Robby. His tour is done, his spirit is free. We, on the other hand, will continue the fight for true freedom for all the other "Robbys" who continue to serve (an estimated two hundred "Robbys" are euthanized every year when they get too old to do their jobs). Congressman Bartlett is equally determined to see the new retirement law implemented.

Many, many thanks to everybody who cared and spoke out on this important issue. Without you, Robby would have been wiped from the annals of our nation's history, just another anonymous, numbered piece of "equipment" who served without complaint and then was disposed of like a junked jeep.

NEW LAW:

Robby was the "Poster Boy" who changed the laws regarding K-9s in wars since WWII.

President W. Clinton signed this new law on November 6, 2000. H.R.5314 became Public Law No: 106 446 amending

Title 10, United States Code, to facilitate the adoption of retired military working dogs by law enforcement agencies, former handlers of these dogs, and other persons capable of caring for these dogs.

The full text of this law can be found on the Library of Congress website:
http://thomas.loc.gov/cgi bin/bdquery/z?d106:h.r.05314:

UPDATE:

June 2002, "Robbie's Law" (P.L. 106-446) used in behalf of Iraqi German Shepherd. "Fluffy" the German Shepherd, born in Iraq, who was acquired, trained and handled by SFC Russell Joyce, 3rd Special Forces, has been flown to the United States and re-united with his handler. Under P.L. 106-446, he was given Honorary Military Working Dog status, and then he was declared "Military Surplus," released to and adopted by SFC Joyce. His story can be seen at: www.k9fluffy.com .

We spoke with SFC Joyce by telephone and e-mail to obtain permission for the statement above; which he graciously gave us.

In return he asked that we list, for your information, the following URLs of a few of the organizations and people who helped him get Fluffy back to the United States:
United States War Dogs Association...uswardogs.org
War Dogs, America's Forgotten Heroes...www.war-dogs.com
Vietnam Dog Handlers Association...www.vdhaonline.org
Viet-Nam Security Police Association...vspa.com/memorial-1.html
(There are over 1,170,000 sites dedicated to War Dogs on the Google Search Engine alone.)

In Loving Memory of

K-9 ROCCO
and
K-9 AXEL

May 22, 2001 and May 27, 2001

Partner Officer Ernest Wolosewicz & Partner Cpl. Greg Manis
Long Beach Police Department
100 Long Beach Blvd.
Long Beach CA 90802
562.570-7260

MEMORIAL SERVICES FOR TWO POLICE K-9'S

The Long Beach Police Department is saddened to announce the Memorial Service for two of the Department's Patrol K-9's. On May 14, 2001, Rocco, with only three months on the job, was critically injured after a fall during a burglary investigation and was euthanized on May 16, 2001. On May 19, 2001, the second K-9, Axel, died at home from a sudden intestinal problem.

The Memorial Service for both dogs will be held on

Thursday, May 31, 2001, at 3:00 p.m., at the Long Beach Police Academy, 7290 East Carson Street, Long Beach. The Long Beach K-9 Officer's Association will be raising funds to replace the much needed service dogs.

Axel and Rocco, two beloved Long Beach police dogs who died in the same week, were memorialized Thursday afternoon before a crowd of officers, K-9s and other mourners gathered at the Long Beach Police Academy. Panting in the hot sun, about 20 police dogs from Long Beach, Orange County and as far away as Pismo Beach sat on mats flanking their officer partners and rows of seated spectators at the service. The animals marked the close of the service with a symphony of loud barking, tugging at their leads as the 21 gun salute commenced.

"I think they want to go chase bad guys," a boy whispered to himself toward the memorial's end. "Some people think an animal is just an animal," observed Debbie Lim, 40, her infant nephew asleep in her arms. "But when they serve us, these dogs become a part of the family." Lim works at a fast food restaurant frequented by many of the K-9 officers. Because dogs are not known for long attention spans, the double funeral was brief, opening with a Police Department color guard and drummer and including remarks from the department chaplain and the playing of taps.

"It was wonderful, very respectful," said Clarice Mooney, widow of Bill Mooney, the Long Beach police chief who started the K-9 unit in the city 23 years ago. The funeral was held near the special cemetery the department and its formidable citizen support group maintain for 30 departed police dogs. Each deceased service dog has a headstone, in which its cremated remains are entombed should the cemetery need to be moved. That has already happened once, when the Police Academy had to move to make way for the Towne Center shopping complex off the southbound San Gabriel River Freeway.

Rocco and Axel will be laid to rest at the cemetery, where each headstone features a photograph of the dog and its handler. The headstones surround a lawn beside the department's kennels, where the dogs stay while their handlers receive training.

On the night of May 14, Rocco was pursuing a possible burglar at the Museum of Latin American Art. A 2½ year old Dutch shepherd whose specialty was tracking people by scent, Rocco followed a trail onto the roof. He leaped onto an aluminum awning which collapsed. Then he struck a railing, which broke his back and left him paralyzed. He was euthanized two days later.

Three days later, Axel, a 7 year old German Shepherd, was found dead in the garden of Cpl. Greg Manis, his partner of four years. A veterinarian later determined that Axel had a rare but lethal intestinal disorder. "My youngest son decided to name his tadpole Axel, so his name will live on."

Rocco's death marked only the third time a Long Beach police dog has died in the line of duty. To lose two police dogs in the same year, much less in the same week, is rare. "It hit us pretty hard," said Officer Richard Lubchenko, who brought his dog, Jaro, along for the funeral but, because of the withering heat, "tossed him back in the air conditioned car with a bowl of water."

Along with a large police presence, there were a sizable number of people who just love dogs and felt the loss of the pair. In what is already a dog loving town, there is a citizens group called the Long Beach K-9 Officers Association which hosted a reception after the funeral.

In Loving Memory of

K-9 ROXIE

AKA Roxanne
LODD
February 12, 1994 - November 6, 2001

Partner: Cpl. Gerald 'Pete' Riess
Delaware River & Bay Authority
Cape May County - Lower Twp., NJ

'Roxie, a black lab, died of a heart attack in the line of duty from work overload after September 11, 2001. Roxanne was used to patrol the authority's various airports, and bridges as well as the ferry terminals. This is dangerous and very hard work. She died of a heart attack the sixth of November while searching cars and luggage of passengers waiting to board the ferry.

Her work load had increased as Delaware River Bay Authority police increased surveillance and detection efforts in the wake of September 11, 2001, terrorist attacks. She died working to protect passengers, doing what she was trained to do. "Roxie" cremains will be buried in the spring (2002) under the flag pole at the Cape May Ferry Terminal. She is also sadly missed by Cpl. Riess' wife, Mrs. Tammy Riess, and their three young children, as well as many others.

March 22, 2002: Cpl. G. Peter Riess graduated with his yellow lab, Molly, and black lab, Holly from Explosive Detection school with a short ceremony and followed by luncheon. Congratulations Pete, Holly & Molly!

Update:

They did not have any type of memorial service for Roxanne. However, the grounds maintenance people did an excellent job of landscaping the area.. I did put her ashes in the ground at the flag pole. If you go to the Cape May side of the ferry, on the piece of ground between the two loading bridges is a flag pole, no longer in use. The memorial is located a few feet from the pole. It is in the shape of a dog bone. If you are ever there, please ask anyone working. I would be honored to show all the memorial.

In Loving Memory of

K-9 SABRE

April 13, 1995 - August 15, 2001

Partner: Sgt. Rod Smith
Tukwila Police Department
6200 Southcenter Blvd.
Tukwila, WA 98188
206.433-1818

Sabre was a fabulous dog, hard working. He fought hard from start to finish in both work and play. He was very attached to me and couldn't stand for me to leave without him. He was responsible for 100 arrests during his 3.5 year career. Known as a very hard dog, Sabre was a small giant. He only weighted 75 pounds, but had the heart of a 115 pound dog. He was loving to my family. We miss him terribly.

Together, Sabre and I forged memories that I will never forget. Those few years we spent together were filled with all the extremes of life. There were many pleasurable moments. Lots of frustration. A bit of pain and many defeats. But most of all, I remember the numerous successes that Sabre afforded me as the only K-9 unit for our department.

In Loving Memory of

K-9 SAM

June 15, 1998
January 5, 2001

Partner: Daryl E. Delagrange, MPO III
High Point Police Department
High Point, NC 27260

Sam was a purebred Belgian Malinois, who worked the streets of High Point from January 14, 1991 until his retirement with honor and distinction on June 15, 1998. He then tried to take life easy, but his desire to work the street never left. Being retired was not for him. When we worked together he would get sick on his stomach if he thought he was being left behind at home. He was four years old when he started his K-9 career and over eleven and a half when he retired. He will always be the oldest working K-9 that the High Point Police Department will ever have. They are now required to be retired by age ten.

Sam was put down with me at his side on January 5, 2001

because he could no longer have quality of life. His life long (service years) vet performed the task. He shed as many tears as I did.

On January 19, 2001, my department held a memorial service for him. A lot of nice things were said about Sam and I. I had only hoped that I had made his life as rewarding as he had made mine. He is truly missed.

Sam was honored by being selected as both "Who's Who of Animals, 1994 and Who's Who of Dogs, 1995." Sam was also honored as "Patrol Dog of the Quarter" by the USPCA (United States Police K-9 Association") for a track he ran back in1993. So, not to relive his 67 apprehensions, he was a great dog and a wonderful partner.

UPDATE:

I am a Housing Authority officer now. In fact, the last six months that Sam spent on the street, we were assigned to the Housing Unit. I still occasionally dabble in K-9 stuff with our new handlers. In fact this last November (2001) our department sponsored a K-9 Seminar for about thirty dog teams across the nation.

I got to assist and that brought back a lot of memories. I decided that when Sam retired I would never work another dog.

Well, that's a short version of my life as a K-9 chauffeur. I loved it and loved my dog. Of course I have always loved dogs. If you want some coincidence, my parents sent their Doberman to WWII and he returned from the Pacific during WWII and two years later my twin bother and I were born. So we grew up around dogs with experience at catching the "bad guys".

I wish that my father would have lived long enough to have seen Sam. He would have loved him to death. Dad was an obedience trainer for the AKC.

In Loving Memory of

K-9 SHADOW

1991   March 2, 2001

Partner   Officer Craig Bunting
Trenton K-9 Police Unit NJ
225 North Clinton Ave.
Trenton, NJ, USA 08609 1091
609. 989 3921

I'm Officer Bunting, trainer of the Trenton Police K-9 Unit. I lost two pets within the last three months, and it has been hard. One was on Christmas day, a Fila (Lector) about 180 pounds that I got for my wife nine years ago for Christmas which made it that much harder. The second one was my K-9 partner whom I met at the dog pound in Trenton and who became the best partner that I ever had since becoming a police officer.

Shadow was his name and his was about ten years old. When you think, coming from the pound you never know. He was abused and left on the streets prior to coming home with my wife and I. He was getting ready for retirement, I had him fixed, teeth cleaned and about one month to go to retire when I found him gone on March 2, 2001.

The vet found a tumor in his heart that was cancerous. He said that nothing could be done. Shadow was a great K-9 partner for six years but it seems like just yesterday that we were put together. So many street fights, burglaries etc. I miss him everyday. There was so much more we could have done together.

In Loving Memory of

K-9 SIRIUS Badge # 17 WTC

LODD
September 11, 2001

Partner: Officer David Lim
Port Authority Police Department NYNJ
World Trade Center NYC

I first saw Dave on TV, covered with gray ash and in shock as he was rescued, tearful and grateful for surviving. Deep in his heart, he knew that he lost his best friend, Sirius, along with many other friends and co workers. It took a week or so to find his name, email and requested a photo of Sirius and Dave. This memorial to Sirius was first on the web. This is how I met Dave.

"One Got By Us"

Officer Lim was in the K-9 office in the basement of the WTC and heard the explosion on an upper floor. Thinking it was a bomb that had exploded David put his K-9 Sirius in the dog crate and told him to stay, he was going to investigate.

David told K-9 Sirius, "one [bomb] must have gotten by us." Officer Lim had no idea what had actually occurred or how the world was rapidly changing for all of us.

The officer started up the stair way directing people out and reached about the 44th. floor when he heard the second explosion. The officer still did not have any idea what was happening and felt that missiles had hit the building. The building evacuation was under way and he was assisting several people down the staircase. Officer Lim stated they could now hear the building collapsing and he was helping a female down the staircase when the whole building came down around them. The officer and others believe they were at about the 5th level in the stairwell that was partly standing after the collapse. The smell of jet fuel was heavy and they elected to go up to the now top of the World Trade Center, the sixth floor. They were eventually tossed ropes to get down and were making their way across the debris when small arms fire was heard.

David stated he first thought that a battle was under way and thought to himself was he going to get shot after living through the building collapse? It was later found the small arms fire was ammunition that was stored that was now being detonated by fire.

David made several attempts to find a way to get to the basement where K-9 Sirius was crated but was rebuffed by fireman and police officers now trying to secure the scene and set up rescue operations. His K-9 Sirius #17 is still listed as missing.

Officer Lim and Sirius were new members of the USPCA having joined in July of this year. They were members of Region 15 and had participated in certification trials. Officer Lim told me that his department has had several offers to replace his K-9. He asked me to pass on to you all his sincerest appreciation for all of your thoughts and prayers. We still hold out hope and pray for those missing. Officer Lim told me that his Department, The New York Port Authority, is missing thirty seven officers as well as K-9 officer Sirius in this attack and he asked me to pass on the following information for anyone who wishes to make a contribution to his Department. The Port Authority PBA is extremely grateful to all those who have offered assistance to our membership in this time of need. We have offers of financial help for the families of members of the Port Authority Police Department affected by the World Trade Center disaster.

COURAGEOUS K-9S!

When Port Authority K-9 police officer David Lim responded to the World Trade Center disaster on September 11, he brought along his trusty bomb sniffing Labrador retriever, Sirius. But when he realized he'd be more effective freehanded, Lim left his K-9 companion inside the building. "Nobody thought these buildings would fall down," he told ET. "At that time, I couldn't think of a safer place for Sirius to be than in the basement while I was up doing the rescues. Of course, now, when I look back, he probably saved my life by just sitting there."

Sirius perished in the tragedy, leaving David alone without his co-worker. "He's very special," said David. "All dogs go home with us. So not only was he my partner, but he was also my pet and my friend." The bond between K-9 and master is a special one. And while David realizes the human tragedy may overshadow the death of his dog, any pet owner can attest to the impact an animal makes on our daily lives. "We were very close. No matter where I went, he went. Whatever I asked him to do, he did. He never complained. Sometimes we'd be working for long hours, searching hundreds of cars or trucks, and he'd just look at me like, 'What do you want me to do now?'"

When Seventeen magazine heard of David's situation, it decided to make a difference. Last Friday in New York City, in front of a roaring crowd, the K-9 police officer was presented with a new dog, BUSTER, at the 9th Annual Seventeen's Star Showcase, a charitable event for 3,000 teens now benefitting New York City Disaster Relief. During the uplifting event, featuring concert performances by EDEN'S CRUSH and 3LW, plus fall and holiday fashion shows by Seventeen's Style Squad,

David took the stage with his family and was presented with his new pooch. "This is a fine example of a new beginning," David said. "Everybody talks about September 11. Let's talk about the future. The future is a new dog that I'll be working with, that'll be just as good as my buddy, Sirius."

"One particular moving piece of film was about a Port Authority officer named David Lim," Tellep said. Lim, Sirius' handler, was one of the few people to climb out of the rubble alive. Unfortunately, his four legged partner didn't. Tellep knew the state was in the process of buying the dogs, and as the local representative of the Public Safety Employee's Association, he brought up the idea of naming one of the new dogs after Lim's missing dog. The union bought the dog. Other organizations, such as various Lion's Clubs, helped raise funds for the other four dogs. Because the $4,000 for Sirius was provided by the union, "in our small way, it was to show solidarity and support to the victims of the 9/11 (attacks) and to the policemen and firemen," Tellep said. The name comes from the brightest star, "Sirius," in the constellation Canis Major, meaning great dog. But it has taken on a whole different meaning since Sept. 11.

Lim, 45, has told his story countless times on shows such as the Today Show, Extra, Entertainment Tonight and has given many speeches. Lim and Sirius, a 4.5 year old, 90 lb. yellow Labrador, started a normal day at 5:30 AM in the basement of the World Trade Center, Lim said in a phone interview from JFK International Airport in New York on Sunday. Sirius is one of two dogs whose job was to check incoming trucks for bombs. But at 8:48 a.m., everything changed when an airliner crashed into the first tower at the World Trade Center. "Oh my god, they got one (bomb) by us," Lim remembers saying to Sirius.

He told the dog to stay put while he went upstairs to check things out. He struggled past falling debris and people streaming down the stairs until he reached the plaza floor. There he saw a dead body lying next to a stage. "I've been a police officer for 21 years and had never seen a dead body like that," Lim said. Soon after, another body landed about 50 feet away from the first one. He called his wife Diane. That's when he learned a plane had hit the first tower.

When he reached the 44th floor, the second plane hit the other tower. "I saw this debris and fire coming toward the window. It blew out the window and knocked me and everybody there down," he said. "When the second one hit, I knew we were in trouble and we were under attack." When he and another fireman were helping probably the last civilian in the building escape from the fragile tower, the world came crashing down around them. "The sound, it was something between an onrushing locomotive and an avalanche," Lim said. "It lasted 15 seconds, but it seemed like forever."

They were on the fourth level at the time and half of the staircase in front of them had disappeared. They started looking for a place to hunker down until they could be rescued and they passed Lim's two cell phones around for people to call their families. Soon after, Lim started smelling jet fuel and they started back up the stairs again. The reached the top of what remained of the World Trade Center on the sixth floor. There they radioed for a ladder team who threw them rope and they climbed down roughly three stories to Ground Zero. There Lim turned around and saw a sight he described as surreal and horrific. "It reminded me of the movie 'Terminator' where they're going through the big junk yard during a battle at the beginning," Lin said. "It looked like a big kid kicked over his Legos."

Lim still believed his dog was alive and was trapped in pockets underneath the rubble. He tried several times to re enter the debris, only to be turned back by firemen and police officers. Finally, some of his fellow Port Authority officers threw him in the back of an ambulance. He cried the entire way to the hospital. Sirius and 37 officers of the 1,000 strong Port Authority were gone. The dog's loss has hit the Lim family hard, especially Lim's 12 year old son Michael. Sirius lived with the Lim's like most K-9 officers. Lim's life, like the country's, has pressed on.

But things are different for Lim. Lim will be getting a new

K-9 next week, but there isn't a World Trade Center to protect anymore. He's had his story published in international magazines, he's received scores of e mails and letters, most of them wishing him sympathy. He's had 160 people offer him replacement dogs. He rang the buzzer on the New York Stock Exchange's reopening day September 17, has met royalty, movie stars and high profile politicians. People even recognize him on the streets. There are plans for Lim to meet Sirius' Alaska namesake in March. Tellep has been trying to organize sponsors to help Lim and his wife travel up for the start of the Iditarod and to spend two days in Fairbanks.

Meanwhile, the Alaska Sirius is beginning what will hopefully be a long career as a trooper K-9. Trooper Lt. Randy Hahn, the statewide K-9 coordinator, went to Alabama to select five dogs who would be suitable for the tough job of a law enforcement K-9. The dogs were matched with the personalities of the troopers selected for the K-9 program. The dogs and their handlers are headed for roughly 10 weeks of training to become dual certified as narcotics and patrol dogs, doubling the number of dogs troopers have already.

Sirius is originally from Holland and knows commands in Dutch, but at the academy all of the dogs will be taught commands in German. After the academy, one of the dogs will go to Sitka, two will be stationed in Soldotna, one in Palmer and Sirius will come to Fairbanks. Sirius has spent the last month bonding with Baker and lives with him, his wife, Tracy and their 3 year old Greyhound Dalmatian mix.

Baker spent 13 years in the Army prior to becoming a trooper. He has experience only in the logistical side of the military's K-9 program in the Pacific area, but he's always wanted to be a handler. "The only adjustment I've really had to make is the idea of working with a partner," Baker said. "He's my partner. I've got to watch over him and he watches over me. It took a few days to get used to."

Sirius Found January 21, 2002

I recovered him yesterday, January 21st. He was in his kennel and from all accounts, was killed instantly. He received full Police Honors when his body was recovered. Everyone lined up and saluted Sirius as we left. All the great machines were silent as we led the procession to the Police Truck. I was given the American Flag that draped his body. I will cherish it always. I will probably get one of those triangle boxes to put it in. The Hartsdale Pet Cemetery has offered to do the cremation and burial of Sirius. Tough day, but at least I fulfilled the promise I made to him on September 11th, 2001. "He waited and I came back."

Westminster Salutes Search and Rescue Dogs Feb. 11, 2002

The Westminster Kennel Club and USA Network have united to donate $275,000 to the National Association for Search and Rescue to create the NASAR K-9 Fund. On Feb. 11, exactly five months after the Sept. 11 terrorist attacks, they will present $275,000 to Michael Tuttle, president of NASAR, during USA Networks live coverage of the 126th annual Westminster Kennel Club Dog Show in the New York Madison Square Garden.

Handlers and dogs representing the heroic search and rescue teams that worked at the World Trade Center and Pentagon will participate in the special salute on the opening evening of the Westminster show. All contributions donated to the fund, including the original donation of $275,000, will be used to train handlers and dogs across the country in the skills needed to respond in a crisis. Donations may be sent to the NASAR K-9 Fund, 4500 Southgate Place, Suite 100, Chantilly, CA 20151

During a break at the Westminster Dog Show in NYC, SAR dogs from around the country were introduced with their handlers. The crowd of 10,000 cheered to the point of frightening the dogs and their partners along with the music from the NYPD marching band. Some of the K-9s were returning to work at the WTC site after their appearance. One officer said he would rather face gunmen than the crowd.

Portrait of K-9 Sirius by artist, Deb Stonebraker of Missouri.

Personal Impression by author (Lulu) Louise Krause

Tuesday:

Bob and I checked out Liberty park the afternoon prior to the memorial service. We wanted to make sure where to arrive early the next morning. The Liberty State Park is very large, and at that time was almost empty. The weather over these two days was beautiful with the sun sparkling on the Manhattan skyline. That was awesome for us because we don't take it for granted. Yes, we could see broken windows in skyscrapers near Ground Zero. A constant reminder of September 11th 2001.

Wednesday:

As we approached the area, we found ourselves in a sea of a hundred or more K-9s. "I WAS IN HEAVEN!" There were Police and Sheriff's K-9 patrol cars from all over the USA. A very large PAPD bus, painted with graphics about Sirius, the Port Authority Police Department and the names of 37 others who gave their lives on that tragic eventful day. You could hear the practice sessions of 2 bagpipe drum corps. Men and women dressed in law enforcement uniforms, including many from the San Francisco Fire Department. It was a military event familiar to us since we attend many USCG events in Cape May, NJ.

Best of all for us, was meeting Dave and his family and his new partner, Sprig, face to face instead of e mail. Sprig, incidentally, knocked me on my BUTT when I stooped down to pet him. Why? Sprig not only has a great nose for 25 or more explosives, but rawhides too. I had one hidden, sealed and in a heavy canvas bag. He knew it was there, a gift for later.

SERVICE: Programs were handed out. Lapel pins and programs were given to guests. There were chairs set up for many guests. Suddenly, TV, photographers and reporters from all over appeared in front of everyone to cover the service. The stage was set with "important" people. There was a display of a framed photo of Sirius' coming home to Dave, American flag encased that covered Sirius on his return home, and the urn holding his cremains. Each handler and his partner approached the table to give respect to Sirius, two at a time. This took an hour or more. A twenty-one gun salute ended the service. A long table was set up to display gifts sent to the Lim family from people who cared from all over the country.

During the service, I never saw so many Law Enforcement officers with tears streaming down their cheeks. From 10:30 AM to 2:30 PM (when we departed for home, and I am sure afterwards) Dave was unselfishly giving individual time to everyone who wanted to speak to him. He was proud of his family, parents, co workers and superiors for all their support. His family patiently watched and waited.

Dave kept his composure and generously made everyone feel very special as though each was the most important person there. He displayed his sincere appreciation of everyone's attendance. Needless to say, emotions were high. The guests acted like one big family comforting each other. I know support was there for the Lim family and others who lost friends and relatives. We were honored to be a part of this celebration of the life of Sirius. ~lulu

In Loving Memory of

K-9 STARKO

May 9, 2002

Partner: MPO II Rick Dietz
High Point Police Department
1009 Leonard Avenue
High Point, NC 27260

Starko was a Belgian Malinois born in Holland who immigrated to the U.S. when he was 2 years old. After we graduated Patrol Dog School on 19 April 1990 he hit the ground running. Among his many accomplishments was that he was the first K-9 to work with the High Point Police TACT Team, and as a result of his work a course was designed and taught at the N.C. Justice Academy for SWAT Dogs and their handlers.

Starko was also in "Who's Who of Animals 1994." The list of his apprehensions, drug finds, and evidence recoveries is probably no greater than most Police Working Dogs, but to me he will always be the greatest K-9 to ever wear a badge.

On 19 April 1997 Starko retired from active duty. His ceremony at the police department was attended by over 70 officers, which was a testament to his ability as a street dog. His retirement years were a blessing. On 09 May 2002 I had to make the decision that all handlers dread.

I had to end my best friend's life. Starko had developed complications from a tumor and had to be put to sleep. I am comforted by the knowledge that I was able to be with Starko as he went to sleep for the last time and he knew that I was there and that he was loved. That was the hardest thing I've done, but I owed him that, because he never left me when the chips were down. He was a very courageous, noble, forgiving, and loving partner and friend and I shall always love and miss him.

In Loving Memory of

K-9 TASHA SAR

October 2001

Partner: Marianne Crowell
West Jordan, UT

K-9 Tasha worked in the WTC after 9/11/01

An illegal attempt to kill predators resulted in the poisoning deaths of a search and rescue dog and a service dog in the hills of Summit County.

Wildlife officials say the heavy doses in the poisoned bait also could have killed an unknown number of wild animals, including birds of prey. Toxicology tests confirmed that two dogs one a German Shepherd rescue dog and the other a Labrador trained to assist a handicapped woman, fell victim to strychnine laced deer entrails most likely meant for coyotes.

The Utah Division of Wildlife Resources is investigating several leads. The first confirmed poisoning occurred Sept. 9 in Forest Meadow Ranch, a spread of private homes and mountain lots about 10 miles north of Park City. On that afternoon, the German Shepherd, Tasha, was training to become one of the elite Rocky Mountain Rescue Dogs, which recently took part in the recovery work at New York's World Trade Center.

Coming down the mountain after finding a "lost hiker" in a training exercise, Tasha came across a pile of entrails and took a bite. Minutes later, the 17 month old dog lost control of her hind legs. Then her entire body seized up and she fell. Tasha's owner, West Jordan resident Marianne Crowell, screamed for help and tried to soothe the frightened animal. On the way to the animal hospital, Tasha died in Crowell's arms.

A week later, a Labrador companion dog named Lucy and her owner, a Salt Lake City woman who relies on dogs to alert her to her seizures and provide her with medical syringes, were hiking in the same area when her dog ate some of the entrails, stumbled to the ground and later died. DWR investigator officer Bruce Johnson said both dogs died within 20 minutes of ingesting the deer entrails, which were heavily laced with strychnine.

"It was a hot enough dose that it will kill secondary and tertiary animals, in the food chain, without question," which would put predators and carrion feeders in danger, he said.

David Lyman, who was training Lucy, said he believes the poison is responsible for the deaths of other wildlife. "We used to sit up there and watch hawks and vultures all day long. After this, there wasn't a vulture in the sky. We're sure it was because of the poison," Lyman said.

Utah dog trainers are shocked by the incident. "It's a sad story, let me tell you," said David Perks, a Rocky Mountain dog handler who recently returned from the World Trade Center site. "Tasha's death has been a hard loss for Marianne and our group. When you lose one of these dogs, it's like losing a person."

Anyone with information about the poisonings or other illegal predator control activities in the area are asked to call Johnson at 801 476 2740.

In Loving Memory of

K-9 TAZ

April 26, 2001

Partner: Patrolman Christopher Kaupe
Fairfax Police Department
144 Bolinas Road
Fairfax, CA 94930

The first Police K-9 to join program "Taz" a male German Shepherd 8 years old, had to be euthanized 4/26/01 due to kidney disease.

After six years of searching buildings, capturing suspects, and walking in town parades, Fairfax Police K-9 Taz passed away this week due to kidney failure. The eight year old male German Shepherd had been ill since Monday, said Officer Christopher Kaupe.

Taz was euthanized at the Marin Humane Society on Thursday after it was determined that the dog had an ailment that could not be cured. Taz was the first dog to work with Fairfax Police. The K-9 worked with his partner Chris, assisting on calls, and also helped other agencies over 60 times. Taz was described by co workers as "dedicated and sharp" and responsible for over 18 captures that would not have been made without him. "Taz was much more than a police dog, he was a mascot for the Fairfax Police force" said Kaupe. "When I would drive around with Taz, children would yell his name, and ask to pet him. He really will be missed."

Taz had led the town parade celebrating the opening of Little League just a month before his death.

UPDATE:

A Fairfax police dog is recuperating today at the Marin Humane Society after she was seriously injured earlier this week by jumping 30 feet from a window during a training session on Alcatraz Island. Storm, a 2 year old German Shepherd partnered with K-9 handler and Fairfax police officer Chris Kaupe, suffered a severe leg fracture that involved hours of painstaking surgery to correct. Although she is expected to go home tomorrow, the dog faces up to eight weeks of rehabilitation and an uncertain future as a police dog if her leg doesn't heal property, officials said.

Kaupe said Wednesday that Storm had just finished performing a bite maneuver, where she is directed by officers to clamp down on a suspect, when instead of coming back down the stairs from the second floor of a structure used for training at the old prison, she ran inside the building. "The only thing we could think of is she went to look for further suspects," Kaupe said. Kaupe went up the stairs after her, and tried to get her to heel, but the dog put her paws up on the window's sill and looked down. "She looked around, she contemplated it, she evaluated it and she thought she could do it," he recalled. "She thought the easiest way down was to jump, and she jumped."

Kaupe and Novato police officer Matt Poore, another K-9 handler at the training, watched in horror as the event unfolded before their eyes. "This dog jumped 30 feet," Kaupe said. "We just couldn't believe it." On the way down, she struck a metal grate. The frantic officers performed first aid, and, after stabilizing her, strapped her to a backboard and rushed to get her immediate care. With a fractured distal femur, Storm underwent two hours of emergency surgery performed by Dr. Andrew Sams, a veterinary orthopedic surgeon with an office in Fairfax.

It was a lengthy procedure since Storm had lost so much of the bone, Sams said. "What makes it challenging is it splintered into multiple pieces," he said. "It doesn't fit back together like a puzzle." Plates and screws were required to stabilize the bone, and a synthetic bone graft was performed to fill in the missing pieces. The procedure went well, and the prognosis is good, Sams said. If the bone heals without loosening the plates or the screws, she is likely to return to duty.

For Kaupe, the experience has been emotionally exhausting, he said, since this isn't the first time his partner has been down. Last spring, he lost Taz, a 8 year old German Shepherd who worked by his side for six years and was credited with more than 18 captures. Taz succumbed to kidney failure. "So it's really rough," he said of Storm's injury. "I've handled dogs for seven years now it's just a pleasure."

The Marin Humane Society's K-9 Care Fund, established to offset expenses incurred by the county's police's and search and rescue dogs, picked up the cost of treating Storm's injury. This time around, however, the fund took a hit, officials said. The surgery, expected to cost anywhere from $4,000 to $6,000, has essentially wiped out the fund. "If a dog gets shot tomorrow, we can't cover it," Humane Society spokeswoman Marissa Miller said. "We want to take care of the dogs that take care of us."

Yesterday at the Humane Society, a timid Storm moved about a bit on her bad leg, which now sports a shaved section where a roughly 15 inch incision held together with nearly 40 staples can be seen. These days, it's quiet time for the dog, giving everyone who loves her time to reflect on how fortunate she was. "When Chris told me how far she fell, I thought, 'Oh, God,'" recalled the Humane Society's Carol Williams Skaggs, who oversees the Humane Society's K-9 program and has worked for years with the officer. "She has got a guardian angel over her."

In Loving Memory of

K-9 TOBY

(Toby von Schmidt)
December 31, 1990 - August 2, 2001

Partner: R. Michael Brouse
Metro Health Police Dept.
11551 Valley View Rd.
Sagamore Hills, OH 44067

Sagamore Hills, Ohio Police K-9 (Ret.) has passed away.
Memorial services to honor Toby
Wednesday, August 8 at 10:00 AM at
Paws Awhile Pet Memorial Park
3426 Brush Rd., Richfield, Ohio.
As his legacy, he leaves behind 5 sons,
THOR - East Cleveland, OH PD
HAWK - Brunswick Hills Twp., OH PD
STORM - Medina City, OH PD
ODIN - Olmstead Twp., OH PD
NEIKO - Bath Twp., OH PD

Above are working police K-9's, protecting & serving us all.

K-9 handlers and their partners were at the grave side, August 8 as the music of Mariah Carey's "Hero" was playing. A minister did a brief introduction and prayer.

The poem "Guardians Of The Night" was read and the country song, "If There Hadn't Been You" was played. After prayers, a police bagpiper played as the ceremony ended.

A beautiful service for our beautiful officer. I am fortunate enough to have one of his daughters. We named her Misha (after Mike Brouse) who gave her to me for work. My husband and I did help with the formation of the SHPD K-9 unit and with fund raising to keep it going. It was run by donations from businesses and residents from 1991 1995.

/s/Judith B. Thomas

CMCA, AMS   Aries Management Corporation.

Update:

Ptl. Brouse has been working for Metro Health Police since Sagamore. He has Toby's one son, Thor and Toby's mate, Kilo. He's not doing K-9 work right now.

In Loving Memory of

K-9 TOBY

July 2001

Partner: Mike Andrel
Darby Township Police Department
Sharon Hills, PA
(Toby in center)

Toby retired from police department when he was age 13. Ruger is still in my heart and Jaeger did have three puppies and we have Yago . I will send you a picture. The day we picked up Yago, we took pictures of Grandfather, Toby, and then Jaeger and Yago, but the bad news is, the next day Toby got very sick and could not walk. We took him to the vet and had to put him down. But I think he waited for his grandson, who is now 11 months old and being trained as another police dog.

Toby was my first K-9 dog. I am looking for a real good picture. I am lucky because I have his son Jaeger now working with me. Jaeger is 6 years old and a patrol and drug dog. I now have one of Jaeger's sons, Yago, one of them is 11 months who will also follow in his steps.

In Loving Memory of

K-9 TOMMY

February 15, 1996 - June 9, 2001

Partner: Patrolman Norm Kekic
Parma Police Department
5555 Powers Blvd., Parma, OH 44129
440.887.7300

Tommy suddenly got sick and passed on. We later discovered he had a brain tumor. He is missed by everyone who loved him and we're in shock over his sudden loss.

On Friday, June 15th, a service was held for Tommy. His true name was Bandit, but he was known as Tommy.

Police officers and many regional K-9 units as well as numerous citizens attended his funeral. It took place at "Paw Awhile".

A second K-9 was added to the force and handled by Officer Wells.

In Loving Memory of

Trooper II - SAR

November 6, 2001

Partner: Special Agent Bobby E. Earls
K-9 SAR - FEMA - Conrail
15 Richmond Dr., Norton, MA 02776

"EVEN THE DOGS CRIED....."

Special Agent Bobby Earls & K-9 Trooper II, joined the search for 9 year old Cory Anderson in a severe snowstorm. Conrail Railroad Police Special Agent Bobby Earls, in full dress uniform stood at attention with nearly 100 fellow officers and firefighters as the casket of 9 year old Cory Anderson was carried into Holy Cross Church in Easton MA in early March. It was cold and blustery, but the weather was nearly spring like compared to that Friday just 5 days earlier when Earls and his dog, Trooper were called in to search for Corey in a fierce snowstorm. The boy had left his home on a wooded dead end near Winnecunnet Pond in Norton on a Thursday afternoon to look for the family's golden retriever during a heavy snowstorm.

The dog showed up at a neighbor's about an hour later, but

Corey, wearing a Boston Bruins jacket and his bother's boots, never returned. The 4th grader's disappearance triggered a massive search involving nearly 500 local and state police, firefighters, volunteers, air boats, & helicopters.

The Norton Police contacted Earls, who had worked search & rescue missions with various area police and sheriff's departments in the past. "The terrain was against us from the start, " Earls said. "There were streams, a lake and some cranberry bogs. They ended up draining the bogs. But he wasn't there."

Earls and Trooper II, both certified by FEMA in search & rescue work, teamed up with officers from the Department of Environmental Police and a state police helicopter to search a heavily wooded area. Their efforts continued unabated for 32 hours through a later winter storm that would dump nearly a foot of snow on the eastern part of the state. "By Saturday, it didn't look good," the 7 year Conrail veteran remembered. "We started to think the worst. There was also some thought that he might have been abducted. I 495 runs right by the area."

That Sunday broke clear and cold, but with the good weather came the bad news. A state trooper aboard a boat spotted the yellow sleeves of Corey's Bruins jacket. Searchers on shore found him curled in the fetal position along a riverbank just 300 yards from his home. He had died of hypothermia.

"The area had been searched before," says Earls. "We probably missed him because of the snow. Once it stopped and the sun came out, it was easier to spot Corey's jacket." The discovery took its toll on the searchers. "Hardened troopers and other law enforcement personnel had frozen tears on their cheeks as they loaded Corey into the body bag," Earls recalled, himself choking up at the memory. "Even the dogs cried."

The railroad special agent and his fellow officers and firefighters would not be able to attend the actual services due to the large number of mourners, so they bid farewell to Cory in their own way, 100 white gloved hands snapped a salute to the 9 year old as the casket carrying his body passed by. "I was honored to represent the Conrail Police department in the search for Corey and at his wake and funeral." Earls said, "I'd do it over again 100 times." K-9 Trooper II retired later that year in August.

In Loving Memory of

K-9 WALKER

SAR
September 10, 1996 - October 7, 2001

Handler: Lou Ann Metz
Summit Search & Rescue Dogs, Inc.
1074 Jones St. Ravenna, OH 44266

Certified Area Search Dog with Summit Search and Rescue Dog Certified Delta Society Pet Partner, Walker was a special guy. He was confident, compassionate, gentle and forgiving. Walker had his own ideas of fun and they did not include repetition or simplicity.

Walker proved to me that although humans "think" they know where scent is, we humans actually have no idea. Walker would turn a deaf ear to me if he had scent, no matter how long or how loud I yelled. He would just keep working until he made his find. He would come running back to me full tilt and hug me with that 100 LB. body and grinning ear to ear.

Walker taught us all the meaning of intelligent disobedience. Being a new handler, I would often feel compelled to change things after reading a book or attending a seminar. Eventually however, Walker figured out what worked and got me trained. I learned to put my hands in my pockets, keep my mouth shut and give Walker the trust he deserved. He never let me down.

As a Pet Partner, Walker spent much of his time with cancer patients at our local hospital. Ever gentle, Walker would quietly sit while the patients or families shared their thoughts with him. Walker seemed to soak up their hugs and their tears and replace them with a smile. He was magical that way.

Walker died much too young at six years of age from bacterial meningitis. I am richer for the experience of being his partner and having him as my teacher.

UPDATE:

Lou Ann is currently working an 18 month old White German Shepherd named Lilly. They are certified with Summit Search and Rescue Dogs, Inc. of Ohio as a Human Remains Detection Team. They are currently working toward a specialization in historical remains detection which they will utilize by assisting in the detection of battlefield remains. Remains such as; Native American burial sites, lost cemeteries and family burial sites.

Lilly is a certified Delta Society Pet Partner, so when we are not searching, we visit patients at our local hospital.

In Loving Memory of

K-9 Sir Wallace

Von Stone Wall
(K-9 WALLY)
September 18, 2001

Partner: Officer Mark Golembiewski
Detroit Police Department
Tactical Service Center
1300 Beaubien   Detroit, MI 48226
313.876.0779

Wally, Detroit Police Officer Mark Golembiewski's K-9 partner, died on September18 of a blood disease.   Mark Golembiewski is a canine officer without a K-9, which is an unfortunate thing to be. He has a dog, a golden retriever, specifically, who's being trained as a bomb specialist.

They've been together six weeks now. But a bomb dog isn't the same thing as a K-9 patrol partner, a teammate who's with you through thick, thin and dark, spooky buildings. K-9s are always German Shepherds, like Wally. The Detroit Police Department paired Wally and Golembiewski in September

1999, and they were together almost every minute until September 18. That's when Wally died.

"Your dog will give his life for you," says Golembiewski, 42, but Wally didn't die in action; in fact, as far as he knows, no Detroit K-9 ever has. Wally had a blood disease.

Golembiewski, a 17 year police veteran and lifelong west sider, has owned dogs as long as he can remember. At one point, he had four full grown golden retrievers and nine pups, the pups being what happens when you have four full grown golden retrievers.

You would think an owner would get used to saying good-bye when he's had kennels full of dogs, but you would be wrong. "It doesn't get any easier," Golembiewski says. "With each one, it's the same feeling." He's a professional, though, and even if he's not completely over Wally, he's ready to take on a new K-9.

The problem is finding one. Dogs aren't in the department budget. The K-9 unit depends on donations, and it's not like 14 month old German Shepherds are getting dropped off at police stations on a regular basis.

Anybody with a likely candidate in the house is invited to call the tactical services department at (313) 237 2600. Maybe the dog is outgrowing your home, or it has turned out to be more than you can handle, or you just think it would look good in blue. For qualified candidates, the police department can offer love, advanced training and real live chew toys. In the meantime, Golembiewski will content himself with Topper, the dog who came from a golden retriever rescue center in Standish. Topper is called Topper because, when he's excited, he spins around like a top.

He's one of five bomb dogs the department started to train after September 11, just in case. Assuming he catches on, he'll be able to detect 14 different odors, none of them desirable in populated areas. Bomb dogs are the field goal kickers of the K-9 world, called upon only occasionally but at particularly high stress moments. Because bomb dogs are essentially part timers, police officers can work and live with a bomb dog and a K-9 simultaneously.

"There's a lot of work involved," Golembiewski says, "but this is the best assignment in the world, assuming you like dogs." And, assuming you can get one.

UPDATE:

Mark now handles TOBY, a Belgian Malinois and TOPPER, a bomb dog.

In Loving Memory of

K-9 WOLF

February 1998 - December 2001

Partner: Det. Keith Crandall
New London Police Department
5 Governor Winthrop Blvd.
New London, CT 06320

Wolf was a handsome, sable, German Shepherd bred in Belgium and born on February 13, 1998. Wolf's sire was a Police Service Dog in Belgium and the handler was the breeder. Wolf's brother, from a different litter was a working dog in Scituate, RI. Wolf began his career with the New London Police Department on March 3, 1999, which was the fourth anniversary of his handler's career. Wolf and his handler, Officer Keith Crandall were trained by NAPWDA and CPWDA Master Trainer, NLPD Sgt. William Nott for 12 weeks and graduated from basic patrol school in June 1999.

By August of that year, Wolf lead Crandall to their first successful track and subsequent area search that resulted in the recovery of a loaded Glock 9 mm handgun and the arrests of the two men committing robberies with it. Another high point in Wolf's career was a track from an armed bank robbery. Crandall will admit that he was angry when Wolf tracked directly to a doghouse in someone's back yard. His anger diminished quickly however when Wolf pulled his head out of the doghouse with the robber's disguise in his mouth. Although the robber managed to escape that evening, hairs in the mask were later analyzed and resulted in conviction through DNA.

Wolf even backtracked a rape victim who walked into the NLPD, lost and hysterical. She had no idea where the assault took place but Wolf was able find the crime scene and her clothing that had been thrown into the woods over a ten foot tall chain link fence.

One of Wolf's best tracks was not even for a suspect. A neighboring town requested his services to search for a suicidal person. A retired Navy Seal who had seen service in the Vietnam War, was suffering from Post Traumatic Stress Disorder and after his closest friend was murdered, decided to end his suffering. He fled police who had been called to help him and ran into the deep woods in the remote area where he lived. Wolf was brought in and within less than a half hour, the man was found. After a conversation with the officers, the Seal walked out of the woods, without incident, scratching Wolf's head and thanking him.

Wolf was large dog with an unforgettable penetrating bark but he was a lover at heart. Everyone in the department loved Wolf and enjoyed having him around the station. One of the secretaries even kept Milkbones in her desk for him.

Wolf was loved deeply by Crandall's wife and daughter. One of Wolf's favorite pastimes was chasing sticks in the stream that runs through Crandall's back yard. Wolf also pulled every black rock that looked anything like a Kong out of the water and dropped it on the shore of stream.

Crandall was promoted to the rank of Detective in October of 2001. Wolf, not yet four years old, was to be transferred to a new handler to finish his career. This however was not to be.

Within six weeks, Wolf died as a result of Congenital Heart Disease; a condition that had gone undetected throughout his career. The veterinarian said the damage to Wolf's heart was massive and he was surprised that Wolf lasted as long as he did, considering his line of work.

Crandall likes to think that Wolf, the ever vigilant partner, held out as long as he needed until Crandall moved on to the next phase of his career, allowing Wolf to move on as well. Wolf will be sadly missed by all.

In Loving Memory of

K-9 "WOODY"

March 2001
who grew up to be a Police K-9
Born June 20, 1988   retired 1998

Partner: Specialist Rusty Graham
Office of the Sheriff Lee County, Florida
14750 Six Mile Cypress Pkwy.
Ft. Myers, Florida 33912

Lee County Sheriff's first drug dog, "Woody" ended his watch after 10 years. A yellow Labrador, "Woody", passed away. They had a heartfelt funeral. Woody was the Lee County Sheriff's Office's first drug dog, and he worked the streets with the same partner, Cpl. Rusty Graham, for over ten years. Graham was deeply saddened by the loss but seemed most upset that Woody will would be forgotten.

An E mail from Rusty:

Thanks for your support. This came from an unexpected source, my friend, K-9 handler, Ezra. Woody was my first police dog. I first became his partner on June 20, 1988. He was my

life for the next ten years. Woody & I went everywhere together, did everything together. We competed and trained across the
United States. He was a great dog.

When I had to say good bye to him, it was without a doubt,
the hardest thing that I have had to do in my lifetime. It's so
hard to let him go, but I have so many memories of him in front
of me. Right now I am looking at a music video made by my
department, especially of Woody, for me. It is full of our times
together. Please stay in touch and thank you from the bottom
of my heart.

In Loving Memory of

K-9 YENTL

October 1999 - November 6, 2001

Partner: Deputy Brian Thompson
Genesee County Sheriff's Department
Sheriff Gary T. Maha
14 W. Main St. Batavia, NY 14021-0151
716.345.3000 Ext. 237

A K-9 was killed when she darted into the path of a tractor trailer. "Yentl" was a 2 year old Belgian Malinois used for drug detection and tracking, by the Genesee County Sheriff's Department. The dog died just before midnight Tuesday after running from her handler outside the sheriff's office. Yentl was put in a patrol car and was en route to the Batavia Animal Hospital when she died, quoted Sheriff Gary Maha.

"She made a lot of hits for us, a lot of drug arrests," Maha said. Yentl was used throughout the county and also assisted surrounding county police agencies when needed. She is sadly missed.

Yentl was born in Holland. She was 2 years old in November

of this year. Our Administrators are the best. I have been so supported by them during all training and work with Yentl and I will always be grateful.

Yentl has accomplished more in 9 months than many do in their whole career.

In Loving Memory of

K-9 ZEUS

LODD
May 20, 2001
Badge # 762

Partner: Officer Robert Thomas
Boynton Beach Police Dept.
100 E. Boynton Beach Blvd.
Boynton Beach, FL 33435
561.732.8116

At sunrise Sunday, police officers Stewart Steele, Robert Thomas and police dog Zeus responded to an alarm at a local pharmacy. The front door to the Medication Station at 141 E. Woolbright Road was open when they arrived at 6:32 and prepared to enter. Four minutes later, Steele radioed dispatchers to say that Thomas had been shot by a man inside the store and that they were heading to Bethesda Memorial Hospital.

Several hours later, following a police standoff and a fire that gutted part of the pharmacy after police tossed in tear gas like chemicals, a police SWAT team went in and found the bodies of Zeus and an unidentified man. Details about what happened in the four minutes after police arrived at the pharmacy   and what caused the fire, are still sketchy, police spokeswoman Sgt. Wendy Danysh said late Sunday.

Police did not identify the suspect Sunday, release his cause of death or reveal possible motives. It's also unclear how Zeus died, Danysh said. The Palm Beach County Medical Examiner's Office will examine the dog today.

Thomas, a 14 year veteran, was wearing body armor, which protected him from the bullet that hit him. He was stable and in good condition at Bethesda Memorial Hospital Sunday evening, according to a nursing supervisor. He was recovering from injuries caused by the impact of the bullet hitting the armor on the front of his torso, Danysh said. But it wasn't clear whether Zeus, a 9 year old German shepherd, was wearing his department issue bulletproof vest.

After Sunday morning's shooting, police surrounded the building. A few hours later the pharmacy building caught fire shortly after police threw two types of chemicals similar to tear gas into the business to try to force the suspect out.

Although firefighters had been standing by as a precaution, the fire damaged much of the inside of the building, specifically on its north side, said Mike Smollen, Boynton Beach Fire Rescue battalion chief. The cause of the fire was unknown Sunday, according to Smollen. "There's no telling what started it at this point," Smollen said. "It could be anything from the guy himself, or I've heard stories that tear gas can start it. We'll just have to wait and see."

Smollen said State Attorney Barry Krischer was on the scene and borrowed a pair of firefighter's boots to inspect the store after the incident. The owner of the Medication Station, David Goodmanson, was out of town Sunday and could not be reached, his son said when a reporter called his home. A small crowd gathered in the parking lot of a strip mall near the store to watch as firefighters and police inspected the building, an independent pharmacy that has a loyal customer base.

John Pacy, a veterinarian who lives nearby, said he walked down to the pharmacy after noticing a police helicopter overhead. He stayed on the scene for a few hours, waiting for police to remove Zeus from the building. "I called the animal emergency clinic and had two doctors on standby in surgery, ready and waiting," he said. Because Pacy, who works at Golfview Animal Hospital in West Palm Beach, was not near his office, paramedics offered their supplies for him to use. But he heard about 11:30 that Zeus had died in the building. "It's tragic," he said. "I wish there was something more we could've done."

Warren Rogers, 50, who lived a few blocks from the pharmacy and regularly used it said it always reminded him of "an old fashioned mom and pop pharmacy." "It's so strange to see smoke coming out of there," he said. It was still unclear Sunday evening what the suspect was doing in the pharmacy, Danysh said, or why he fired shots. Drugs and cash were stolen from the pharmacy in a February burglary, she said.

Delray Beach police are investigating a May 14 incident during which a man pointed a gun at a Walgreen's pharmacist and demanded the prescription drug OxyContin. Danysh could not say whether this incident was related to the drug. A child who answered the phone at Thomas' home Sunday said there was no adult available for comment.

Thomas, 42, became Zeus' trainer in 1994, when the department imported him from France. Most police dogs live in their handlers' homes. "Zeus was a sweet family dog. He was a sweet animal and a good worker," Danysh said. His death was being mourned by a force he had served since 1994.

Officers are treating Zeus' passing as a death in the family. Zeus was the second Boynton Beach police dog to die on duty; the first was killed nearly 20 years ago when a Florida Highway Patrol trooper shot the dog during a chase. Zeus was trained to detect narcotics as well as to search areas, buildings and articles, track suspects and control crowds.

Together, Thomas and Zeus earned numerous accolades in

police dog competitions, crime fighting and in the community, visiting local schools to teach students about police dogs. "It's so hard in that situation, not just for the officer but for his family and everyone who knows the dog," Danysh said, Zeus will be mourned and honored as any human would be. "We have lost an officer," she said.

May 22, 2001

A Boynton Beach teenager with a history of burglary and weapons arrests was identified Monday as the burglar killed inside a pharmacy during a Sunday standoff with police. James Connelly, 17, was found dead inside the Medication Station after tear gas canisters fired by the police SWAT team ignited the building. A police dog also died inside the blazing building. Connelly exchanged gunshots with a Boynton Beach police K-9 officer inside the pharmacy, police said. The officer was hit in the stomach, but his bulletproof vest stopped the bullet. It was unclear whether Connelly died from gunshot wounds or the fire. The Medical Examiner's Office said a cause of death has not yet been determined.

The officer, Robert Thomas, 42, was released from the hospital on Monday after being treated for a severe bruise to his lower right abdomen caused by the bullet, spokeswoman Wendy Danysh said. A bullet also hit his right pinky finger. If Thomas returns from medical leave before the conclusion of the investigation, he will be placed on paid leave.

Of the seven times Connelly has been arrested since 1998, six of them were by the Boynton Beach Police Department, state records show. Charges against him include burglary, armed burglary, auto theft, grand larceny and carrying a concealed firearm. Boynton Beach did not release many details of Sunday's standoff and particularly on their decision to repeatedly fire canisters of tear gas into the business. Danysh said she could not release details about how many times Thomas fired or how many tear gas canisters were fired into the business because the incident remains under investigation.

Three of the aluminum tear gas canisters were found inside the business, while a fourth ricocheted, ending up outside, according to the Boynton Beach Fire Department. It's unknown how many others were destroyed by the fire. The state Fire Marshall's Office is investigating. The State Attorney's Office also is investigating the incident, as is customary in police related shootings.

The standoff began when police responded to a burglar alarm at the pharmacy at 6:17 a.m. and found an open door. Thomas, another officer and the police dog, Zeus, went inside to investigate. When Zeus located Connelly inside a room, Thomas was shot in an exchange of gunfire. The officers ran out but were unable to get Zeus to follow. SWAT members were called, and the area was closed off. Police called for Connelly to come out.

When he refused, they fired several canisters of tear gas into the building. About 9:15 a.m., the building erupted in flames and was put out after 30 minutes. Connelly and the police dog, Zeus, were found in a back room, in what appeared to be a storage closet, said Boynton Beach Deputy Fire Marshal Bob Borden. Connelly had a puncture wound to his upper left eye possibly from a dog bite, Borden said.

The tear gas canisters are hot after being fired and sometimes emit sparks, Borden said, which can easily start a fire. The fire could have spread quickly if the pharmacy had oxygen containers, alcohol bottles or other flammable substances, he said. "It's one of the hazards of this type of procedure," he said. Fire investigators have not yet determined where or how the fire started. The business had no rear exit and no sprinklers but didn't violate city fire codes, Borden said.

After his release from the hospital Monday, Thomas talked about losing Zeus his fellow officer and friend. He got the dog when Zeus was only 18 months old and has spent nearly seven years with him. He said that once he realized he was OK, he started thinking about his dog and was overcome by a rush of emotion. "It was like losing a family member, it was like losing another officer   it was tough," Thomas said. Thomas called Zeus a hero."He was definitely telling me somebody was in there," he said. "I know what he's going to do for me. He won't back down and I know he'll give his life for me   and he did just that."

Sept. 4, 2001

On Tuesday, officers introduced the dogs to the public. Ceasar, a 2 year old male German Shepherd, and Ully, a 16 month old male German Shepherd, joined the Police Department about three weeks ago and are undergoing the required 400 hours of training.

Ceasar, who was bred in Belgium, and Ully, who hails from the Netherlands, join the department's two other dogs.

"A lot of animal lovers came forward and wanted to do something," police spokesman Sgt. Thomas McCabe said. "People just kept sending money. The dogs cost about $4,500 each. "

2002

Index 2002

In Loving Memory of

FRISKO

January 10, 1998 - September 8, 2002

Officer James Henasey
Mounted Police New Castle Police Department
3601 North DuPont Hwy.
New Castle, DE 19720
302.571-7900

Frisko was an 18.3 hands high, 2000 lb. Clydesdale born January 10, 1998 at Carson Farms in Listowel, Canada. He was purchased by the New Castle County DE [Mounted] Police Dept. on March 1, 2001 and was brought to Carousel Stables to begin his police training. Frisko arrived barely green broke with nothing, but an aggressive attitude. He quickly took charge of his turnout field and became a leader among all the horses, an odd feat, since Frisko was the youngest horse in the unit.

Frisko also became a favorite with the public, who often came to the stables to visit the police horses. He began his police training April 1, 2001. It was clear from the beginning, that he was eager to work and attack any obstacle. As his rider, I began training the same day with absolutely no experience with horses and no riding ability. Learning to ride a horse was tough on Frisko, because of his rough gaits, but his confidence in the ring made it much easier to learn.

During our training, I found that it wasn't a challenge to make Frisko a good police horse; it was a challenge for me to keep up with his advancement in the training. In his seventh week of training, we competed in the Devon Police Equestrian competition and took seventh place. After training, Frisko continued to advance and lead the other horses. He competed in the National Police Equestrian competition in 2001, placed fifth in the obstacle course competition and helped the team to a second place finish. He again competed in the Devon police competition in 2002, and placed third. Frisko never backed down from anything I asked him to do. I always thought he could get better and better, and I think he did too. During the summer of 2002, Frisko contracted a hoof infection that became extremely serious. He under went a surgery at the New Bolten Center in Pennsylvania. Frisko was admitted to the hospital and became a favorite among the doctors.

The doctors explained the seriousness of the operation and the expenses involved. Dr. Krause, his surgical doctor, knew the police unit had a limited budget, and she and the other doctors within the hospital donated the majority of their services to help save Frisko. Shortly after returning home from the hospital, Frisko seemed fine and eager to get back to work. Sunday, September 8, 2002, Frisko was in his stall. In a matter of 20 minutes, he laid down and died of toxic shock, caused by the antibiotics he needed to survive.

As his rider, I wanted him to be tough and to do the things I asked. He did that and much more. Up until his death, he never showed his pain and was never lame and continued to go out and work with me. He had a heart of gold and unfortunately not the body to go with it. The saddest part about losing

Frisko was that he had the confidence to do anything I asked, just as a true friend and partner would do.

UPDATE:

Jim is waiting for another Clydsdale from Canada. The Mounted unit just received brand new RED uniforms.

In Loving Memory of

K-9 ADDIE

SAR
May 10, 1994 - October 22, 2002

Partner: Chief Ranger Shane Petty
Tennessee State Park
2314 River Road
Henry Horton State Park
Chapel Hill, TN 37034
866.836-6757

Tennessee state parks lost one of its best officers this week: Addie, a search and rescue dog. Park rangers told News 2, Nashville, the bloodhound's super senses led to a large number of finds in the state of Tennessee, and when Addie wasn't catching bad guys or saving lives, she was visiting more than 8,000 school kids across the state teaching outdoor safety. She died this Tuesday.

News 2 first met Officer Addie and her partner, Chief Ranger Shane Petty, back in 2000. "She's been in on over hundred searches." On that day, Addie and Shane had just finished successfully tracking two teenagers who had escaped from the Middle Tennessee juvenile detention center. Tuesday night, Officer Addie passed away from natural causes. "She stretched out, laid her head in my lap, and breathed her last breath. Sad the way she went," said Petty. With a tear in his eye, Petty told News 2 his partner of eight years left behind a legacy few dogs can touch.

"I've been in a lot of tough situations. She saved my life that night." Petty told News 2 he was tracking a gunman through the woods when Addie suddenly signaled that the bad guy was close. Instead of moving forward, Petty waited for backup. "The guy told me, 'If you'd come over that hill, I'd have shot you.'" And when it comes to finding people, few bloodhounds had a better nose than Addie. "We've made a lot of communities safer, chased bank robbers, mass murderers." Officer Addie came from good stock. Petty said her grandmother, Sally, was one of the bloodhounds who tracked and found James Earl Ray when he escaped from Brushy Mountain Prison in 1977. "It killed me. I have her picture on my dresser."

Petty's got tons of memories, including those of a partner who loved to gobble up Velveeta after a job well done. "A lot of people can say this is just a dog, but this is my partner. She was a family member, also." Addie was buried in Henry Horton State Park, where she lived. It's there a small plaque will be placed in her memory for now.

Officially named Adeline, Addie was born May 10, 1994, at Brushy Mountain State Prison. Chief Ranger Shane Petty acquired her when she was ten weeks old. (Her great grandmother, Sandy, tracked down James Earl Ray when he escaped from Brushy Mountain in 1977.) Addie was named for Adeline Wilhoite, who, in 1845, purchased land along the Duck River for a grist and saw mill which later became Henry Horton State Park.

Her name is fitting for, technically, Addie is owned by the State of Tennessee to aid in locating lost campers and hikers in the Tennessee State Parks. Her head was as big as a soccer ball. Her sleepy eyes are slits (Who needs them anyway with such a nose?), and she had to throw back her head and let her skin slide back so she could see you. Her ears hang down to her throat. Her soft tawny fur covers her skin, which hung in loose flapping sheets all over her head. When you pulled it up slightly from her neck it felt like thin crust pizza dough. In fact, everything about was Addie was loose, from her long, supple legs to her swinging tail.

This loose skin is called a cape and enables the bloodhound to twist out of brambles, thickets, and barbed wire fences when it is on the trail. When the dog is working the cape slides forward and partially covers the eyes making it difficult to see. Like her skin, Addie's attitude was loose most of the time, too. When you first saw her lying on the ground, she looked deceased and could probably maintain this posture for hours on end. (She may sleep up to 20 hours a day.) That is, until it's time to work. "When she lies around like that, she's storing up energy," observed Petty. When he snapped on Addie's long leash, however, she resurrected and staggered up on all fours sweeping the ground with her nose. When Petty got in his vehicle, turns on the blue lights and backs around by her pen to pick her up, Addie started baying, whining and moving around excitedly.

Addie has been used not only in Marshall County but Maury, Williamson, Rutherford and other surrounding counties as well. She has assisted in locating suspects accused of parole violations, D.U.I., armed robbery, drug trafficking and arson, plus a prison escapee from Louisiana and a burglary ring suspect. She has also trailed a "Peeping Tom" on two occasions. She has trailed people through woods, fields, hollows, and creek beds to houses, trees and thickets. Once, she located a person hiding behind a chimney on a roof.

Addie located people not by their footprints, sweat or body odor, but by millions of skin cells which fall off human bodies. She could catch a scent of a person on horseback or on a bicycle. She could even trail a person through water if the water was slow moving. The faster a person runs, the more skin particles break free and fall to the ground. It is estimated that a bloodhound can smell up to 2 million times better than humans. The length of a bloodhound's ears are important also. Called "leathers," the ears should hang below the nose. The ears brush the ground and actually move scent particles into the nostrils especially on cold, damp days.

Roger Caras, author, naturalist and bloodhound owner, wrote a book about bloodhounds titled "Yankee," and affectionately calls them "slobber chops." According to Caras, a bloodhound can pick one person out of tens of thousands and almost never becomes confused. For many years, the record for trailing a criminal was held by the bloodhound Nick Carter. In the early 1900s, he followed a trail that was 105 hours old, which led to the conviction of the fugitive. Since that time, his record has been more than doubled to over 210 hours old, almost nine days old. Some dogs will follow human scents for up to 50 miles, and one trailed a person for 138 miles and found them.

The breed is so respected that bloodhound tracking is considered acceptable evidence in U.S. courts. Only once were Addie's abilities challenged in court. When Petty pulled out his record book of more than 900 documented practice trails, however, there were no more questions. Addie's success rate of "finds" is about 78%, which is extremely high for a bloodhound. For Addie and other bloodhounds the sport ends once the trail terminates. When Addie finds someone, she may jump on them, but would never attack them. She is just saying in her own way, "This is it! This is the one I have been looking for!" Then, she expected her reward, which was a piece of cheese. Some bloodhounds prefer dill pickles or Milky Way candy bars' wrapped or unwrapped. "Most of the time you just chase them and chase them and they'll end up hiding in the bushes, and she knew it. When she gets close and knows they're hiding, she wagged her tail and whined. Most people had rather be shot or sprayed with Mace than attacked by a dog," says Petty.

Tracking criminals was not all that Addie did, however, Petty and Addie were involved with project K.E.E.P.S. (Kids Exploring Environmental Programs Successfully) and the "Hug A Tree" program, which teaches survival skills for those who are lost and disoriented when outdoors. As the finale, Addie tracked a child who hid nearby.

Sometimes Addie's searches were more than play. Once she found a mother and two children (ages two and six), who had wandered from their rural home in Marshall County. Petty and Addie tracked them for about three miles through a thick cedar glade in the dark. When they found them about 1:00 a.m., they were crying, scared, and scratched from head to toe. The children were barefooted.

Addie and another bloodhound based out of Cleveland were the only two tracking dogs in the state certified through the Tennessee Emergency Management Agency. Addie did not become the fine bloodhound that she was on her own. She had an excellent bloodline, yes, plus talent and desire, but she would not have become what she is without skill, patience and trust from her handler.

From the moment he brought her home and took her on her first trail run, Petty has focused on her training. When Addie was just a puppy, she and Petty attended the Crater Criminal Justice Academy in Petersburg, Virginia together. After the initial training, Petty read books on bloodhound training, but credits much of his knowledge to Phillip Wendt.

Wendt was a charter member of the North American Search Dog Network and owned a bloodhound while living in southern New Jersey. There he helped rescue mentally impaired people who wandered from the facility near his home. Together, he and his dog experienced more than 1,000 trails. Over the years, Wendt has helped other bloodhound teams get started. "I have worked with 50 or more bloodhound teams, and there are only two that I am proud of. One of them was Shane Petty and Addie," says Wendt. "Shane is an outstanding handler." "The problem with most teams is the trainer, not the dog," Wendt continued. "I have seen very few bloodhounds that won't trail, but some trainers try to out think the dog. Eighty percent of the training is trust."

Wendt explains that once the harness is on the dog, the trainer must learn to follow. If the dog loses the scent or seems confused, the trainer must be patient and trusting enough to let the dog work it out. The dog is the boss. Even though bloodhounds are wonderful for police work and search and rescue, they do not make good family pets.

According to "Choosing a Dog" by Nancy Baer and Steve Duno: "the bloodhound is a dog with a relentless, determined mind set. The bloodhound will follow a scent forever and ignore everything else, including you. Choosing a bloodhound for a family pet would be like using a bulldozer to drive to the corner store." Petty concurs, "There's just no sense of obedience there. This is the reason why Addie was rarely off her line. If she once caught the scent of a rabbit, deer or any other animal, she would follow the scent without regard to where she was going." Fortunately, for Addie, there's a brain bigger than hers at the other end of her line. And, thankfully, for Petty and Middle Tennessee, there's a nose bigger than a human's at Addie's end of the line.

Being the 1st Search and Rescue Dog for TN State parks, Miss Addie was an icon for our state. She did much good for many. She also meant a great deal to this family, personally. Addie, of course, used her God given ability in her job of search and rescue. Shane, as handler, had to learn to read and interpret her communications. Our entire family was an intricate part of this training. We frequently "got lost" in the woods, in rock crevices, and/or buildings; then, with her reward of cheese in hand, waited for her to find us. While on an actual (real) search, our two girls and I anxiously awaited her arrival home to congratulate her with her deserved "cheerleading". Consequently, the entire family was bonded with this creature. She is greatly missed. Officer Petty told News 2 he has a new bloodhound he's training. Her name is Ellie Mae, and he hopes she can serve him and the people of Tennessee half as well as his former partner.

In Loving Memory of

K-9 ARGUS

Dog # 596
June 29, 2002

Partner: Constable Brian Moss
Burnaby Royal Canadian Mounted Police
Canada

Burnaby RCMP are mourning the loss of one of their own after a police dog died last Saturday. Argus, Police Service Dog #596, passed away after he was rushed to a veterinary hospital when his partner, Const. Brian Moss, found him lying on his kennel floor. Argus worked with Moss on the Burnaby dog unit for the last 18 months during which time the K-9 tracked down many criminals. Born in Quebec, Argus was introduced to Moss in April 2000 and was a big part of the officer's family. The dog was especially loved by Moss' two young sons. Moss describes Argus as a loving and very sociable dog whose greatest love outside of police work was swimming. "If Argus wasn't a dog, he would have been a fish," Moss said.

In Loving Memory of

K-9 ASKO

August 17, 2002

Partner: Officer Ken Greenleaf
Redondo Beach Police Department
401 Diamond St.
Redondo Beach, CA 90277
310. 379-2477

It is with great sadness that I announce the passing of K-9 Asko. During Asko's career he has had two spinal surgeries causing him, of course, to slow down. Asko was given six months to live after his last surgery which would have been May of 2000. Two years later, Asko was still with us. During the past two weeks Asko has been losing all his motor skills and was dragging himself throughout the house and yard. He was getting to the point where he could not hold his bladder or bowel movements. The decision was made to put him down. My decision was supported by my trainer and veterinarian. At 7:30AM this morning, K-9 Asko was put to sleep. He passed away with his head in my lap and a kong ball in his mouth. He will be missed.

Asko was hired on October 11, 1993 and retired a full seven years later on October 11, 2000. He was the first Redondo Police K-9 to be cross trained for patrol and narcotics. He has won competition in both patrol and narcotics. He apprehended suspects from simple assault, burglary to murder. He was truly a remarkable dog. Asko was my second K-9 and a great dog. I now have Basko as my K-9 partner.

Poem especially for dear ASKO

Wherever crime was festering,
There's one who stopped it fast.
He won most competitions
and he never came in last!
He's quick, he's sure, he's Asko
The police dog, K-9 champ.
And once he has his jaws shut
they hold tighter than a clamp!
He's has a sense of humor
But at work he wastes no time.
No messing 'round for Asko
When he has his mind on crime.
For every situation
There's an action he must do.
When tracking things or people
He can sniff out any clue.
The furry coat of Asko
Is brown and black and gold.
His eyes are bright and accurate,
His talents manifold.
He will always be remembered
For he was one of the Best!
It was a sad day in Redondo.
Asko was laid to Rest!
Poem by: Ken Greenleaf

In Loving Memory of

K-9 BEAR

September 23, 2002

Partner: Capt. Scott Shields
Marine Safety Service
225 Rector Place
New York, NY 10280

The morning of September 11th started out as one of the most beautiful of the year. Scott Shields was at his sister's home in Greenwich Connecticut watching television with his then eleven year old golden retriever named Bear at his side as he watched the live broadcast of planes crashing into the World Trade center. Scott jumped into his car and made the wild ride down to Chambers Street in 38 minutes a ride that usually takes 90 minutes. As chief safety officer for many of the New York City Harbor events his car is always filled with disaster equipment and ready for response to any type of disaster.

Trained in marine safety and emergency management by the National Guard, FEMA, and The American Red Cross, Scott as

one of the first rescuers to respond to the attacks; used his
extensive background in emergency management to organize
harbor activities, utilizing boats for rescue and emergency transportation efforts and communicating with other craft for assistance the first few days of the incident.

   Scott boarded the U.S. Coast Guard ship, Katherine Walker
(tied up to Rockefeller Park in Battery Park) and proposed a
plan to Capt. Steve Whitlock, it's commanding officer, to evac-
uate and then shuttle firemen around the gridlock on the West
side highway. Scott also assigned DEA agents to assist Dr.
Barbara Kalvig (chief veterinarian for the World Trade Center
response), to set up Veterinary Medical Assistance Teams
(VMAT) for the Suffolk County SPCA; the only organization
that provided treatment for the Search and Rescue Dogs that
worked Ground Zero.

   A New York State Senate Proclamation states "Captain
Scott Shields and his companion "Bear" were the first K-9 crew
to arrive under that leaning facade that became known as
Ground Zero, working tirelessly in the search and rescue mission, locating the body of the beloved FDNY Chief Peter Ganci
with his friends firefighters T.J. Munday and Jean Paul Augier
as chronicled in Dennis Smith's best selling book Report From
Ground Zero, on page 111 and remaining at Ground Zero for
six months assisting with the recovery efforts.

   A day after the attack stories of Bear walking through the
rubble carrying his dad's helmet in his mouth brought a smile
to the dog tired rescue teams. A wonderful picture of Bear getting a drink of water that second afternoon on the site was
taken by AP photographer Beth Kaiser.

   To quote firefighter Jean Paul Augier in a Comcast interview; who actually made the find of Chief Ganci and made one
of the few live finds that day (the head of Customs) "it was like
being on the moon, Bear was working as hard as we did, the
debris field was so large it was like trying to find a needle in a
haystack. Bear was phenomenal. To see this dog climb up and
over these pieces of steel and crushed concrete was amazing. I

wanted to keep the dog with me as long as I could, but there were too many firemen trying to latch on to him." When asked how much do you credit Bear with ? "everything!" Bear was injured on his back by a jagged piece of metal that first night and after being treated at a triage center on the site he went right back to work.

Months later the area around this wound became cancerous and he received treatment from Dr. Jennifer Chaitmen a vet who had donated her services down on the site and had promised she would take care of him forever. Dr. Chaitman kept that promise as Bear was to die of multiple forms of cancer almost a year later with over $15,000 worth of treatment for this hero.

Scott is proud to say he was "surrounded by my friends in that hell we called the World Trade Center." One such friend was Andrew Furber a welder, sculptor, and poet. Andrew had volunteered on the fireboat, John J. Harvey, a 1932 one hundred and thirty foot fireboat with the five largest mobile water pumps in the northeast. The Harvey had been sold for scrap by the city of New York for $50,000 ten years earlier. Rebuilt with the efforts of dedicated volunteers like Andrew Furber a month before the WTC the Harvey was asked to be the committee boat for the tug boat races in New York Harbor. Her Captain, Huntley Gill decided at the last possible moment that this old lady of the harbor, who was only there to sound her horn and start the race would also participate. Scott was on the bridge when Huntley said "awh let's race" and threw the telegraph down full ahead to the engine room. Tim, the engineer who had dedicated the last few years of his life to rebuilding her (and was often asked to work on other boats at much more money) must have read Huntley's mind and pushed the engines to their max. The old lady of the harbor who was only there as a courtesy came in first against all the new boats in the harbor.

On a national public television show "The Day the Towers Fell." Scott describes that morning and what his friends did that day. "We lost all the water downtown, stuff was still falling from all the buildings still left standing and fires still engaged the surrounding structures. There was no way to fight the fires and pieces the size of trucks were falling off, and then the fireboats started arriving and then the Harvey came, scrapped for fifty thousand dollars by the city. The Harvey can pump more water than any New York City Fireboat. She ran lines back in along North Cove between the Financial Center Buildings and into where The World Trade Center was, and she became a hero," and a legend.

Andrew Furber helped lay those water lines and then courageously went inside (the buildings were still falling). Andrew worked with Scott and Bear those first days. November 19th, 2001 he wrote this about their work: " Scott worked with his dog Bear on finding bodies buried in the pile, and I worked as a steel worker cutting steel and helping firemen extract bodies after they were found. Bear shares the same characteristics as Scott. Just observing him on the pile and comparing him to some of the other rescue dogs, he was clearly in his element. He was at peace, agile, and didn't slow down until it was time to rest.

Other dogs I noticed behaved erratically, emotionally, and were apparently so overwhelmed with the amount of possible bodies that they were less effective. Watching Scott and Bear interact told volumes about their relationship and personalities. Scott and Bear were clearly working really hard, putting in extraordinary hours and focused on saving lives. I could not imagine how poorly Bear must have been since all of us had dust masks, but he had his nose right down in the thick of it the whole week. A New York State Senate Proclamation stated "within every community there exist certain individuals who through their hard work, dedication and service play an instrumental role in protecting the lives of citizens, Capt. Scott Shields and his dog Bear displayed the human values of bravery and dedication as a member of the fire fighting community, achieving success."

Bear was given the honor of leading New York City's Fifth Avenue Columbus Day Parade. Bear was first marching at the

head; in front of governor Pataki, Mayor Juliani, and both
Senators Clinton and Schumer. On November 17th, 2001, Bear
and Scott were presented with "The Heroes Award" by the
International Cat Society" at the Westchester County Cat Show.
Scott says that this was the first time he laughed since the inci-
dent "just the irony of the cats giving a dog an award."

Scott and Bear worked with some of these men on the site.
We honored their heroism here at Bear's memorial service a
month later with a presentation of "The Bear Search & Rescue
Fondation Award" for extraordinary service to humanity. A
hundred others we saw do extraordinary things those days were
also honored.

In Loving Memory of

K-9 BEAR

LODD
November 12, 2002

Partner: Deputy Scott Devereaux
Pocahontas County Sheriff's Department
Havelock, IA
712.335-3308

A black Labrador retriever used by Pochontas County as a drug dog was found Saturday dead of gunshot wounds. The dog, Bear, had been reported missing by his handler Deputy Scott Deverearux. "Bear, a five year veteran K-9, was found in a ditch." said Sheriff Bob Lampe.

Bear was a successful drug dog and had also located several missing children. The agency is offering a reward for information. No further information on the above, sorry to say.

In Loving Memory of

K-9 BEAU

February 15, 1997 - September 19, 2002

Partner: Deputy Johnny Eubanks
Okaloosa County Sheriff's Office
1250 North Eglin Parkway
Shalimar, FL 32579
850. 651-7702

The Okaloosa County Sheriff's Office recently lost a member of our family. K-9 "Beau" passed away on September 19, 2002 after battling an unexpected illness. Beau was a 5 year old Belgian Malinois handled by Deputy Sheriff Johnny Eubanks. Beau began his law enforcement career with the Okaloosa County Sheriff's Office in 1999. He was certified through the United States Police K-9 Association and was trained in narcotics detection, tracking, and all phases of criminal apprehension. A special tribute is being planned for a later date.

More about the K-9 Unit

Dogs and their handlers must constantly train to maintain the performance standards for which the Okaloosa County Sheriff's Office K-9's are renowned. The Belgian Malinois and German Shepard breeds have proven to be well suited for the many tasks that Okaloosa County K-9's must perform. The unit has three German Shepherds, "Rocky", "Rex" and "Valko," and the rest are Belgium Malinois. Many people instantly associate "police dogs" with drug detection, but that is only one of the many jobs that the K-9's perform well.

In Loving Memory of

K-9 BEXAR

March 20, 2002

Partner: Officer Brian Griffeth
Garland Texas Police Department
P.O. Box 469002
217 N. Fifth St. Garland, TX
75046-9002
972.205-.2000

Bexar has served heroically and has received numerous awards throughout his career. Griffeth and Bexar hold the unique distinction of apprehending over 100 criminals during their partnership. The Garland Police Department K-9 Unit currently has four handler/K-9 teams offering 24 hour coverage to Garland.

Police K-9 dogs, properly trained and handled, give police officers one of the finest non- lethal aids in the prevention and detection of crime. The Garland K-9 Units provide the maximum amount of safety to officers, citizens, and suspects while investigating criminal activities, especially in instances of felony offenses. Statistics show that the proper use of a K-9 unit reduces the number of officer involved shootings in a police department.

Bexar was a great dog, with 139 apprehensions. He found over 400 pounds of drugs in his career and he was my second dog. We worked the streets together since January 1995. I never regretted a moment of time that I spent with him. "He was a joy to be around and work with."

UPDATE:

I just finished training my new partner. His name is Czar and he is a sable colored shepherd, 21 months old and full of life. I forgot what it was like having a young dog around with all that energy!

In Loving Memory of

K-9 BO

March 1, 2002

Partner: Officer Brian Bunch
West Plains Police Department
302 E. Broadway
West Plains, MO 65775
417.256-2244

Bo was born in Holland and brought to Somerset, TX for narcotic training. He was almost six years old. The first week in February I noticed Bo was having problems with his balance. The vet checked his ear, felt he had an inner ear infection. Feb. 27th, Bo lost his balance again and fell. The vet thought it was something else and I took him to the Missouri University at Columbia.. Bo went lethargic, I carried him into vet's office. Vet felt he had a severe inner ear infection

On February 28th, I was contacted by vet and was told he had a massive tumor in his lower brain stem and it was inoperable. On March 1, I picked my partner up. I brought him to

West Plains and he was put out of his misery. I took him to my hometown of Cabool and buried him at my family's farm.

MEMORIAL SERVICE

The West Plains Police Department held a Memorial service for "Bo" on Friday, March 8, 2002. Bo was with the Police Department for six years from 1996 until 2002. During that time he had 160 drug seizures in 307 call outs while working with patrolman Brian Bunch.

Royce Fugate, City Administrator. presented Brian with a plaque recognizing Bo's achievements. A plaque was also presented by the County Sheriff's office and the South Central Drug Task Force. Joey Hiett, Dept. Chaplain, made some remarks. Veteran's Memorial at People's Park Memorial Service for Police Dog "Bo." Book Discussion Group is being organized at The West Plains Public Library recognizing Bo's achievements. A plaque was also presented by the County Sheriff's Department.

In Loving Memory of

K-9 BRESTON

2002

Partner: Officer Steve Junge
Last Vegas Metro Police Dept.
4511 W. Cheyenne Ave. Suite 401
N. Las Vegas, NV 89030
702-229.3441

Steve lost his partner, Breston in 2002. This department lost 5 K-9s in that year. Steve is a 12 years with the Las Vegas Metro Police Department, 7 years a K-9 handler, two time recipient: Unit Citation, Valorous Conduct and one Meritorious Service Award. Trial Chairman and organizer, Defensive Tactics Instructor. Partners; K-9 liaison to Nevada Task Force #1 FEMA Team that responded to New York City during the World Trade Center disaster, with his patrol dog partner, Breston. A total of 4 K-9s were involved with the NYC WTC disaster, including Dak, Breston, Zorro & Matjo. Zorro and Matjo are also deceased.
UPDATE
Steve has a black lab named SAM as his present partner.

In Loving Memory of

K-9 BRIGG

July 1991 - October 26, 2002

Partner: Sgt. Rod Mamero
Payson Police Department
303 N. Beeline Highway
Payson, AZ 85541
480. 503-6000

Payson's first Police K-9 "Brigg" passed away on October 26th from complications of surgery and unknown illness at an animal hospital in Phoenix. Brigg was born in Russia and purchased through a grant from the state of Arizona. Brigg trained with his handler, Sgt. Rod Mamero, with the Maricopa County Sheriff's Office in Phoenix. He trained in Patrol and Narcotics detection.

Brigg had countless narcotic finds totaling in the hundreds of thousands of dollars. He also had many suspect apprehensions, finds, and deterrent cases. Brigg served with honor until an injury during a building search forced him into duty as a home dog in the Mamero household. Brigg will be remembered for his courage, hard work, and being a beloved member of the family.

In Loving Memory of

K-9 BUBBA

August 30, 2002

Partner: Cpl. Keith Baumann
Anne Arundel County Police Department
8495 Veterans Highway
Millersville, MD 21108
410. 222-8525

Bubba was like my best friend.
We worked together every night
that I went to work for six years.
He is already missed very much.

Bubba, the Anne Arundel County police dog who assisted in
more than 100 arrests during 11 years of service, died over the
weekend after a long bout with cancer. The German Shepherd
made headlines for helping apprehend thieves and purse snatch-
ers. But his friendly way with others made him so popular that
hundreds of people chipped in to pay for his medical treatment.

"It was his personality that made him," said Cpl. Keith Baumann, Bubba's handler. "He was so social and friendly with people." Bubba managed to postpone retiring for two years after the life threatening disease was diagnosed in 1999. "He took his medicine and kept on going," Baumann said.

One night after Bubba received chemotherapy, he and Baumann responded to a call that three men breaking into vehicles in Glen Burnie had run from police. Bubba chased them behind a department store, and Baumann made the arrest. Bubba was trained to use force if necessary. But off duty, he was a different dog, living with Baumann and his family.

When police funds for treating Bubba ran out, the Society for the Prevention of Cruelty to Animals called for help and more than 650 people responded with donations totaling about $30,000 to help Bubba. "He was the epitome of German Shepherds," said E. Joseph Lamp, a member of the society's board. "He was such a tough guy. He was tall and strong and had all of the Rin Tin Tin type color in him, with the mixture of brown and black." The fund raising drive got the attention of the U.S. Secret Service, which invited Lamp, the Baumann family and Bubba to the White House a few years ago. They toured the grounds, then Bubba waited in the car while Lamp and the Baumanns peeked inside the Oval Office and played with President Clinton's chocolate Labrador, Buddy.

When cancer forced Bubba to retire, he would wag his tail as Baumann put on his uniform, then follow his former handler to the door. Baumann would pat the dog on the head, then go to work with another German Shepherd. "It was kind of sad to leave my old partner there at the door," Baumann said. When Baumann returned from work, Bubba was waiting. As Bubba's health worsened, he tried to get around, but his spine was deteriorating and he often fell. Baumann had Bubba euthanized August 30. Baumann is adjusting to life without his former partner, and if his new partner or any of the other four legged members of the county's K-9 unit fall ill, nearly $20,000 remaining from Bubba's fund will be available to help pay for treatment.

In Loving Memory of

K-9 BUDDY

January 3, 2002

55 W. 125th St., 14h Floor
NY, NY 10027

Former President Bill Clinton's dog Buddy was killed Wednesday by a passing car outside the family's Westchester County, New York, home. The former "first dog" was struck at about 12:15 p.m. on Route 117, a busy two lane street close to the Clinton's' home on Old House Lane in Coppice. According to police, Buddy was struck by a vehicle driven by a 17 year old girl after "playfully chasing a contractor" who had just left the residence.

Secret Service agents rushed after Buddy when they saw him chasing the contractor's van off the property, and arrived at the scene moments after the dog was struck.. The agents immediately took Buddy to Coppice Animal Hospital, where the dog was pronounced dead. No members of the Clinton family were at home at the time of the accident. A spokeswoman for the former president said that the Clinton family is "deeply saddened" by Buddy's death. A family statement said Buddy was "a loyal companion and brought us much joy. He will be truly missed."

The dog's namesake was Clinton's great uncle, Henry O's "Buddy" Gresham, who died in June of 1997. Clinton said at the time that Gresham was a father figure to him, in addition to having been a dog trainer for 50 years. Buddy, a chocolate Labrador retriever, was frequently seen at the president's side at the White House and on travels, and joined Clinton when he moved to New York one year ago.

NEW LAW

(Previous to this military K-9s were euthanized at the end of their tour of duty.)

Robby was the "Poster Boy" who changed the laws regarding K-9s in wars since WW II. President W. Clinton signed this new law. November 6, 2000, H.R.5314 became Public Law No: 106 446 amending Title 10, United States Code, to facilitate the adoption of retired military working dogs by law enforcement agencies, former handlers of these dogs, and other persons capable of caring for these dogs. the full text of this law can be found on the Library of Congress website:

http://thomas.loc.gov/cgi bin/bdquery/z?d106:h.r.05314:

Update:

Former President Clinton revealed in Northern Ireland that his new dog will have an Irish name. At the opening Wednesday in June 2002, of a peace center named for him, Clinton encountered a chocolate Labrador retriever and told the crowd that his own chocolate Lab will be called Seamus, spokeswoman Julia Payne said. Seamus, pronounced Shay' muss, is the Gaelic form of James. The dog is still being trained at the Maryland kennel where he was born in February and is expected to join the former president at his Coppice home later this month.

At the kennel he was called B.B., for Bill's Boy, while Clinton decided what to name him. Clinton's White House dog, Buddy, was killed by a car in Coppice in January, an event the ex president said was "by far the worst thing" to happen to him after leaving office. Seamus was sired by Buddy's nephew, and breeder Linda Renfrew said he seemed much like Buddy, "except that I think he's probably a bigger eater. From what I have seen of him, his sole ambition 24 hours a day is to eat." Clinton was in Enniskillen, Northern Ireland, to open the Clinton Center, which is designed to be a base for Catholic Protestant reconciliation work and international study of the Irish conflict. Clinton's interest in Northern Ireland encouraged the Good Friday peace pact 4 years ago.

In Loving Memory of

K-9 BUDDY

December 27, 2002

Partner: Deputy Mike Roberts
Hillsborough County Sheriff's
5808 Wilkins Rd.
Tampa, FL 33610
813. 247-8000

The Sheriff's Office regrets to announce the death of one of it's honored K-9s, Buddy. Buddy died unexpectedly at his handler's, Deputy Mike Roberts residence on December 27, 2002. Deputy Roberts and Buddy, who had worked the previous night shift, had just completed playing in the back yard with the family. When Deputy Roberts checked on Buddy in his kennel about twenty minutes later, the K-9 was discovered not breathing. Buddy was rushed to an emergency veterinary clinic and pronounced. A necropsy will be conducted, today at a clinic in Kissiminee to determine cause of death. Foul play is not suspected. Buddy was a 3½ year old German Shepherd that was brought in from the Czech Republic. He had been on the K-9 unit for 2 years. He was certified in tracking and narcotic detection. He was just re-certified on December 8th. Buddy's last catch was on December 12th, when deputies pursued a stolen car. Several Sheriff's cars were crashed into including Deputy Robert's vehicle. Despite a heavy rain, Buddy tracked down two suspects in a field. Sergeant Mark Olive, K-9 stated, "Buddy was one of our finest dogs. His forte was tracking, he will be missed." Deputy Roberts is a 14 year veteran of the office and a 2 year veteran of the K-9 unit. He will start training a new dog as soon as it is selected.

Buddy, a German Shepherd was born in Czech Republic in 1999. He began working as a Sheriff's Office Patrol Dog in January 2001. He is also trained as a Drug detection dog. He will be missed by all, especially by his handler, Deputy Mike Roberts.

In Loving Memory of

K-9 CAESAR

October 24, 2002

Partner: Officer A. L. Crouse
Wilson Police Department
120 N. Goldsboro St.
Wilson, NC 27894-0010
252.399-2323

WINNER 2001 FIRST QUARTER PATROL

On February 6, 2001 while on routine patrol in the city of Wilson, North Carolina at 2300 hours I was requested to head to Kenly, NC in reference to an armed robbery that just occurred at an Exxon Service Station. A black male had entered the Exxon station around 2245, waited for everyone to leave and then approached the clerk at the register and demanded all the money in the cash register. The suspect never showed the clerk a gun but had his hand in his jacket pocket like he had a gun. The clerk gave the suspect all the money in the cash register and then he ran out the door.

A Kenly Police Officer who was close to the Exxon responded to the area. While checking the area the Kenly Officer
observed a black male who met the description of the robbery
suspect. The black male observed the Kenly Officer and started
to run. The Kenly Officer started a foot chase with the suspect.
While running through a mobile home park the Kenly Officer
fell down, the suspect kept running.

I arrived on the scene around 2325 and Sgt. Parker showed
me the place the suspect was last seen. The location where the
suspect was last seen was crossing the road at Darden and
Goldsboro Street. I deployed K-9 Caesar in the intersection.
Caesar located a scent and followed it through a car parking lot
heading west. Caesar crossed the parking lot and into a wooded area. We went through the wooded area and up a small hill
coming out of the woods onto the northbound side of I 95.
Caesar continued following the scent across all four lanes of I 95
and into another wooded area. We traveled about two hundred
yards through the wooded area, making a turn heading south.

K-9 Caesar came out of the woods at the on ramp to I 95.
After casting a little bit Caesar continued across the on ramp
and off ramp of I 95, still heading south. Caesar entered another wooded area, were we went another three hundred yards
before making another turn heading west. In this wooded area
I lost my hand held radio although I did not know it yet. After
making the turn, we came out of the wooded area and crossed
Hwy. 301.

Once Caesar crossed the first lane and into the second lane
he made a small turn in the lane and headed north/west down
the road. We went about one hundred yards and Caesar made a
hard left turn down a dirt road heading south/east. Caesar followed the scent down the dirt road for at least six hundred yards
coming to another wooded area. We went up a small hill and
entered the wooded area. Caesar went through the wooded area
for 200 hundred yards coming to a stream. Caesar crossed the
stream and went down a hill coming to some railroad tracks. At
the tracks Caesar made a left turn heading east down the mid-

dle of the tracks. Caesar went down the tracks for about three hundred yards made a left turn and went up a hill. Once on top of the hill Caesar made another left turn and headed back the way we had just came. We went almost to the location where we had entered the wooded area and Caesar made a right turn going back through the stream and into the wooded area. Caesar came out of the wooded area right around the dirt road. Caesar made a small turn heading north/east across an open field. While in this field we lost our second backup officer (the first one had gotten tired and changed out with the second officer) We went about a mile through the field until we came to a fence with barbed wire on it. As I was looking for a crossing location I could hear sticks breaking and dry leaves being stepped on.

I ordered who ever was making there to call out and give up, I was a K-9 Officer and would send the K-9 unless they showed themselves. The unknown noises grew louder, as if someone was running. I too began to run down my side of the fence attempting to locate a spot I could put my partner over the fence. After about one hundred yards I could no longer hear the noise from the other side of the fence. I thought the suspect had lain down and was hiding. At this point I was able to locate a crossing point. I was able to put my partner over the fence.

Caesar started to track and air scent back the way we had come. Caesar was pulling really hard going through the wooded area and then began to bark and the tracking lead went slack. Turning on my flashlight I observed a black male lying in the leaves with his hands under him. I ordered the suspect to show me his hands. The suspect advised that he had the money and was sorry and to "please don't let that dog bite me." Johnson County deputies who had been off in the area had seen my flashlight and with the Officer from Kenly had rushed through the wooded area and took the culprit in custody without further incident. The subject Caesar had tracked was the armed robbery suspect from Exxon and had $674.00 on him that was taken in the robbery. The suspect had just been released from prison a week before for armed robbery.

I took K-9 Caesar back to the wooded area where I thought I had lost my hand held radio. I put Caesar into the wooded area and did an article search for my radio. Caesar was able to locate my radio without any trouble.

UPDATE:

Al is now working with Maximus and will train in January 2003.

In Loving Memory of

K-9 CASTOR

June 28, 2002

Partner: Sgt. Frank VonCannon
Asheboro Police Department
205 E. Academy St.
Asheboro, NC 27203
336. 626-1300

Castor came to the Asheboro Police Department in 1989. We were assigned to a street level Narcotics Unit. For almost six years then back to patrol until 1998. We transferred to the Vice/Narcotics Unit until Castor retired in 2001. Castor was very active in the schools. He loved kids and the more kids the better. He had several large narcotics bust for the small town we live in. We seized over 400,000.00 in cash and drugs over the years.

In June of 2002, while enjoying retirement, Castor had what the vet said was a stroke. Two weeks later, he left our family. He will be missed by all, including my two kids. They were not even born when Castor came to me. He was a hard working friend and will be missed.

In Loving Memory of

K-9 CHAS

June 10, 2002

Partner: Officer Edward Potanovic
Yonkers Police Department
730 E. Grassy Sprain Rd.
Yonkers, NY 10710
914-377.7388

On June 1, 2002, my partner Chas was diagnosed with cancer. He was placed off duty but spent his remaining days by my side. On June 10, 2002 Chas succumbed to his illness. He will be sorely missed by my family , but more so by me, his partner, the members of the K-9 Unit and the entire department.

Chas was donated to the Yonkers Police Department in June of 1995 by the late Marty Walshin. He was named after the Police Commissioner's father, the late Charles Cola Sr. Chas and I served as a K-9 team and provided the City of Yonkers with seven years of faithful service.

The teamwork was a valuable asset to the Yonkers Police

Department. In 1998 P.O. Potanovic and Chas entered the prestigious U.S. Police K-9 Association Trials in Warwick, New York. Chas won 1st place overall and took home 6 trophies that year.

During his career Chas made many arrests most of which were felonies. He was responsible for the apprehension of 25 burglars and won accolades for the capture of a day time burglar wanted for over 20 entries throughout the city. Chas recovered over $5,000 from a bank robbery. He was also personally responsible for removing several guns from the streets. In addition to being a valuable asset, Chas was a great K-9 and a best friend."

"Chas, we will never forget you, and thank you for being part of our family.

Love Daddy, Mommy Ashley and little Eddie"

In Loving Memory of

K-9 CHELSEA

June, 1997 - August 2002

Partner: Officer Bo Currey
Montgomery County Police Headquarters
2350 Research Blvd.
Rockville, MD 20850
240.773-5000

Chelsea was half Lab and half Chesapeake Bay Retriever. She LOVED the water, working and running. She would retrieve anything you could throw. She also had a really keen nose and was an explosive detection specialist.

Chelsea enjoyed swimming and playing after her job was done. She joined the K-9 unit in 1999. Chelsea developed lymphoma in June of 2001. She continued treatment until complications set in August, 2002.

UPDATE:

New Partner: K-9 Greger, a Belgian Malinois.

In Loving Memory of

K-9 CHUCK

May 8, 2002

Partner: Sgt. Wes Barnes
Anderson City Police Department
Anderson City, SC 29622
800. 859-6397

The Anderson County Sheriff's Office is investigating the death of a police dog found dead at his Anderson County home on Wednesday afternoon. Anderson Police Sgt. Wes Barnes' family found Chuck, a 7 year old Belgian Malinois, that served the police department for six years, dead in the yard of the family's home. Sheriff's Capt. Dale McCard said no foul play is suspected, but officers are investigating since the dog had no apparent health problems.

An autopsy will be conducted to determine the cause of death, he said. The Anderson Police Department plans to hold a memorial service for Chuck next week.

The Department's K-9 Unit consists of five Officers and five

Dogs who have completed training in specific areas. These Officers are providing a Valuable and Necessary Service to Uniformed Patrol and Vice/Narcotics Officers by Assisting in the Detection and Seizure of Drugs, Explosive Devices, and by Assisting in the Apprehension of Fleeing Suspects.

Police grieve loss of K-9

By the time Anderson Police Sgt. Wes Barnes got around to asking the question Sunday night, the answer was quite clear. He was just a dog, so what's the big deal? The big deal, for Sgt. Barnes and a group of about 40 people who turned out at a memorial for Sgt. Barnes dog, Chuck, was a life devoted to snuffing out crime and protecting local residents.

Chuck, 7, died suddenly May 8 after six years with Sgt. Barnes and his family. In the process, Sgt. Barnes said, the Belgian Malinois taught him about trust, being himself, and caring for children. Chuck even was there for him in his darkest hours of alcoholism and addiction.

Local law enforcement officers brought their own K-9s to the service, held at Chris Taylor Park, and shared a hug with Sgt. Barnes. In the back of their minds was a simple, yet loaded, question: what happens to dogs when they die?

"I can't believe God would take them to a place where we couldn't be with them," said the pastor of United Methodist Church. Sgt. Barnes said Chuck, who had slowed down a little but still seemed very healthy, passed away in his favorite cool spot. He said it was still unclear why he died, although no foul play is assumed.

Mr. Stutler led the ceremony, which included Bible passages, religious songs and a blessing for the beasts and the children. With several police dogs sitting patiently next to their handlers, Mr. Sutler explained that the dogs demonstrate selfless service, courage, forgiveness and other exceptional qualities. Of all the species God has created, we as humans seem to have the most trouble with trust, while our K-9 friends seem to do it the best.

Sgt. Barnes said Chuck also would protect a child over me

without hesitation. He learned this lesson when he went to spank his son one day and Chuck nipped him in the rear. Chuck's passing is something Mauldin police officer Chris McCord knows he'll have to face someday, even if he doesn't like to think about it. He brought Billy, a black lab he had for four years, to the service.

"They become your children, your best friend, I can't imagine what he's going through." Chuck's last duty was to find a gun that was used to shoot a 14 year old boy. He did this in no time.

Sgt. Barnes said that he never known a kinder soul than a red, black and tan dog named Chuck. He plans to spread Chuck's ashes in the mountains of North Carolina.

In Loving Memory of

K-9 CLARK

April 27, 1994 - April 2, 2002

Partner: Officer Scott Petersen
Ledyard Police Department
11 Lorenz Parkway
Ledyard, CT 06339
806.464-9416

K-9 handlers have even a more special bond with their partner. Clark was eight years old. He passed as result of kidney failure. He was trained for both patrol work and narcotics detection. We worked on the road together for more than four years. He was a very special friend, companion, and partner. Clark was very loyal and protective, but also very social, particularly with children. His passing came while riding in a Ledyard Police cruiser, for one last "tour of duty."

A memorial service for K-9 Max and K-9 Clark was held on April 26, 2002.

Double loss, double sadness.

In Loving Memory of

K-9 COSMO

May 27, 2002

Partner: Officer Greg Thomas
Gilbert Police Department
1025 South Gilbert Rd.
Gilbert, AZ 85296
480.503-6000

Former Gilbert Police K-9 Cosmo passed away on Memorial Day, Monday, May 27, 2002. She was almost 11 years old. Cosmo was Gilbert's first police dog and started with the Department in 1993. Like our current K-9s, Cosmo came to us directly from a police K-9 kennel in Holland. She was less then 2 years old at the time.

We attended the Arizona Department of Corrections K-9 Academy. In April 1996, Cosmo and I were certified for narcotics detection and patrol work. During our three years together, Cosmo was integral to several large drug busts, including a 1,500 pound seizure of marijuana on a traffic stop during an assist to US Customs. Cosmo also made eleven apprehensions of various fleeing felons during her career.

On one occasion, Cosmo located two burglars hiding in the second story of a home. When confronted, the suspects started to flee. I sent Cosmo on one suspect and she clamped onto his leg. Seeing this, the other suspect jumped right off the second story. I'm not sure who had the worse leg injury, but they both limped to jail.

Cosmo competed in numerous K-9 competitions during our partnership. Cosmo won 5 trophies in 6 different trials in Phoenix, Tucson and Las Vegas. In 1998, Cosmo won first place in tactical obedience over some 50 dogs competing in the Phoenix K-9 Trials. At just under 9 years old, Cosmo developed an eye disease that caused progressive blindness. This, in addition to a leg injury during an apprehension, led to her eventual retirement in May 1999.

K-9 UNIT HISTORY

The Gilbert Police Department K-9 Unit was started in 1993 with a grant from the Criminal Justice Enhancement Fund (CJEF). The goal of the program at the time was to reduce Gilbert's escalating trend of street crimes and drug use. CJEF funds were accepted to purchase a narcotic detection / patrol K-9. The first K-9 member of the Gilbert Police Department came to us all the way from Holland; a German Shepherd named "Cosmo."

After intense training in drug detection, obedience, building searching, and tracking, Cosmo joined the fight to keep Gilbert safe. In November 1996, Cosmo was injured during the apprehension of a suspect after a vehicle pursuit. When the suspect abandoned the vehicle and fled on foot, Cosmo knocked the suspect off his feet. The suspect landed on top of Cosmo and ripped a rear tendon in the dog's leg. Cosmo never gave up, but never fully recovered from the injury and suffered a permanent limp.

In May 1999, Officer Thomas made the difficult decision to

retire Cosmo after she was diagnosed with a degenerative eye disease. Cosmo worked for the department for six years, making hundreds of arrests and seizing over 2,000 pounds of illegal drugs. Cosmo also competed in numerous K-9 trials through-out Arizona and won many trophies. The Department let Officer Thomas keep Cosmo and she enjoyed a relaxing retire-ment. Cosmo will always be remembered as Gilbert's first K-9. Farewell Cosmo.

UPDATE:

Officer Greg Thomas and K-9 Otto have been working together since February 1999. Otto is a Belgian Malinois born July 1997 in Holland. Otto is the newest member of the K-9 Unit and was assigned to Officer Thomas for training when K-9 Cosmo's retirement grew imminent. Otto's high energy, assertiveness, and persistence in searching out drugs made him an easy choice for a career in police work.

In Loving Memory of

K-9 DAK

July, 2002

Partner: Officer Michael R. Horn
Las Vegas Metro Police Department
K-9 Div. 4511 W. Cheyenne Ave. Suite 401
N. Las Vegas, NJ 89030
702. 229-3441

One of the most treasured of friends, K-9 Dak was put down on July 17, 2002. He had a tumor on his heart. Mike lost his other partner, Duke a month before. Mike is a 21 year veteran with Metro and also 16 years with the K-9 unit. He is a Patrol Dog Trainer, and a Medal of Valor recipient. He has been partners with Dak, a 8½ year old German Shepherd for 4½ years. Mike also holds the title of Judge-Polizeischutzhundprufung, he is President of "Friends for Las Vegas Police K-9s." As well as a member of the Nevada Task Force #1 FEMA Team that responded to the World Trade Center.

In Loving Memory of

K-9 DALLAS

January 4, 2002

Partner: Officer Paul Ossella
University of Connecticut Police Department
126 North Eagleville Rd.
Storrs, CT 06269
860.486-4800

The sympathy cards are piled high on the desk of Police Officer Paul Ossella. Hundreds of people wrote to express sympathy for the loss of his partner, Dallas, who died January 3. Dallas was no ordinary police officer. He was a K-9 cop. "Dallas was a great patrol dog," says Ossella. "He was very protective of all the officers on the force and made a great impact on the community he served." Dallas, a German Shepherd, was the third patrol dog employed by the University of Connecticut Police Department. He had worked with Ossella and the department since May 1999.

During this period, Dallas and Ossella performed many services: searching buildings, recovering evidence, and controlling crowds. These services were sometimes extended to the surrounding communities of Coventry, Willimantic, the State Corrections Department, and the Connecticut State Police. "Dallas's presence on a call would put everyone's mind at ease," says Ossella. "Dallas was a great tracker, so he would make parts of the job much easier." Dallas also performed many demonstrations. "He was a very social dog," says Ossella. The two visited E.O. Smith High School in Storrs to talk about drugs and alcohol, gave a skills demonstration at the African American Cultural Center on campus, and also competed in the K-9 Olympics."

UPDATE:

The University of Conn. Police have obtained another dog for training and eventual deployment in the community. Benny, the new German Shepherd, will start the 14 week State Police K-9 training program on Feb. 18. Ossella will accompany him throughout the program.

In Loving Memory of

K-9 DANDY

December 1, 2002

Partner: Capt. Mark Reid
Hopkinsville Police Department
112 West First Street
Hopkinsville, KY 42240
270.890-1500

Hopkinsville police were collecting donations today to buy a headstone for one of the department's original police dogs after the animal died over the weekend. At the recommendation of a veterinarian, the retired K-9 Dandy was euthanized Saturday, officials said. The dog suffered from a degenerative disc and had become paralyzed about midway down his back, according to Cpl. Mike Wood, public information officer. "He couldn't walk unless someone helped him," Wood said.

Dandy's handler, Capt. Mark Reid, buried the dog this weekend on his family's farm in South Christian. Dandy was a German Shepherd. He was 13 years old and had been retired from police work for about four years. After being retired, he became a family pet for Reid. The dog came to Hopkinsville in 1992 from the Czech Republic. Dandy and another German Shepherd, Enzo, were the first two K-9's purchased for the department. Enzo died in early 2001.

Dandy was trained to locate felony suspects by scent and sight and was used to search buildings and track people out-doors. He also was trained to protect police officers. During his six years of police work, Dandy was credited with 29 felony apprehensions. In seven of those cases, he had to physically stop a suspect. Wood said he was collecting donations today from police officers who wanted to help buy a headstone for Dandy. Citizens who want to make a contribution should contact Wood at 502 890-1500.

In Loving Memory of

K-9 DANNY
and
K-9 WINSTON

September 19, 2002

Partners: Officer Frank Sorrentino & Partner: Officer Dan
Southwell
Las Vegas Metropolitan Police Department K-9 Unit
4511 West Cheyenne
North Las Vegas, NV 89030
702-229.3441

Officer Sorrentino retired his German Shepherd, Danny, earlier this year. He serviced 4 years on patrol with Officer Sorrentino. Danny died due to cancer.

Officer Sorrentino currently handles K-9 Iwan, Belgian malinois for patrol and K-9 Jake, a black lab, for drugs.

Officer Dan Southwell - no further information.

In Loving Memory of

K-9 DASTY

June 10, 2002

Partner: Nick Henderson
Evansville Police Department
15 New MLK Jr. Blvd.
Evansville, IN 47708
812-436.7948

Evansville police officer Nick Henderson didn't think anything of it when his K-9 partner, Dasty, got hurt during a chase earlier this month. The dog was going over a fence while chasing a fugitive, and he came down on his belly, eliciting a loud yelp. Dasty then got up and continued his chase. "He'd fallen and hurt himself plenty of times before," Henderson said.

Less than a week later, Dasty, a decorated police dog and Henderson's partner, died of complications from that fall. The fence had punctured his bladder, causing an initial discomfort that doctors couldn't identify. By the time they could, it was too late. The loss hit Henderson hard. The officer, who recently was named the department's police officer of the year, had ridden the night shift with Dasty for more than three years, during which time the dog lived with Henderson's family.

Everybody has come up to me and said, 'Sorry for the loss of your dog,' but it was a lot more than that," he said. "He was my partner for three years; I drove around in my car with him for eight hours a night, then I'd take him home at night and feed him, and I'd wake up that afternoon, (and) my little boy would be outside with him, just throwing a stick and playing ball." The whole family has taken Dasty's death to heart, Henderson said. But none has taken it harder than the dog's partner, who described his best experiences on the force as those where he worked with Dasty.

A particular highlight, he said, came when the duo was awarded one of their three "Catch of the Quarter" awards from the United States Police K-9 Association for capturing a suspect barricaded in a Washington, IN home. "(The man) ran inside and said he wasn't going back to jail, and he was taking someone with him," Henderson said. "Dasty went in and searched the house and found that the guy had climbed over a wall and buried himself in the insulation; Dasty drug him out by the arm so we could see his hands and see that he was unarmed and arrest him."

In his five years on the force, Dasty found and seized more than $275,000 in illegal drugs and currency and won several awards in USPCA trials. Now that Dasty is gone, Henderson said he expects to continue working in the K-9 department of the police force. "The hard part's going to be going to work and driving around without my partner; it's going to be an awfully lonely 8 hour shift."

In Loving Memory of

K-9 DUCHESS

March 28, 2002
LODD

Partner: Deputy Josh Payne
Anderson County Sheriff's Department
305 Camson Rd.
Anderson, SC 29625
864.260-4400

My name is Don Hodges Jr. I am a Master Deputy K-9 Handler with the Anderson County Sheriff's Office. I was given one of the memorial cards today for K-9 Duchess. She and her handler Deputy Josh Payne were my partners. The grief we went through during that rough time period was awful. Several times I heard members of the local community say " But it was just a dog".

To them it was just a dog but to me and other dog handlers they are a part of us just like a child is. We as handlers work long hours for little pay or recognition and that suits us. My dog

'Chief' is my friend and my partner. The day will come when he is laid to rest and when that happens I can say without a doubt "Well done thou good and faithful servant."

Thank you says so little, but the cards will keep Duchess in our minds and hearts. She was not just a dog. SHE WAS MY FRIEND.

An Anderson County sheriff's deputy accidentally shot his own dog this weekend as the two chased after a man who had fled from Iva police. Duchess, a bloodhound who had been with the Sheriff's Office for a year and a half, was shot by her handler, Josh Payne. At 3:16 AM, Saturday, Mr. Payne tried to return his .40 caliber handgun to its holster after chasing down a man who fled through the woods on S.C. 413, Sheriff's Capt. John Skipper, said that Mr. Payne was holding a flashlight on the suspect with one hand and Duchess' leash and the weapon with the other hand when the dog jumped, causing Mr. Payne to squeeze the trigger of the gun causing it to accidentally go off.

Duchess was struck in the hind quarter and the bullet traveled through her body. Mr. Payne and other officers tried to render first aid to the dog and transported her to an emergency veterinary hospital in Greenville, but she died later the same day.

"This is one of those unfortunate things that happen in law enforcement," the captain said. The two had responded to a call that a car being chased by Iva police had wrecked at S.C. 413 and Wilson Creek Road. The car had sped away from Iva officers who tried to pull it over because its tail lights were out.

Iva Police Chief Jimmy Ray Sutherland could not be reached about the case Monday. A passenger in the car, whose name was unavailable, was arrested at the scene of the accident, but the driver fled. Mr. Payne and Duchess responded to the scene to help find the suspect, along with fellow officer Brian Andreas and his dog, Spike.

The officers found and arrested the driver, whose name was also unavailable, about 30 to 40 yards from the road, hiding in a culvert. "They drew guns on him, but they did not shoot at the suspect," Capt. Skipper said. Mr. Payne has worked with the Sheriff's Office K-9 Unit since 1999 and was Duchess' sole handler. The bloodhound lived at Mr. Payne's home and had become a part of his life. Duchess was allowed to tag along with Mr. Payne and his wife on their honeymoon about two months ago. "Dogs are your partner," A private funeral is planned for Duchess later this week.

UPDATE:

Deputy Payne is up and running with Duchess' sister, Lucy. Lucy was approved for duty after 2 months.

May, 2003: Don is on his way to Washington D.C. for the National Police Memorial Services. He is taking 2 black ribbons for K-9 Duchess and for K-9 Chuck. A year has passed since the end of a training track. However, she did love to play with a empty water or soda bottle too. While we go to the memorial services to honor our fallen human partners, let us not forget our four legged partners who also paid the ultimate sacrifice.

Greater love has no one than he who lays down his own life for a friend and well done thy good and faithful friend.

In Loving Memory of

K-9 DUKE

July 25, 2002

Partner: Deputy Brian Thompson
Genesee County Sheriff's Office
Sheriff Gary T. Maha
14 W. Main St.
Batavia, NY 14021-0151
716-345.3000

The Genesee County Sheriffs Department is looking for a
new drug sniffing dog, after the second death of a K-9 in recent
months. Duke, a German Shepherd, had been with the department for just three weeks. He died on the operating table, during what was supposed to be routine dental surgery."The surgery was winding down, after 2½ hours," said Genesee County
Sheriff Gary Maha of the events leading up to the death. "All of
the sudden for some unknown reason the dog went into cardiac
arrest." Efforts to revive the dog proved futile.

Maha says Duke's death was particularly tough for his handler, Deputy Brian Thompson, because of what happened to K-9 Lentil, the department's previous K-9. She was hit by a tractor trailer and killed last November. The department is now searching for a new K-9.

In Loving Memory of

K-9 EBO

LODD
December 19, 2002

Partner: Officer Doug Haymans
Washington Metro Transit Police
600 5th St. North West
Washington, DC 2001-2693
202.962- 2696

Our condolences to Officer Doug Haymans and the Metro Transit Police Department on the loss of K-9 Ebo who was killed on December 19th, 2002 while on duty near the Branch Avenue, Metro Station. Our thoughts are with you.

Police win awards in the U.S. Police K-9 Association's Region Three trials. Metro Transit Police recently racked up several awards during the U.S. States Police K-9 Association Region Three Trials. Hosted by the Montgomery County Police Department, the trials tested police officers' and their K-9 partners' abilities to work together in apprehension situations and contraband detection simulations. The trails also tested the K-9 partner's ability to follow and obey commands.

The first place team award went to Sgt. George Colvin and Officers Douglas Haymans, Earl Brown, and Paul Ludwig and their K-9s Boris, Ebo, Condor, and Hutch. The Distinguished Patrick Cahill Award, the third place overall award, the second place criminal apprehension award, and the second place obedience award went to Officer Haymans and K-9 Ebo.

In Loving Memory of

K-9 FANG

April 22, 2002

Partner: LT. Dan D'Annunzio
Trumbull County Sheriff's Dept.
150 High St.
Warren OH 44481
330.675-2508

The policy of the Trumbull County Sheriff's Office is to utilize a professionally trained K-9 team to assist in the daily operations of the department. The K-9 team is a valuable law enforcement tool for use in criminal apprehension, evidence location, narcotics detection, building searches, tracking, article search, search and rescue and promoting favorable public relations. The K-9 team goes through rigorous training in Freemont, Ohio for six weeks and is certified by the State of Ohio in patrol and narcotics. The team is also certified by the North American Police Work Dog Association. The dog "Fang" was imported from the Republic of Czechoslovakia.

On April 22, 2002, the Trumbull County Sheriff's Department lost our K-9 FANG. Fang was still on active duty; as he was for the last six years. He passed early in the morning from intestinal problems during surgery. Fang was a dog that loved his job. He gave his all every time he was needed. We did more demos than I can count and everyone loved him. Fang was also a member of the SWAT Team with the county. Fang's biggest bust was 2.25 million dollars worth of cocaine.

He also tracked a 72 year old woman who escaped from a nursing home at night in 40 degree weather. Several people had been searching for some time before Fang was called upon. He found her in a short amount of time. She was taken to the hospital and treated for exposure. Without him, she might have not made it. That is just some of the things that Fang did in his time with us.

My heart goes out to LT. Dan. I was not his handler, but I feel a great loss now that he is gone for I was his decoy. We had a special bond and I will miss him greatly. Fang didn't like many people, but he liked me. I feel like I have lost a friend. Officer Mike A.K.A.; Fang's Decoy.

In Loving Memory of

K-9 FAX

April 23, 2002
LODD

Partner: Officer Brian Harpp
Lake County Sheriff Dept.
3811 S. Liverepool Rd.
Hobart, IN 46342
219.755.3392

    Lake County Sheriff John Buncich announced this morning that Lake County K-9 Fax died after undergoing emergency surgery and treatment for wounds received while the K-9 was defending two Lake County Officers who were attacked by a vicious Pit Bull. Sheriff Buncich stated that early this morning, at approximately 12:26 AM, Lake County Officers Nate Jazyk, Brian Harpp and K-9 partner, Fax, responded to a call in reference to a suspicious vehicle in the wooded area of the 49th Ave. & Wilson St.

    The area is well know as a dumping ground for stolen vehicles. Upon arrival and while searching the area, officers located a 4x4 maroon vehicle, parked without lights. As the officers approached the vehicle the driver activated the 4x4 and started to drive towards the officers, with bright lights, on disregarding the officer's instructions to stop. Officers again instructed the driver to stop. The driver finally stopped and the driver exited the vehicle walking towards the officers. As the male subject walked toward the officers, he mumbled something and immediately afterwards a large Pit Bull jumped from the vehicle and attacked Officer Harpp and his K-9 partner Fax. K-9 Fax immediately defended the officer and a vicious fight took place between the Pit Bull and German Shepherd, Fax. The male subject was instructed to call off the Pit Bull or risk the dog being shot. Both dogs were finally separated and the Pit Bull was placed in the 4x4 by the male subject. The officers then placed the male subject under arrest for resisting law enforcement, disorderly conduct, public intoxication, battery on law enforcement and criminal trespass.

As Officer Nate Jazyk was attempting to place the male subject under arrest the male subject began to resist. While Officer Jazyk was struggling with the subject the Pit Bull managed to jump from the vehicle and rush Officer Harpp and his K-9 partner, Fax. Officer Harpp drew his service weapon and shot and killed the attacking Pit Bull.

The male subject identified as Robert L. Dorman Jr., age 38, of Gary, was taken to the Lake County Jail. K-9 Fax, was rushed to the Calumet Emergency Veterinary Clinic where he later died from complication of injuries sustained during the performance of his duty, defending and protecting his partner from harm. Fax's full name is Fax vom Wimbachtal . He would have been 8 years of age this July. Fax has been the K-9 partner of Officer Harpp since he was 1 1/2 years of age and has been in service as a regular patrol K-9 for approximately 6 years. Residents have placed flowers at the site of the dog-fight, and the police have lowered their flag to half staff. An official ceremony will be held May 10, 2002.

CROWN POINT:

Officer Brian Harpp stood among dozens of his fellow officers and their families, fighting back tears and remembering his K-9 partner. Fax, a 6 year old German Shepherd and a member of Lake County police's K-9 Unit, died Tuesday after a fight with a pit bull.

During a service for Fax on Saturday morning at the Lake County Law Enforcement Memorial, Harpp talked about the dog that was like a son to him; the dog he took to work in the morning and brought home at night. "You were my friend, my buddy, my pal," Harpp said, quoting a poem for Fax titled 'My Partner.' "You loved to wrestle and pal around, but you knew it was time for work when I put my uniform on. Together we protected our town."

About 75 people attended the service, including Sheriff John Buncich, Police Chief, Mike Arredondo, dozens of Lake County police officers and several officers from other area police departments. Members of the county's K-9 Unit lined up with their dogs and saluted Fax. "He was my best friend. He was my son," Harpp told them. "Fellow K-9 brothers, take a moment to look down at your partner. Give him a hug and a kiss for me. Give him the love and protection he gives to you."

Chief Arredondo delivered the service's opening remarks. "These dogs are there to protect, but (police officers) see them as family," Arredondo said. "... These dogs are very special." The 20 minute program ended with a 21 gun salute by the Lake County Tactical Team and a bagpipe rendition of taps. During the gun salute, police dogs chimed in with barking.

"Fax deserves all of this," Harpp said. "He was an excellent dog." For several minutes after the service, Harpp received hugs and words of consolation. When it ended, Harpp talked about losing the dog he's worked with since 1996. "All kinds of people are trying to help me out," he said. "A guy came over and tried to give me a little female German Shepherd. I appreciated it, but I couldn't accept it. It's hard right now."

Fax died after fighting a pit bull to keep it from attacking

Harpp and Officer Nathan Jazyk. Harpp and Jazyk were in Calumet Township trying to handcuff the pit bull's owner when the owner ordered his dog to attack the officers, police said. Fax didn't die from fight injuries; he died from a heart attack after surgery at the Calumet Emergency Veterinary Clinic in Schererville, according to police.

Police officials said a new trained dog for Harpp would cost between $5,000 and $10,000. But for Harpp, there is no price tag for replacing Fax. "He knew every word I said, and I understood him," Harpp said. "It was like two people talking."A Gary man has offered to give his dog to the Lake County Sheriff's Department as a replacement for the German Shepherd that died after a fight with a pit bull. "I know how attached a person can get to a dog," said Dwight Taylor, 46. "When I saw that story about the police dog that died, it reminded me of my dogs." Taylor said Wednesday he was willing to give his 11 month old German Shepherd mix, Ol' Boy, to Officer Brian Harpp, whose K-9 partner, Fax, died from complications during surgery.

The Lake County Commissioners, however, voted Wednesday to buy a new dog to replace Fax. The dog fight took place Tuesday as police were investigating a report of a suspicious vehicle. While Robert Lee Dorman Jr., 38, was being arrested, his pit bull lunged toward Harpp and Fax. Harpp shot and killed the pit bull, and Fax was taken to a Schererville veterinary clinic. His wounds were not life threatening, but he died from a reaction to the anesthesia. Dorman has been charged with criminal recklessness and criminal mischief.

Lake County Commissioners honor fallen police dog

Officer receives $5,000 check to replace K-9 Fax, killed in mauling.

Lake County police Officer Brian Harpp wiped tears from his eyes Wednesday as County Commissioners honored his fallen police dog, Fax. The voice of County Commissioner Frances DuPey, whose son has been a county police handler for seven years, wavered as she read the tribute and announced a $5,000 gift to Harpp to buy a new K-9 to replace Fax, who was mauled by a pit bull April 23 in the line of duty. She said the board commended Fax, "for his valiant efforts and valor in the line of duty while protecting officers of Lake County, Indiana which resulted in his sacrificing his life."

"I appreciate the check," Harpp told the audience at the commissioners meeting, "but it is not what I'm looking for. I think everyone knows what I want and cannot have." DuPey said she understood. "I was very touched by what happened," she said. "A police dog is like a family member. We hope this money will help toward the purchase of a new dog, which many people don't realize the officer himself has to purchase."

Harpp replied, "On behalf of myself and the office of the sheriff, I appreciate the support I've received from everyone who is helping me get through this period." Harpp, Officer. Nathan Jazyk and K-9 Fax were investigating an intruder parked in a field near 49th Ave. & Wilson St. when the truck driver released a pit bull that attacked Fax. Harpp was forced to shoot and kill the pit bull. Fax later died of injuries from the mauling. The pit bull's owner, Robert Lee Dorman, 38, of 4606 Woodbridge St., Gary, IN has been charged with criminal mischief.

In Loving Memory of

K-9 FLAME

SAR
1995 - February 16, 2002

Handler: Helen Young
Iowa Search & Rescue
710 W. North St.
Madrid, IA 50156

Helen Young with Iowa Search and Rescue recently lost her beloved K-9 partner, Flame. Flame was diagnosed with cancer at the age of seven and within two weeks left us. Flame was an ambassador for SAR K-9s, as you can see in the picture. He was certified in Air scent wilderness, water and evidence. Flame gave ISAR four years of service and helped find closure for many families. The members of ISAR miss him almost as much as Helen does.

In Loving Memory of

K-9 FRESCO

June 7, 2002

Partner: Officer Derek Welch
Dumas Police Department
124 E. 7th St.
Dumas, TX 79029
806-935.3998

On June 7th early in the morning, somewhere between 1:30 AM and 7 AM, an unknown suspect entered the back yard of Officer Welch's property. They took K-9 Fresco from his gated pen. Officer Welch's personal family pet Lexi was taken as well. Lexi is a 6 month old Belgian Malinois K-9 prospect. K-9 Fresco was a 2½ year old Belgian Malinois imported by Global Training Academy from Holland in August of 2001.

The next day at approximately 4:30 PM, K-9 Fresco was discovered by the animal control officer near the entrance to the city dump. He was rolled in a tarp, dead of unknown injuries. K-9 Fresco was a narcotics detection dog, imported but not formally trained for patrol work. He was lured from his home while his handler was working to protect others. He was killed and dumped like a piece of trash, set there near the entrance for his handler to find him.

K-9 Fresco had been with the Dumas Police Department since October of 2001. K-9 Fresco was responsible for making several small narcotics cases. He recently was certified USPCA and NPCA. At the time of his death, he held three separate certifications for narcotics detection. A necropsy was performed on K-9 Fresco, but the results were unable to determine a cause of death. Investigators from the Dumas Police Department have been unable to develop a suspect in the case of the fallen officer.

K-9 Fresco will be missed terribly by those who had the opportunity to know and love him. He was irreplaceable.

The Dumas Police Department has lost one of its own over the weekend. Narcotics K-9 "Fresco" was taken from his partner's home and later found dead. All that's left of Fresco is the football he used to chew on and the memories his partner has of their days together on the narcotics unit.

"It's difficult to explain, unless you've been a K-9 handler before. You're with your dog 24 hours a day, 7 days a week, very rarely are you two not together. Whether it be at the house or on patrol in the car," said officer Derek Welch. A brief separation of the two ended up in tragedy. "The chief of watch at the time had assigned Officer Welch another patrol car, because his was down. So, the animal was unable to go to work that night and as a result it was left at the officer's home," said chief Dale Alwan.

Welch says usually Fresco's kennel is kept latched so he can't get out. On Friday morning, he found the door open and Fresco gone. The next day, Welch received word of Fresco's whereabouts. "He was rolled in a gray tarp, rolled outside a dumpster. Fresco also had a chip or chunk missing out of his left ear and I just rolled him over and saw that he was missing the tip of his left ear and I knew it was him," said Welch.

"I don't know at this point whether there was foul play or not. We're waiting on some reports to come back in," said Alwan. Until then, all the officers who worked with Fresco can only remember his contributions. "It was a benefit to the city of Dumas and its people and the police department and in our efforts in enforcing narcotics laws," said Alwan. As for Fresco's partner, he's handling his loss day to day. "It's tough to realize he's not coming back," said Welch. Chief Alwan says Fresco wasn't the only dog missing. Welch's personal dog was also taken, but later found shot twice in the leg. That dog is expected to recover.

Alwan also tells us that if this is found to be a direct act of criminal conduct, the person or persons responsible will face some stiff consequences. It'll be considered a third degree felony. This can mean two to ten years in prison as well as a fine of up to $10,000. Who killed Fresco? No further investigations have been done.

The local animal hospital called today and said they thought they had Lexi (girl). We went and checked and it was her. She had been brought in by a farmer on Saturday. She had been shot twice with a .22 caliber weapon of some sort. She is alive, but she will have to undergo at least one if not two or three surgeries to get her back to normal. She was shot in the right hip which shattered the bullet and broke her leg. She was also shot in the right front leg which fractured that leg as well. She has been sedated and her surgery is scheduled for first thing in the morning. She has a good chance of living a healthy long life if everything goes all right. Not sure how I will pay for the surgery, but I will worry about that later.

I have to go talk to my chief regarding burial of Fresco in the local cemetery and have a grave side service. Now concerning the burial site, marker and casket. I think I have a friend that can maybe build a makeshift casket. Anyway, thank you so much for the time, effort and money you spent on the cards, it means a lot to me. I will keep you posted on anything further.

Lexi is our personal dog, she is all ours as we purchased her from a breeder in Colorado a few months after I got Fresco. She is all ours, we call her Lexi Lou, but she answers to LuLu. As for the vet expense for Lexi, I have no idea where it is coming from except payments maybe. It will run $600 $800 plus follow up appointments.

The Police Department will have a new recruit joining their team soon. This recruit will have four legs, fur and a tail. The Dumas City Commission gave approval Monday to allow the police department to purchase a new police K-9 within budget. Dumas Police Chief Dale Alwan said the police department will look into three agencies and academies from which the dog may be purchased. These agencies are Global Training Academy in Somerset, Texas, Hill Country Dog Center in Pipe Creek, Texas and K-9 Concepts Inc. in Broussard, La. The dog will be trained for narcotic detection and tracking. Alwan said the last dog was trained only in tracking.

This police dog will replace the dog that died on June 8. The police investigated his death and weren't able to develop much of a case because autopsy results were inconclusive. Alwan said the case is still open if anyone has any information about it. The new police dog will be trained to find missing children, fleeing suspects and missing elderly people, Alwan said. The academy will train the dog using controlled aggression techniques.

If the police department decides to purchase a dual purpose dog, it will cost about $8,000. Mayor Rowdy Rhodes likes the fact that the police department wants to focus more on searching for and stopping drug offenders. Commissioner Mike Milligan even brought up the issue of what would happen if Buckie Eager, the officer who would handle the dog, left the Dumas Police Department later. Alwan said Eager seems to want to stay with the department for a long while, but with any employment situation there are no guarantees. Alwan said Eager is happy to have the opportunity to be the dog handler.

Alwan also discussed warranties the academies offer. If the city is unhappy with the dog's performance within a year's time frame, the police department may return the dog to the training academy. This warranty includes the fact that if the dog handler leaves and the K-9 does not take well to another handler.

It will be awhile before the dog becomes an active member of the police force. The Dumas Police Department must choose an academy, wait for the next academy opening, see how the dog and the handler bond together and wait for the dog and his handler to become certified. During the bonding process, the handler and the dog work and live together on a regular basis. "We want to make sure Officer Eager bonds fully with the animal," Alwan said.

RESPONSE:

Dear Editor,

In response to the front page article in the Nov. 21 issue of the News Press I would like to reply with the following: To those of us who knew and loved Fresco; which as many of you know is the K-9 that was found dead near the entrance to the city landfill June 7th, not 8th 2001, we know that the city may be able to buy another dog, but Fresco was irreplaceable.

In this article the News Press referred to the new prospect as a member, I hope if a human member of the department were to pass away, a bit more respect would be given to him than was to Fresco when he died. Just so the community knows this will be the second time the city has owned three different dogs and they utilized a handler owned dog at least three times prior to that, so in essence this will be the sixth dog in service with the city.

Fresco was not trained in tracking; Fresco was certified by Global Training Academies, The United States Police K-9 Association, and the National Police K-9 Association as a narcotics detection dog. He had basic imprinting for apprehension work, but was not even remotely trained in tracking.

As a citizen, a parent of small children and a grandchild of elderly people I would like to know how this new dog will respond and what it will do when this police dog locates 95 year old Grandma Flicker who has Alzheimer disease and wondered off from the Shady Pines Nursing Home, because every police dog I have seen including those used by the prison system bite when an apprehension is made at the end of a track. Poor Grandma. Hope this dog does something different than the rest.

In closing I would like to say that Fresco was a good dog who was known and loved by many in this community and he got absolutely no respect when he was killed, the News Press might as well do an article on the department getting new cars because a dog is viewed by them as a piece of equipment and not a member. Look at K-9 Concepts website at www.K-9concepts.com and educate yourself a little.

Remember Officer Welch was happy with his employment at one time as well, until the fact, that to date, a memorial service has not been conducted for Fresco. The fact that he was not recognized for his contribution to this community, however small it may have been was like spitting in his face and the face of his partner. (Good luck to you Buckie, hope it goes better for you than it did for others.) Fresco's memory still lives within many in this community who had the opportunity to get to know and love him.

/s/ Cathy Welch , Dumas TX

In Loving Memory of

K-9 GROLL

July 23, 2002

Partner: Officer Celeste M. Robitaille
Stratford Police Department
900 Longbrook Ave.
Stratford, CT 06615
203-385.4134

The Stratford Police unveiled a monument last Thursday to two of their fallen officers, police dogs Groll and Harley. An honor guard of K-9 units from around the state, and the Stratford Police Honor Guard, was present to show support and dedicate the memorial. "They are fearless, loyal and loving," said Chief Michael Imbro of police dogs. "Their passing impels us to recognize the short amount of time we have."

Officer Celeste Robitalle, Groll's handler, said, "I'll never forget the day I met Groll for the first time. He was a skinny, hyper German Shepherd who wouldn't listen to a word I said. I know Groll is in good company with K-9s Shadow, Max and

Jack." Detective Jack Cratty read a poem, "Guardians of the Night," from the North American Police Working Dog Association website. The author is unknown.

K-9 Groll was the department's patrol dog. K-9 Harley was a narcotics dog. The monument is made of black marble and bears the names of all Stratford's police dogs since the program's inception in 1985. "It is one of the most successful programs we have implemented over the years," Imbro said. "Just the presence of a trained K-9 and his handler makes a criminal think twice." The department plans to replace the two dogs it lost recently and add a second patrol dog. Each dog will cost $6,000.

The department has received some outside help in raising funds for the new dogs. Erica Pazkowski, a Bunnell High School freshman, raised $5,024 toward the cost of a new narcotics dog. "[She started collections at] the end of January," said Vicki Spada, Erica's mother. Capt. Andrew Knapp said, "Vicki Spada and her daughter Erica Pazkowski went above and beyond the call of duty. Pazkowski collected money at Flood Middle School, Stop & Shop and other locations, and also received mail in donations. "She really liked Harley," Spada said. "She always looked forward to seeing him. She's an animal lover. She says the K-9s are a very important part of the police department." Spada and Pazkowski have two dogs at home.

Just one example of Groll's work:

On February 4th, Officer Robitaille assisted the Valley Street Crime Unit with the execution of a search warrant in Shelton Connecticut. On arriving at the residence, a male suspect standing outside, hit an officer in the face and fled on foot. Officer Robitaille ordered the suspect to stop or she would release her K-9 partner, Groll. The suspect stopped running and surrendered. During the search K-9 Groll detected various narcotics and paraphernalia that was hidden throughout the apartment and even a bag of marijuana that was thrown off a second story balcony.

Police Officer Celeste Robitaille knew there was something terribly wrong with her police dog, Groll, recently when he failed to run over to her as she laced up her boots for work. "Groll was a very social and loving dog, but when it came to work he was all business," said Robitaille. But instead of gearing up for work that fateful day, the German Shepherd K-9 officer looked over at Robitaille and lay back down on the ground.

Robitaille immediately knew the cancer Groll was diagnosed with on July 1st, had finally overtaken him. It was July 22. Groll died the next day. He was 6 years old and had been working with Robitaille and Stratford police since 1997. Groll's death hit Robitaille hard. He was more than just a partner Robitaille and K-9 Groll were only apart for one week since she first got him more than four years ago. "We were a good team," she said.

In tribute to Groll, the officers on Robitaille's shift placed black mourning bands on their badges, customarily done when an officer dies in the line of duty. Supervisors also lowered the flags at police headquarters to half staff. "That was an indication of how much he was loved by the guys here," Robitaille said.

K-9 Groll was an integral part of the Police Department, said Capt. Mark DeLieto, Robitaille's shift commander. "You had confidence in that dog," he said. He assisted in 690 police calls, resulting in 143 arrests and the seizure of drugs and cash. The dog also provided assistance for Bridgeport, Milford and Trumbull police, as well as the Federal Drug Enforcement Administration. Robitaille's patient work with Groll was a critical factor in his becoming an effective K-9, DeLieto said. "As successful as a dog is, it is mainly because of its handler," he said.

Acting Chief Michael Imbro has said the department hopes to replace Groll by the fall. Robitaille has volunteered to be the trainer and handler for the department's next K-9. But, for the time being, Groll remains a strong presence in Robitaille's life. "I still sense him. Sometimes I turn around and think he is still following behind me it has been difficult," she said.

In Loving Memory of

K-9 HALLE

SAR

November 6, 2001 - April 28, 2002

Partners: Jason & Dana Berry
Greater Houston Search Dogs & Houston Fire Department
817 Dollins St.
Katy, TX 77493
281. 391-9264

Our beautiful Halle died on Sunday 4/28/02. Halle was a wonderful 48 pound black female lab. She was a shining star for Greater Houston Search Dogs and will be missed by all who worked with her. She was born 11/6/01 and her short life has touched us all. God decided that she had more important things to do. She is our angel and she will never be forgotten. She is with us, my parrot calls, "Come on Halle" as soon as we walk in the door each day. We know she is happy and want to honor her life.

One of the youngest members of our team fell several stories from an open window to her death on Sunday. This is the first loss for Greater Houston Search Dogs and a very heart breaking loss for all our members. Halle was the perfect search dog. The one dog you wish you could find. Her handlers are the type of people you wish you had a hundred of them on a team.

I am announcing this to all so that Halle did not die in vain. Her handlers, Jason & Dana want to try and prevent accidents such as this by increasing awareness among all handlers. Please look at all potential hazards in your training and search environment. Dogs do not always understand they can fall and hurt themselves.

Jason & Dana are professional fire-fighters and understand safety issues, yet this happened to their dog. It was a freak accident. Dana watched helplessly as her dog fell to the ground. They performed CPR yet Halle died in their arms.

In Loving Memory of

K-9 HARLEY

January 23, 2002

Partner: Officer Robert Skrutsky
Stratford Police Department
900 Longbrook Ave.
Stratford, CT 06615
203-385.4100

Police have lost an officer known for nosing around in garbage and bugging colleagues for treats. Eccentricities aside, this officer was known as a standout narcotics detective and an integral member of the force. Harley, a black Labrador, specializing in narcotics detection, died after a brief heart illness. He was 9 years old. Harley, who joined the department in 1994, partnered with Detective Robert Skrutsky and worked on more than 600 cases.

Harley and Skrutsky were also popular figures at community events, performing more than 500 Demonstrations for schoolchildren and other civic groups. Skrutsky was unavailable for comment. LT. Thomas Rodia of the narcotics unit said Harley was "Good at finding things you couldn't see." During one drug raid, officers came up dry, Rodia said. But Harley kept scratching and sniffing at the staircase. After removing some panels from the stairs, sure enough, the drug stash was uncovered.

Capt. Paul Aurelia, commander of the Detective Bureau said that during another raid, officers found minor drug paraphernalia, but not the big haul they were looking for. Harley kept scratching and clawing at the back of a closet, and closer inspection showed the closet had a false back leading into a room stocked with the means for growing marijuana. "he was very accurate. There was no mistake with his nose." said Aurelia.

When Harley wasn't catching bad guys or entertaining schoolchildren, he often could be found lying on the floor in the department hallway. "He had the best job in the whole place." said Aurelia.

Captain Andre Knapp, department spokesman, said the department plans to replace Harley as soon as possible. With the passing of Harley, there is now one German Shepherd on staff trained in patrol work and narcotics detection. But finding a replacement so universally loved may be hard. Every day about 4 PM Harley would come by Knapp's desk and scratch at the bottom drawer, looking for treats. "Because he was a Labrador and specifically trained for narcotics he didn't have the aggressive tendencies that dogs trained for patrol work had," Knapp said. "He was just a good dog. An excellent dog." Rodia said.

MEMORIAL SERVICE FOR K-9 GROLL & K-9 HARLEY

The Stratford Police unveiled a monument last Thursday to two of their fallen officers, police dogs Groll and Harley. An honor guard of K-9 units from around the state, and the Stratford Police Honor Guard, was present to show support and dedicate the memorial. "They are fearless, loyal and loving," said Chief Michael Imbro of police dogs. "Their passing impels us to recognize the short amount of time we have."

Officer Celeste Robitalle, Groll's handler, said, "I'll never forget the day I met Groll for the first time. He was a skinny, hyper German Shepherd who wouldn't listen to a word I said. I know Groll is in good company with K-9s Shadow, Max and Jack." Detective Jack Cratty read a poem, "Guardians of the Night," from the North American Police Working Dog Association website. The author is unknown.

K-9 Groll was the department's patrol dog. Harley was a narcotics dog. The monument is made of black marble and bears the names of all Stratford's police dogs since the program's inception in 1985. "It is one of the most successful programs we have implemented over the years," Imbro said. "Just the presence of a trained K-9 and his handler makes a criminal think twice." The department plans to replace the two dogs it lost recently and add a second patrol dog. Each dog will cost $6,000.

The department has received some outside help in raising funds for the new dogs. Erica Pazkowski, a Bunnell High School freshman, raised $5,024 toward the cost of a new narcotics dog. "[She started collections at] the end of January," said Vicki Spada, Erica's mother. Capt. Andrew Knapp said, "Vicki Spada and her daughter Erica Pazkowski went above and beyond the call of duty.

Pazkowski collected money at Flood Middle School, Stop & Shop and other locations, and also received mail in donations. "She really liked Harley," Spada said. "She always looked forward to seeing him. She's an animal lover. She says the K-9s are a very important part of the police department." Spada and Pazkowski have two dogs at home.

In Loving Memory of

K-9 HOJEE

Von Silberwiese - Badge #27813 Ret.
July 28, 1994 - June 10, 2002

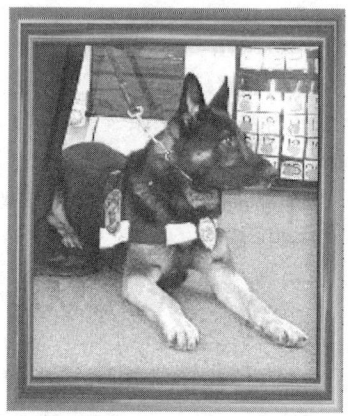

Partner: Chief Chris Wallace
Brookings Police Department
898 Elk Drive
Brookings, OR
541-469.3118

The Brookings Police Department's K-9 force consists of a Belgian Malinois named Robby. His handler is Officer Donny Dotson. The K-9s primarily ride on patrol nightly and get involved in a variety of cases. They do everything from sniffing out illegal drugs, to chasing down and holding fleeing suspects.

The Brookings Police Department is mourning the death of a fellow officer this week. On Monday morning, Hojee von Silberwiese, a six year police dog of the force, died, and his passing is being felt not just throughout the police department, but throughout the community.

Hojee, perhaps the most well known officer on the Brookings police force, was put to sleep after a short, valiant battle with a spinal disease. Brookings Chief of Police Chris Wallace felt the loss the hardest. He handled the 8 year old German Shepherd from when he was a pup until he "jacketed him up" for the final time on Monday.

"When you're a handler, you spend more time with your dog than you do with your wife and kids," Wallace said quietly during an interview Monday. He said he would often get home with Hojee late at night after his family was asleep, so he would wind down in front of the television with him by his side. And Wallace said he would wake up and get ready for work with Hojee raring to go after his wife and children had left for work and school. Because of that bond, Wallace said he had to spend part of Monday with his young daughters who had known Hojee as their only dog.

At work, Hojee was easily the most well trained and effective officer on the Brookings police force, Wallace said. He was certified as a police K-9 officer by the time he was 2, an incredibly early age. Hojee was effective in any realm in which he was placed, Wallace said. He was a great tracker. He was cross trained in narcotics detection and he was an outstanding public relations officer.

"His tracking instincts were phenomenal," Wallace said, explaining his ability to find either people or drugs that others could not. Wallace said Hojee tracked down one particular area felon twice within weeks and discovered a cache of marijuana when other officers and dogs couldn't. The chief also said Hojee became a trusted partner and loyal friend. "You get in a few situations where you get him protecting you or another officer and that bond just gets stronger," Wallace said.

"K-9 Hojee was one of us," said LT. John Bishop, who had also known Hojee since he was a pup. "When we did search warrants, I can't tell you how much more at ease we were when he was with us. "Those dogs save our lives. They keep us from getting hurt." In addition to his daily duties in law enforcement, Hojee visited with Brookings Harbor school children through the department's Safety City and similar programs. Wallace said Hojee's popularity was also felt well beyond the department. He said a woman at the Azalea Festival ran up to him with tears in her eyes asking for another "Hojee" trading card. "She said her son had a card he went to sleep with every night and he had just worn it out," Wallace said with a smile. He gladly obliged the request.

"On a certain level, he was the community's dog. God just allowed me to handle him," Wallace said. That kind of loyalty is why Hojee's death has hit the department so hard. When the time had come for Hojee to be put to sleep, Wallace, Bishop, John McKinney, one of Hojee's trainers, and Donny Dotson, an officer who handles K-9 officer Robby, were present.

"There's going to be very few times you'll see four officers with tears in their eyes, but (Monday) was one of them," Bishop said. Wallace said the toughest thing he has ever had to do was take Hojee's badge off for the final time. He said it was difficult because Hojee's mind was still very sharp, he just couldn't control his hind legs.

"One thing I would like to say to the community is a sincere thank you, Wallace said. "We've gotten a lot of messages from the community about Hojee." Wallace brought out a framed poem he received while he was handling Hojee. Bishop read the poem, "Guardians of the Night," that Wallace said was a perfect description of Hojee.

"Trust in me my friend for I am your comrade.
I will protect you with my last breath.
When all others have left you, and the loneliness of the night closes in,
I will be at your side.
Together we will conquer all obstacles and search out
those who might wish to harm others.
All I ask of you is compassion, the caring touch of your hands.
It is for you that I will selflessly give my life and spend my nights

unrested.

Together you and I shall experience a bond only others like you will understand.

When outsiders see us together, their envy will be measured by their disdain.

I will quietly listen to you and pass no judgment.

Nor will your spoken words be repeated.

I will remain ever silent, ever vigilant, ever loyal.

And when our time together is done and you move on in the world,

remember me with kind thoughts and tales.

For a time we were unbeatable.

Nothing passed among us undetected.

If we should ever meet again on another field, I will gladly take up your fight.

I am a Police Working Dog and together we are

Guardians of the Night."

"That was Hojee," Bishop said. The Brookings City Council, through a request from the police department, voted Monday to erect a memorial to Hojee and other K-9 officers who served the force.

In Loving Memory of

K-9 HUNTER

August 20, 2002

Partner: Sgt. Larry Schroeder
Montgomery County Sheriff Dept.
330 W. Second St.
Dayton, Ohio 45422
937. 225-4357

Hunter was a great K-9 and partner. He recovered over 4.5 million in cash and another 10 million in drugs. I would have to say he did his part in the war against drugs. I have his son Magnum a 2½ year old Labrador, he is so much like his father and a great bird dog and drug dog. I am looking for a yellow female pup now to carry on the Hunter line. And yes there will be a Hunter Jr.

My dad used to call HUNTER his grandson. My parents kept him while we were in Mississippi for Christmas. My dad spoiled him. I was in a cruiser crash and was unable to get a hold of Cindy to come and get him before they took me to the hospital, so I call my dad to come and get Hunter. When he got there the other officers tried to get Hunter out of the car and he about ate them alive. My dad walked up to open the cage door and got him out with no problem. They were 'big buds' till the end.

Sgt. Larry Schroeder of the Montgomery County Sheriff's Department, here in Dayton, Ohio lost his retired black lab this past Saturday. His dog HUNTER, a black lab of fourteen years passed away of natural causes. Hunter served the department for over eight years.

He worked with Deputy Shirley Doran from 1991 to 1994, Deputy Officer Randy Duff from 1994 to 1995 and Deputy Larry Schroder from 1995 to 1999. Larry ended up working with K-9 Jake, another black lab on the Drug Task Force from 1999 to April 2001, until being promoted to Sgt. in the Montgomery Sheriff's Dept.

He had patrol dogs from 1967 through 1994 and drug dogs from 1991 to present. At the time between 1991 to 1994, they had three labs in service. After 1994, only one drug dog.

The department has had three patrol/narc K-9s since September 2001 and have made many drug finds and apprehensions since they hit the street in December. K-9 Jake is working with his new handler on the drug task force.

In Loving Memory of

K-9 HUNTER

July 15, 1999 - April 19, 2002

Partner: Deputy Brian Biegel
Sarasota County Sheriff's Department
2071 Ringling Blvd.
Sarasota, FL 34237
941. 861-5800

Not a day goes by that I don't think about him. He was my life, my partner, but most of all, he was my best friend. Hunter had a heart defect from birth called cardiomiopthy. His heart was enlarged and his aorta was small. Hunter worked through a ten week training program plus four months on the road with just 1/3 of his heart functioning. Most people don't realize what these animals mean to us as K-9 handlers. I felt like I lost a part of me when Hunter passed. It was a difficult time.

K-9 Hunter was born in Budapest Hungary. He was a sable German Shepherd. In four months, Hunter had nine criminal catches. He located over six pounds of marijuana, one hundred hits of XTC, thirty grams of cocaine and two handguns. He also was used in the seizure of a 1993 BMW 325i. Hunter was nationally certified in the detection of marijuana, heroin, cocaine. He also trained in the detection of meth amphetamine and XTC.

He will be missed for his excellent work, but more so for his unconditional love and service. Hunter died of heart problems.

UPDATE:

I'm happy to tell you; I have a new partner, K-9 Ozzi, a 2½ year old Belgian Malinois.

In Loving Memory of

K-9 IKE

March 21, 2002

Partner: Sgt. Gary Kamp
Lee County Sheriff's Myers
14750 Six Mile Cypress Pkwy.
Ft. Myers, FL 33912
239-477.1193 & 239 -477.1335

Ike is sadly missed by Sgt. Kamp.

In Loving Memory of

K-9 IKE

November 26, 2002

Partner: Officer Chester Eads
Rockingham County Sheriff's Department
1088 Hwy. 65
Wentworth, NC 27025
336.634-3232

Ike, a 7 year old IPO trained Belgian Malinois died from stomach cancer. Although the cancer had progressed unknowingly to the point that it was beyond treatment, Ike worked with as much energy, desire and dedication as he did when first assigned to the Sheriff's Department K-9 division. Ike was all business when on duty and when off duty a member of the Ears family.

Matthew, Deputy End's 7 year old son, loved playing with Ike. Ike would snatch a toboggan hat off of Matthew's head and run away with it so Matthew would have to chase him. The 60 lb. dog's favorite thing, though was jumping six feet in the air into the arms of handler, Ears for acknowledgment of a job well done.

Ike was only with the department for three years due to his extended training and certification in tracking, but during his three years, he had his share of apprehending suspects that would have gotten away without his keen nose and the confiscation of illegal narcotics. The most serious incident Ike was involved in occurred in May 2001. Ike was sent into a house with the Special Response Team to locate a male suspect after a seven hour standoff and deployment of tear gas. Ike went in and gave his handler notice of interest to a closet, the suspect came from under a pile of clothes and fired from the closet striking a Special Response Team member in the stomach. The team member sustained only a bad bruise thanks to his vest. The male suspect was shot in the arm and surrendered. Without K-9 Ike drawing attention to the closet, more severe injuries could have been sustained.

Ike will truly be missed by the K-9 Division as one of the best to protect and serve. Ike was certified IPO and had a degree in tracking which he demonstrated in his performance. Ike was also the motivation for a school to raise money and purchase three ballistic vests for Rockingham County's K-9s. What was so unusual was the school was not in our county but a neighboring county. The saying was " We like Ike!" Sound familiar from history?

In Loving Memory of

K-9 IWAN

March 10, 2002

Sgt. Cory Mason
Danville Police Department
147 W. Main St.
Danville, IN 46122
317.745-2486

Iwan, a Belgian Malinois who helped the Danville Police Department track down bad guys for the last five years, died when he was struck by a truck. "It is kind of sad around here this week," said LT. Jerry Cunningham. Police said after Iwan got off duty Sunday, the dog got out of the gate at the home of his handler, Sgt. Cory Mason. Mason and other officers searched the neighborhood until about 3 a.m.

After dawn, the dog was found dead along U.S. 36 near Hendricks County Road 525 West. Later in the day, a truck driver called police and said he had hit a dog. "Iwan was kind of goofy. He was playful around the station and liked to explore the trash cans. He was a great dog. "But when Cory told him to bite, he was like a land shark," Cunningham said.

March 14, 2002 Police dog's death linked to fire truck.

A Police Department dog killed last weekend in a traffic accident actually was run over by a Fire Department fire truck, police said Wednesday. Police LT. Jerry Cunningham admitted he skirted the truth in a news release when he said Iwan, a Belgian Malinois, was hit Sunday night by "a vehicle traveling along U.S.#36." Cunningham said he intentionally hid the identity of the fire truck "for obvious reasons." Danville Police Chief, Garry Edwards, did not return phone calls Wednesday.

Iwan, purchased for the department in 1998 with $8,000 donated from a local business, was used to find narcotics, for rescues & to run down suspects. The Belgian Malinois (pronounced mal an wah) breed is a member of the shepherd family.

Since 1998, Sgt. Cory Mason had worked with Iwan. The two were on duty Sunday until the evening hours, when they returned to Mason's home near U.S. 36 & County Road 525 West. Iwan was put in his pen.

Later that night, Mason noticed the gate open and the dog missing, and he began to search for Iwan. Others helped him look for the dog until about 3 a.m. On Tuesday, Cunningham said a truck hit the animal. He said the driver of the truck called police and said he had hit a dog. But when questioned Wednesday, Cunningham changed his story. "The Fire Department said they had a run on a car fire on Sunday night," he said. "On the way, they thought they hit a dog. The next morning, the firefighters learned the Police Department was looking for an escaped animal. "They put 2 & 2 together." Cunningham said.

Donations will help pay for a new police dog. March 26, 2002, Kroger Co. and Milk Bone have donated $5,000 to the Police Department to help replace Iwan, a highly trained narcotics and attack dog killed March 10 in a traffic accident. Chief Garry T. Edwards said the donated money would help the department buy a new dog and help pay for specialized training for the animal and its handler, Sgt. Cory Mason.

"The new dog will cost $8,500. We also need funds to pay room and board for Sergeant Mason during the four weeks of intensive training with the new animal," Edwards said. He said the new dog would be purchased from a Michigan kennel specializing in dogs trained for law enforcement. Edwards said Iwan was insured for $7,000. The department has filed a claim with the insurance carrier. "This donation will be a big help to us," said Edwards.

On March 10, Iwan, a Belgian Malinois that had worked with Mason for five years, got out of his kennel and ran into the path of a Danville fire truck on an emergency run. Mason and other Police Officers found the dog's body the next morning.

Officials of Milk Bone, a maker of dog biscuits, have helped police departments nationwide obtain more than 145 dogs, said Jeff Golc, Kroger's manager of public affairs. The grocery chain is happy to offer aid, too, he said. The joint donation was made Monday at the East Main Street Kroger. "We are pleased to be able to help the department replace the dog. We like to be good citizens."

In Loving Memory of

K-9 JAMBO

February 8, 2002

Partner: Officer Jeff Jouanicot
San Leandro Police Department
901 Est 14th St.
San Leandro, CA 94577
510-577.3201

Jambo made his 58th and final arrest on February 5, 2002 and was euthanized three days later as a result of the injuries sustained while fighting with the suspect. Jambo's handler, Officer Jeff Jouanicot, became involved in a brief struggle with a suspect who then fled on foot. Jambo was sent to apprehend the suspect who was caught and stopped as he tried to climb a fence. Jambo pulled the suspect down off the fence and the suspect landed on top of Jambo. The suspect struggled with Jambo and Jambo held the suspect until Officer Jouanicot arrived. Officer Jouanicot took the suspect into custody after a brief struggle with the assistance of Jambo.

It was later learned that Jambo had sustained internal bleeding as a result of the struggle with the resisting suspect. Jambo apparently had an unknown tumor on his spleen, which burst during the struggle. The cancer was determined to be inoperable and Jambo was put to sleep on February 8, 2002.

Jambo was a very gentle dog with the public but all business when he was dealing with suspects. He was very well known in the community for his numerous public appearances as well as the many visits to local schools. Not only the department but also the public will miss him as well.

(End of Watch: February 8, 2002.)

Jeff has been a police officer for 18 years and is assigned to Patrol as a K-9 handler. His partner was Jambo. Together they worked swing-shift where they assisted in searching for hiding suspects. Jeff is also a member of the SWAT team and has worked in the Criminal Investigation Div. as a Robbery Detective. Jeff has also been a Field Training Officer and a Crime Scene Technician.

In his off time he enjoys camping and boating with his wife and 2 daughters.

Personal Message: Help Jambo and I take a bite out of crime.

In Loving Memory of

K-9 JAZZ

December 27, 2002

Partner: Officer Tony Balzano
Portland Police Department
109 Middle St.
Portland, ME 04101
207. 874-8300

I just lost my retired K-9 partner, JAZZ, to spinal cancer. It was the hardest thing I ever had to do, deciding to have him put down, two days after Christmas! He was 10 years old. We had worked together for 8 years.

I now have a new partner, my third over the 18 years of my career.

In Loving Memory of

K-9 JET

March 20, 2002

Partner: Sgt. Gabriel Cebada
Gallup Police Department
451 State Rd. 564 Gallup, NM 87301
505.726.0926

My K-9 Jet, after nine years of service as a narcotic police dog was retired to me. He lived happily with his other police K-9 companions and family. Unfortunately after so many years of dedicated service, his aged body could no longer keep up with his still bright and playful mind.

It was almost as if he still expected to go to work daily, not realizing he was too old. He passed away this week (March 20, 2002).

Sincerely, Sgt. Gabriel Cebada

In Loving Memory of

K-9 JETTA

Search & Rescue
March 27, 2002

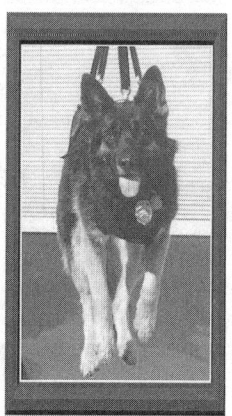

Handler: Patrick Horn
Spanish Lake Fire Protection District MO
The Missouri Region C Technical Rescue Team K-9 Division

Tribute to a Friend   Who Am I?

My career began at the FBI Academy in Quantico, Virginia. From there I moved to St. Louis to my new home. I began my training with my new handler and started my new job with the Spanish Lake Fire Department. I have my own union card from the International Association of Firefighters Local 2665. I'm loyal, trustworthy, dependable and give unconditional love. I have touched the hearts of over 25,000 people at public demonstrations and I have stood shoulder to shoulder with fellow firefighters and police officers at memorials.

I have been to hospitals and licked the faces of terminally ill children and brought smiles to the faces of elderly people in nursing homes. I'm also the mascot for the Missouri Children's Burn Camp. I have marched in parades, been to D.A.R.E camps and many other functions for the department. I have taught in High Schools, Colleges, Police and Fire Academies and the FBI. I can rappel from a 5 story training tower, fly in a helicopter, and jump from a rescue boat.

My job is to find you whether you are alive or have perished. I have been talked about, laughed at and criticized for what I do. I don't know anything about politics, department rules or disciplinary procedures. I have found a 6 year old girl, a 7 year old girl, two 14 year old boys, and an elderly Alzheimer's patient who walked away from his nursing home. I have assisted in two 1st degree murder convictions, and one 2nd degree murder conviction. Because of me our state now has laws to protect others just like me.

I have received the Firefighter of the Year Award. I'm the only employee of my kind who has received an Outstanding Service Award from the Director of the FBI, Louis Freeh. I have assisted in finding 15 drowning victims, several suicide victims and so on.

I have looked for the remains of our Governor on a mountainside, and was called to duty to go to New York to look for our fellow brothers and sisters. To those of you I have helped, I bring closure, comfort and relief. I'm proud of the job I've done and live for it. I have done my duty and others like me will carry on the tradition. For those I have met along the way of my career I want to thank you for your support. For the non believers, you now believe in what I do.

Who Am I? I am Jetta Search and Rescue K-9 Spanish Lake Fire Protection District Missouri Region "C" Technical Rescue Team K-9 Division.

K-9s CODY, CINDER, ALI, MOSES, & PRICE came Friday morning to pay their respects to Jetta, a 10 year old German Shepherd, who died Wednesday. She suffered a ruptured disk in her back, perhaps from an old injury, and had to be euthanized. Jetta wasn't just Horn's best friend. She was a rescue and recovery dog, called a "legend" and even a "firefighter" by her human companions.

Jetta is credited with finding missing children and an elderly Alzheimer's patient who walked away from his nursing home. She helped with three murder convictions, found fifteen drowning victims and has searched for remains after the plane carrying Gov. Mel Carnahan crashed. She has looked for just about every missing or murdered child the area has lost in recent years: Arlin Henderson, Gina Dawn Brooks, Heather Kullorn, Angie Housman.

Inside the bays of station house No. 1 of the Lincoln County Fire Protection District in Troy, MO, the Rev. Glenn Davis, chaplain of the Wright City Fire Protection District, stood next to the casket and led the group in prayer. "Whether the hero is a man on two feet, or his companion on four feet, they are heroes who are worthy of honor," he said. As they left the firehouse, the firefighters and police officers and their dogs filed past Jetta's closed casket, where she lay with her badge and orange rescue vest. Some paused and saluted.

A funeral procession accompanied the casket to the Horns' house, southwest of Troy, where family members had dug a grave alongside a creek. A recording of bagpipes playing "Amazing Grace" wailed from a boom-box. Firefighters carried Jetta's casket down two lines of firefighters and police officers. Under a grave side tent, the firefighters folded the flag from Jetta's casket. Fair gave the flag to Horn and hugged him. In a cold, steady rain, Davis led the group in another prayer. "Bless all of those who have lived their lives answering the alarm," he said. "Bless all of those who will bring comfort to those in crisis. Bless Jetta, who has been called home by the master's alarm, called to comfort."

Jetta began her training at the FBI Academy in Quantico, Virginia and then moved to St. Louis to live with Horn and his wife, Lincoln County firefighter Keli Horn. Jetta was one of the founding members of a group called the Missouri Region C Technical Rescue Team, and through her work, was the only rescue dog to get an Outstanding Service Award from the director of the FBI.

In Loving Memory of

K-9 JIMMY

SAR - WTC 9/11/01
May 17, 2002

Rescue & Recovery K-9
Handler: David Vitalli
1162 Union Ave.
Newburgh, NY 12550
845.566-4417

Jimmy, the search and rescue dog, died in his sleep yesterday morning. He was 8 years old. Jimmy's story appeared in the Record last October. With his best friend and owner, David Vitalli of Newburgh, the German Shepherd dog searched for survivors at Ground Zero in the aftermath of the attack.

For three weeks, the man and dog picked their way through the smoking wreckage, looking for survivors. Tethered to David's torso, Jimmy sniffed for the scent of distress , a sign that someone was alive. He breathed in the dust, the debris and the soot in a tireless effort to save someone. In the end, the man and dog found no one. And, in the end, death found Jimmy.

"He breathed in so much of that bad air," said Dee Dee Hurlburt, David's mother and partner in the family's security business. "He developed respiratory problems about a month after the Ground Zero search." Jimmy's health gradually deteriorated. The breathing problems took a toll on his good heart until it gave out in the dark hours yesterday morning.

"Thursday afternoon, I sat with him," said Dee, who takes care of the four dogs that form the backbone of their business. "I told him, 'You don't feel so well, do you, Honey.' I brushed him, and we talked for awhile." He was the best of their dogs, said David. At Ground Zero, he would nudge David on, even in the face of such defeat.

"He tried so hard," said Dee. "He never gave up. David had to carry him out of the rubble to get him to leave."

Yesterday, David carried his best friend's body away for the last time.

Jimmy paced in his kennel as he watched David load the Hummer. Ice. Ropes. Respirators. First aid kits. Boots. Dog food. Jimmy knew. He knew they were going to work. "Semmot! Kereshed! Semmot! Kereshed!" David said the Hungarian commands over and over to his 8 year old search and rescue dog to prepare him for the job ahead. It is the language Jimmy learned as a pup in Budapest, before coming to David when he was a year old. "Rescue! Bark! Rescue! Bark!" It is shorthand for "Find someone who is still alive! Bark to tell me where!"

Jimmy paced. It would be like before. Like the time he and David went to Oklahoma City to find the person who was still alive. To bark so David knew where to dig. Jimmy found the person. Many persons! He barked many times. "Nana la kausch! Nana la kausch!" David would say it, over and over. "Good boy! Good boy!" Jimmy stood by as his 32 year old master, David Vitalli, said goodbye to his family at their Town of Newburgh home and the three other shepherds who would stay behind. Then Jimmy settled into his car cage as David drove the

Hummer out of the driveway onto Union Avenue and headed south. They were going to New York City. They were going to Semmot! Kereshed!

It was Sept. 11 at 7 p.m. They would be there by 8. Troop T of the state police had cleared the way for David and Jimmy, and for the thousands of other volunteer rescue workers pouring into the city to find, to save, to bark.

For three weeks, the German Shepherd would work, strapped to David's torso. For three weeks the dog would sniff and the man would dig with his bare hands. For three weeks they would go into holes where there was something, something! Could it be someone alive! Man and dog would push themselves, trying, trying. But in the end, there would be no nana la kausch. There would only be exhaustion and collapse and the salty tears on David's face for Jimmy to lick away.

Jimmy is one of four search and rescue shepherds that David Vitalli uses in the operation of Vortek Corp., his Newburgh based security business, which provides guards for hire. But David and the dogs also help police agencies. They search for missing persons. The dogs sniff for bombs. They smell out drugs.

But the World Trade Center wasn't business. This was volunteer work. David could help. And he knew that Jimmy was the most indefatigable worker. If there was a live person to be found, Jimmy would do it. He was trained for such jobs with the use of pseudo scents, made for such purpose. In New York City, he was to smell for the scent of distress. It's the odor of a chemical the body gives off in a high stress or trauma situation.

That's what Jimmy seeks when David gives the rescue command. But when David and Jimmy arrived at Ground Zero, it was another smell that overwhelmed the shepherd: the smell of death. His nose was in chaos, the scent of distress from rescue workers competed with the scent of corpses. All this, on top of the fire smell he'd noticed way up town, as far north as the Harlem River Drive. He'd begun walking in circles in his cage, his nose in the air. What was this that David was bringing him to? David parked near Ground Zero, but it would be several hours before Jimmy was let out of the Hummer. The earth was too hot. Days later, the heat would still burn Jimmy's pads and would cause David's boots to melt to his feet.

The broken glass and twisted metal were everywhere. Fire erupted from this hole, that hole. Piles of rubble collapsed without warning. Jimmy had no boots to protect his feet. His shaggy coat would catch fire too easily. He would have to wait until 2 a.m. Wednesday before David let him out of the Hummer to begin his job. But how to smell through all the debris in the air, the powdered concrete, the smoke, the dust? The dog and man stood in total darkness, in two feet of ash, of broken bits of things. Broken bits of bodies.

David attached his dog's leash to a harness around his own chest. Dog and man were tethered together. The dog's ID is tattooed in his ear. He wears a metal tag on his collar. David wrote his own name and Social Security number on his arms, his calves, the front and back of his torso. Dogs don't care what happens to themselves when they're on a search mission. And Jimmy was on a mission. He didn't notice the cuts on his feet, the singed fur, the stinging eyes, the fires, the hoses, the sounds. So many dogs, so many men and women searching, searching. More than 1,100 dogs by one estimate. Labs, poodles, beagles, mutts, shepherds, rottweilers. The handlers took their dogs off the "bark" command. It was too chaotic. There was too much reason to bark. The scents of stress and death were everywhere.

Instead, Jimmy just stopped and stood still when he came upon a scent. Every few feet, he stopped. Then David would go down, into a hole, to check. Is it? Is it? Body parts were sent out by the bucket brigade, who sifted through the debris, millions of tons of debris, with their hands, looking for something that could be identified as a child's father, a man's wife, a son, a daughter. The people with posters lined the site, just beyond the yellow tape.

Time and again, David took his dog out of the debris to the street for a break, a sense of normal. But there was no normal.

"Have you seen this person?" they asked David. "My daughter wears an ankle bracelet, she has a barrette in her hair, my son has a red stone in his ring. Take this picture of him. Take my phone number. Call. Please call. "David's pockets bulged with their posters, their pieces of paper. "Can I hug your dog? Can I pet your dog? I love him. Thank you, thank you for looking."

On one of the days, who knows which one? a little girl, no more than 6, wrapped her arms around Jimmy's neck. "Is your dog looking for my daddy?" she asked David. "Yeah, honey." "Will you come to the party we're going to have when you find my daddy? Will you bring your dog to the party?" Oh, God. The water brought into the site for the rescuers was often luke-warm, but the people behind the yellow tape made sure the dogs had cold water. Jimmy lapped their offerings, poured into David's respirator mask for the dog to drink from. "Thank you, dog, thank you."

Veterinarians walked through the crowd of rescuers carrying oxygen, asthma pumps, IVs, gauze, sutures. Some dogs died, David heard. He doesn't know for sure. Booties were distrib-uted for the dogs, sent down from a company in Canada. Leather to protect the feet, Velcro to hold them on. Jimmy wore them for a 12 hour shift , which one? which day? which night? but the wet metal was slippery. He lost his footing, slid in the ruins. David removed them and Jimmy went back to work on his naked, sore, blistered feet. As the days wore on, the dogs grew depressed. They weren't finding, rescuing, barking. The living person is their goal, and it is also their reward. Jimmy was failing, failing. He was not nana la kausch. He was bad.

Still, he nudged David back when they went out for a break. Try more. Try harder. The dog pushed himself to the point of collapse. David carried him out of the rubble to rest in the Hummer with the air conditioner on. Just a little fresh air. Just a little break. David heard that one of the dogs found a white pigeon alive in the rubble. The rescuers named the bird Hope, it was said. The man and the dog went back to work. Again. And again. And then they stopped. After three weeks, they stopped. Jimmy was sick. A growth on his back had gotten worse. The vet wanted to remove it, to test it. David knows the results. He isn't talking about it. But Jimmy knows. He knows his final mission was a failure. He didn't find. He didn't bark. He wasn't nana la kausch. And it is Jimmy's daughter, 2 year old Nieka, who will be with David the next time he loads the Hummer and says, over and over, Semmot! Kereshed! Jimmy rests his head on his paws as he looks mournfully through the bars of his kennel door. His work is not entirely ended just yet. His David needs the tears licked away from his face once again.

Losing Jimmy was as hard to me as if I was losing a member of my family, though he really was a part of my family. No matter how large the task, or the type job we where on he was always ready to go. Even though I saw his health going at "Ground Zero" he wanted to keep searching. He did not want to stop. Many times he kept me going even when entering Hell as I saw it. I hope and pray that the poem on the back of the card is true. That some day I will see my best friend again.

Thank you again and God Bless.

(David Vitalli, handler)

In Loving Memory of

K-9 JOURIE

September 18, 2002

Partner: Officer Keith Bush
Tampa Police Department
One Police Center
411 N. Franklin St.
Tampa, FL 33602
813. 276-3717

K-9 Jourie died of heat stroke. He was three years old. He broke out of his protective kennel by chewing it and ran around in the heat which caused heat stroke. He was found by the side of the building, too late to help.

He is sadly missed not only by Officer Bush, but the entire department. He was not working on the street very long, but did have three street apprehensions.

Officer Bush is now working with a German Shepherd, named FALCO.

In Loving Memory of

K-9 JUNO

July 7, 2002

Partner: Deputy N. R. (Ray) Shearin
Vance County Sheriff Office
156 Church St.
Henderson, NC 27536-5574
252-738.2200

Juno has died. The 10 year old German Shepherd retired form the Vance County Sheriff's Office 2 years ago because of illness. She died Sunday at home. Ray Shearin, A K-9 officer, is still grieving. He was Juno's handler for three years.

"A lot of people knew that dog," he said this week in an interview. Juno lived with Shearing, his wife, Jonnie, and their 4 year old son, Brandon. "That was his dog," Shearin said. "That was his girl. She was like a member of the family." Juno had cancer and had to leave the department in March 2000. "It had started eating away at her spine and her back," Shearing said. "It was inoperable. She couldn't work anymore. I think she did good to live two years."

Shearin buried her under an old oak tree that has been in the family home place for many years. "I fixed a graveyard. It was kind of like a shady spot. She's under that. We live off the road a ways." No one else is buried there. "Just her. To be honest with you, I hope I don't have to go through that again."

Shearin now works with Rex, another German Shepherd. Juno was a full fledged deputy and earned several commendations during her tour of duty, which stared in 1993. Jay Swilley was her first handler.

"She didn't get no paycheck, but she was still there, just as good," Shearin said. She and Shearing graduated together from a six week training school in March 1997. Juno was certified through the National Police Work Dog Association. Shearin said she found missing children and elderly people in Vance County.

Juno discovered a bank robbery suspect hiding in an attic in Warren County in 1999. The Warren County Sheriff's office gave her a commendation for that. "It was so many things she did," Shearin said. "Juno was all purpose. she located several pounds of narcotics in Fayetteville. She has several misdemeanor and felony arrests."

Deputy Juno serviced Vance County for seven years. Juno had a switch, according to Shearin. "She knew when it was time to work, and when it was time to play." she liked to ride in the front seat of the patrol car, not the back, and Shearin let her do it, sometimes.

"Juno was the kind of dog who was easy going until it was time to bite somebody," he said. She enjoyed going to elementary schools and playing with the children. Shearin had a way he wanted to end this story.

"She was my partner, but, most of all, my friend, and she will be greatly missed."

In Loving Memory of

K-9 KASEY

May 13, 2002

Partner: Officer Rick Quigley
Coral Springs Police Department
2801 Coral Springs Dr.
Coral Springs, FL 33065
954.346.1201

A good friend of mine and a long time K-9 handler and trainer from Coral Springs, FL Police Department, Rick Quigley, suddenly lost his dog yesterday. A little over a week ago his dog, "Kasey" yelped after jumping a hurdle in training. After some muscle relaxing medication no change was noted. Yesterday a specialist diagnosed two crushed vertebrae. The vet told me this could not be fixed. "Kasey", a four year old German Shepherd, had to be put down.

Recently "Kasey", a cross trained patrol/narcotic detection dog, alerted to a large quantity of cash in a vehicle, which is now in forfeiture proceedings.

I will never forget "Kasey.

In Loving Memory of

K-9 KEMO

October 18. 1995 - August 2, 2002

Partner: Sgt. John Bullard
Independence Police Department
223 N. Memorial Dr.
Independence, MO 64050
816-325.7872

Loss of a Friend

On August 2, 2002 Independence Police K-9 Kemo lost his battle with cancer. In the latter part of June, Kemo began losing weight and having problems with his rear legs. Numerous tests were conducted with no clear cut answers. Dr. Schrock, Dr. John and all of the staff of John Veterinary Clinic did a great job of comforting Kemo and his family while they waited for test results. Kemo was referred to the University of Missouri Veterinary School in Columbia, MO. Again numerous tests were conducted, consultations were made with other doctors, other clinics, even other veterinary colleges in an effort to determine what was causing Kemo's problems.

On August 1, a series of more invasive tests were conducted. The conclusion of those tests revealed a highly aggressive cancer in Kemo's spinal column. The prognosis for treatment of this type of cancer would have been at best temporary. The cancer left Kemo in a great deal of pain and the inability to walk. The decision was made that Kemo would leave this world with all of the dignity that he had brought to it.

Kemo's body will be temporarily loaned the University of Missouri Veterinary School in Columbia, MO where research may be conducted hopefully to help create a cure so this type of tragedy will not occur again. Eventually, Kemo will be laid to rest at the site of the Independence Police Department's K-9 Training Facility.

Kemo was born on October 17, 1995 in Holland with the registered name of Iron Vom Grauen Stahlhammer. Kemo's career began with the Independence Police Dept. in October of 1998 when he and his handler, Sgt. John Bullard, attended basic handler's school at Vohne Liche Kennels in Denver, IN. Since that time Kemo has responded to 2082 K-9 calls for service.

He assisted in 133 public demonstrations for school kids, neighborhood block watch groups, & others showing off his skills for finding narcotics and making apprehension to 16,312 members of the community. His criminal interdiction work helped in apprehending 26.5 criminals (the .5 was because Kemo had to share one apprehension with the rookie, K-9 Haas.)

Between the two K-9s, the person that was going to run, couldn't quite give up fast enough. Kemo had 112 narcotics finds with one of them being the largest load of marijuana ever confiscated by the Independence Police Department. That find resulted in the removal of 100 pounds of marijuana from the streets of Independence and the seizure of the van that was transporting the marijuana in the gas tank.

Kemo left a lasting impression on anyone who ever caught

him during a training session. He also left a lasting impression on a couple of officers who happen to get in his way during a criminal apprehension.

Kemo will be missed by his mom, Konnie, his brothers and sisters, Jennifer, Jim, Michelle, Ian, Andy, Jared, Erik and his little buddy Budrow. He will also be missed by many other co workers, friends, school kids, neighbors etc. Kemo will especially be missed by his dad, John. Going to work won't be the same without him. No one to talk to, no one to help watch the people in the cars beside us, no one to put his muddy feet on my seat or to steal a french fry from my hand. Especially no one there to watch out for me or to provide me with that rather moist lick up the side of the face as if to say "Hey let's go get the job done."

Just one last comment to make, and that is to Terry. Hey Brother, I'm sending you a good partner and a good friend, but he is only on loan to you until I get there. You two patrol those heavenly streets and be sure to watch over the rest of us yet to come. You two take good care of each other and while you're at it work with him a little bit and see if you can get him to spit that damn sleeve.

Good Bye, best friend~~

Officers say goodbye to Independence police dog Kemo, who died Aug. 2 from cancer. He touched the lives of thousands of children, uncovered hundreds of pounds of illegal drugs and aided in dozens of searches for dangerous criminal suspects. On Aug. 2, Independence Police K-9 officer Kemo lost his life to a rare form of spinal cancer.

Kemo's partner and handler, Sgt. John Bullard, said his dog was more than a pet, more than a partner and more than a friend. "I think it is hard for people who do not work close with animals the way we do to understand," Bullard said. "There is a very special bond between an officer and their K-9 partner. It has been very touching for me, for my family and for the other guys in the unit."

K-9 officers live at home with their handlers. The dogs ride in the back of a patrol car with their heads resting inches from their handler's shoulder. "They are right there with us, 24 hours a day. We spend more time with the dogs than with our own families," Bullard said. Kemo was born in Holland in 1996 and trained in Indiana. He received his commission with the Independence Police in 1998 and was partnered with Bullard.

In his career, Kemo did more than 130 public appearances and demonstrations for thousands of school children and neighborhood groups. He was trained as both a narcotics dog and for patrol duties that included locating suspects hiding from police. "His big claim to fame is probably a hotel search we did with the DEA in January 2000," Bullard said. "As soon as we exited the car, he did a bee line for this van in the parking lot. It was a textbook example of a vehicle search." Kemo's keen nose uncovered 100 pounds of marijuana concealed in the gas tank of the van. He has also found drugs concealed in the steering column of a passenger car and dozens of other places.

"They (the dogs) can find drugs in places we would never look. Criminals can be very ingenious," Bullard said. Besides sniffing out narcotics, Bullard said the K-9 officers protect the lives of their handlers and other police officers. The dogs are sent into dark woods, basements, empty buildings and other places where possibly dangerous criminals are hiding from police.

"That is probably the hardest thing for us, to send our K-9 into a situation where they could be seriously hurt or killed. If you think that doesn't affect us, it does, believe me," Bullard said. "But, if it is to protect the life of an officer or a citizen, then that is their job. They would give their lives for us, without hesitation."

Kemo has served the last four years with no major injuries or problems, Bullard said. Then, this June, he began to fail very suddenly. "He was dropping weight pretty fast, and we noticed him dragging his left rear foot," Bullard said. "He must have been in pain long before that but he never showed it. He was a very stoic dog." Local veterinarians ran tests and put Kemo on medication, but he continued to lose weight. Eventually, Bullard took Kemo to the University of Missouri School of Veterinary Medicine in Columbia, Mo. Lead physicians there tested again and recommended new medicines.

"Nothing was working. The pain just got worse and he kept losing weight," said Bullard. Finally, Kemo fell to 20 pounds under his former weight, even with double servings of food. The MU veterinarians performed a CAT scan and finally found the cause of Kemo's decline, a rare form of cancer attacking his spinal cord and nervous system.

"We made the decision to have him put to sleep the next day," Bullard said. "We wanted him to go with as little pain and as much dignity as possible." Kemo's body was left with researchers at MU to explore the nature of his rare cancer. He will be cremated and returned to Independence later this month. Bullard wants to have a proper resting place waiting for him.

"We had the idea to do a memorial for the K-9 officers a long time ago. We just never had a permanent place to do it," he said. Now, the K-9 unit has taken over a building on Missouri 78, just east of Blue River Community College. The building was donated by the Little Blue Valley School District, which occupies another building on the property.

The planned memorial site is a 42 foot gravel circle with a 50 foot flag pole standing in the center. Bullard and other K-9 unit officers went Friday to select a memorial stone for the site. The stone will be engraved with a picture of a German Shepherd, the breed of many police dogs, including Kemo.

"We just feel it is right that they should have a memorial to recognize the contribution they make to the department, to the community and to the fight against crime," Bullard said. Kemo's name will be engraved with the names of two other lost K-9 officers, Arco, who died in July 1996, and Jake, who died in June 1997.

The K-9 unit is still collecting contributions to pay for the memorial site and to complete renovations of the new facility, kennels and training grounds. Contributions can be sent to FOP/Coins for K-9s, c/o Sgt. John Bullard, 2150 Independence Center, Independence, Mo., 64057. Additional funds are also needed to pay for the cost of purchasing and training two new police dogs. One dog will fill Kemo's place and the other will take the position of K-9 Larry, who retires later this month.

In Loving Memory of

K-9 KILO

July 28, 2002

Partner: Officer James White
Derby Police Department
229 N. Baltimore Ave.
Derby, KS 67037-1601
316.788-1557

K-9 Kilo, a six year old Belgian malinois, was put to sleep after suffering from severe heat stroke. Kilo had been with handler Jim White and the Derby Police Department since 1997. He was trained in narcotics detection, tracking, trailing and patrol work.

In Loving Memory of

K-9 LARS

November 1992 - February 22, 2002

Deputy Lucian C. Hudson
Eric County Sheriff's Dept.
10 Delaware Ave.
Buffalo, NY 14202
716. 858-7088

Lars was born in Czech Republic and purchased by the sheriff's office with drug seizure money. Brought to the U.S. Deputy Hudson and Lars were together 6 years. Earned their NYS BMP certification as a police K-9 team. Lars was trained in area & building searches, criminal apprehension, tracking, crowd control, officer protection and drug detection.

Erie County Sheriff's Office K-9 Dog Lars, a 10 year old Czech Republic German Shepherd died unexpectedly from natural causes on Saturday, February 16, 2002. Lars was the first trained duel purpose, patrol and narcotics K-9 dog in the history of the Erie County Sheriff's Office. He was trained to the level of ZVV1 in the Czech Republic and received his narcotics training at the Amsel Kennels, under the direction of Owen Tober of Akron, New York.

The K-9 worked with Federal, State and Local Law Enforcement agencies: FBI, DEA, State Police and Town and Village Police Departments. Lars and his handler did many K-9 Demonstrations at the Erie County Fair, local schools, Boy and Girl Scout meetings and Senior Citizen groups.

The K-9 Drug Awareness Program for Middle and High Schools evolved as a result of having this specialized K-9 dog. Lars was trilingual, he understood his commands in Czech, German and in English. During his long career the K-9 alerted on large amounts of Marijuana, Crack Cocaine, Cocaine, Heroin, and a variety of other drugs. Some of the most memorable finds he was involved in are:

26 Kilos of Cocaine in suitcase for the DEA.

Two suit cases with 15 lbs. Marijuana Buffalo International Airport.

65 hits of Heroin hidden in engine compartment of Chevrolet S 10 pickup truck.

The first time, after Lars finished narcotics school, he assisted the Career Criminal Task Force, and found $4700.00 in cash & 2 oz. of Crack Cocaine.

Apprehension of suspect hiding in soybean field in the Village of Springville.

Lars and his handler also did many demonstrations for schools and organizations. K-9 Lars was placed in service from June of 1994 until February of 2002.

Deputy Sheriff L. C. Hudson, handler for Lars, will have a memorial for him, to be held March 20, 2002 at 11:00 a.m., at the Colden Fire hall, Town of Colden. The Colden Fire hall: Rt 240 (State Road) Corner Gutkunst Road, Town of Colden.

In Loving Memory of

K-9 LAUREN

SAR
January 21, 1991 - January 1, 2002 1:15 AM

Handler: Helen Young
Iowa Search & Rescue

It is with sadness that I report the loss of ISAR's K-9, Lauren, partner of Helen Young. Lauren joined ISAR after spending three years living in a crate. Despite her great love for Helen and members of ISAR, she just did not care to find anyone.

Helen soon retired Lauren from searching. That, however, was not Lauren's last contribution to ISAR. She was called upon many times to help break ISAR K-9s of aggressive behavior. Lauren would just look at their aggression as if to say, "What is our problem?" She was an awesome help to our organization.

Before her recent retirement, she taught obedience classes with Helen for the Humane Society. ISAR members that knew her are not going to be the only ones to miss her. Although she never found anyone, Lauren most certainly earned her place in heaven.

In Loving Memory of

K-9 LEX

LODD
December 10, 2002

Partner: Officer Bert Combs
Portland Police Bureau
1111 S. W. Second Avenue
Portland, OR 97204
503. 823-2154

"LEX" in Latin means "LAW"

"Pretty darned appropriate for a police dog!" On Tuesday, December 10, 2002, at 12:07 p.m., "Lex," the K-9 partner of Officer Bert Combs died of an apparent heart attack while tracking a suspect. After apprehending the suspect, Lex returned to his handler, Officer Combs and died.

Lex was a 7 year old German Shepherd and 6 year veteran of the Portland Police Bureau. He was also one of two Portland Police Bureau K-9's trained as a member of the SERT team. Lex was responsible for the capture of 126 suspects during his six years with the Portland Police Bureau.

Lex is the third dog trained by Officer Bert Combs since he joined the K-9 unit in 1986. Officer Combs is a Master Trainer of police dogs in the State of Oregon. "Lex was very dedicated to his work and to me. Out of all his captures, none really stands out. They were all bad guys and some were quite dangerous, but Lex made their captures "routine." I never had a suspect challenge me when Lex was barking and wolfing during a confrontation. They always gave up and submitted to arrest. That truly is the benefit of having a police dog as a partner. Bad guys will fight with officers, but very rarely will they fight with a German Shepherd. I cannot help but wonder if any of those 126 captures that Lex made actually saved my life, or kept me from getting hurt. If Lex had not been there, would one of those suspects have made the decision to take me out? I guess I will never know.

I do know I loved the little guy and I'd like to think the feeling was mutual. He was a hell of a police dog.

This Sunday 4/13/03 I start work with my new partner, Brutus. We just finished training on Wednesday and we're both ready to go.

In Loving Memory of

K-9 MAJOR

February 10, 2000 - June 9, 2002

Partner: Officer David Thurman
KY Department of Fish & Wildlife
#1 Game Farm Road
Frankfort, KY 40601
800-858.1549

One of our K-9 Officers dogs was found deceased after the handler returned home from Church. Foul play is not suspected, as his hunting dog was in the same pen with his work dog, and is doing fine.

Unfortunately, this is a severe blow to the program at a personal level. The officer, David Thurman, is a twenty year veteran with the Kentucky Dept. of Fish & Wildlife. He was assigned as one of three officers in the state for the pilot test program. This gave him a new outlook on work. He recently completed training with Indiana Fish & Wildlife. Dave & K-9 Major, were just beginning to work as a very successful team.

I thank you for putting my partner and friend on this site and am sending this picture to put on. Major was a Lab/Rhodesian Ridgeback mix K-9 with very keen senses. A very fine K-9, partner and friend. His time with us was short, February 10, 2000 to June 9 2002, but in his short time he touched a lot of lives, employees, school kids, sportsmen and women across the state of KY. He had in his short time out of school, 3 months, found a lost woman, and a bad guy, and a few cases of evidence recovery (shot shells, police baton, shotgun.) Thanks again for your site.

There is a true bond in our K-9 ranks that most would never understand. This was a personal favorite, because his breed ranking in intelligence and obedience was 52 and my fellow officers laid a track in school that ended on this camp site, and then took our picture. It was a reminder to us both to work harder at what you do to be better.

Update:

My new K-9 partner's name is "GLORY." She was born on the 4th of July. She is a shiny little black female lab, 48 pounds with the heart and drive the size of Texas. I met Glory about a month after I lost K-9 Major. I was not really sure that I wanted to do the K-9 work anymore. Thanks to my new partner, and numerous other K-9 officers from around the nation who e-mailed me, I knew I needed to keep doing this.

So "Glory" and I began to start our career together as a team.

In Loving Memory of

K-9 MARK

LODD
May 18, 2002

Partner: Deputy Bert McCue
Osceola County Sheriff Dept.
400 Simpson Rd.
Kissimmee, FL 34744
407-348.2222

At work and at play, 24 hours a day, police dog, Mark was at the side of Osceola County deputy sheriff, Bert McCue: sniffing out illegal drugs, tracking down escaped prisoners and even entertaining schoolchildren. Mark, a 6½ year old German Shepherd who died Saturday, was honored Thursday outside the Osceola County Sheriff's Office with a memorial fitting for a fallen officer.

"He was just a gentle, gentle dog," said McCue, teary eyed as he twisted a tissue in his hands. "I spent more time with him than anybody. I could trust him 100 percent. He was there for me, never failed me." Mark was euthanized after a deputy accidentally ran him over with a car while the dog was chasing down a man accused of kidnaping and beating an ex-girlfriend.

Mark had served with the department since 1998. He helped with 75 drug seizures, including finding a kilo of cocaine in a vehicle earlier this month. Mark also participated in 33 felony arrests. He was one of five dogs owned by the department.

Police and their K-9 partners traveled from Ocoee, Apopka, Orange County and other surrounding areas to attend the memorial. They covered their stars with black tape, as they would do for any fallen comrade. People lined up to offer condolences to McCue, who was given a plaque bearing the police dog poem "Called to Give My All."

Staff Sgt. Jason Campbell drove from Patrick Air Force Base with a military dog, Dasty, to salute the fallen dog. He called K-9 units a brotherhood. "He [the dog] helps you grow," said Campbell, who operates the kennel on the base. "When you've got problems you can call on him and he'll listen. He teaches you about life."

Seminole County Sheriff's Sgt. Karen Mills, who brought her dog, Bolo, said police dogs are true partners and co-workers to the people with whom they work. "They're there for you when you need them, ready to give their lives for you," she said.

The dogs are talented and invaluable on the job, said Orange County Sheriff's Sgt. Ed Durant, who brought his dog, Shadow. He said whenever a dog dies, it's considered "another officer down." McCue already has been given another dog, named Fritz, to care for and to try to bond with as a new partner. He'll never forget his old partner, though. "This means a lot," he said, looking at the crowd of people at the memorial. "I want them to know it's for Mark."

Service scheduled for fallen K-9 May 23, 2002

A memorial service is scheduled today for Osceola County Sheriff's Office K-9 Mark after the dog was struck by a deputy's patrol car. Deputies transported K-9 Mark to a veterinary hospital in Orlando, where they learned the dog had a broken back, and therefore, he was put to sleep. The service will begin at 9:30 a.m. in the courtyard in front of the sheriff's office at 400 Simpson Road. The public is welcome to attend.

In Loving Memory of

K-9 MASE

LODD
Badge # 546
May 4, 2002

Partner: Cpl. Garry Begg
Langley Royal Canadian Mounted Police
22180 - 48A Avenue
Langley, B.C.V3A 887
604. 532-3200

Langley RCMP are saying good bye to a lovable colleague and friend who was adored by local children. Police service dog Mase was killed on Saturday, May 4, while trying to apprehend a man who led police on a hazardous chase. "He was quite a popular dog with the kids," Langley RCMP Cpl. Garry Begg said of Mase. "He was a very gentle dog with little people."

The Langley RCMP use police dogs to track suspects from crime scenes, look for missing people, for public relations activities, and to help apprehend suspects. Mase was killed at the end of a police pursuit that started around 4:23 a.m. in north Langley, at 202nd St. and 91 Ave., when a suspected impaired driver refused to stop. The chase headed down the freeway and ended at the Kensington Overpass & the Lougheed Highway, when the suspect's car collided with the overpass guard rail.

As the driver tried to free himself from the car and run away, the Langley RCMP dog handler released Mase. The dog jumped onto the hood of the suspect's car, but when he went to jump down, Mase accidentally jumped the wrong way and went over the railing of the over pass to the highway below. He sustained massive injuries and attempts to revive him at a veteri-nary clinic were unsuccessful. Police Dog Mase, Badge #546, was pronounced dead.

"It was totally accidental," said Begg, adding that the dog simply made an error in judgment. Five year old Mase had been a police dog in Langley for three years, and lived with his han-dler. "He was part of their family," said Begg. "He was with his partner for 24 hours a day." Langley RCMP had two police dogs, but Mase and his handler had been scheduled for a trans-fer to New Brunswick. Both the officer and the dog will be replaced.

A small ceremony for the lost police dog will be held by the Langley RCMP detachment. The driver of the car that started the chase, a 28 year old Vernon man, is in custody, and is facing charges for refusing to stop for police.

Crime fighters:

K-9 cop new top dog RCMP Cpl. Mike Landry may have a new partner, but he'll never forget Mase.

RCMP Cpl. Mike Landry lost a long time friend and part-ner recently. Langley police service dog Mase died while trying to apprehend a man who led police on a pursuit. Landry, an RCMP dog handler, said joining up with his new dog Czar, a 2½ year old German Shepherd, has been therapeutic for him as he mourns the loss of Mase.

But while he sees a bright future with his new partner, he

will always remember his old one. "Mase loved kids and loved the general public as well," Landry said. "We spent a lot of time in the local schools in Langley and in the schools in Surrey as well. It's going to take time with this new dog, but in Mase's memory, I want to make this dog as good as he was. Maybe he'll never take the place of Mase, but I think this is an excellent dog."

Mase died May 4 during a police chase which started in North Langley when an impaired driver refused to stop. The day is burned in Landry's memory. "It was just a little bit after 4:00 and I was off duty heading home from Langley to Surrey, when a call came over the air of an erratic driver with front end damage in the Walnut Grove area. To make a long story short, I didn't go home. I went to check on the car. I figured if it was stolen that we may get a foot chase or a pursuit. After I found him, the driver didn't want to stop."

The pursuit headed down the freeway and ended at the Kensington Overpass & Lougheed Hwy., when the suspect's car collided with an overpass guard rail. As the driver tried to free himself from the car and run away, Landry released Mase. The dog jumped onto the hood of the car, but when he went to jump down, he went over the railing of the overpass and tumbled onto the highway below. Mase suffered massive injuries and died later at a veterinary clinic. Five year old Mase had worked in Langley for three years. The driver of the car, a 28 year old Vernon man, is in Langley RCMP custody and is facing various charges.

Meanwhile, Landry is struggling to carry on. "The whole week's been hard," Landry said. "It's a hard thing to do, to leave the other guy behind and get bonded with this guy." Landry, who lived with Mase, said they had been a team for four years. Landry said Mase was a great companion, and an even better police dog. "He had caught several hundred culprits, drugs and stolen articles and everything he was a great service to the community."

Landry is looking ahead to a future in Moncton, NB with

Czar, who has been a working police dog for the past six months. Czar has trained for five months at the RCMP Kennels in Innisfail, Alta. The pair transfer to New Brunswick on Monday.

The handler sees a lot of Mase in Czar. "They are very similar in personalities," Landry said. "This guy is very energetic, likes to bark, tracks very well, searches very well, and from what I can see so far, he is going to bond fairly well with me. At the same time, he is quite sociable, and I like that in a dog."

While the Langley RCMP uses dogs to track suspects from crime scenes, look for missing people, and to apprehend suspects, they are also vital in public relations purposes. "We can do a lot of public demonstrations with kids and Boy Scouts like we did with the other dog," Landry said. The bonding process between the handler and the dog takes time. "It depends with every dog, but usually, the bonding takes over several months, but you can usually see a lot of the bonding occurring over the first few weeks," Landry said. "If they are tough or independent dogs, it takes a bit of time."

The two will come together as constant companions. Like Mase before him, Czar will live with Landry and become part of his family when the two move to Moncton. As he knelt down and stroked Czar's fur, Landry said "Now I've got Czar in the back of the truck, and he's taken a little bit of the place of Mase. He'll never replace him, but he is my partner. I do have to go back to work, and I'm very, very happy to have this dog."

In Loving Memory of

K-9 MAX

March 27, 2002

Partner: Sgt. Michael J. Ravenelle
Ledyard Police Department
11 Lorenz Parkway
Ledyard, CT 06339

I deeply regret to inform all that one of our brothers, K-9 Max was put to rest last night, the 27th of March 2002, after a brief illness. I purchased him as a young pup at twelve weeks old. He began some basic training at the age of four months. K-9 Max was the first Police Service Dog for the Town of Ledyard CT. He had served the town faithfully since 1992.

Max represented the Ledyard Police Department at countless public and schools demonstrations. He was responsible for locating numerous felons and illegal narcotics. I am very proud to have served alongside of Max. He not only protected me, but every officer and citizen of Ledyard during his ten years service. He will truly be missed.

Max was not only my partner. He was a true and loyal friend. Thank you for your support, Sgt. Michael J. Ravenelle

Ledyard's Max, the town police department's first police dog who retired two weeks ago after serving the department for a decade, died Wednesday night just days after it was discovered he had cancer. Max was purchased by Sgt. Michael Ravenelle in 1991 from a Westbrook breeder and was sworn in at the Ledyard Police Department in 1992. At the time, there was no K-9 program in place at the department, but Ravenelle developed an interest in police dogs and decided to buy one. When he found Max, he had no idea how to train or handle a police dog or whether Max would rise to the occasion. Most dogs used by police departments are bred and trained in Germany or Czechoslovakia where there are established training academies.

Michael got extremely lucky There'll never be another one like him. After purchasing Max, Ravenelle approached Sgt. William Nott, who heads the K-9 team at the New London Police Department. Nott helped Ravenelle train Max and the dog was soon on the job, though it was a few years before the town began chipping in for his expenses. They didn't really give Michael a budget until Max was 4 or 5.

During his police career, Max was involved in the seizure of more than seven pounds of drugs, including marijuana, cocaine and crack cocaine, and more than $4,500 in cash and weapons. He helped in two homicide investigations and located a number of wanted and missing persons. For Ravenelle and his family, who have lived with Max since he was a puppy, the dog's death has been difficult. Their oldest boy, who's 11, is taking it kind of tough because Max's been around as long as he has.

Max retired from the police department just two weeks ago, Ravenelle explained. Days later he stopped eating and, one day, collapsed. Ravenelle took him to a veterinarian, who diagnosed the dog with colon cancer. On Wednesday night, Max was euthanized.

When Max retired he became the Ravenelle family pet. They

never even knew about Max's illness. There's a big, empty hole in their hearts. As far as home life goes, he would never leave Michael's side. He would lie on the bath mat while I took a shower. The Ravenelles still have plenty of K-9 companionship around the house, though. Max recently fathered a litter of seven puppies, which are just three weeks old, and Ravenelle is already training another dog, Nikko, who lives with the family. It's like a zoo!

Another Ledyard K-9, which retired a year ago, is also suffering from a serious illness, Ravenelle said Thursday. The police department anticipates having a burial ceremony for both dogs within the next two weeks. The dogs will be buried outside the department's headquarters. The Ledyard Police Union is accepting donations on behalf of Ravenelle to help defray medical expenses.

In Loving Memory of

K-9 MAX

July 2, 2002

Partner: Trooper. Dennis Sullivan
MA State Police K-9 Section
164 Pond Street
Stoneham, MA 02180
781 279.1283

Trooper Dennis Sullivan most recently lost his retired K-9 Max. "Sully" (Sullivan) went to the basement to say hello to his old partner and saw that he was in distress. His tummy had twisted (flipped). Even as Trooper Sullivan sped to the local vet, ole Max would lift his head when he heard the siren activated to clear traffic. He would lift his head to answer that last call to duty and then passed the Rainbow Bridge. He was one of the greatest dogs the MSP has had.

My present partner is K-9 Konan.

In Loving Memory of

K-9 MIDNITE

(Missouri Midnite Shadow)
July 5, 1989 - August 6, 2002

Partner: Officer Gary White
Raytown Police Department
10000 E. 59th St.
Raytown, MO 64133
816.737-6016

Midnite said, "Crime prevention is something you can really get your teeth into." I would like to thank everyone who help me with my loss of K-9 Midnite who was put down 8/6/02 due to illness. Midnite was a black lab & Ridgeback mix who was 13 years old.

Midnite was special to me and my family. He was my first K-9 and took all the mistakes I made in stride. He started as a family pet and my daughter took a while getting over that I made him a working dog, but became proud of his duties as a K-9. He was able to again become a family pet in 1994 when I started my second dog, Knitro.

Midnite enjoyed a retirement and eating M&M's that he got hooked on while working with me. I want to give Paul Thompson a big heart felt thanks for being with my family and me when Midnite got his last ride in the patrol car on 8/6/02.

Midnite, you will be missed and you are special. Keep Jake, Bill, Basco, Arco, Kai, and Kemo and all the other K-9s company up there.

In Loving Memory of

K-9 MONTY

May 20, 1993 - May 9, 2002

Partner: Officer Rich Garner
Whitehall Police Department
3731 Lehigh St.
Whitehall, PA 18052
610.437-3042

Whitehall police now have a triple threat in keeping crime and vandalism down: patrol cars, bike patrols and K-9 dogs. The township patrol division reported one of its police dogs is responsible for the apprehension of a suspect involved in a shooting incident in Allentown June 1. In a report submitted to the commissioners, Chief Dennis L. Peters said 3 township police officers assisted Allentown police in apprehending a suspect involved in a shooting.

A police officer's partner, K-9 Monty, located the suspect on a city rooftop. It allowed police to quickly take the suspect into custody. "Without Monty, it is doubtful the suspect would have been located," the report said. There were eight K-9 dog deployments in June.

ALL ABOUT MONTY

Monty was a long haired German Shepherd from Czechoslovakia. Before joining the Whitehall Police Dept. in April 1996, he went through several weeks of intensive training with his handler, Rich Garner. Monty has assisted in several arrests in areas of tracking, building searches, crowd control, and narcotics. Along with police work, Monty also gave many demonstrations for the public. He seemed to take pride in his "demos" and got along exceptionally well with all who attended, especially children. Monty is a wonderful partner who will be missed by all at the police department. He retired to the home of Rich and continued to be loved by his family eternally. "They do not fear bad news; they confidentially trust the Lord to care for them, they are confident and fearless and face their foes triumphantly. (Psalm 112:7 8)

ALL ABOUT RICHARD H. GARNER

Officer Garner has been a police officer since March 1989. He has a new partner, "NANUK," who joined the force in 9/2000. They are both members of the ERT team, and Nanuk lives at home with Garner's wife, and 4 children and Snickers, "family cat." Rich enjoys wrestling, football, weightlifting and coaching youth sports. Notice: Avid fan of the Pittsburgh Steelers. Nanuk also misses Monty very much, who passed away due to lung cancer.

A memorial service was held today at the Whitehall Township Municipal Building for Police K-9 "Monty". Monty was recently diagnosed with an advanced stage of lung cancer and was euthanized on May 9, 2002. Monty was born on May 20, 1993 in Czechoslovakia and joined handler Richard Garner and the Whitehall Township Police Department in April 1996, after several weeks of intensive training.

He retired in September 2000 and took up residence with

Garner's family.

Monty was a patrol and narcotics dog, and assisted in many arrests in Whitehall Township and surrounding jurisdictions. Monty was called upon to do building searches, tracks, crowd control, and narcotics work. Monty and Garner are members of the Whitehall Township Emergency Response Team, which has been recently integrated into the Lehigh County Municipal Emergency Response Team (MERT).

Monty was also involved in numerous demonstrations every year at various events such as carnivals, church groups, schools, and pet stores. He took pride in his demos and interacted well with all people, most especially children. Monty's handler, Patrolman Richard Garner, is an eleven year veteran of the Whitehall Township Police Department. He is the senior patrolman on the night shift platoon where he patrols with his new K-9 Nanuk.

Monty's service was attended by several members of the Whitehall Township Police Department and officers and K-9 patrols from Easton, Palmer Township, Allentown, and the Pennsylvania State Police. Chief Dennis Peters, Officers Paul Davis and Jeffrey Coleman spoke at the service.

Handler Richard Garner spoke words of thanks to all who attended and reflected on his days with Monty while fighting back tears. Officer Karen Bailey read a moving poem entitled "Guardians of the Night." Ashley Zuber played "America the Beautiful,", "Amazing Grace" and "Taps" on the bagpipes. Channel 69 News and several other news agencies including the Whitehall Coplay Press were also in attendance.

Rich Garner stated that Monty's illness came on quickly the week leading up to May 9, 2002. Garner noticed Monty was not feeling well earlier in the week and was not eating well. He took Monty to the Allentown Animal Clinic where he was given an exam. His x rays showed an advanced stage of lung cancer.

Today we said good bye to a hero, teacher, and friend. Monty will never be forgotten for his service to Whitehall Police and the citizens they protect and serve. Monty set the standard for all present and future K-9's to follow.   He was a true "Guardian of the Night."

A hush fell over the room as Whitehall Township Patrolman Richard Garner prepared to share stories about Monty, the German Shepherd he had taken care of, and who had taken care of him, for the last six years. Garner started to thank everyone who had come to the memorial service for Monty, but he couldn't finish his sentence. He bowed his head and cried, and the audience of about 50 people, some of them K-9 officers like himself, applauded. "He was one of the best partners I ever had ...," Garner said later. "He was always there for me."

Officers and dogs from Palmer Township, Easton, Allentown, Emmaus and Coplay and from the state police attended the service Friday at the Whitehall municipal building. As in a ceremony for any fallen officer, there were stories from colleagues, such as Patrolman Jeffrey Coleman's recollection of what happened when an unruly mob surrounded officers quelling a disturbance at a Whitehall High School football game. The crowd parted "like the Red Sea" when Garner let Monty go, Coleman said. "His presence parted a crowd that would have taken at least 10 officers to disperse."

Whitehall Police Chief Dennis Peters said Monty had been trained in patrol work and drug detection. During his career, he was frequently lent to other departments. The department now has two dogs; Nanuk, a German Shepherd trained in patrol and drug detection who lives with Garner, and Ylan, a Belgian Malinois taught to detect explosives.

Garner recalled that one of his first tracking experiences with Monty came after a man in a vehicle rammed cars on MacArthur Road outside the Lehigh Valley Mall, then ran away and hid in a truck behind the Salvation Army building. Monty found him. Garner said dogs are described as tools in police work, but they eventually become more.

"Once you start working with them and you know that they're there for you, and you know that they will protect you no matter what, that bond becomes tighter and tighter," he said.

K-9 Nanuk is Rich's new partner.

In Loving Memory of

K-9 PEDRO

August 9, 2002

Partner: Officer Robert Miner
Midvale City Police Department
655 W. Center St.
Midvale, UT 84047
801. 255-4291

The Midvale City Police K-9 Unit suffered a loss of K-9 Pedro this summer. Police Service Dog (PSD) Pedro died August 9, 2002 due to a sudden illness. PSD Pedro joined the Midvale Police K-9 Unit in July of 1998. He made his way to Midvale from Czechoslovakia where he entered the Police Academy for K-9s.

Pedro was a certified Patrol and Detector dog, handled by Officer Robert Miner. Pedro's presence will be missed.

In Loving Memory of

K-9 NASH

(Nash Du Clan D'Signeur)
December 1, 2002

Partner: Officer Ian Nelson
Pocatello Police Department
911 N. 7th Avenue
Pocatello, ID 83201

Nash was a European German Shepherd born 03/21/97 and died 12/21/02. Officer Ian Nelson of the Pocatello Police Department in South Eastern Idaho got Nash as a partner in October 1999. In the summer of 2000, Nash came down with carbon monoxide poisoning and was almost lost, however, through the use of a good vet and steroids Nash became a survivor. After his bout with carbon monoxide, Nash was never the same.

He had continual health problems with his stomach and intestines and frequently had bloody diarrhetic and vomitous episodes and remained on medications until the spring of 2002.

Nash's health continued to go down hill along with his work performance with increased failures.

Officer Nelson faced the tough decision of making a request to retire his partner due to health. Officer Nelson's request was denied and due to disagreements in the status of Nash's health, Officer Nelson was removed from Nash and the K-9 unit and labeled as having been less than honest about Nash's health.

The day after Nash was removed from him, Officer Nelson met with the Chief of police to tell him that he was not being dishonest about Nash's health and that if Nash was going to be kept working, he would die within a year. Nash was turned over to a new and inexperienced handler and died 12/21/02.

Officer Nelson describes Nash as a true hero, dedicated, stubborn, take no crap from anyone type of dog. Nash was also gentle as a puppy when he wanted to be and a loyal best friend. Nash was also Officer Nelson's daughter's best friend as the two of them shared a different special relationship that only the two of them could have.

During his three year tour, Nash did Officer Nelson and the City of Pocatello proud by locating over two hundred narcotic finds, numerous apprehensions, and a minimal two street bites (one of them an officer who admittedly erred after Nash was deployed).

Because of his demeanor, Nash was given numerous nick names by his fellow officers such as Sgt. Nash, Cujo, and the one that ended up sticking with him Nash Hole (because he had a habit of being an asshole when anyone, but Officer Nelson came with a hundred yards of his car or kennel.

Nash's last act of loyalty to Officer Nelson was to pass away, clearing Officer Nelson's name from being dishonest about his health. Today, if you ask Officer Nelson's daughter where Nash is, the answer is "he's up in heaven with God, keeping all the bad guys out." Nash was a member of the Nelson family and was loved and will be missed by Officer Nelson, his family and the community of Pocatello, Idaho.

Officer Nelson was not reinstated to the K-9 unit, but says

he and Nash will be partners again in heaven one day when both of them will be retired together. Nash was buried on December 4, 2002.

UPDATE:

Ian is no longer with the K-9 unit, but he has 3 dogs at home. They are a chocolate lab, TYMBRE, Yellow lab, DYLAN and a German Shepherd, MAGNUM (he's the old fart of the trio) all above quoted by Ian.

In Loving Memory of

K-9 NERO

February 17, 2002

Partner: Trooper (retired) Jerry Schenck
Nebraska State Patrol
3600 N. Academy Rd.
Grand Island, NE 68801
308.385-6030

Retired Nebraska State Patrol dog Nero, who was known for his drug seizures, died suddenly Sunday afternoon. Jerry Schenck, the retired trooper who handled Nero, said the dog was about 13 years old and had been in good health.

He suffered an embolism, which caused his body to fill with blood, Schenck said. Nero, a Dutch shepherd, was the first patrol dog to join Troop C, which has its headquarters in Grand Island.

He began his work in May 1992 with the badge number 337R and retired with Schenck in December 1997. During his six years of service, he helped seize approximately fifty million dollars worth of drugs. Schenck said, "Drugs were his forte, he was a great drug dog." He was also used to track suspects in buildings or large open areas and was trained to protect Schenck and other law enforcement agents.

Nero also loved children. Schenck said he often took the dog to schools to give demonstrations and to talk about the dangers of drug abuse. He said he could let Nero go into a crowd of children to play and be petted, which is a rare trait for a police service dog. "He loved going to schools," Schenck said.

The duo also had a business for a few years called Nero the Hero, he said. Together, they did drug searches at schools. "As Nero got older, I let him be a dog," he said. No special services are planned for Nero. Schenck said he buried the dog on Monday on his acreage at 1030 McMartin Ave. "I buried him as my family," he said.

In an e mail sent to The Independent on Monday, Schenck wrote, "Nero was my friend and partner, and he left me with many, many great memories."

In Loving Memory of

K-9 NIKKI

November 9, 2002

Partner: Officer Tim Tonsor
High Point Police Department 1009 Leonard Ave.
High Point, NC 27260-5321

Nikki was Tim's second dog, a Beauceron, looked like a Doberman on steroids. Nikki was a great dog and about four to five years into his K-9 work, he developed cancer of the jaw and had to have surgery which caused him to be retired, he couldn't bite that hard any more. Tim kept him at home after that. Nick as I called him, was a phenomenal tracker. I think he went through his career with about a 50% tracking success, which is very, very high.

Beauceron K-9s

The Beauceron, a rare French dog that is almost unknown outside of France. The Beauceron is still used to herd on farms in France. They are the most preferred dog in France for this work and are said to have been at one time, palace dogs. There is an ancient painting showing two Beaucerons guarding the throne of a French king. The official name of the breed is Berger de Beauce but is commonly referred to as the Beauceron.

The Beauceron's physical appearance is described as, "A strong dog, but without heaviness...". They can stand 24 to 27 inches high and weigh up to 110 pounds, about the size of a Doberman pincher. They are a working dog and give off an aura of strength, freedom of movement, and liveliness. The color of these dogs is either black and tan with distinctly located tan markings or harlequin which includes random patches of gray in the coat. The eyes can commonly be multicolored and the ears are held high on its head. A distinct feature of this dog is the double dew-claw on each their hind legs. These dogs commonly live to be about 10 to 12 years old.

The temperament of a Beauceron makes them very easy to train. They are used by the French police and army in the same way that German Shepherds are used in the United States. They are very calm dogs and follow commands very well without hesitation. This was demonstrated well during both major wars in Europe. The military used them on the front lines to run messages without being deterred by exploding bombs or artillery. In pictures the Beauceron is shown jumping over the heads of troops in a foxhole while in route to his destination. These dogs were also used to pick up trails, detect mines, support commando actions, find wounded, and carry food or ammunition to the front line.

The following is from The Encyclopedia of Dogs by Fiorenzo Fiorone: "Regarding the mental capacity of this breed, Boulet d'Elboet (the creator of the Griffon which bears his name) has observed: The intelligence, the obedience, and the activity of the Beauce are proverbial. He is also a faithful guard and brave defender, and his herding instinct seems to be inborn transmitted through the centuries..."

Despite their strong and intimidating appearance, the Beauceron is very tolerant by nature and is a great family pet.

The Beauceron can survive in an apartment if it is sufficiently exercised. They are moderately active indoors and usually do best with a large yard to romp in. The Beauceron should be given lots of attention and exercise. This breed of dog needs a job to do most of the time and lots of space to use his energy.

These dogs do not tend to be one person dogs. They tend to choose one person as their master which may not be the person intended. They are very obedient and will obey commands from all members of the family if it is trained to do so. Beaucerons are sociable with other dogs they know but are very territorial and will not tolerate an intruder. They instinctively try to herd animals standing together like horses, goats, ducks, and almost anything else. Beaucerons require a strong disciplinary figure who can take the time and patience needed to properly train such a dog.

In Loving Memory of

K-9 Pete

Kleetuus Proud Pete II
May 2, 2002

Partner: Deputy Henry Sheldon
Otsego County Sheriff's Criminal Patrol Division
P.O. Box 326 - 172 County Highway #33 West
Cooperstown, NY 13326
607.547.4271

Pete was my partner for 7½ years. He would be nine in August, 2002. The best way to describe Pete...

"faithful friend,
loyal partner,
dedicated officer"
He was a honored law enforcement officer
and beloved family member.
He will be missed by our family,
department and community.

Pete, the K-9 officer, died a week ago today at the age of 8, and his human partner, Otsego County Sheriff's Deputy Hank Sheldon, is in mourning. "He was with me day and night, and I can't tell you how much I miss him," said Sheldon, 44.

The sheriff's department is going to hold a funeral service in a week or so, he said. Pete died of cancer. "After all that time with Pete, I don't think I could start with another dog," he said. The department will get another dog, but the new recruit will have a hard time living up to Pete's reputation for finding lost toddlers and tracking down suspects, Sheldon said. "He was a great tracker," he said.

Pete, a German Shepherd, and Sheldon met in 1995 when Pete was 1½. "He was donated by Monica Van Blarcum of Otego," Sheldon said. Pete was untrained but seemed smart and willing, so he and Sheldon went to K-9 schools together. "The first few months we had obedience training to make sure I had him under control. After that we went to the Bureau of Municipal Police K-9 Academy," he said. For 3½ months, the partners worked on obedience, building searches, article searches, tracking, handler protection, then graduated as a K-9 unit.

During this course, Pete learned how to apprehend fleeing suspects, not an easy task in New York state, Sheldon noted. "In this state, a dog has to use 'reasonable force,' the same as a police officer," Sheldon said. If a suspect wants to give up after being chased, the dog is not allowed to take him down, but must circle him and confine him to that circle until help arrives, he said. Pete mastered this concept and began active duty in 1995. "He and I went to every school in the county, and the kids loved him," said Sheldon, the county's Drug Abuse Resistance Education officer.

Times at schools were relaxed, but there were tense times in the field, Sheldon recalled. Pete, who was fast afoot and 85 pounds, was ready. When a very young boy in Otego toddled away from home one summer day, Pete tracked him a half mile or more and helped volunteer firefighters return him home, Sheldon said. "Then there was the burglary at Klumm's Liquor

Store in Richfield Springs. "We got called in, maybe eight hours after the fact," said Sheldon. "Pete started sniffing around, then led us across Route 20. He took us through a park, down a side street, along a sidewalk and right up to the front door of a house. "He had his nose only a few inches away from the doorbell when we took over," Sheldon said. Inside, were surprised burglars, who were placed under arrest, he said.

Another time, near Goodyear Lake in the town of Milford, state police were trying to arrest a convicted rapist who was wanted on a parole violation, Sheldon said. "As the trooper went in the front door, the bad guy ran out the back door. The trooper called us in because he knew we were on duty, and Pete tracked this guy all the way to the back of Wightman's Lumber yard," Sheldon said. "He was just entering the back of the lumber yard when Pete spotted him, so I gave the alert command." At that, Pete began barking, forewarning the suspect that where there's bark, there might be bite.

"Now this guy would have run away from me, but as soon as he heard Pete, it was all over," Sheldon said. And that's the way it was most of the time, he said. Just Pete's presence was enough to subdue most suspects.

Otsego County Sheriff Donald Mundy termed Pete "a very valuable part of our department, especially as a tracker. Everyone liked that dog." The department soon will begin to search for another dog, he said. Sheldon said that at home, "Pete was a pet, a member of the family. We used to plan our vacations around his schedule."

When Pete moved into Sheldon's home, he quickly grew to love the three boys, then 11, 9 and 5 years old, Sheldon said, and he got along with the two cats and made himself at home. "He had this habit of sleeping only about 20 minutes in any room. He'd lie down on my wife's side of the bed for 20 minutes, then moved off to one of the boy's rooms for 20 minutes, and kept on moving like that during the night. "At first, it kept us up, hearing him move off like that, but we got used to it," said Sheldon. "I came to think it as his way of watching over us, making sure everybody was OK during the night."

Memorial service   May 31st, 2002 at 10:00 AM

Everything went well... as well as could be expected. It was a nice service. I sent a thank you and reply to an email letting you know the cards came...thank you again so much for them. I gave your cards to the NY State Police & Southern Tier Police K-9 Association. Should they every have a funeral too. There was a picture and caption in the paper. About 100 people attended with K-9 teams there. It was nice.... Hank

In Loving Memory of

K-9 Preston

August 7, 2002

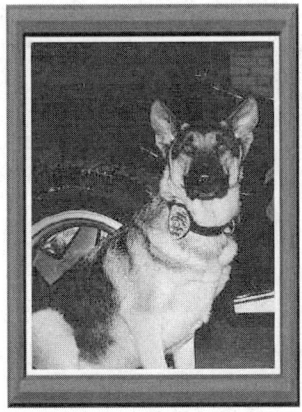

Partner: Officer Ginger Robertson
Springfield Police Department
321 E. Chestnut Expressway
Springfield, MO 65802-3899
417 864.1810

Officers - family and friends bury K-9 Preston

A member of Springfield Police Department for just three years, K-9 Preston was bred for the work. Hearken Preston came down the hill from Rivermonte Memorial Gardens, led by a police escort. Preston served the Springfield Police Dept. for three years before he slipped three back discs and had to retire in 1994. But oh, did he ramble, when he rambled.

Preston was the first police dog brought into service for the city force in twenty years when he was commissioned in 1991. As a police vehicle bore his coffin to the Lakeland Pet Cemetery, about 35 people and dogs waited to honor the dog who had served without hesitation. Before the tent where we gathered, a black granite monument with Preston's image etched into it introduced the six law enforcement dogs already buried there.

"They faced danger at a single command, willing to give their lives for the officers they loved and trusted," the inscription read. "We thank them for their heroism and we honor their memory."

Officer Val Hewett, who helped train Preston, gave a eulogy. At times, it was hard to hear her voice, softened by emotion. "I was able to be there when the training process for Preston started," she said. "It was so awesome." Preston's partner, Ginger Robertson, explained later that she went to Darlene Cavin's Hearken Kennels near Rogerville to train a black Labrador retriever to be her police dog, but the Lab just didn't take to the work. Preston, in his kennel, thought that was fine.

I kept going out there with my Lab, and this scrawny looking shepherd kept trying to get to me." Robertson said, "He was going to be my dog, no matter what." In time, Robertson and Cavin agreed with Preston. "Magic" the Lab wasn't destined to be a police dog. Preston was.

"His line had been bred for service for 30 years." Cavin said. Hewett has one of Preston's sisters and five more of his siblings went into law enforcement. Hewett eulogized Preston, a handsome dog reflected in photos at a table near the funeral tent. She remembered when she backed up Robertson on a call and found Preston sitting forlornly alone in the front yard of a house. "I saw the devastation on Preston's face, it was like "What do I do ?"

Robertson remembers the incident too. Preston always sat in place as commended. "I tackled the guy and the guy ran. I was in the back yard fighting the guy, and Preston never moved."

Hewett also remembered the time she was helping Robertson train Preston and wore the "bite suit: the padded suit used to help train the dog for the field. "I'd run into the yard," she said, and try to behave as a perpetrator. She recounted the time she'd thought she'd fool Preston by putting her arms over her chest, only to be bitten in the rear end. "That's when we changed to a full body bite suit."

Then there was the time mad cap Preston sat on the accelerator of a golf car, he and Robertson were riding at the Ozark Empire Fair. As they barreled toward a parked semi truck, Robertson managed to pry the 115 pound dog off the pedal just in time to avoid sailing underneath. As Rivermonte personnel prepared to bury Preston after the service, Robertson gathered the cloth and memorabilia from the table near the funeral tent.

"He was a wonderful dog." she said as she folded the cloth. "And he was my best friend."

In Loving Memory of

K-9 Ralph

SAR
January 10, 1992 - October 10, 2002

Partner: Dave Krumm
Kellogg, IA
50135-9614

Ralph was one of ISAR's first certified dogs and he served us well for 9 years. Ralph served ISAR and his community well, he was present at so many call outs and was never wrong. When Ralph said someone was there, you could rest assured he was right on the button. Whether it was articles, drowning victims or lost people, Ralph was right. Perhaps it was because Dave and Ralph were together 24 hours a day 7 days a week. Dave gave Ralph numerous searches every day, because that was the game that made them both the happiest. Ralph was responsible for ISAR's first live find. He was the role model all tenured ISAR members strove to be like.

When Dave retired Ralph we all hoped he would change his

mind and bring him back into active service. From the time he was a baby Ralph helped Dave do everything he did. Even tearing up the old kitchen floor was not a problem for him, just stand back and let him work. I also remember Dave working on the roof and by his side....even at that height was Ralph. (huge two story house) The dedication Ralph held for Dave was astounding. He would find anything from jewelry to grave sites. How many handlers trust their partners enough to take their billfold containing a couple hundred dollars and throw it blindly into a field and ask them to find it. Trusting them enough with that much cash? No one else in our organization but Dave. Yes, Ralph did not let him down. When I work my dogs, my memories of Ralph often help me solve problems I am working on. I feel sorry for future members of ISAR that never got to meet Ralph. They are missing a great opportunity. I will always remember Dave waltzing across a field puffing on a pipe and Ralph running ahead, finding every time. I know through the years Ralph will continue to come to mind and I will smile, always hoping someday, I can earn the right to say, my partner and I are almost as good as Dave and Ralph were. I will always recall Dave looking down at Ralph and Ralph looking back in admiration and Dave saying "Are you ready... 'PUP.'" (even the age of 10, Dave ALWAYS called him "PUP")

Ralph left us all Oct 10 cradled in Dave's arms from cancer. He fought a long and hard battle and now rests high on a hill overlooking the pond Dave and he fished in almost every day. It has been five months since ISAR lost Ralph and I still expect to see him when I go to ISAR functions. I still can not think of his powerful black figure running through the woods without tearing up. I don't think I ever will get over him and he wasn't even my partner!

In Loving Memory of

K-9 REX

April 5, 2002

Partner: Officer Jason Pace
Mountain Home Police Department
103 W. 9th St.
Mountain Home, AR 72653

The Mountain Home Police Department reported the loss of a K-9 member of the force, Rex, who was killed Friday after apparently being struck by a vehicle on Highway 62 West. Rex, a Belgian Malinois, was the department's first K-9. His handler, Officer Jason Pace, was preparing for the 11 p.m. shift and noticed Rex missing from his fenced yard at about 10:30 p.m., according to a press release from Mountain Home Police Chief Carry Manuel.

Officers from the MHPD and Arkansas State Police started searching for Rex. A short time later, Trooper Joel Eubanks located Rex after he apparently was hit by a vehicle near Pace's residence. The dog was normally housed in a kennel on the officer's property, but occasionally was released into the fenced yard for exercise, Manuel stated. On Friday, Rex escaped by jumping the 4 foot fence. Rex was a valuable member of the Mountain Home Police Department, Manuel stated.

Since August of 1998, he was involved in 619 drug searches241 arrests and 25 searches for suspects. The K-9 and his handler assisted other officers 319 times. Rex and Pace received a letter of commendation for tracking and saving the life of a man in the Clarkridge area. Rex and Pace were the first members of the department's K-9 unit. Later Nero and K-9 handler Officer Robert Harden were added.

"Rex was much more than a dog; he was a law enforcement K-9 and a great asset to the law enforcement effort in our community," Manuel stated. Green dogs are dogs that can be used for all kind of work, like Sport, Home Protection Police work and more. Those dogs are biting and have a high ball drive, but have to be trained for the category of work what they have to do.

Officer Pace writes:

It is with deep regret, that I must tell you this. I got ready for work as I usually do. I went out into the back yard to get my partner and he did not come to me. I started looking for him and he was no where to be found. I radioed other officers to come and help me look for him. They found him. He had been hit by a car and he was dead. This is really hard not only for me but for others at the Police Department who have grown to love Rex. He was a great partner and he will be missed tremendously by me.

He was born in Holland on the 9th day of August 1995, He died on April 5th. At approximately 11:30 PM. Thank you for your site and thank you for caring about K-9's. I know in my heart that he will never be able to be replaced. But I do love K-9s and I want to get back into it.

Rex was the first member of the Mountain Home Police K-9 Unit. He was purchased with local business donations. After five weeks of training at Vohne Liche Kennels in Denver, IN, he currently was being used for narcotics, tracking building searches and criminal apprehension. Rex was 7 years old.

The name of Belgian Malinois comes from the city of Malines in north central Belgium, where the breed originated. This breed of dog has short hair and a mahogany colored coat with a black face and ears. The average Malinois ranges between 22 to 26 inches at the shoulder and weight 40 to 80 pounds. Ken Licklider is a master K-9 trainer who trains passive response K-9s instead of aggressive response. When a K-9 find narcotics its passive response is to sit down next to the narcotics.

In Loving Memory of

K-9 RIK

LODD
June 5, 2002

Partner: Deputy James Schiffler
Bonneville County Sheriff's Dept.
605 North Capital
Idaho Falls, ID 83402
208. 529-1350

On June 5, 2002, Bonneville County Deputies and Search & Rescue were called out to assist with the disappearance of a 14 year old girl. Information provided that the girl had been kidnaped from her home and was left tied up at an undisclosed location. The girl managed to escape and call for help. With the information received concerning her kidnapper, a warrant was obtained. The Bonneville County SWAT team was called out to assist with the warrant.

Deputy Jim Schiffler and his K-9 Rik responded to the call out. The suspect was spotted in a work truck and a tri county pursuit ensued. Deputy Schiffler and K-9 Rik were involved in the pursuit. The truck ended up on a forest service road and turned onto a dead end. The truck got stuck and the suspect bailed. It was unknown at that point if the suspect was armed, although he had access to firearms.

Deputy Schiffler deployed K-9 Rik to apprehend the suspect. K-9 Rik engaged the suspect, who then pulled a gun. The suspect shot and killed K-9 Rik. Sgt. Todd Raymond of Bonneville County was also shot in the leg. Deputies returned fire, as the suspect took his own life.

Sgt. Raymond is in fair condition at EIRMC. It is believed by deputies at the scene that K-9 Rik had saved Sgt. Raymond's life and possibly the lives of the other deputies as well. Rik was a 2 ½ year old male Belgian Malinois. Rik had been a deputy K-9 with the Bonneville Sheriff's Office for almost a year.

In Loving Memory of

K-9 RINGO

January 27, 2002

Partner: Deputy Brad Brocker
Faulkner County Sheriff's Office
801 Locust St.
Conway, AR 72032
501.450-4914

Friends, family and citizens gathered to bid farewell to Faulkner County's K-9 Ringo in a short but emotional ceremony Friday. "This was not a dog, he was a member of the Faulkner County Sheriff's Office and is due the respect of any law enforcement officer in the country," Sheriff Marty Montgomery said. "We're here to acknowledge and show our respect to one of the officers that's served you." Ringo was just as devoted to saving lives and stopping criminals as any human officer, the sheriff said, adding he was also just as willing to give his life in the name of duty. "There's not a doubt, Ringo was dedicated," he said.

Ringo died Sunday as his partner, Deputy Brad Brocker, rushed toward a veterinarian's office. He found the dog alive but ill in his pen about 11:30 a.m. Brocker said on the way to get help, Ringo pawed at his shoulder, licked his hand, then laid down and died. Foul play is not suspected.

During the memorial, Brocker sat red faced and wet eyed as his wife consoled him, and his young son held a stuffed dog also named Ringo. Sitting on the table flanked by flags at the front of the room was a picture of Ringo, his lead, a baton. An urn filled with his ashes and a plaque featuring "Guardians of the Night," a poem for police dogs.

Standing at the table, Montgomery said he and his department were thankful for the "respect, dedication and service given to the community by Ringo." He then asked Brocker to join him at the front of the courtroom. "It's hard to understand the partnership between a K-9 and his partner," the sheriff said.

The officers live, work and play together and become inseparable, he said. "Brad, on behalf of the Faulkner County Sheriff's Office, we give you our condolences on the loss of a member of your family and a member of the law enforcement community," Montgomery said. "I would like to present to you Ringo's badge as a memento of one darn good officer." The two then exchanged a hearty hug.

Sniffles could be heard from various attendees as Taps was played. As if he understood, K-9 Tony with the Conway Police Department also began whining, although his partner, Officer Clay Smith, tried to quiet him with treats. The Sheriff's Office does plan to get another K-9, but in the meantime Ringo's death leaves the department with only one K-9, Rom Tom.

Update on Ringo:

The Faulkner County Sheriff's Office is mourning the loss of a member of its law enforcement family: K-9 Ringo. The 8 year old Belgian Malinois died Sunday as his partner, deputy Brad Brocker, was rushing him to the veterinarian. Brocker said he heard what sounded like people talking near Ringo's pen about 4 a.m. Sunday. The normally active dog was barking and Brocker went to check on the situation. "I went outside and checked but didn't see anything," Brocker said. "And Ringo calmed down and was fine." Brocker said his bedroom window faces a store parking lot and it's not unusual for him to hear people talking, so he didn't think any more about it. Then about 11:30 a.m., Brocker checked on Ringo and found him "curled up in a fetal position and his stomach was completely bloated and hard as a rock."

The deputy scooped up the big pooch and the two headed to the veterinarian. "About halfway there, he put his paw through the cage and put it on my shoulder," Brocker said. "I put my hand back there to pet him, he licked it and then laid down. I think that's when he died."

Ringo's body was sent to the state Crime Lab and preliminary reports show he died of natural causes, according to Jack Pike, public information officer for the Sheriff's Office. Toxicology reports should be complete by Friday and reveal the exact cause of death.

Brocker said when he found the ailing dog, there was a film on Ringo's water and it had a peculiar smell, but he doesn't know if the film could be poison or just dog saliva. A water sample and the water dish were collected by a detective for further testing. Ringo has been with Brocker for almost three years. The dog was originally trained in Holland by that country's military police before coming to Arkansas for more specific training with Brocker. They met and trained in Brockwell (Izard County) and Ringo was certified in narcotics detection, patrol, tracking and prisoner transport.

He participated in 135 narcotic detections, including the November discovery of 36 grams of methamphetamine found in a hidden compartment of a vehicle's back seat. He also performed 16 successful tracks. One of the most noteworthy was in April when he found an elderly Mayflower lady who had wandered from her home and was found, by Ringo, face down in a thicket. Pike said Ringo was also instrumental in calming a disturbance in the Detention Center last year.

Ringo's estimated worth was $10,000 to $12,000, Pike said. The department plans to get another K-9, although it is not in the budget. It was not known Monday if the insurance policy the department had on Ringo would pay for another dog. Ringo was purchased with $5,000 donated by American Management Corporation and smaller contributions from other businesses and individuals.

Ringo will be cremated and a memorial service will likely be held Friday, although the time and place has not been set. The Sheriff's Office has one other K-9, Rom Tom, whose partner is Deputy Ursula Westmoreland.

The Faulkner County Sheriff's Department K-9 Unit did consist of two handlers and two Belgian Malinois (Rom Tom and Ringo). Each K-9 team has completed extensive training in a wide variety of areas including narcotics detection, tracking, article recovery, prisoner transport and crowd control.

The K-9 Unit performs daily patrol operations and is subject to call out when needed. The K-9 teams work closely with the Special Response Team, schools and other law enforcement agencies. If another agency requests assistance from the K-9 Unit a team will be dispatched to provide whatever service is needed.

In Loving Memory of

K-9 RIO

June 25, 2002

Partner: SPO Christopher Mahlstadt
Des Moines Police Department
Narcotics Unit #25 East First St.
Des Moines, IA 50309
515-283.4824

If dogs wore shoes, Kirby would have some big ones to fill. Des Moines police didn't think they could afford another dog for the narcotics unit after Rio, an English Springer Spaniel dubbed the "$2 million dog" for his drug sniffing talents, died last month. So police officials in St. Paul, Minn., dispatched Kirby, a 4 year old male Labrador, to provide backup.

"It was put out on a Web site that Rio had to be put down, and St. Paul said they had a dog available and they'd donate it to our department," said Des Moines police Sgt. David Brown. Officer Chris Mahlstadt, who was Rio's partner in the local drug wars, said Des Moines has had a good relationship with St. Paul.

A dollar changed hands, & Kirby changed departments.

Like Rio, Kirby was rescued from a dog pound and trained in detection of illegal drugs. Rio was trained by a Minnetonka, MN, police officer. He joined the Des Moines force in July 1994. On his 10th day on the job, Rio found $119,000 worth of marijuana, said Mahlstadt. Rio was nearly 10 years old.

During his eight years in the department, he was credited with about $2 million worth of illegal drug seizures and won several trophies in competitive trials. He had an operation for a cancerous growth last winter and appeared to be doing well. Officers said he suddenly stopped eating, his weight dropped, and he appeared to be in pain. He died June 25.

Officer Warren Steinkamp said of Kirby, "He's full of energy, and he loves to work." "It's nice to have (a dog) assigned to the narcotics unit," Brown said.

Sgt. David Brown of the vice and narcotics section said, "I've had a lot of tough assignments in the past but I've never had to put one of my subordinates to sleep before." A pound puppy, recruited from a Minnesota animal shelter because of his interest in tennis balls, Rio was trained by a Minnetonka, MN, police officer. He joined the Des Moines force in July 1994. On his 10th day on the job, Rio found $119,000 worth of marijuana, said his long time handler Chris Mahlstadt.

Drug dogs commonly are rewarded for their work by being allowed to play with a favorite toy. As a puppy at the pound in Minnesota, Rio showed intense interest in a tennis ball when an officer came in search of high spirited animals to train. During his eight years in the department, Rio was credited with about $2 million worth of illegal drugs and won several trophies in competitive police trials, Mahlstadt said.

"He was a very nice dog," said Brown. "He liked the bad guys as well as the good guys." Rio is the last of his kind on the department, at least for now. Brown said the department's three dogs are cross trained in drug detection and will take over Rio's duties.

K-9 Oby, the department's other easy going drug sniffing

dog, died last fall. He was retired in 1996 after six years on the force. Rio will be buried next to K-9 Oby in a pet cemetery south of the city.

In Loving memory of

K-9 ROCCO

October 10, 2002

Partner: Deputy David Miller
Allegan County Sheriff's Department
112 Walnut St.
Allegan, MI 49010
269. 673-0500

We here at Northern Michigan K-9 are very sad to announce the death of K-9 Rocco of the Allegan County Sheriff's Department. On October 10th after successfully tracking and locating a lost 3 year old child, K-9 Rocco was struck and killed by a car.

Rocco had been a member of the Allegan Co. Sheriff's office since November 2001, and had recently graduated again with his new handler Deputy David Miller. Our hearts and prayers go out to all involved.

More About Allegan County Sheriff's Dept.

K-9 UNIT Allegan County is pleased to present its newly expanded K-9 Unit, led by Sgt. Bud Randall. The newest members of the unit are a 3 year old German Shepherd named "Bosco" and his handler, Deputy David Holmes, and a 2 year old Dutch Shepherd, "Rocco" and his handler Deputy Cory Hunt. The dogs were selected based not only on their drive to do the work, but they also must be very social animals, since they are used to perform public demonstrations of their abilities for school children and civic groups. These teams join veteran K-9 team Deputy Scott Tatrow and his dog Jock, a Belgian Malanois.

The Allegan County Sheriff's Office has had a formalized K-9 Unit since the early 1980's when the ACLEA (Allegan County Law Enforcement Association) donated the funds to purchase a K-9 for the department. The purchase of subsequent dogs and training aids has historically been done through grants, donations and drug forfeiture proceeds. The only expenses to the taxpayers are for dog food and veterinary services.

The dogs are all dual purpose animals, meaning that they are trained in patrol work such as tracking and building searches, as well as in narcotics detection. The K-9 teams are assigned to the patrol division and are made available to any law enforcement agency who may have need for their services.

In Loving Memory of

K-9 ROOKIE

LODD
December 27, 2002

Partner: Patrolman Jack Neapolitan
Boardman Police Department
8299 Market St.
Youngstown, OH 44512
330.726-4144

The silence of a bright chilly morning was broken as more than 50 cruisers pulled up in front of township police headquarters, tires squeaking in the snow. Police K-9 officers were barking through the slight cracks left in the cruiser windows. The dogs were honoring one of their own Rookie, a fallen German Shepherd who was afforded all the rights of a human officer.

"Perhaps Rookie captured more hearts than bad guys," were the words penned by the K-9's handler, Boardman patrolman Jack Neapolitan, referring to the many demonstrations the duo put on for students. Rookie was struck and killed by a vehicle

December 27 in the driveway of Glenwood Middle School. Neapolitan, who was given a few days leave after the death, stood in front of the crowd where grown men were weeping and where a young boy proclaimed, "Rookie will remain ever loyal."

The boy, Billy Martin Jr., is a Niles sixth grader and founder of the Bite the Bullet program, which provides protective vests to police K-9s. He acknowledged that "a vest can't protect a police dog from everything." No charges were filed against the motorist. Police said the vehicle driven by a 17 year old boy from Boardman was traveling about 20 MPH when it hit the dog. The driver's visibility may have been hampered by ice on the windshield. Neapolitan and his K-9 had stopped at the school for an exercise break about 10:35 p.m.

The dog was born five years ago in Romania and then put through his paces during countless hours of training, with Neapolitan right by his side. The team was certified in April 1999, and worked in the patrol division, as well as sniffing out drugs in a special Drug Enforcement Agency detail. But Rookie was also a tracker.

"You might think this is too much for a K-9, but we will miss his enhanced senses," said Boardman police Chief Jeffrey Patterson. "I think the funeral today helped Jack with a little closure." Officers traveled from as far as Port Clinton to take part in a procession from Boardman Park to the police station.

The uniformed men circled the seating area of the township meeting room and saluted during the ceremony. Trustee Thomas Costello also said his good byes, while Warren police officers Chris "Skippy" O'Rourke, and former K-9 officer Michael Krafcik both spoke about their love of the animals. "When I worked the blue division, nobody talked to me. Nobody cared," said O'Rourke. "Now with Aron, everybody stops me, asking about the dog."

It was Trumbull County Sheriff's Lt. Dan D'Annunzio, who has lost two K-9s, whose voice cracked a bit while he read a poem:

"The one absolutely unselfish friend
That man can have in this selfish world,
The one that never deserts him,
The one that never proves ungrateful
or treacherous ... is his dog."

K-9 Rookie's Service

K-9 Rookie and Officer Neapolitan served with the Boardman P.D. since 1991. They worked Patrol as well as narcotics investigation. Rookie began in 1999. He was a male GSD from Romania and lived with his partner. His commands were in German. He was trained in drug detection, tracking, building and are searches as well as apprehensions of criminals. He will be sadly missed by all.

In Loving Memory of

K-9 RUDI

April 1, 2002
LODD

Partner: Officer John Jenkins
Las Vegas Metro Police Dept.
4511 W. Cheyenne Ave. Suite 401
N. Las Vegas, NV 89030
702-229.3441

The first Metro Police dog that died in the line of duty will be buried Monday alongside other K-9 veterans in a service with the department's honor guard. Police Service Dog Rudi was crippled on March 28 when the police car he was riding in while heading to a call was struck by another car.

Rudi, a two and a half year old Belgian Malinois who started his duty in September, 2002, was euthanized Monday, April 1st. "When we lose a dog, it's pretty devastating. It hurts," said Sgt. Todd Fasulo of Metro's K-9 unit. "We're talking about a dog that is trained to protect his handler. The dog rides with the officer all day and lives at the officer's home."

Officer John Jenkins was driving on Nellis Boulevard with the police car's lights and sirens on, going to investigate a call about a man with a gun. Another K-9 officer and dog were at the scene, but Jenkins and his two dogs were called to assist in tracking down the suspect. As Jenkins drove into the intersection of Nellis Boulevard and Stewart Avenue, a car driven by James Herrin struck the right side of Jenkins' police car, according to an accident report.

Herrin was cited for failure to use due care upon approaching an intersection and failure to yield right of way to an .emergency vehicle. Police are waiting on the results of blood tests, the report states. Jenkins was injured and taken to University Medical Center. Fasulo went to the accident scene and saw Rudi. "I went to pull him out of the car, he stood up and instantly went right back down," he said. "We thought it was a broken leg." But a veterinarian that night determined Rudi had a dislocated hip and a fractured hip. It wasn't until the next day that more extensive X rays determined that Rudi's back was broken.

A veterinarian waited to see if the swelling would go down and Rudi's paralysis would subside, but when it was determined that Rudi was permanently paralyzed, the decision was made to put him to sleep, Fasulo said.

"We knew Saturday, but the officer was still recovering and we wanted to wait until after Easter," Fasulo said. Jenkins was still recovering from his injuries Thursday and was not available for comment. The other dog was not injured in the accident.

Metro's K-9 unit has 26 dogs consisting of patrol, bomb detection and drug detection dogs. The dogs can cost up to $5,000 each and including training, the cost can total $15,000 to $20,000. Rudi was a patrol dog. The dogs are more than just tools to the officers who handle them. Fasulo said they really become part of the officer's family. "The officers are with the dogs more than their families," he said. "Rudi was a good dog. He was an up and coming dog."

Monday, April 8th   3 p.m.   Craig Road Pet Cemetery
Goodbye to K-9 Partner

Las Vegas police officer John Jenkins said it was going to be one of the hardest things he has had to do deliver the eulogy for his late partner, a 2½ year old Belgian Malinois named Rudi who was killed in the line of duty. "These dogs mean the world to us," the teary eyed K-9 officer told dozens of officers and their families from around Southern Nevada who attended Monday's service. "They serve the community. They're totally selfless. They're the most loving creatures in the world."

Rudi was euthanized last week after being injured in a traffic accident, becoming the Metropolitan Police Department's first police dog killed in the line of duty. The K-9 unit has been in existence since 1959, originating under the former Las Vegas Police Dept. As with police dogs who die of natural causes, Rudi was given a funeral at the Craig Road Pet Cemetery, complete with a "seven dog salute." Handlers of seven other police dogs instructed their partners to bark for several seconds before silencing them.

Because Rudi died while on the job, the department's honor guard was present to fold the American flag draped over Rudi's casket and to play "Taps." Jenkins, in his eulogy, said he was responding to a call March 28 with lights and sirens on when he was broad-sided by another vehicle at an intersection. "I was knocked unconscious, and the first thing I could remember is hearing my dog howl in pain," he said. Jenkins reached his arm back to grab him and see where he was hurt. Rudi opened his mouth and gently closed it around the officer's forearm, he said. "He looked up at me to say, 'Dad, I'm hurt.' "

Rudi's hip was shattered in the accident, and he lost all feeling below his neck. Jenkins also was injured in the crash and attributes Rudi's presence for preventing him from going into shock. Jenkins still is recovering from his injuries and had to have another officer help him stand up as he spoke.

Officer Mike Horn, the K-9 Unit's trainer, told attendees at the service that it was hoped Rudi's hip could be reconstructed and that he would live out the rest of his life as a pet. Horn said on one visit to the veterinarian clinic, Rudi stood up straight, despite his injuries, when his handler came to visit. "He held that position for 15 minutes as John talked to him," he said. "He basically said, 'I'm OK, Dad. I'll be fine. I can go to work.'"

Rudi never recovered any feeling below his neck, however, and the decision was made to euthanize him, Horn said. Rudi had been with the department since May 2001. Horn described the dog as the "Michael Jordan of the police dog world." Horn said he secretly hoped he would someday handle Rudi, citing the animal's keen nose for tracking down bad guys.

In an interview, Horn acknowledged that Rudi, to other people, is just another dog. But, he said, the service was important to officers in K-9 units, who made up the people in attendance Monday. "They're our partners," he said. "We spend more time with these dogs than any other human being."

In Loving Memory of

K-9 RUDY

April 19, 2002
LODD

Partner: Officer J. R. Perez
Oxnard Police Department
251 South C Street
Oxnard, CA 93030
805-385.8290

About 200 people, including K-9 officers from as far away as Bakersfield and Las Vegas, gathered Tuesday to pay tribute to Rudy, an Oxnard police service dog stabbed to death during an arrest nearly two weeks ago. A police honor guard flanked a portrait of Rudy on the stage of the Oxnard Performing Arts Center during the emotional, one hour memorial.

"Today is not a sad day," K-9 trainer Rodney Spicer told the group. "It is truly a great day. It's a great day because we're here to honor a hero." Rudy was stabbed to death April 19 as his handler, Officer J. R. Perez, attempted to arrest an Oxnard man. "April 19 was one of the hardest days in my career as a police officer," Perez said from the podium. "I lost my friend, my partner, and a member of my family."

Police said Timothy Knight, 20, fleeing from another officer during a traffic stop, ran into a nearby house and knocked over his 92 year old grandmother. Knight was spotted about 30 minutes later, and brandished a knife at officers before Rudy was sent after him and was stabbed, police said. Rudy continued to subdue the man until officers were able to handcuff Knight, and then collapsed from his injuries and died a short time later, police said.

"Rudy was doing his job until the end," said Oxnard police Sgt. Bill Lewis II. Since Rudy started duty in July 2000, he performed about 3,000 assists and was directly responsible for 13 arrests, Lewis said. The 4 year old Belgian Malinois excelled in police dog training, Spicer said.

"Rudy had a very sensitive nose and he loved to search," Spicer said. "He loved to send people to jail. He was truly an exceptional dog." Perez recalled the first time he saw Rudy. "He was an 80 pound ball of brown fur with more energy than anything I'd ever seen," he said. "Later, I discovered Rudy was also 80 pounds of heart, dedication and love."

Rudy is the first Oxnard police service dog killed in the line of duty since the department's K-9 unit was established in 1980, Lewis said. A local auto dealer and an Oxnard resident have donated the estimated $8,500 needed to purchase and train another service dog, which Perez will handle, Lewis said.

In the days after Rudy's death, Perez was unsure whether he wanted to continue to be a K-9 officer, Lewis said. But Perez, who dreamed of being a K-9 officer as a child growing up in Oxnard, will be matched with the new dog when selected.

Memorial service for Rudy on Tues., April 30th, at 10 A.M.

It will be held at the Oxnard Performing Arts Center. The suspect who killed Rudy is still being held in our county jail. He had a court hearing yesterday and tried to get released or his bail reduced. The judge denied both and he is still being held on

$500,000 bail. Our District Attorneys's office is pursuing this case very strongly, however at this point he is still only facing 8 years in prison. I have been told that the D.A.'s office will not accept any plea bargains and will insist that he do the maximum time.

UPDATE:

New Partner, K-9 Beemer
I received my new partner last week. His name is "Beemer", and he is a three year old Belgian Malinois. We started our month long training last week at Gold Coast K-9 in Ventura, CA. So far things are going well. He has the makings to be a great police dog. Suffice it to say that even though he is my new partner, "Rudy" will never be replaced or forgotten. On the other side of the coin, the suspect who may have killed "Rudy" had his preliminary hearing last week on June 13th. The suspect's arraignment is set for June 26th, and a trial date will be set soon after.

All five dogs in the K-9 unit are male and were raised and initially trained abroad. Senna, Buck, Levi, and Rudy are Belgian Malinois; Argos is a Dutch Shepherd. They all respond to commands in Flemish (Dutch). Although the dogs receive initial training in their home country, once they are imported to the United States, the K-9 teams undergo extensive training together at Gold Coast K-9 Training Center.

UPDATE:

Tim Knight, who killed K-9 Rudy, pled guilty April, 2003 and will be sentenced May 8t, 2003.

05/01/03: Tim Knight, who killed Rudy, pled guilty last month and will be sentenced May 8th, 2003.

05/08/03: "Dog killer gets 4-year sentence"

In Loving Memory of
K-9 RUDY

LODD
November 7, 2002

Partner: Deputy John Trevor-Smith
McKinley County Sheriff Department
2105 E. Aztec Ave.
Gallup, NM 87301
505. 863-1410

SO NM & PSD RUDY PHI, PSP 1, PSP 2 were searching for a violent felon who had beaten a family member with a shovel and apparently was also armed with a knife. They were performing an off lead track in a remote location in western NM when, according to first reports, the perpetrator who was laying in wait either stabbed or strangled the dog (necropsy reports pending). Deputy Trevor Smith was working his way to Rudy, but the rugged terrain in the high mesa area slowed him down and on his arrival the dog was dead and the perpetrator had fled again.

My thoughts are with John as he and this dog were close as could be seen in their work. A very happy team that was responsible for 21 felony apprehensions so far this year. John and Rudy had won many awards as K-9 competitions and were an absolute for a real team also.

It is especially a loss to the sparse law enforcement in western New Mexico. The incident occurred on reservation lands and the FBI are investigating the occurrence.

In Loving Memory of

K-9 SASHA

February 22, 2002

Handler: Officer Kent Reisenauer
The Anaconda-Deer Lodge County Police
800 S. Main St.
Ananconda, MT 59711

Someone fatally shot the Anaconda Deer Lodge County police department's drug sniffing dog "Sasha" and dumped the body near her handler's home, law enforcement officials confirmed Wednesday. Investigators have made no arrests and have not determined if the killing was revenge by drug dealers, Chief Tom Blaz said. "We haven't had any recent cases that were a direct result of working the drug dog, but it was no secret that's what the dog was," Blaz said.

Sasha, a 3½ year old female black Labrador, had been shot once in the head, probably at close range, Assistant Police Chief Mark Blaskovich said. The body was left in an area next to Interstate 90 often used to dump animal carcasses and other refuse. The department made no announcement of the killing, and officials still withheld some information Wednesday. Blaz confirmed the death only after area residents called a number of news organizations, who inquired about the dog's death.

Sasha's handler, Officer Kent Reisenauer, said she disappeared Friday after he let her out for exercise. He lives in Opportunity, just west of Interstate 90, and said Sasha's body was found about 1½ miles away. An area resident out for a walk found the body and called him. "She never left the yard, or if she did she didn't go far," Reisenauer said Wednesday.

He declined to speculate on who killed Sasha. Blaz would not say whether investigators recovered the slug from the dog's body. Blaskovich said the body was near the carcasses of two calves that had been there some time, but said it was unlikely that Sasha was shot by a rancher for chasing livestock. "Normally the owners (of livestock) would shoot the dog and call us," he said. Blaskovich said the department acquired Sasha from Texas almost two years ago at a cost of about $3,400 for training and transportation.

Sasha is missed by 2 sons of Officer Reisenauer...who sleep with Sasha's picture on the headboard of the beds.

In Loving Memory of

Don Vom Ederbergland

K-9 SGT. DON

February 10, 1996 - January 1, 2002
LODD

Partner: Officer Ron Ross
McLoud Police Department
P.O. Box 1250
McLoud, OK 74851
405.964-3325

Sgt. Don was a member of the McLoud police department for 1½ years. He was partnered with Officer Ron Ross on December 2000, when Sgt. Don was given his commission and badge #7, Sgt. Don and Officer Ross were partners ever since.

He is credited with removing a lot of drugs off the streets. He was active in the McLoud school system and loved the attention he received from the students. He also was a very lovable and personable dog who loved what he did and gave his life doing what he loved, protecting his partner, Officer Ross.

Sgt. Don was a very valued member of the Ross family and will be missed deeply by the Ross' as well as the McLoud police department family. Sgt. Don was born on Feb. 10, 1996, in Germany and given name Don Vom Ederbergland. He was purchased by Rebecca Mosenthal of West Virginia. She trained him to be one of the best police dogs, Ms. Mosenthal then received a job assignment that would not allow her the opportunity to take Sgt. Don with her so she donated him to the McLoud Police Department where he remained until he gave his life protecting his partner Officer Ross.

The new year had a rough start for the McLoud Police Department after its police dog died Tuesday from multiple gunshot wounds. Officer Amanda Tackett said the dog, Sgt. Don, was the partner of K-9 Officer Ron Ross. Tackett said the four legged officer was shot several times at about 10:45 p.m. New Year's Eve.

After the shooting, Ross immediately took Sgt. Don to a local veterinarian where he was stabilized before being taken to the Veterinary Emergency and Critical Care Center of Oklahoma City, she said. Tackett said early Tuesday that Sgt. Don was in a coma and breathing with a respirator. "We're just praying and hoping for the best," she said. But the dog died later that afternoon.

An investigation into the shooting incident is being conducted by the Pottawatomie County Sheriff's Office. Under Sheriff J.D. Hodges said no arrests had been made by Tuesday afternoon. Hodges said Ross apparently was either loading or unloading Sgt. Don from his patrol car when a neighbor's dog distracted the animal.

The K-9 reportedly escaped the officer and began barking and growling at the other dog on the neighbor's porch, Hodges said. The neighbor then allegedly shot the dog. He said the McLoud officer had already taken the dog for emergency care when Deputy Will Dodd arrived. A statement was taken from the alleged suspect, he said. Hodges said no arrests were made for a number of reasons. "We did not see the shooting take place," he said. "We didn't get a statement from the McLoud officer until today (Tuesday)." Hodges said laws regarding weapons are different in the rural areas than in the city.

"There is a right to protect a person's property," he said. "Our deputy handled the situation properly." He added that the question of whether the alleged suspect knew Sgt. Don was a police dog or if he was on duty has yet to be answered. That factor could play a role in punishment if any charges are filed in this case. Hodges said the investigation will be turned over to the district attorney once it is completed.

Jan. 5, 2002

A McLoud man faces a felony charge in the shooting death of a McLoud police dog. Tommy Dale Delk, 50, of 11655 Highway 177 is charged with injury of a police dog, and in the alternative, killing of a police dog. The charge was filed Friday in Pottawatomie County District Court, shortly after Sgt. Don, the police dog, was buried in a Spencer pet cemetery. The shooting of Sgt. Don occurred New Year's Eve. The dog died Jan. 1.

On the count of injuring a police dog, Delk is accused of injuring and disabling Sgt. Don. Felony information alleges Delk shot Sgt. Don several times with a semi automatic rifle during the commission of a misdemeanor. That misdemeanor is listed as reckless conduct with a firearm, "creating an unreasonable risk of great bodily harm to others and demonstrating conscious disregard for the safety of defendant's neighbors by firing his semi auto rifle in the direction of his neighbors." felony information reads.

In the alternative of count one, the district attorney's office filed a charge of killing a police dog. On that count, Delk is accused of killing Sgt. Don by shooting him multiple times. A probable cause arrest affidavit was filed with the charges. The shooting of Sgt. Don reportedly occurred as his partner, McLoud K-9 Police Officer Ron Ross loaded his dog into a patrol car. While doing so, Ross noticed a "dark, pit bull type dog running up to him as if to attack Officer Ross," the affidavit said.

The dog appeared to have broken loose from a chain in Delk's house or yard, the record shows. The affidavit indicates Ross affirmed that Sgt. Don leaped from the patrol car to protect him, then chased the neighbor's pit bull back to the Delk's yard. Officer Ross went to retrieve Sgt. Don, the affidavit indicates, but because of previous encounters with his neighbor, Ross "screamed as loud as he could that there was a police dog there, multiple times before Delk began shooting," the affidavit claims.

At the time of the shooting, Sgt. Don had a police badge atop his collar, the affidavit reads, and the area where the two dogs were was well lighted. Ross indicated Sgt. Don was shot "multiple times from his back as he was going to Officer Ross away from Delk's house" the affidavit reads.

Some of the shots were reportedly fired in the direction of Officer Ross and his house. After the shooting ceased and Sgt. Don was shot, the affidavit claims, "Officer Ross heard immediately, among other things, laughter coming from the Delk's porch area." Ross reportedly sought immediate veterinary care for Sgt. Don, but the K-9 later died.

The affidavit reports that Delk told sheriff's deputies at the scene that he shot eight to 10 rounds from his SKS semiautomatic rifle. None of Delk's dogs were reportedly injured. The probable cause warrant also claims that Delk knew Officer Ross had a police officer and knew Sgt. Don was a police dog.

Pottawatomie County District Attorney Kay Christiansen attended the funeral for Sgt. Don Friday. The service was held at Precious Pets Cemetery in Spencer, where the Tecumseh Police Honor Guard as well as officers and K-9s from various law enforcement agencies attended. "He (Sgt. Don) is considered a downed officer," Christiansen said. If found guilty of either charge filed against him, Delk faces punishment of a fine up to $1,000 and/or imprisonment for up to two years.

Words will never be available to describe how loved and respected Sgt. Don was. Thank you for caring. Officer Ron Ross

#3 McLoud Police Department.

UPDATE:

I wanted to say thanks for all that you had done back in January of 2002 for my partner and I just thought I would come by and take a few minutes to honor all the other fallen K-9 Heroes. I did get another K-9 his name is Rex and he's a 1 year old German Shepherd with a lot of heart and right now goofy as can be! Well, thank you again!
/s/Ron Ross

UPDATE:

My wife and I moved to Hot Springs, Arkansas and are just waiting on a start date from Hot Springs Police Department. I resigned from McLoud in April. I now have a German Shepherd. He was 6 months old when I got him in February of 2002. I have started training him in narcotic detection and handler protector, But I do believe he is just going to be a house dog, not sure I want to go through something happening again.
/s/ Ron Ross
Mountain Pine, AR 71956

In Loving Memory of

K-9 SHADOW

June 4, 2002

Partner: Officer Peter McClelland
Yarmouth Police Department
1 Brad Erickson Way
W. Yarmouth, MA 02673
508.775-0445

He was a frequent visitor to schools and senior citizen homes an enthusiastic tail wagging ambassador for the Yarmouth police department. He excelled in state, national and international competitions and captured more than 100 felons trying to outrun the police over his 14 year career. Shadow, a Belgian Malinois, also had his share of legal problems, landing his handlers in federal court three times when convicted criminals sued over a dog bites.

Nonetheless, the K-9 member of the Yarmouth police department was a well recognized and popular figure in town. Shadow was recently euthanized because of a debilitating and degenerative spine disease. While most police dogs are retired before age 10, Shadow continued working until a few months before his death at age 14 1/2.

"It was one of the hardest things I've ever had to do," says Officer Peter McClelland, who worked with Shadow since first picking him from a litter of puppies. It was Shadow's ability to concentrate, his quickness to obey commands, his agility and his intelligence that made him stand out, according to the dog's handlers. The special relationship he had with McClelland also made him unique.

Police dogs are trained to track people, locate drugs, locate cadavers and control crowds. This leads some people to view them as tools, much like a gun or can of pepper spray, or something akin to a search tool. McClelland never shared that perspective. "The relationship between Peter and Shadow was unique, maybe one of the most incredible relationships between a police officer and a K-9 that I've ever seen," Deputy Chief Michael Almonte says.

"Peter brought out the best in that dog like he brings out the best in the people who train with him," added Barnstable police officer Sean Roycroft. He had gone to North Carolina to select a puppy in anticipation of his German Shepherd's retirement. McClelland observed the puppies at play, got down on his hands and knees to play with them himself. He decided on a red coated male.

"I'll take that one" It was a last minute change of mind that brought Shadow into McClelland's life.

Official honors

Shadow's contribution to Yarmouth was recognized last year in the form of a declaration from the state senate honoring his 14 years service. Shadow had 200 confirmed tracks, everything from suspected criminals to lost children and lost senior citizens as well as 100 captured suspects.

Last year's Annual Blessing of the Animals held in Yarmouth was dedicated to Shadow. "There wasn't a dry eye in the place when people saw Shadow with his gray muzzle standing there next to Peter," says Penny Schiller, Yarmouth animal control officer. "Peter and Shadow had an incredible connection, and one of the reasons for that is Peter really loves his dogs. He works with them constantly. They are an integral part of this life."

The Shadow file

Shadow was the K-9 partner of Peter McClelland, a Yarmouth officer, for 14 years. McClelland bought Shadow from a breeder in North Carolina when Shadow was 7 weeks old.

In 1992, the pair was judged the best of 26 K-9 units at regional trials in Orleans. In September 1997, Duane Gomez was badly bitten after police broke open a vehicle and sent Shadow in after him. Shadow's handlers were cleared of any wrong-doing in January 2002. Another suspect, Shane Orton, had a run in with Shadow after a night of drinking in October 1997. Shadow found Orton, who was hiding from the police, and bit his leg.

Three years later, a jury ruled the officers acted reasonably when they caught Orton. In June 2000, jury awarded $1 in damages to a man bitten by Shadow. Jerome Jarrett was wounded by the dog while fleeing police in 1994.

Shadow helped track an alleged burglar in Yarmouth in August 2001. The search ended when Shadow found Patrick Bishop in the bushes. A campaign to raise money in support of Shadow raised $2,500 for Independence House.

Court upholds use of police K-9 force

Yarmouth officer's use of dog to bite and hold suspect ruled appropriate by U.S. appeals panel. A two year legal battle over whether a Yarmouth police officer used excessive force when sending his dog after a fleeing suspect ended in victory yesterday for the officer. A three judge panel of the First U.S. District Court of Appeals ruled that Officer Peter McClelland did not use undue force nor violate the civil rights of Jerome Jarrett in 1994, when his dog bit and held Jarrett during a foot chase.

"Shadow has been exonerated. I am happy beyond words," said McClelland yesterday afternoon when word of the decision reached him. "Having this hang over my head all this time has not been easy. My whole career was put in doubt," he said.

"This decision will become the standard for all other decisions involving police K-9s," said Leonard Kesten, who represented McClelland and the town. "It will become a sort of Miranda rights for police K-9s," Kesten said. "There can be no doubt now that a K-9 is not deadly force, and that there are appropriate circumstances in which police can release a dog to bite and hold a suspect," he said.

Shadow, a Belgian Malinois, died earlier this year after serving the town of Yarmouth for nearly 14 years. He and McClelland won honors in regional, national and international competitions throughout his career. Yesterday's decision represents the last of three cases brought against McClelland and the town as a result of Shadow biting suspects during police chases. In the other cases, which were filed after Jarrett's initial victory, juries in U.S. District Court in Boston rejected arguments that McClelland erred in sending Shadow after fleeing suspects.

In all three cases, Shadow bit and held the suspects until McClelland ordered the dog to release them, as he was trained to do. All three suspects received stitches as a result of the bites. Shadow bit Jarrett in December 1994 during a police chase that began when police tried to pull him over for speeding on Route 28. Police said Jarrett, who was also a suspect in an armed robbery case, admitted jumping out of the car and scaling a nearby fence to avoid police. He was later convicted of the armed robbery charge.

McClelland and Shadow were called to track Jarrett through a nearby residential neighborhood. McClelland unleashed Shadow after spotting Jarrett and shouting a warning to stop or have the dog released on him.

In June 2000, a jury in U.S. District Court in Boston awarded Jarrett legal fees plus $1 after finding use of the bite and hold technique, common among police dogs, was akin to deadly force. That jury also took the unusual step of writing a note to the Yarmouth police department recommending that its police dogs be trained to only bark at suspected criminals. The appeals court decision, written by Judge Juan Turruella found that other federal courts have ruled that use of a police dog does not constitute deadly force. McClelland acted within departmental regulations concerning use of force in sending his dog after Jarrett.

Jarrett's original complaint against McClelland and Shadow should have been dismissed because McClelland was protected by "qualified immunity," which protects officials from civil damages as long as their actions don't violate established statutory or constitutional rights.

The appeals court took a further step in noting, "all the evidence supports the conclusion that Officer McClelland was exceptionally well trained. The uncontradicted testimony was that Officer McClelland and Shadow were one the highest rated K-9 teams in the nation. They had even been recognized internationally."

In Loving Memory of

K-9 SKIPPER

SAR
December 16, 2002

Partner: Karen Hardesty
Oklahoma K-9 SAR & Heartland SAR
Parson, KS

I think this is the picture of me holding Skipper. Duchess had picked her up and shaken her. It was like shaken baby syndrome. She also had one puncture in her shoulder. When the vet drew blood on her Sunday she found Skipper had Addison's disease which stops the production of adrenaline. She crashed so fast the vet couldn't do anything for her. Skipper was donated to us in June of 95 after the Oklahoma City Bombing.

When I first met her she was standing up on a fence grinning at me. She had a remarkable smile. Skipper was a tracking fool. She thought every search was for her and that everyone in the world was put here just to pet and talk to her. Skipper was a talker. She would tell me when people came to the house and talked a lot of the time. Skipper would track for anyone, it did-n't matter to her who was on the end of the lead.

She was so expressive there was no doubt in your mind she had found what you were looking for. I have very few good pictures of her, she was always moving. To get her to rest on a long search I would have to hold her and make her take a break. She never wanted to miss anything. We will miss her. I dreamed she was still alive the other night and had just been asleep. The house is too quiet without her.

In Loving Memory of

K-9 TANGO

August 30, 2002

Partner: Ptl. William Sierchio
Barnegat Township, NJ
Chief E. J. Smith
900 West Bay Avenue
Barnegat, NJ 08005
609. 698-0080

K-9 Tango was a 10 year old male German Shepherd. He was with the Barnegat Township K-9 Unit since its inception in January of 1996. Tango retired from service in December of 2001 due to the advance of a degenerative myleopathy in his spine. He was euthanized August 30th from complications of the disease.

Tango and his handler Ptl. William Sierchio attended the Dover Township Police Patrol Dog Class #3 as well as the NJ State Police Scent Dog Class #3 both in 1996. He certified with the U.S.P.C.A. and the N.A.P.W.D.A. in patrol, narcotics and tracking. Tango was responsible for countless narcotic searches, tracks and public demonstrations in Barnegat as well as surrounding towns.

Tango will best be remembered as a fearless, proud, and loyal patrol dog. He left a lasting impression on all who knew and worked with him. The Barnegat Township P.B.A. Local 296 is in the process of establishing a K-9 memorial for Tango. He will be greatly missed but never forgotten.

In Loving Memory of

K-9 BARRY & K-9 TANK

November 20, 2002 - June 1, 2002

Partner: Officer Carol Catizone
Department of Corrections

My heart is aching. I had to do one of the hardest things I have ever done in my life at 2:00 P.M. today. I took my former partner/patrol dog "Barry", Belgian Malinois, to be put to sleep. Barry has always been an extremely hyper dog who required a very strong handler. While we worked in the prisons together, he was the best prison dog in our entire region.

But he always was a extremely high maintenance dog, meaning you had to work with him every day to keep him safe and in control. If he felt you were, in the smallest way, weak or not feeling well or whatever, he would take advantage of the handler. K-9 Barry & K-9 Tank protected their fellow officers (as they were certified officers even though they were dogs), their handler and the public during their many years of service in the many maximum security facilities they were brought into.

In Memory of my partners, K-9 Barry, Belgian Malinois and K-9 Tank, Rottweiler who stood up against the worst environments and situations to ensure the safety of staff, myself, and the public. You are missed more than you will ever imagine. All my love & respect,

Senior Corrections Officer Catizone (Former K-9 Patrol Dog Handler/DOC)

My eyes are your eyes,
To watch and protect you and yours
My ears are your ears,
To hear and detect evil minds in the dark
My nose is your nose,
To scent the invader of your domain
And so you may live,
My life is also yours.

In Loving Memory of

K-9 TASJA

July 1, 1994 - June 13, 2002
"Semper Fi, Tasja"

Partner: Officer Terence Garrison
High Point Police Department
1009 Leonard Avenue
High Point, NC 27260-5321

Tribute to TASJA
SEMPER FI TASJA
A few days ago, I had to put my K-9 partner, Tasja, down. I know I did the right thing and that I had no other choice. Tasja and I had simply had been dealt a bad hand that we couldn't beat.

The situation, Tasja's kidney failure was beyond my control, and even that of our top notch vet, Dr. Harvey Goho. Even so, it was the hardest thing I have ever done and thus far, the saddest day of my life. Tasja, a small but excessively feisty Malinois was above the par. Most handlers, like any parent out there, feel this way, but in my case this is entirely true.

Her numbers speak for themselves. She was never in a situation where she disappointed me. Her only fault, if it can be considered such, was her overly aggressive nature. She was a fearless, tireless being who even in the end, didn't know what it was to quit. In the days before her death, she found over 10 bundles of heroin and apprehended a bad guy.

Is that exceptional for a police working dog? I think so. You see, she was dying even then, her toxin levels should have incapacitated her according to our vet. But she was an incredible dog, Why should her death have come about in a way any different from how she lived the rest of her life?

So it is with a heavy heart that I mourn the passing of my partner, my friend. I suspect she will have been the greatest dog I will ever have had the privilege of handling. During her career, Tasja recovered the following:

$413,718 in narcotics,

$53,340 in cash,

$28,852 in property.

 83 criminal apprehensions

43 public information programs performed

26% successful tracking average, an impressive record!

Tasja was my K-9 partner for the City of High Point for a tragically short 4.5 years.

K-9 Officer Tasja was, by all accounts, a loyal ball of energy. From the day she came to the High Point Police Department to the day she was put to sleep, Tasja gave her all, officers said at a memorial service held in her honor Monday afternoon.

Officers from patrol to vice narcotics filled the City Council chambers in City Hall to pay their respects to Tasja, who died of kidney failure last month. From finding drugs to returning lost equipment to officers, Tasja was a big part of the department, Chief Blair Rankin said during the service.

Rankin recalled the time in September when Tasja captured a robber and recovered his gun as one of the highlights of her five and a half year career.

Police also honored Starko, a retired K-9 who died in May. Starko was one of the department's first police dogs. "They are more than just dogs to us handlers," said Officer Tim Tonsor, the department's dog trainer, in opening the service.

"They are our companions, the officers' last resort and the citizens' savior." Tonsor, who trained Tasja when she came to the department, described the dog as tenacious. But last month, the dog's kidneys began to fail. Her handler, Officer Terence Garrison, had to have her put to sleep.

A visibly shaken Garrison was presented with a plaque memorializing Tasja. He called his partner always faithful and loyal. "Our personalities matched," he said. "She was very outgoing."

Terence Garrison and Tasja.

Garrison recalled the day Tasja found a missing toddler and took her home. The little girl had crept out the back door of her house while her father slept. Detectives found the little girl, but had no idea where she lived. Tasja was called in to find the girl's home. She led a track straight to the girl's back door.

During her police service, Tasja recovered more than $495,000 worth of property, narcotics and cash. "She was like a nuclear powered Energizer Bunny," said Officer Daryl Delagrange. Delagrange read the eulogy at the memorial service. He called himself Tasja's biggest fan.

The day Tasja was brought to High Point, Delagrange was one of the first people to meet her. "I thought, 'What a sweet dog,'" he said. But on the ride from the airport to the department's kennel, Delagrange said Tasja transformed from "Barbie to Witchblade."

Delagrange said she was aggressive and ready to work. "We thought we were going to have to feed her with a slingshot." "Tasja was the alpha male of a pack of dogs," he said. "If Supergirl showed up to claim her dog, I'd understand."

In Loving Memory of

K-9 TAZ

March 19, 2002

Partner: Officer Scott Ptacek
Franklin Park Police Department
9545 W. Belmont Ave.
Franklin Park, IL 60131
847-671.8200

"Taz was my partner for seven years at the Franklin Police Department. He developed cancer and lived only about five weeks after having his spleen removed. He was a good partner. We did a lot of drug secures and searches. I will miss him for my remaining six years with the police force."

Taz, the 7 year old German Shepherd who worked for the Franklin Park Police Department for more than six of those years, was put to sleep March 19, about a month after it was found he had cancer. After the cancer was detected, Taz, whose illness was the subject of the March 20 main Images feature, had his spleen removed, but there was nothing else doctors could do for him.

Scott Ptacek, the officer who trained Taz, worked and lived with him, said a week earlier that he would not hesitate to have the dog put to sleep once the cancer got bad enough to cause him great suffering. Flags flown at the Franklin Park Police Department and Village Hall, which have been at half staff since the March 5 death of longtime resident/village historian Rodger Hammill, will continue that way. Park residents are hopeful that another dog will be added to the force.

Deputy Police Chief Jack Krecker said several factors probably should be considered before a decision is made about adding another dog. "Things have changed quite a bit since we got our two dogs," Krecker said. At that time, there weren't many departments in the area with dogs, and our dogs helped out in other towns as well as in Franklin Park. Krecker said area police departments have since added their own dogs.

"My opinion is that the departments should all get together and work together where the dogs are concerned," he said. "It's possible that there are now so many dogs out there that they're not all getting the type of street work they need. I just think we need to look at every aspect of this before making a decision." Krecker said purchase of another dog would run $8,000 to $9,000. The same amount would be needed for training, and the department also would have to pay for food and medical care of another dog.

You also have a $25,000 (police) car that can only be used for one man and one dog, he said. And, you have a lot of calls that you can't use that officer for because the dog is in the car. You're not going to send that officer on a traffic call or to transport a prisoner.

Losing Taz has been an emotional thing, and that's the hard part. The question now is do we try to get approval (from the Village Board) and go out right away and get another dog, or do we wait and take a look at the whole picture. We have to be responsible to the taxpayers.

In Loving Memory of

K-9 TITAN

March 12, 2002

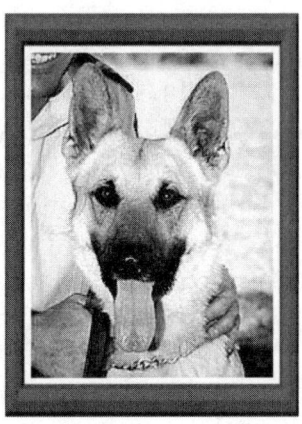

Handler Snr-Sgt. John Casey
Queensland Police Service K-9.
Australia

The state's top police pooch, instrumental in the dramatic capture of the Childers arson murderer Robert Long, died this week. Six year old Titan had a heart attack during surgery after he was injured at training on Tuesday night.

The K-9 hero and his handler clashed with Long in bushland 30km from Childers in June 2000 after tracking the itinerant fruit picker. The feats of the German Shepherd endeared him to people around the world. During the struggle, Long stabbed Titan, cutting his paw, before turning on his handler and slashing his face.

Today is the first time Titan's photograph has been allowed to be published as Special Emergency Response Team members cannot be identified. Titan's death has devastated his handler and the close knit 60 strong dog squad. State co ordinator Snr Sgt John Casey said Titan was responsible for apprehending many criminals after graduating in 1998. "These two were unique, an excellent handler who is totally dedicated to being a policeman and dog handler and a dog who was very strong," he said.

Sgt. Casey said dog squad duties were very physically and mentally demanding. "A dog must have a high drive to retrieve and defend its handler and other police and community also have to rely on the dog and the handler to protect them well," he said. "They must have a steadiness under gunfire, be physically fit and around two years old. "We are so short of dogs and to lose one of our best will affect the whole squad because he won't be replaced easily." Police dog Titan, who caught the Childer's back-packer murderer, died days before Long was convicted.

In Loving Memory of

K-9 TORI

December 14, 2002

Partner: Chief Don Perkins
Clay Township Police Department
8207 Arlington Rd.
Brookville, OH 45309
937 833 4015

I am sad to report that the Clay Township, Ohio Police Department has lost a valuable member of its Department, K-9 Tori. On 12/14/2002, Chief Don Perkins' K-9 and best friend, K-9 Tori, passed away suddenly and unexpectedly from an irreversible seizure late in the evening.

Tori, an approximate eight 8 year old yellow lab, started their K-9 program in 1996 as a Narcotic Detection K-9, and was purchased from donated funds. After two K-9 handlers moved to other departments, Chief Perkins found himself to be the only one interested in taking Tori on as his K-9 partner.

K-9 Tori had many accomplishments while serving the

community in and around Montgomery County, Ohio and will be sorely missed. Keep Chief Perkins in your thoughts and prayers during this troubling time.

In Loving Memory of

K-9 TURBO

April 22, 2002

Deputy Sherri Bagwell
Bay County Sheriff's Office
3421 Hwy.#77
Panama City, FL 32405

Turbo had spent many years on the streets and the last two working with the DARE program in the schools. Turbo was a clown and had a lot of personality, but his bite was strong and his nose was good. He loved to beg for "treats" out of the "junk machine," and could outsmart just about anybody. He loved his toy, his friends and his handler. He was euthanized Friday due to severe hip problems at 9 years of age. He will be greatly missed by those of us who loved him.

Today, we mourn the loss of a 8 year Bay County Sheriffs Office veteran. Sheriff's Office K-9 Turbo passed away Friday, April 19, 2002 after a debilitating illness. Turbo was born in Largo, Florida and joined the Bay County Sheriffs Office after extensive training in Bay County with his handler, Deputy Sheriff Sherri Bagwell.

During his career, Turbo was responsible for the apprehension of numerous suspects with his tracking abilities but excelled in his abilities to search out and locate illicit narcotics which led to hundreds of drug arrests. Turbo was assigned to the Field Services Division in 1995 where he spent three years working Patrol. In 1998, his social skills were recognized and he was assigned to the D.A.R.E. Program where he spent his remaining years, working with the children of the Bay County School System giving thousands of hours helping them to learn about the dangers of drug and substance abuse.

Turbo was buried at a country site near his home with a small service attended by his family and friends of the Bay County Sheriff's Office.

In Loving Memory of

K-9 TYLER

September 1,1989 - October 1, 2002

Partner: Sgt. Ron Labarriere
Kenner Police Department
500 Veterans Blvd.
Kennere, LA 70062
504.712-2200

K-9 Tyler, became a member of the Kenner Police Department, most of all he became my partner and BUDDY. He served as the department's only narcotic detector dog from February 1992 until August 1999. At that time he retired and became a full time family member. K-9 Tyler was loved by all who met him. He will be greatly missed. He is now in a better place and best of all, he is not hurting. He can now run again, to catch his "giftie," which he loved very much.

I am sorry to inform you that we have lost another wonderful K-9 partner. On October 1st at 4:40 AM my first K-9 partner, K-9 Tyler, known to a lot of you as "Big T" passed away.

K-9 Tyler was in service from February 1992 until July 1999 with the Kenner Police Department.

At that time he was retired due to hip problems.

In Loving Memory of

K-9 TY

SAR

January 2, 2000 - September 12, 2002

Partner: Karen Hermanson
Jewell, IA 50130

Ty was only 2 years old when handler, Karen Hermanson had to have her put down. She suffered from a degenerative muscle disease. Unfortunately, Ty was just approaching the stages to become a certified K-9 with Iowa Search & Rescue. She had gone through almost two years of training and had become confident in air scenting, cadaver and article searches.

It was not only a horrible loss for Karen, but a devastating blow to ISAR to loose such a young search dog. Karen had worked hard with TY and we sympathize with her in her loss. It is always difficult to deal with the loss of a pet and especially hard when that pet has become your partner during the many months of training.

In Loving Memory of

K-9 WILLIE

September 29, 2002

Partner: Officer Peter M. Morgan
Waterbury Police Department
255 East Main St.
Waterbury, CT 06702
203. 574.6921

K-9 Willie was a working patrol dog for the Waterbury Police Department with Officer Peter Morgan for three years. Earlier this year, Willie was diagnosed with a bone disease in his front elbow. On September 29, 2002, Willie's condition worsened to a point to where he had to be put down. Willie was 6 years old. During his three year career, he made several suspect apprehensions and narcotic finds for the police department. He will be sadly missed by Officer Morgan and the Waterbury Police Department.

UPDATE:

Officer Steven Flaherty, Jr. who accompanied Officer Morgan sent thanks for support when K-9 Willie was put down. He said; "I am also a K-9 handler on the Waterbury Police Dept, and I have had my partner for almost 7 years. I was with Pete at the time we put Willie down, and he took it very hard.....and to know that there are citizens out there who care for us and our partners is very comforting..... Thank You," Officer Steven Flaherty Jr., Waterbury Police Dept.

In Loving Memory of

K-9 WINDY

SAR
December 22, 1994 - October 22, 2002

Partner: Kathy Reed
Grinnell, IA 50112

Windy was a gentle giant and just loved to be cuddled as most newfy's (Newfoundlander) do. Although she grew a lot larger than other ISAR newfs, she displayed a beautiful black and white coat that was unmistakable. She was a beautiful dog. Even with her great size she moved with grace and agility. It was amazing. She was the first Newfoundland I ever saw run.

I remember hiding for her in the woods in the winter and she would find me and lay on me. She certainly kept me from getting cold! She was a certified K-9 with ISAR and served us well. Windy's enemies were brooms and vacuum cleaners. Her friends were many, children, kittens, divers on the Linn County dive team, police officers and grieving families at Search Call outs. She is fondly remembered by oh, so many people.

In Loving Memory of

K-9 WOODROW

Badge No. 537
May 24, 2002

Partner: Officer Joseph Arrison
Philadelphia Police K-9 Academy
8501 State Rd.
Philadelphia, PA 19136
610 685.8088

Police dog killed in too hot car

A city police dog died last week after being accidentally left inside a patrol car for more than four hours with the windows up, officials said today. When found shortly after 12:30 p.m. last Friday, Woodrow, a 5 year old German Shepherd assigned to Officer Joseph Arrison of the K-9 Unit, was already dead, police said.

Arrison, a 28 year veteran who has been in the K-9 Unit for 15 years, has been temporarily reassigned pending the results of an investigation by the Internal Affairs Division. Police said.

"It's a tragic, tragic incident, and the officer is devastated," said Capt. Alan Kurtz, who commands both the K-9 and Mounted Units. The loss has deeply bothered Arrison, investigators said. Efforts to reach him today were unsuccessful.

The accident occurred after Arrison and Woodrow finished their shifts about 8 a.m. last Friday, police said. Arrison, 49, of Northeast Philadelphia, stopped at K-9 Unit headquarters at the Police Academy on State Road to drop off his cruiser and transfer Woodrow from his compartment in the back of the police car to Arrison's personal car for the drive home. K-9 Unit officers are permitted to take their partners home and receive a stipend from the city for their care. Arrison routinely took Woodrow home after work, officials said. Before moving the dog, however, Arrison stepped inside headquarters to complete some end of shift paperwork and have a cup of coffee.

He left a short while later but forgot about Woodrow, who was still inside the cruiser, investigators said. Last Friday was a warm day, topping out at 85 degrees. By the time Woodrow was spotted by another police officer, the temperature was already reaching 80. The police car's windows were up, so the temperature inside the vehicle was well above that because of the searing sun, investigators said.

A necropsy indicated Woodrow died of heat exhaustion, according to police. Charles Spencer, a director of the Pennsylvania Society for Prevention of Cruelty to Animals, said that warm weather and closed vehicles can be a recipe for tragedy. "It only takes a short amount of time," Spencer said.

Kurtz, the K-9 Unit commander, said Woodrow's death may spark changes within the unit. Kurtz said he was looking into the possibility of installing heat sensors inside K-9 Unit vehicles that would automatically drop the windows slightly, start a fan, and set off the vehicle's siren when the temperature became excessive while a dog was inside.

K-9 Unit officers and their dogs develop close bonds, both on duty and at home, where the animals often become members of the family. Investigators said Arrison was stunned when con-

tacted at home about Woodrow's death. There are no plans for
a departmental burial for Woodrow, Kurtz said.

K-9 officers pay last respects to Woodrow, German Shepherd
'will be sorely missed,' cop says

He was one of the guardians of the night. Woodrow, a 5 year
old German Shepherd, fought crime, protected his human partner, and was an asset to the police force. Yesterday, in the grass
field of the Police Academy exercise yard, K-9 officers from
throughout the Philadelphia area gathered to pay respects to the
revered K-9 officer, who died when he was left in a hot police
car for about three hours by his partner, Officer Joseph Arrison.

The attendees, police officers in their K-9 uniforms and
police dogs, stood solemnly as Capt. Allen Kurtz, K-9 commander, read a short anonymous poem that has been used for
years by the K-9 Unit:

> *My eyes are your eyes, to watch and protect you and yours.*
> *My ears are your ears, to hear evil minds in the dark.*
> *My nose is your nose, to scent the invader of your domain.*
> *And so you may live, my life is also yours.*

On May 24, Arrison had gone home, leaving Woodrow in a
squad car at Police Headquarters. The heat in the rear of the
vehicle reached 94 degrees and killed Woodrow, police said.
Though the status of the investigation is still continuing, police
believe it was just an unfortunate accident. Arrison, who is still
in service, just made a mistake, police say.

Arrison and Woodrow were constant companions ever since
becoming partners a year ago. "Joe would take his dog wherever he went," Kurtz said. Police say Arrison was too upset to
attend the service. He has Woodrow's cremated remains and
will choose where to bury the ashes. Woodrow entered the service only a year ago in July. During his brief time with the police
he became one of the most decorated dogs in the K-9 Unit. He
was responsible for 10 arrests and many drug confiscations,
police said.

Officer Robert Wyszynski described Woodrow as easygoing and peaceful. Wyszynski said he used to play ball and hide and seek with Woodrow in the exercise yard. "He was a good police dog who loved his handler," said Sgt. Paul Bryant, head trainer of the K-9 Unit. In the exercise yard, a fenced off K-9 memorial is set up, listing all the police dogs in the unit that have died.

The board stands behind a statue of a police dog with a police badge on a chain around its neck. Woodrow's name and police No. 537 was added. "He will be sorely missed," Wyszynski said.

Police officer Michael Andrel in Darby Township Pennsylvania adores his partner. Yeager is a highly trained German Shepherd who rides on patrol with Andrel. But Yeager doesn't leave the squad car for every call. Sometimes he has to stay in the back of the car, even on hot muggy East Coast summer days. That can be dangerous. But Andrel has a weapon to protect his partner a device called the Hotdog, a temperature monitor used in K-9 unit police cars. The sensor's thermometer measures air temperature inside the car. When it reaches 85 degrees, the horn of the vehicle begins to beep.

How the Hotdog works. It's not just a warning device. Hotdog, which is manufactured by law enforcement equipment maker Criminalistics, is hooked into the car's electrical system. When temperatures reach 88 degrees inside the cruiser, the horn blares even more frequently, then a fan is activated near Yeager's cage and the windows are automatically rolled down. On a 78 degree day, the temperature inside a shaded car is 90 degrees. A car parked in the sun can reach 160 degrees in minutes. For a dog, heatstroke death takes just 15 minutes.

The Hotdog system has been used by Andrel and other K-9 units in Darby County during the past three years and now other police departments elsewhere are finding a need for the device.

Tragic incident.

Police in Pennsylvania say they think the Hotdog device

could have saved Woodrow, a Philadelphia police dog with the
K-9 unit who died in July 2002 when his handler accidentally
left him in the car on a day when the temperature topped 85
degrees. As a result of the tragic death of Woodrow, a 5 year old
German Shepherd, the Philadelphia Police Department is
implementing the Hotdog system.

All the units were donated by music publisher and
Philadelphia philanthropist Kal Rudman. He is also donating
two new dogs for the police department and another German
Shepherd to replace Woodrow.

For every pooch.

But the Hotdog is not just for police departments. It's available to purchase for $328. If you want one with a pager that
alerts you to the car's temperature, the price is $598. You can
buy the device at Criminalistics' website.

Heat stroke is a life threatening medical emergency that
occurs when an overheated dog's body temperature soars four
to seven degrees above the normal range of 100 to 102.5
degrees Fahrenheit.

What to look for:

Excessive panting
Brick red oral membranes
Weakness
Loss of coordination, or collapse

What to do:

Contact your veterinarian, who may direct you to begin cooling
the dog yourself or to bring it to the clinic.
If you begin cooling your dog, use cool, not ice cold, water &
a fan to bring the dog's body temperature down to 103.

How to prevent heatstroke:

Never leave a dog unattended in a car during warm weather.
Keep your dog inside on hot, humid days, particularly if the

heat regulation mechanisms are compromised by age, heart, lung disease, or a pug nose.

If you leave your dog outside, provide plenty of fresh water (with a backup supply if one bowl tips over) and access to shade at all times of day.

Don't shave long-haired dogs in hot weather. Hair coats operate as air filled buffers shielding the dog's skin from heat.

In Loving Memory of

K-9 ZEUS

LODD
October 29, 2002

Partner: Officer Mitch Waters
Indianapolis Police Department
IPD K-9 Section - 901 N. Post Rd.
Indianapolis, IN 46219
317.327-6696

A dog in the Indianapolis Police Department's K-9 Unit died Sunday night, shot down after attacking an IPD officer. Zeus, a 2 year old Dutch shepherd, attacked Officer Brett Seach sometime after 10:30 p.m. Sunday. Police hoped Zeus would help them find a man who had run away after Seach pulled his car over.

Zeus tracked the suspect to a porch, but in the struggle to catch the man, Seach ended up shooting Zeus twice after the dog bit his forearm and biceps and caused deep puncture wounds, according to a police report. Zeus is the second dog to die from officer fire in IPD's K-9 unit, which is one of the largest in the country and has operated since 1960. An undercover narcotics officer killed the first dog, Valco, on July 17, 2000, during a drug raid on the Near Northside. The officer did not know Valco was a police dog.

Only a few dogs die each year in the line of duty, said Joan Hess, assistant to the director of the U.S. Police K-9 Association in Springboro, Ohio, the country's largest K-9 certification group. She said she had never heard of a dog being killed by officer fire. IPD has 11 bulletproof vests for its 33 dogs, but officers prefer not to use the vests because they make the dogs hot and tired, said LT. Paul Ciesielski. The vests usually go on when an armed suspect is present, he said.

Zeus and his partner, Officer Mitch Waters, were called to the traffic violation Sunday night and found the suspect in the 3700 block of Rural Street. Waters had let go of Zeus' leash to take a lawn chair the suspect was using to poke the dog. Seach was providing cover for Waters at the time Zeus attacked him, but Ciesielski did not know if Seach had his gun drawn. A dog might run at an officer with a gun pulled, and Dutch Shepherds are known to be more excitable than other dogs in K-9 units, Hess said.

Zeus and Waters, a nine year IPD veteran, graduated from training and began patrolling together in August. Waters plans to hold a private burial for Zeus. The suspect, 18 year old Michael A. Dobbins, was arrested later and faces preliminary charges of auto theft, resisting arrest and battery on a law enforcement animal. Seach and Dobbins were treated at Wishard Memorial Hospital and released.

In Loving Memory of

K-9 ZEUS

July 23, 2002

Partner: Officer Robert Schnelle
New York Police Department
140 - 58th St.
Brooklyn, NY

Zeus, the most highly decorated police dog in NYPD history, has died, the department announced yesterday. The end came suddenly on Tuesday morning for the 10 year old German Shepherd, who spent most of his life chasing down criminals, solving murders and recovering the remains of people buried under the rubble of terrorist bombs, unforgiving hurricanes or building collapses.

He died at the North Bellmore, L.I. home of his former handler, Police Officer Robert Schnelle. Zeus had been a full time family pet since his retirement from active duty two years ago. "He was a great dog, a happy dog, a sociable dog. He was one in a million," said a somber Schnelle.

A cancerous tumor on his spleen suddenly ruptured Tuesday morning, causing internal bleeding that claimed his life, Schnelle said. Zeus was just 8 weeks old when he was teamed up with Schnelle.

He was the first NYPD dog to search for victims when the World Trade Center was bombed in 1993. In April 1995, he worked steady 12 hour shifts in the rubble of the Oklahoma City bombing. That August, Zeus helped solve an 8 year old murder by sniffing out a corpse buried four feet beneath earth and concrete in the back yard of a Queens home.

In 1996, he was on duty in Atlanta, during the Olympic bombing. He also helped with hurricane duty in St. Thomas and Puerto Rico that year and in the Dominican Republic in 1998.

News of Zeus' death was particularly sad for Schnelle's two sons, Joseph, 9, Nicholas, 7, who learned about it when they returned from camp, Schnelle said. Zeus had kept the boys company during the day while their dad patrolled the city with 2½ year old Atlas, who succeeded Zeus and also lives at the Schnelle home.

Even Atlas feels the loss. "They were like father and son," he said of Zeus and Atlas. "He knows he's not around."

In Loving Memory of

K-9 ZEUS

September 9, 1995 - September 28, 2002

Partner: Officer David Denton
Middletown Township Police Department
5 Municipal Way
Langhorne, PA 19047
215.750-3845

Grieve Not For Me

K-9 Zeus served the community for five years and was a loyal partner to Officer David Denton. I unfortunately found Zeus in his kennel on that uneventful morning in distress. A common complication, he had flipped his stomach. I rushed him to an emergency Veterinary clinic. Due to complications from the surgery, Zeus died later that day.

Zeus was due to work on the day of his death and do a demonstration for the public. During his career, Zeus was instrumental in apprehending suspects that committed crimes against society. He was also responsible for locating a missing child five miles into a wooded area.

His death is a tragedy for Officer Denton and a great loss to this department. We are having a memorial for Zeus on October 29th.

In Loving Memory of

K-9 ZUCCO

LODD
October 30, 2002

Partner: Officer Michael Hughes
New Orleans Police Department
Harrison & Marconi Streets
New Orleans, LA 70124
504 483.2040

A bank robbery suspect chased by police into a Lakeview neighborhood Wednesday fatally shot a police dog before emerging from beneath a house and surrendering to police SWAT negotiators about six hours later, authorities said. Two other men, including a suspected getaway driver, also were arrested in the case. All three were booked with attempted bank robbery, a federal charge that carries up to 20 years in jail, the FBI said.

The police dog, a Belgian Malinois named Zucco, died of a gunshot wound shortly after being taken to a veterinary hospital, police said. "It's tough. It's like one of your own going down," said Sgt. Harold Chambliss, a long time K-9 member who works in the same unit as the dog's handler, Officer Michael Hughes. Hughes "is devastated," Chambliss said.

The K-9 unit was responding to an incident that began when a man with a revolver confronted a bank employee opening the Hibernia Bank at 7033 Canal Blvd. shortly before 7:30 a.m., and forced him inside, FBI spokeswoman Sheila Thorne said. The man, joined inside the bank by a second man carrying a shotgun, ordered the employee to open the bank's vault, the FBI said, but the employee said he wasn't able to, and the two men left. The alarm sounded, and two N.O.P.D. officers detailed to a Lakeview Crime Prevention District responded quickly and spotted two suspects on foot.

Police arrested Darius Copelin, 20, 4601 Stephen Girard St., in the 800 block of Turquoise Street in Lakeshore, and recovered a shotgun. Police spotted the other suspect, Andre Cassimer, 19, 3704 Garden Oaks Drive, Algiers. He emerged from a nearby driveway, jumped a fence and disappeared.

Police quickly surrounded the block, and Hughes led Zucco from yard to yard to track the man, police spokesman Capt. Marlon Defillo said. When they got to a house at Walker and Memphis streets, Zucco picked up a scent and started to go under the house, officers said. That's when he was shot. Hughes picked up the dog and rushed to a police unit.

Two neighborhood boys, ages 12 and 8, watched from the front window of their house across the street. "He had the dog in his arms like this," the older boy said, making a cradle with his own arms. Authorities evacuated residents from the house and two adjacent to it as the SWAT team tried to negotiate with Cassimer, first by megaphone, then with a microphone they dropped beneath the house, Defillo said. After a few hours, he began talking with negotiators and asked whether he could talk with his grandmother, officers said. Shortly before 1:30 p.m., he agreed to crawl out from under the side of the house and surrender to negotiators, police said.

"We waited him out and he finally got tired," Defillo said. A handgun was found under the house, police said. After the federal charge is resolved, Cassimer, also faces a state charge of killing a police dog, which carries a possible three years in jail, Defillo said. A third man, Calvin Anthony Scott III, 22, 5947 Providence St., was arrested later Wednesday afternoon. Authorities allege Scott was the getaway driver.

The loss of a man's best friend.

A memorial ceremony Thursday, November 7, 2002. The ceremony for Zucco, a 4 year old Belgian Malinois, was held at 10:30 a.m. at the New Orleans Police Department K-9 compound in City Park at Harrison Avenue and Marconi Boulevard. It was a perfect fall morning, not cold but crisp, with a sky so blue it could bring tears to your eyes. Thursday was the kind of day I think of as "dog weather."

On such a day, a dog will lift his nose and breathe in deeply, savoring the possibilities. It was the right kind of morning to pay tribute to Zucco. At the New Orleans Police Department K-9 compound in City Park, the air was laced with rich aromas coming from the stable next door, and dozens of police officers stood waiting for the ceremony to begin, their uniform shirts matching the color of the sky. A plaque next to the wooden urn told the police dog's story: "In memory of K-9 Zucco," it said. "A 4 year old Belgian Malinois who was killed in the line of duty on Oct. 30, 2002, while he and his handler, Police Officer Michael Hughes, were searching for a bank robbery suspect."

Dogs & Heaven

The service was held in the shade of a pecan tree, in the training yard where Zucco had learned the skills he needed to become one of New Orleans finest. The Rev. David Julian, police chaplain, gave the invocation, and after his prayer, he told how Zucco had returned to his handler's side after he was shot. "Zucco was faithful to the end," he said. "He was a faithful member of the New Orleans Police Department."

Police spokesman Capt. Marlon Defillo thanked the crowd for coming to the service and for their concern for Zucco and his partner. Then he read the poignant "Dog's Poem After Death," about a dog who tells his master he will wait for him outside the pearly gates because, "I'll miss you so much, if I went in alone it wouldn't be heaven to me."

'Part of the family.'

Police Superintendent Edwin Compass spoke of Zucco's courage and dedication. "These animals aren't just animals; they're part of the family," he said. "It's a sad day for the New Orleans Police Department, because he was one of our own."

A wreath of white carnations trimmed with blue ribbons was brought forward while the lonesome sound of "Amazing Grace" played on bagpipes filled the air. After the 21 gun salute, an officer played taps on the trumpet, and as the echo began, dogs in a nearby building began to bark, saluting Zucco in their own way.

When the service was over, people lined up to offer their condolences to Hughes, saying the awkward things you say to a man who has recently lost someone he loves. I asked him if he would get another partner, and he said yes, that in a few weeks he'd have a replacement dog. Could another dog replace Zucco? I asked, knowing the answer as soon as I asked the question. "No," he said, smiling sadly. "Not Zucco. Never."

CREDITS:

Articles, photos for Heroes All Without Question

Adjoa Adofo, Inquirer - Philadelphia
Al Wheless, Henderson Daily Dispatch
Al Recker Whitehall Press
Alex Breitler, Record Searchlight
America's Most Wanted
Andrea Cavanaugh, Ventura County Star
Andrea Pedtke, Muncie, IN newspaper.
Andy Starnes, Post Gazette - North Huntingdon, PA.
Andy Cordan, News 2 Nashville
Angela Ascopella - Norwalk CT
Anne Koch, Seattle Times
APBnews - Wayne Culley
Armando Rios, Bulletin (AR)
Becky Worley, Tech Live -Darby Twp. Sharon Hills, PA
Beth Kaiser (photo) NYC
Beth Quinn, The Times Herald-Record
Brenda M. Culler, Sandusky Register
Brenda Conyeers, Hillwboro Press
Brent Israelsen, The Salt Lake Tribune
Brian Bullock, Curry Coastal Pilot
Candance Heckman, Seattle Post Intelligencer
Carol Williams-Skaggs, The Marin Humane Society
Carolina Procter, The Times (IN)
Cathy Welch, TX
Charita M. Goshay, Repository
Charmaine Smith, Anderson Independent Mail
Cheris Hodges, News & Record (NC)
Chris Snyder, Connecticut Post
Chuck Fieldman, FranklinPark, IL
Cindy Clayton, The Virginian-Pilot
Clay Lambert, Palm Beach Post
Daily Telegraph UK

Dani Davies Palm Beach Post
Darla McFarland, The Examiner
David Riley, Kentucky New Era
David Eck - Enquirer Contributor
Denise Rasch, Las Vegas
Derek Welch, TX
Don Ratzlaff, Hillsboro, KS14
Dusty Simon, OH
Elaine Porterfield, Seattle Post Intelligencer
Emily Shartin, Globe Staff
Eric Carpenter, The Orange Country Registerr
Erin McKay Langley Advance.com (Canada)
Florida Parishes Bureau
Gabriel Baird, The Baltimore Sun
Gary Thompson, Las Vegas Sun
Georgina Gustin, The Day.com
Gloucester County Times
Gretchen Ertl, AP Photo
Hal Dardick, Chicago Tribune
Hilda Munoz, Jerse Journal
Hugh McDiarmid, Jr. Free Press
Ian Berry, Anderson Independent-Mail
J. Reese, MHS (photo)
Jaime Jenkins, The Shawnee News-Star
Jan Ackerman, Post-Gazette (PA
Jason Hagey, The News Tribune
Jay Newcomb, Repository
Jennifer Midberry - Philadelphia Daily News
Jennifer P. Brown, Kentucky New Era
Jennifer Upshaw, MHS
Jessica Heslam, MA
Jim Watson, NAPWDA Perry Ohio
Jim Fitzgerald, Assoc. Press
Jim Cortina, CPWDA Director, photos
Joe Atkinson, Courier & Press (IN)Patrisha de Leon - Manlagnit

John Luke The Times (photo)
John Lynch, www.news-journal.com
Joseph Gelarden, Indianapolis Star
Joseph C. Garza Tribune Star
Kansas News - The Topeka Capital Journel
Karen Jeffrey - Yarmouth, MA
Karen Grunden, Tribune Star
Kate Leckie, News Post MD
Katherine Leal Unmuth - Sentinel Staff
Kathleen Sweeney, Times-Union
Kay Ledbetter, TX
Keith Paul, Las Vegas Sun
Ken Carolan, The Trentonian
Kirk Beldon Jackson, The Morning Call
Lauri Zachry TX
Leesville Daily Leader Louisiana
Linda Medura, Gazette Correspondent
Lindsey V. Corey, Savannah Paper
Lisa Teachey, Harris Co. TX
Mark Harrison, Seattle Times
Mark Pino, OSC News Gazette
Michael Baker - The Facts (TX)
Michael S. Wirtz, Inquirer - Philadelphia
Mike Tobin & James Ewinger
Mike Anderson - Tribune-Herald
Missoulian Newspaper - Ananconda Leader
Nancy Wride, Times
Neal Rubin, Detroit News
Nicole Gaudiano, The Bergen Record
Noah K. Murray Asbury Park Press
Patrick Avery, Messenger-Inquirer
Paula Doneman, The Courier Mail Newspaper, Australia
Pete Hartt, Stowe VT
Philip Messing, NY Post
Ptlm. Jefferey Coleman, Whitehall Twp. PD.
Rachel Stein (MD)

Rachel Kim, TX
Rail Cop Spring 1999 Newsletter
Randolph Courier-Tribune (NC)
Randy Howell, Officer, NC
Rene Stutzman - Sentinel Staff
Rita Venable News 2 Nashville
Ron Frehm, AP PhotoBeth Ipsen, Fairbanks Daily News-Miner
Russ Hess, USPCA
Ryan Oliver, Review Journal
Samatha Huseas, Log Cabin
Sarah Coffee, The Patriot Ledger
Sarah Overstreet, New Leader (MO)
Sarah Schulz, The Independent Com
Seamus McGraw, Indianapolis - APBnews.com
Sheila Stroup, The Times-Picayune
Sheri Tabachnik - Asbury Park Press
Stacey Burns, The News Tribune
Stefano Esposito, News Tribune
Steven Scarpa, Statford, CT
Sue Weibezahl Onondaga County Press
Susan Erler, Times
Terri Sanginiti, Staff Reporter - Delaware On Line
The Tennessee Tribuen
The Jersey Journal
The Trentonian
The Times Herald-Record (NY)
The Messenger
Thomas J. Gibbons, Jr. - Inquirer Staff
Tim Hrenchir, The Capital Journal
Tom Spalding, Indianapolis Star
Tom Alex, Register Staff Write (IA)
Tom Grace, Daily Star (NY)
Travis Baker - Sun Staff
Valerie Schremp, Post Dispatch
Vanessa Ho, Seattle Post-Intelligencer
Walt Philbin, The Times-Picayune

Wayne Culley APBnews.com
Whitney Friedlander, Missourian Newspaper
William Bygrave, News Chief (FL)
www.community-focus.com
Yvonne Latty, Philadelphia Daily News
If I left anyone out...I am sorry. I will add in Book #2 coming
in 2004.